THE EUROPEAN UNION SERIES

General Editors: Neill Nugent, William E. Paterson

The European Union series provides an authoritative library on the European Union, ranging from general introductory texts to definitive assessments of key institutions and actors, issues, policies and policy processes, and the role of member states.

Books in the series are written by leading scholars in their fields and reflect the most up-to-date research and debate. Particular attention is paid to accessibility and clear presentation for a wide audience of students, practitioners and interested general readers.

The series editors are **Neill Nugent**, Professor of Politics and Jean Monnet Professor of European Integration, Manchester Metropolitan University, and **William E. Paterson**, Honourary Professor in German and European Studies, University of Aston. Their co-editor until his death in July 1999, **Vincent Wright**, was a Fellow of Nuffield College, Oxford University.

Feedback on the series and book proposals are always welcome and should be sent to Steven Kennedy, Palgrave Macmillan, Houndmills, Basingstoke, Hampshire RG21 6XS, UK, or by e-mail to s.kennedy@palgrave.com

---

General textbooks

Published

... ... ean
Union [Rights: Europe only]

Desmond Dinan **Europe Recast: A History of European Union** [Rights: Europe only]

Desmond Dinan **Ever Closer Union: An Introduction to European Integration (4th edn)**
[Rights: Europe only]

Mette Eilstrup Sangiovanni (ed.) **Debates on European Integration: A Reader**

Simon Hix **The Political System of the European Union (2nd edn)**

Paul Magnette **What is the European Union? Nature and Prospects**

John McCormick **Understanding the European Union: A Concise Introduction (4th edn)**

Brent F. Nelsen and Alexander Stubb **The European Union: Readings on the Theory and Practice of European Integration (3rd edn)**
[Rights: Europe only]

Neill Nugent (ed.) **European Union Enlargement**

Neill Nugent **The Government and Politics of the European Union (7th edn)**

John Peterson and Elizabeth Bomberg **Decision-Making in the European Union**

Ben Rosamond **Theories of European Integration**

Forthcoming

Laurie Buonanno and Neill Nugent **Policies and Policy Processes of the European Union**

Magnus Ryner and Alan Cafruny **A Critical Introduction to the European Union**

Dirk Leuffen, Berthold Rittberger and Frank Schimmelfennig **Differentiated Integration**

Sabine Saurugger **Theoretical Approaches to European Integration**

Esther Versluis, Mendeltje van Keulen and Paul Stephenson **Analysing the European Union Policy Process**

Also Planned

The Political Economy of European Integration

Series Standing Order (outside North America only)
ISBN 0–333–71695–7 hardback
ISBN 0–333–69352–3 paperback
Full details from www.palgrave.com

Visit Palgrave Macmillan's
EU Resource area at
www.palgrave.com/politics/eu/

D1630789

The major institutions and actors

Published

Renaud Dehousse **The European Court of Justice**
Justin Greenwood **Interest Representation in the European Union (2nd edn)**
Fiona Hayes-Renshaw and Helen Wallace **The Council of Ministers (2nd edn)**
Simon Hix and Christopher Lord **Political Parties in the European Union**
David Judge and David Earnshaw **The European Parliament (2nd edn)**
Neill Nugent **The European Commission**
Anne Stevens with Handley Stevens **Brussels Bureaucrats? The Administration of the European Union**

Forthcoming

Wolfgang Wessels **The European Council**

The main areas of policy

Published

Michelle Chang **Monetary Integration in the European Union**
Michelle Cini and Lee McGowan **Competition Policy in the European Union (2nd edn)**
Wyn Grant **The Common Agricultural Policy**
Sieglinde Gstöhl and Dirk de Bievrè **The Trade Policy of the European Union**
Martin Holland **The European Union and the Third World**
Jolyon Howorth **Security and Defence Policy in the European Union**
Johanna Kantola **Gender and the European Union**
Stephan Keukeleire and Jennifer MacNaughtan **The Foreign Policy of the European Union**
Brigid Laffan **The Finances of the European Union**
Malcolm Levitt and Christopher Lord **The Political Economy of Monetary Union**
Janne Haaland Matláry **Energy Policy in the European Union**
John McCormick **Environmental Policy in the European Union**
John Peterson and Margaret Sharp **Technology Policy in the European Union**
Handley Stevens **Transport Policy in the European Union**

Forthcoming

Karen Anderson **Social Policy in the European Union**

Hans Bruyninckx and Tom Delreux **Environmental Policy and Politics in the European Union**
Jörg Monar **Justice and Home Affairs in the European Union**

Also planned

Political Union
The External Policies of the European Union
The External Economic Relations of the European Union

The member states and the Union

Published

Carlos Closa and Paul Heywood **Spain and the European Union**
Alain Guyomarch, Howard Machin and Ella Ritchie **France in the European Union**
Brigid Laffan and Jane O'Mahoney **Ireland and the European Union**

Forthcoming

Simon Bulmer and William E. Paterson **Germany and the European Union**
Brigid Laffan **The European Union and its Member States**
Baldur Thórhallson **Small States in the European Union**

Also planned

Britain and the European Union

Issues

Published

Derek Beach **The Dynamics of European Integration: Why and When EU Institutions Matter**
Thomas Christiansen and Christine Reh **Constitutionalizing the European Union**
Robert Ladrech **Europeanization and National Politics**
Cécile Leconte **Understanding Euroscepticism**
Steven McGuire and Michael Smith **The European Union and the United States**

Forthcoming

Christina Boswell and Andrew Geddes **Migration and Mobility in the European Union**
Wyn Rees **EU/US Security Relations**

Understanding Euroscepticism

Cécile Leconte

palgrave
macmillan

First published 2010 by
PALGRAVE MACMILLAN

Palgrave Macmillan in the UK is an imprint of Macmillan Publishers Limited, registered in England, company number 785998, of Houndmills, Basingstoke, Hampshire RG21 6XS.

Palgrave Macmillan in the US is a division of St Martin's Press LLC, 175 Fifth Avenue, New York, NY 10010.

Palgrave Macmillan is the global academic imprint of the above companies and has companies and representatives throughout the world.

Palgrave® and Macmillan® are registered trademarks in the United States, the United Kingdom, Europe and other countries

ISBN 978–0–230–22806–1 hardback
ISBN 978–0–230–22807–8 paperback

This book is printed on paper suitable for recycling and made from fully managed and sustained forest sources. Logging, pulping and manufacturing processes are expected to conform to the environmental regulations of the country of origin.

A catalogue record for this book is available from the British Library.

A catalog record for this book is available from the Library of Congress.

10 9 8 7 6 5 4 3 2 1
19 18 17 16 15 14 13 12 11 10

Printed in China

Contents

v

List of Figures and Tables

Figures

Tables

Acknowledgements

I wish to thank a number of people for the assistance and support they have given me. Friends and family have been a considerable source of encouragement – notably Manuel, whom I especially thank for his careful reading and very useful suggestions. I would also like to thank the series editors, Neill Nugent and William Paterson, and my publisher Steven Kennedy, for their helpful feedback and encouraging comments and to all at Palgrave Macmillan who have contributed to the realization of this book.

The various Eurobarometer reports produced by the EU have been invaluable in compiling this book. To avoid cluttering the text, references have been abbreviated to EB for regular Eurobarometer, FEB for Flash Eurobarometer, SEB for Special Eurobarometer and CCEB for Candidate Countries Eurobarometer.

CÉCILE LECONTE

List of Abbreviations

ALDE	Alliance of Liberals and Democrats for Europe
ASEM	Asia-Europe Meeting
ATTAC	Association for the Taxation of Financial Transactions and for Civic Action
CAP	Common Agricultural Policy
CCEB	Candidate Countries Eurobarometer
CDU	Christlich-Demokratische Union
CEC	Conference of European Churches
CEO	Corporate Europe Observatory
CFP	Common Fisheries Policy
CFSP	Common Foreign and Security Policy
COMECE	Commission of the Bishops' Conference of the European Community
COREPER	Committee of Permanent Representatives
CSU	Christlich-Soziale Union
EAW	European Arrest Warrant
EB	Eurobarometer
EBU	European Broadcasting Union
EC	European Community
ECB	European Central Bank
ECE	Eastern and Central European (countries)
ECHR	European Convention for the Protection of Human Rights
ECJ	European Court of Justice
ECR	European Conservatives and Reformists
ECSC	European Coal and Steel Community
EDC	European Defence Community
EEA	European Economic Area
EEC	European Economic Community
EFDG	Europe of Freedom and Democracy Group
EMS	European Monetary System
EMU	Economic and Monetary Union
EP	European Parliament
EPP	European People's Party
EPP-ED	European People's Party-European Democrats

ESDP	European Security and Defence Policy
ETUC	European Trade Union Confederation
EU	European Union
FEB	Flash Eurobarometer
GDP	Gross Domestic Product
GUE–NGL	Group of the United European Left/Nordic Green Left
IGC	Intergovernmental Conference
IND–DEM	Independence and Democracy Group
JHA	Justice and Home Affairs
MAI	Multilateral Agreement on Investment
MEP	Member of the European Parliament
MNP	Member of National Parliament
NAFTA	North American Free Trade Association
NATO	North Atlantic Treaty Organization
NGO	Non-governmental Organization
OECD	Organisation for Economic Co-operation and Development
OEEC	Organisation for European Economic Co-operation
OMC	Open Method of Coordination
QMV	Qualified Majority Voting
SEA	Single European Act
SEB	Special Eurobarometer
SPD	Sozial-demokratische Partei Deutschlunds
TEC	Treaty Establishing the European Community
TEU	Treaty on European Union
UEN	Union for a Europe of Nations
UK	United Kingdom
UKIP	United Kingdom Independence Party
UN	United Nations
WTO	World Trade Organization

Introduction

To anti-Europeans' regret, Henry Kissinger's prediction that the disappearance of the Soviet threat and Germany's reunification would bring about the end of European integration (1996:749) proved wrong. EU institutions' and German political elites' commitment to European integration proved much more robust than realist theorists like Kissinger thought. However, twenty years after the end of the Cold War, the political context in which European integration is proceeding has changed considerably. A telling indication of this was incidentally provided by the much-awaited ruling of the German Constitutional Court, delivered in June 2009, in which it declared that the Lisbon Treaty was compatible with German Basic Law. While this ruling was hailed in the rest of the EU as paving the way for a swift ratification of the treaty in Germany, it triggered some strongly critical remarks in the country itself. Former foreign minister Joseph Fischer, for instance, qualified it as 'Eurosceptic' and 'backwards-oriented' (2009). In fact, much of the Court's ruling is permeated by an unusually distrustful tone towards the Union, reminiscent of British Eurosceptics' hostility towards a European 'super-state'. In this ruling, the Court explicitly considered, for the first time, the possibility of Germany's withdrawal from the EU, if the EU were to develop into a federal state without reaching a corresponding level of democratic legitimacy (BVerfGE 2009:s.264). This illustrated the extent of the change in mood towards European integration that occurred in Germany and in many other EU countries during the 1990s and early 2000s. In this respect, recent developments in EU politics over the last few years have confirmed the significance of Euroscepticism and how the latter affects the different dimensions of European integration.

For a start, the EU's institutional reform, which aims at improving the EU's decision-making capacity and enhancing its coherence as an international actor, has been rejected by voters on several occasions, notably in the Dutch and French referenda on the EU Constitutional Treaty in 2005 and in the first Irish referendum on the Lisbon Treaty in 2008.

A second aspect has been the impact that Euroscepticism has had

1

in recent years on all the major EU institutions. In the first half of 2009, the Czech presidency of the Council was almost derailed by Eurosceptic forces in the main ruling party and by parochial domestic rivalries, which brought about the fall of the incumbent government. In the 2009 European elections, strongly Eurosceptic parties attracted large sections of the electorate in some countries: roughly a third of voters in Austria and the Netherlands, a quarter in the UK (without including the Tories) and a fifth in France. Above all, turnout reached a historic low (43 per cent), which was interpreted as either indifference or hostility towards the EU among large numbers of voters. This seemed to affect the representativeness of the European Parliament (EP), precisely at a time when the German Constitutional Court, as discussed above, was questioning the ability of this institution to adequately represent voters (BVerfGE 2009:s.279). As far as the European Court of Justice (ECJ) was concerned, it attracted intense criticism in 2008. Following several of its rulings involving internal market legislation, the ECJ was criticized by trade unions across the EU for undermining workers' and unions' rights. Furthermore, the authority of the ECJ was clearly contested in the German Constitutional Court's Lisbon ruling (see p.160). As regards the European Commission, the aftermath of the 2005 and 2008 referenda illustrated its difficulties in promoting the Union's general interest, in a context where any controversial proposal might fan Euroscepticism in the member states.

Furthermore, the two biggest achievements of the EU, the completion of the internal market and the eastern enlargement, have triggered backlash reactions in the last couple of years, which have been exacerbated by the financial and economic crisis that broke out in late 2008. The internal market, a core pillar of the EU, was threatened by protectionist tendencies, notably in France and the UK. While state aid to the automobile sector was made conditional upon the preservation of French jobs, British workers were demonstrating against the temporary transfer of Italian workers to plants in the UK. In parallel, surveys have highlighted the mixed feelings of public opinion towards the latest enlargements. While a large majority of citizens welcomed the resulting increased mobility within the enlarged EU, 56 per cent thought that enlargement had contributed to job losses in their country, and 50 per cent thought it had increased feelings of insecurity (FEB 257:23). Besides, xenophobic reactions against Romanian residents in Italy (in 2008) and Ireland (in 2009) have endangered the principle of the free movement of persons in the EU. These reactions were reminiscent of French concerns over a potential 'invasion' of Polish service providers (the notorious 'Polish plumber') during the 2005 referendum campaign on the EU Constitutional Treaty.

Finally, the impact of the financial and economic crisis on the evolution of public support for continued integration is uncertain. For the time being, no uniform pattern has emerged. While the crisis seems to boost pro-European support in Sweden (to join the Eurozone) and in Iceland (for EU accession), public opinion in the UK seems to be evolving in an opposite direction. In the past, support for EC/EU membership declined after the two oil shocks of the 1970s and the economic recession of the early 1990s; today, there is uncertainty about the impact of prolonged economic recession on the evolution of support.

These different examples show that Euroscepticism is a generic and encompassing term, which applies to a large variety of actors and discourses.

Origins and definitions of the term

Euroscepticism is a rather recent term. It was not used during the first decades of European integration, when opponents of integration were referred to as nationalists, 'anti-marketeers' (for opponents to the common market in the UK) or simply as communists, Gaullists, etc. However, some of the core concepts of Eurosceptic discourse already existed, such as 'Eurocrat' – a term which appeared in French dictionaries in the mid-1960s (during the de Gaulle era) and which conveys the idea of a gap between European elites and the average citizen. Euroscepticism is a term that originated in a specific context, that of British public debate on the EC in the mid-1980s. First published in an article in *The Times* in 1985 (Harmsen and Spiering 2004), as the completion of the common market was about to become the top priority on the EC's agenda, it initially referred to the 'anti-marketeers', who at that time comprised most of the Labour party and a fringe of the Conservatives. It was popularized later by Margaret Thatcher's so-called 'Bruges speech', given in 1988 at the College of Europe. In this speech, which was to become a 'key building block in the development of British opposition to the European Union' (Usherwood 2004:5), Thatcher outlined the core tenets of her vision of the future of the EC. From the early 1990s on, as domestic debates on the EU became increasingly polarized in the context of the Maastricht Treaty's ratification process, the term Euroscepticism expanded to continental Europe, where it became a 'catch-all' synonym for any form of opposition or reluctance towards the EU.

This reminder of the origin of the term highlights the first difficulty encountered when trying to define Euroscepticism: to what extent does it refer to a specifically British phenomenon? As explained later in the book, Euroscepticism has a specific meaning in the British context, where it refers to a form of cultural anti-Europeanism broader than 'EU-scepticism' (Harmsen and Spiering 2004). In fact, the meaning of Euroscepticism varies according to country context. While it always refers to some form of hostility towards the EU, this hostility does not necessarily apply to the same dimensions of European integration. For instance, Euroscepticism in Austria is driven, to a large extent, by negative perceptions of EU enlargement and opposition to Turkey's EU accession. In the UK, this dimension of Euroscepticism is not significant, as most Eurosceptic discourses express hostility towards a 'European superstate' and to Economic and Monetary Union (EMU). Similarly, Swedish public opinion displays a rather positive evaluation of the latest EU enlargements, compared with other older member states (FEB 257: 32–5), while being more reluctant towards political integration, notably in the field of foreign policy.

Second, the meaning of Euroscepticism also varies across time, as it evolves in parallel to the successive developments of the EU. Opposition to European integration in 1957 mainly implied opposition to the setting up of the common market; by contrast, opposition to the Maastricht Treaty in 1992 amounted to hostility towards political integration (as embodied, for instance, by the Common Foreign and Security Policy (CFSP)). In this respect, the notion of 'revisionists' can be used to refer to those Eurosceptics who oppose European integration as it evolved after the Maastricht Treaty (Flood and Usherwood 2007:6).

Third, Euroscepticism is a very plastic notion that originated in media discourse; like populism, it is compatible with any ideological position, from the extreme left to the extreme right. It is not an ideology: it does not express a single, stable set of ideas, putting forward a comprehensive worldview. Like populism, it also has a normative dimension, as it is often used in inter-party competition to disparage political competitors. Indeed, it is quite telling that even well-known Eurosceptics, such as Czech President Vaclav Klaus, do not label themselves 'Eurosceptics' but rather 'Euro-critics' or 'Eurorealists' (as in the 2001 *Manifesto of Czech Eurorealism* presented by the Czech Civic Union (ODS), of which Klaus is a former leader). In this respect, the flurry of terms that have emerged in order to refer to different forms of Euroscepticism (Eurorejects, Europragmatists, Eurorealists, etc.) does not contribute to a clear understanding of the phenomenon.

Perhaps a useful starting point is the literal meaning of the term 'scepticism'. Historically, scepticism is a philosophy that developed in ancient Greece in the fourth century BC. Initially outlined by Pyrrhon, scepticism is a mindset: sceptics do not accept the validity of any belief or opinion *a priori*, without submitting it to a free and critical examination. The sceptic abstains from judgments and advocates distancing oneself from one's own opinions and beliefs. Scepticism developed in opposition to any form of dogma or theoretical thinking, to which sceptics opposed practical experience and common sense. In this respect, scepticism is a safeguard against intolerance and against the possible subversion of idealism into fanaticism. However, this mindset has its downsides. Indeed, sceptics have been accused of discrediting any form of universal truth or ethics, as their reliance on practical common sense has led them to emphasize the respect of local norms and traditions. The insistence of sceptics on respect for diversity against uniformity may lead to a form of moral relativism and conservatism.

If one retains this definition, Euroscepticism does not necessarily mean hostility towards European integration. Literally, Eurosceptics are those who submit the issue of European integration to a sceptical examination: support for European integration should not derive from any theoretical or normative belief (for instance, the belief that an ever closer union between the peoples of Europe is necessarily a good thing) but must be assessed on the basis of practical cost/gains analysis and according to its respect of national (political, cultural, normative) diversities. In this sense, the Eurosceptic opposes, to the 'dogma' of an ever closer union, a pragmatic stance, evaluating European integration on its merits.

However, in today's political and academic discourse, Euroscepticism has come to be equated with different forms of opposition to European integration. A seminal early definition proposed by Paul Taggart, and initially applied to Euroscepticism among political parties, equated Euroscepticism with 'contingent and conditional opposition to European integration as well as total

and unconditional opposition to it' (1998:364). This initial definition, which covered a broad range of attitudes towards the EU, was
later broken down into two different forms of opposition by
Taggart and Szczerbiak. Whereas 'hard Euroscepticism' refers to
'principled opposition to the EU and European integration' (as it is
being articulated by those parties or actors advocating a withdrawal
from the EU or opposing EU accession), 'soft Euroscepticism'
expresses a 'qualified opposition' to the EU, reflecting dissatisfaction with EU policies or with the current EU trajectory perceived to
be contrary to the national interest (Taggart and Szczerbiak 2002).
Other typologies have been put forward, outlining different degrees
of opposition to European integration, such as Kopecky and
Mudde's (2002) distinction between Euroscepticism (expressing
principled support for membership but dissatisfaction with the EU's
current development) and Europhobia (expressing principled opposition and dissatisfaction), or Flood and Usherwood's six-point
continuum of party positions, ranging from simple rejection of the
EU to a maximalist position advocating a federal Europe (2007:6).

Before turning to the definition retained in this book, it is important to clarify, in Taggart and Szczerbiak's words, 'what
Euroscepticism is not' (2003:12).The first question addressed by
the two authors relates to dissatisfaction with one or several EU
policies: can this be equated with Euroscepticism? To answer this
question, they put forward a distinction between 'core' and 'peripheral' EU policies. For instance, while opposition to EMU or to major
EU treaties can be equated with Euroscepticism, opposition to less
central policies, such as the CFSP or the Common Fisheries Policy
(CFP), cannot. However, as the authors point out, the categoriza-
tion of policies as core or peripheral depends on subjective perceptions. For instance, dissatisfaction with the CFP is widespread in the
UK, while being a non-issue in other countries. Similarly, among
French political elites, the CFSP is a core component of the traditional French understanding of the EU as a relevant power in international relations (the *Europe-puissance* concept). In a similar vein,
as the authors point out, opposition to EU enlargement does not
necessarily correlate with Eurosceptic orientations. While Euro-
enthusiasts may oppose enlargement as a process that could dilute
the EU and prevent institutional deepening, Eurosceptics may
support it precisely for the same reasons. However, this is, again, a
question of context and type of actor. While opposition to enlargement tends to be correlated with a more principled opposition to

further integration among national MPs (MNPs), it tends to be associated with pro-European positions (in the sense of institutional deepening) among Members of the European Parliament (MEPs) (Katz 2002:19). Consequently, in order to assess whether opposition to specific EU policies is an expression of a broader type of Euroscepticism, one has to analyze the actors' positions within their specific context.

The second question to be addressed is whether criticizing the EU 'for being insufficiently integrationist and/or undemocratic' is a form of Euroscepticism (Taggart and Szczerbiak 2003:15). As the two authors rightly point out, criticizing the EU for not being supranational or democratic enough cannot simply be equated with Euroscepticism. Indeed, to advocates of a federal Europe, the institutions of the European Economic Community (EEC) were not supranational enough and the European Commmunities, centred mainly on economic goals, did not live up to the plans of a political union. Eugen Kogon, a former anti-fascist and European federalist, expressed this disillusionment with the EEC when he wrote, in 1957, that the Rome treaties had little to do with the political unification of Europe (quoted in Loth 1989:602). More than thirty years later, federalist hopes were dashed again as the Maastricht Treaty set up the EU on the basis of a pillar structure, with reduced powers for supranational institutions in the second and third pillars. As a result, some advocates of a federal Europe, such as the Belgian Green Party, voted against the Maastricht Treaty (Taggart and Szczerbiak 2003:15, note 28). Similarly, one can criticize the EU for being insufficiently democratic because it is under-developed as a union of citizens. Typically, pro-Europeans who articulate this type of criticism call, for instance, for an extension of the powers of the EP as a way to democratize the EU. Such was the case for the British political scientist and former MEP David Marquand, author of the famous notion of the 'democratic deficit' (see Marquand 1979). Indeed, an intra-systemic criticism, what Flood and Usherwood call the 'reformist position' (2007:6), does not necessarily equate to Euroscepticism. What counts is how actors argue their position and which options they put forward in order to palliate the EU's shortcomings. Again, the issue of context is of crucial importance here. For instance, the notion of subsidiarity (which is now put forward as the panacea for the EU's alleged democratic shortcomings) does not have the same meaning in the 1984 Spinelli project for a European constitution, where it was a cornerstone of federal

Europe, as it does in the 2009 programme of the Bavarian Christlich-Soziale Union (CSU), where it is a code word for the repatriation of EU powers to states or regions. In a similar vein, references to 'freedom' in the British debate on the EU often denote a Eurosceptic position, as it stands for national independence against Brussels' authority.

Keeping these clarifications in mind, in the remainder of the book we will use the term 'hard Eurosceptic' (or 'anti-European') for those parties or actors who oppose EU membership as a principle. In contrast the generic term 'Eurosceptic' will be used for that broader range of groupings or individuals who accept the reality of EU membership, while expressing hostility or deep reluctance towards the 'basic political arrangements' (Easton 1975:437) underlying the EU political system, which they do not consider as fully legitimate, such as: the pooling of sovereignty; the delegation of state powers to supranational institutions; the primacy of EU law over national norms (including constitutions); and the underlying telos of an 'ever closer union' (as the first objective of the European Economic Community (EEC), mentioned in the preamble of the Treaty establishing the European Community (TEC)). Moreover, what Eurosceptic discourses often have in common is a non-acceptance of the *sui generis* character of the EU as a union 'of states *and* citizens' (which distinguishes the EU from interstate international organizations). Those who conceive of EU citizenship and a (hypothetical) post-national democracy as consubstantially illegitimate might be qualified as Eurosceptic. Finally, we qualify as Eurosceptic those parties (essentially from the radical right or radical left) who do not explicitly oppose EU membership, while nevertheless questioning, to varying degrees, the core values on which the Union is based (for instance, market economy, free competition and non-discrimination).

Objectives and thesis of the book

This book aims at providing the reader with an understanding of the dynamics underlying opposition to European integration. By doing so, it pursues a twofold objective. First, there is a need to clarify current debates on Euroscepticism and to debunk widespread, misleading and often normative assumptions about this phenomenon. Current developments in European integration have attracted a lot of political and media attention on Euroscepticism, often leading to the diffusion of mistaken or un-nuanced views on the issue. Examples include the commonly held assumptions that there has been a general decline in public support for European integration since Maastricht, that Eurosceptics are necessarily 'losers' of the Europeanization and globalization processes, or that voters are more Eurosceptic than political elites. Thus, the book also aims at providing answers to simple questions, such as: Do latest EU referenda and declining turnout at European elections express voters' views on the EU or do they mainly express protest against governments? How can cross-country differences in levels of Euroscepticism be explained? Why are women more Eurosceptic than men? And so on.

Secondly, the study of Euroscepticism has generated a vast and rapidly expanding library of materials from such disciplines as political science, political sociology, history, media and communication studies, cultural studies, and translation studies, to name a few. This diversity of perspectives on Euroscepticism has shed light on the different facets of Euroscepticism. This book aims to be the first attempt to bring together and connect these different perspectives, in order to offer a comprehensive analysis of Euroscepticism, as it is being articulated by a variety of actors (political parties and voters, the media, national institutions, civil society organizations, etc.).

In this respect, I argue that Euroscepticism is too often viewed either as a marginal phenomenon articulated by non-mainstream actors (such as protest-based parties or the tabloid press) or as an irrational behaviour on the part of ignorant voters, who 'vote against Europe' in order to sanction national governments. Consequently, it is often analyzed exclusively as the expression of an 'elite/public' divide. By contrast, this book argues that public Euroscepticism is embedded in a much wider context, in which mainstream political elites, national institutions and domestic mass media act as filters of collective perceptions of 'Europe'. Indeed, successive chapters highlight the mainstream dimension of Euroscepticism, as it is articulated by government parties' leaderships, the quality press, and other entities.

Moreover, it argues that students of Euroscepticism must widen their perspective across time and space. From a chronological point of view, collective perceptions of the EU are influenced by different temporalities: that of accession processes but also countries' relationships with 'Europe' in the course of history. From a spatial point of view, perceptions of the EU are influenced not only by national filters, but also by regional factors and global trends. Like the EU itself, Euroscepticism must thus be understood from a multi-level perspective. In that respect, it can be analyzed as a symptom of the broader societal changes and adaptational pressures which confront European societies.

Organization of the book

Why study Euroscepticism at all? The chapter that follows explains that, far from being a marginal phenomenon, Euroscepticism has a concrete impact on the process of European integration – on day-to-day decision-making as well as on successive institutional reforms. It also highlights a consequence of Euroscepticism that is seldom taken into account: its impact on the EU's standing in international relations and on how it is perceived by third countries' actors. Ultimately, it is argued, the nature of the EU and how it will develop will be determined by the extent to which governments take Eurosceptic positions or stick to their official commitment in favour of further integration.

The two following chapters underline the multi-faceted nature of Euroscepticism. Chapter 2 highlights the different varieties of Euroscepticism, by breaking it up into its different dimensions and by showing how they have evolved over time. Chapter 3 explains cross-country variations in levels and meanings of Euroscepticism, as well as regional differences within countries as far as perceptions of European integration are concerned.

The following chapters focus on different categories of actors. Chapters 4 and 5 emphasize the elite dimension of Euroscepticism. Chapter 4 analyzes Euroscepticism among domestic political elites, by focusing especially on mainstream political parties. It highlights the ambiguity of political elites' initial commitment to European integration, shows how they have reacted to the phenomenon of Euroscepticism from the 1990s on, and explains how their stance on the EU is evolving as a consequence. Chapter 5 addresses Euroscepticism from the point of view of those national institutions that are in charge of the implementation and enforcement of EU law. It sheds light on more subtle forms of Euroscepticism, as national institutions use their position as gatekeepers in the implementation of EU law to resist some of the changes implied by Europeanization.

The three following chapters focus on public opinion, the media and civil society. Chapter 6 analyzes the dynamics of popular or public Euroscepticism, as it is expressed in opinion surveys, EP elections and EU-related referenda. Chapter 7 centres on one category of public opinion makers: domestic media. By expanding the study of media Euroscepticism beyond the case of the tabloid press, it shows how the quality press can contribute to diffusing softer forms of Euroscepticism, while new media play an increasing role in patterns of opinion formation on EU issues. Chapter 8 focuses on civil society actors. It explains why traditional organizations hitherto strongly supportive of European integration, like churches and trade unions, might be becoming more sceptical towards the current trajectory of the EU. It also addresses social mobilization and grassroots organizations, like those of the alter-globalization movement, and analyzes whether their criticism of the EU can be equated with Euroscepticism.

Chapter 9 introduces a theoretical perspective by assessing, on the basis of the book's main findings, how relevant different theories can be in explaining Euroscepticism. By relying on classical theories of support for political regimes, it aims to clarify the nature of prevalent support for the EU amongst public opinion. It also evaluates the respective relevance of rational-choice versus constructivist approaches in explaining the underlying logic of Euroscepticism. Finally, it assesses to what extent the study of Euroscepticism can improve our understanding of other forms of opposition to global trade liberalization and international governance. Finally, Chapter 10 introduces a prospective perspective, by considering how Euroscepticism might evolve in the years to come and how the EU might respond to this challenge.

Chapter 1

Why Euroscepticism Matters

When Margaret Thatcher made her famous speech to the College of Europe in Bruges on 22 September 1988 it was seen as a radical manifesto and a defining cornerstone of Eurosceptic discourse. But if we compare her denunciation of the EU's alleged regulation excesses

> The Community is not an end in itself ... [It] is a practical means by which Europe can ensure the prosperity ... of its people ... [Working more closely together] does not require power to be centralised in Brussels or decisions to be taken by an appointed bureaucracy ... [We do not want] a European super-state exercising a new dominance from Brussels ... Our aim should not be more and more detailed regulation from the centre. (Thatcher 1988)

with the text of the European Council's Laeken declaration of 15 December 2001 on the future of the European Union,

> [C]itizens also feel that the Union is behaving too bureaucratically ... What citizens understand by 'good governance' is opening up fresh opportunities, not imposing further red tape. What they expect is ... better responses to practical issues and not a European super-state or European institutions inveigling their way into every nook and cranny of life. (European Council 2001)

these two quotations sound surprisingly similar. What was considered a Eurosceptic discourse in the Thatcher era has now become common parlance in relation to the EU. Indeed, as this chapter will show, Eurosceptics have played a significant role in the integration process as agenda-setters and 'entrepreneurs of contentious issues' (Usherwood 2004:14). As such, they have influenced, in part, the terms of the debate on European integration and the definition of the EU's agenda.

It is argued here that Euroscepticism matters for three main reasons. First, the EC was founded as a compromise between different, even competing views as to its nature and its finalities. Today, the issue of the debate is whether the Union will further develop into a supranational, political community or 'spill back' towards more traditional forms of interstate cooperation. At stake is thus the endurance of a unique system of multinational governance and pooled sovereignty between states. Second, the debate between Eurosceptics and advocates of political unification has implications for global governance. Indeed, if the EU were to be reduced to a mere free trade area, as many Eurosceptics in and outside the EU wish, it is unlikely that the agenda for a more regulated trade liberalization would be supported by other major players on the world stage. Third, Euroscepticism can be analyzed as one of the symptoms of the transformation of democracy in a globalizing world. Not only did Eurosceptics raise the key question of legitimacy at the EU level, thus playing a crucial role in the development of a more democratic EU, public Euroscepticism as a sociological phenomenon also sheds light on the challenging impact of market integration on national democracy and on the relationship between state and society.

The chapter begins by explaining how Eurosceptics in national governments can exert an influence on EU-level decision-making and argues that specific features of the EU institutional system tend to compound this influence. In a second section, the chapter analyzes how Euroscepticism influenced the evolution of EU governance and changes in the balance of power between EU institutions, in a context where there is no clear support for supranational solutions among governments. A third section assesses the impact of Euroscepticism on the EU's external relations and on how it is perceived by third country actors, showing how competing views on the future of the EU interact with a more global debate on the future of global governance. The chapter concludes, in the fourth section, by analyzing Euroscepticism as a welcome thorn in the EU's side, as it prompts the EU to confront not only its own democratic deficit, but also how this deficit affects democratic governance at the domestic level.

Eurosceptics: channels of influence in the EU

Although Eurosceptic parties' electoral weight is significant, their influence on decisions affecting the EU is mainly indirect, as it is channelled through national governments. In this respect, some of the institutional features of the EU allow for a disproportionate influence of Eurosceptic orientations on the integration process, not only in day-to-day decision-making, but also in 'history-making decisions' (following Peterson and Bromberg's typology (1999:10)) that determine the shape of the EU and the direction of the integration process. Moreover, the impact of Euroscepticism on the integration process is compounded by the more frequent use of referenda (as opposed to parliamentary ratification) in order to settle debated EU issues (at least in the case of EMU and the EU Constitutional Treaty).

A limited influence in the EU's institutional triangle

On average, Eurosceptic parties, be they of the hard or the soft sort, appeal to roughly one-fifth of the EU's electorate. While electoral support for hard Eurosceptic parties in national elections remains very limited, with 4 to 5 per cent of the vote, the mean electoral score for Eurosceptic parties (both soft and hard) oscillates between 15 and 20 per cent (Taggart and Szczerbiak 2002:16–24; Ray 2007:165). This corresponds roughly to the proportion of Eurosceptic representatives in the EP (see pp.130–1). This significant electoral weight, however, does not translate into direct influence on EU-level decision-making within the EU's institutional triangle (the Parliament, Commission and Council).

Regarding the EP, the overwhelming majority of overtly Eurosceptic MEPs are confined to small Eurosceptic groups. This small influence is further reduced by their limited ability to engage in party networking at the EU level, as there are no Eurosceptic transnational party federations. Furthermore, the most Eurosceptic groups in the EP are characterized by low levels of internal cohesion. For example, the overall cohesion rate of the Independence and Democracy (IND-DEM) group between 2004 and 2009 was only 47 per cent (compared with 91 per cent for the pro-European Greens) (Votewatch.eu 2009). Besides, the most Eurosceptic groups are rarely part of a winning majority during EP votes. Between 2004 and 2009, for instance, the radical left-wing GUE-NGL (United European Left-Nordic Green Left) and the radical right-wing IND-DEM were part of a winning majority in 52 per cent and 46 per cent of cases respectively, compared with 86 per cent for the main group European People's Party-European Democrats (EPP-ED) (Votewatch.eu 2009).

As far as the European Commission is concerned, Eurosceptics have a limited influence on the formation of the College of Commissioners. Since Commissioners are appointed on the basis of a list of candidates pre-selected by national governments, in agreement with the Commission's President, there is little probability that a strongly Eurosceptic candidate might end up in the College. Besides, the fact that the EP now organizes hearings for individual commissioners, in order to test their competences and overall commitment to their future portfolio, might act as a filter, preventing controversial and/or overtly Eurosceptic candidates from accessing the College. Certainly, not all Commissioners are Euro-enthusiasts. The case of Frits Bolkestein, whose nomination as Dutch Commissioner in 1999 triggered a controversy in the Netherlands over his allegedly Eurosceptic position (Harmsen 2004:108), illustrates this. More fundamentally, governments have sometimes prevented the nomination of strongly Europhile politicians from accessing the Commission's presidency, as John Major did with Jean-Luc Dehaene in 1994 and Tony Blair with Guy Verhofstadt in 2004.

Concerning the Council, any direct influence of hard or strongly Eurosceptic elements is limited by two factors. First, being mostly protest-based parties, strongly Eurosceptic parties in the EU are rarely represented in governments. Second, most of the Council's work is prepared by COREPER-level ambassadors and by the Council's working groups and thus remains relatively immune to the turmoil of domestic politics. Despite being a diplomatic organ, the Committee of Permanent Representatives (COREPER) is permeated by a strong culture of compromise. Member states' representatives share a commitment to ensuring the performance and smooth functioning of the Council, which influences the defence of national interests (Lewis 1998). Similarly, the Council's working groups, composed of national civil servants, have developed specific transnational communication networks which do not rely on a narrow definition of national interests (Beyers and Dierickx 1998).

In this context, Eurosceptics' main channels of influence in the EU are national governments. First, there might be Eurosceptic factions among mainstream incumbent parties (as in the case of the British Labour and Conservative parties, the Italian Forza Italia, etc.). Second, coalition governments may include Eurosceptic coalition partners (examples include the Communist party in French governments and the extreme right parties Lega Nord and

Freiheitliche Partei Österreichs (FPÖ) in the Italian and Austrian governments). Third, governing parties might be tempted to toughen their stance in the Council in order to confront a strong Eurosceptic opposition in domestic politics (as the British Labour party did during negotiations on the Lisbon Treaty in 2007). Consequently, institutional devices giving single governments a disproportionate influence in decision-making are likely to compound Eurosceptics' impact on the integration process. Three such devices are examined below: the rotating EU presidency, voting systems in the Council and provisions on treaty reform.

The rotating Council presidency: a platform for Eurosceptic governments?

The rotating presidency of the Council can certainly provide Europhile governments with a good opportunity to attempt to further integration (as was the case in the Dutch presidency during the Maastricht Treaty negotiations, for example). Moreover, national presidencies can boost the popularity of the EU in the country that holds the presidency, as has been argued elsewhere (Semetko *et al.* 2003). However, the rotating presidency (which is maintained by the Lisbon Treaty, except for the European Council and the External Relations Council) can also be a serious challenge for the EU.

Indeed, it endows a single government, for a six-month period, with the responsibility of managing the daily business of the EU, of acting as a broker between all the actors involved, of displaying leadership skills and of representing the EU on the world stage (see Schout and Vanhoonacker 2006). Consequently, domestic governments face a difficult task. They still represent national interests at the EU level, but, at the same time, their presidential role requires the ability to rise above the fray and avoid an overly parochial, narrow-minded defence of one's preferences, especially in times of crisis or when crucial decisions are on the agenda. This is the case, for instance, during Intergovernmental Conferences (IGCs), when amendments to existing treaties are negotiated.

Certainly, several factors limit the room for manoeuvre of any government holding the presidency. First, the presidency's ability to influence the EU's agenda is limited, at least in the first pillar of the EU, by the Commission's monopoly on legislative initiative. Moreover, member states have unequal resources (in terms of EU expertise, staff, etc.) enabling them to influence the EU's agenda according to their preferences (Hix 2005:81). Second, peer pressure and the wish to have a 'successful' presidency might deter them from taking initiatives that could harm their own country's reputation. Third, other actors, such as the Council's General Secretariat, other national delegations, and the Commission, have to be taken into account by the presidency when it tries to broker deals (Schout and Vanhoonacker 2006:1054).

In this context, peer pressure and 'path-dependency' logic limit the ability of Eurosceptic segments inside governments to push their agendas. This was illustrated, for instance, by the 2003 Italian and 2009 Czech EU presidencies. In both cases, government coalitions were deeply divided over European integration and the main coalition party (the Italian Forza Italia and the Czech ODS) included significant Eurosceptic factions. Furthermore, both presidencies were scheduled at times when crucial decisions had to be made on EU institutional issues: the first three months of the IGC on the EU Constitutional Treaty in 2003, and the deadlock over the ratification of the Lisbon Treaty following the Irish referendum of 2008. In fact, both presidencies could only delay institutional reforms; they were not able to prevent them. While the Italian presidency tried to oppose significant institutional reforms during the 2003 IGC (the extension of EP powers in the adoption of the EU budget, the extension of the scope of qualified majority voting (QMV) to judicial cooperation, etc.) (Quaglia and Moxon-Browne 2004:19), it could only postpone them until the end of 2003, when the Irish government took over. Similarly, the Czech presidency in 2009 found itself in a paradoxical situation. It was expected to negotiate a deal with the Irish government in order to overcome Irish voters' hostility towards the Lisbon treaty, whilst Czech President Vaclav Klaus had used every possible means (including lodging a complaint before the Czech Constitutional Court) to block the ratification of the treaty in his own country (Král, Bartovic and Řiháčková 2009:23–5). Eventually, the Czech government negotiated the deal, which paved the way for a second referendum and the entering into force of the Lisbon Treaty.

However, the presidency can be used as a platform by Eurosceptic actors. This was the case, for instance, with Vaclav Klaus' speech in the EP on 12 February 2009 at the beginning of the Czech EU presidency, as he made his case against political integration and the current EU institutional system, in a speech strongly reminiscent of Margaret Thatcher's Bruges speech. Furthermore, EU presidencies can be used by segments inside governments or the state apparatus to push through Eurosceptic initiatives, as was illustrated by the French presidency in the second half of 2008. While the French presidency was hailed by many as a case of successful leadership, the Mediterranean Union Initiative, launched by the French government, triggered considerable controversy in the EU. Initiated by Henri Guaino, adviser to French President Nicolas Sarkozy, this project initially aimed at revitalizing links between southern EU countries and partner countries from North Africa and the Middle East. Initially called the Mediterranean Union, it was conceived – and rightly perceived – as a rival to the existing Barcelona process (managed by the European Commission on behalf of the EU) and as a way to circumvent EU institutions in a region of traditional French influence. Moreover, it left out non-Mediterranean EU countries. Strongly criticized by other member states' governments (such as German Chancellor Angela Merkel, who warned against a 'splitting' of the Union) and lukewarmly welcomed by the European Commission, the project had to be amended to get rid of its most Eurosceptic elements. Renamed 'Union for the Mediterranean', it is now being developed within the existing EU framework of the Barcelona process and encompasses all EU members. This is a good example of how peer pressure and path dependency limit a presidency's ability to circumvent the EU institutional system. However, even in the revised version of the project, the Commission clearly appears to be marginalized in the Union for the Mediterranean, which is co-presided, on a rotating basis, by one EU member state and a partner country. Moreover, the Commission is not officially represented in the secretariat of the organization.

Decision-making procedures in the Council

Alongside the rotating presidency, the decision-making procedures in the Council, which allow one member state, or a small group of member states, to paralyse the Union's entire decision-making process, tend to give a disproportionate influence to Eurosceptic parties or factions inside governments. Such is the case with unanimous voting (as opposed to QMV), which remains the rule in several areas.

Certainly, whether the extension of the scope of QMV in the

Council enhances the EU decision-making capacity can be debated. On the one hand, decision-making in the Council is strongly permeated by a consensual political culture and formal voting is rare. Between 1998 and 2004, for instance, the Council formally voted in less than 20 per cent of cases. Moreover, decision by consensus tends to remain the rule, even when the treaty provides for QMV (70 per cent of cases over the same period) (Hayes-Renshaw *et al.* 2006). On the other hand, treaty provisions on QMV can be used by governments that support the adoption of a proposal to put pressure on reluctant governments, if the latter could lose in a formal vote.

Indeed, unanimous voting has historically allowed soft Eurosceptic governments to impose their views on others. The first instance of this was the so-called 'empty chair crisis' triggered by French President Charles de Gaulle in 1965, in order to prevent the extension of the scope of QMV, which was foreseen in the TEC. For a long time, the ill-named Luxembourg compromise (adopted in 1966) has allowed individual countries to veto significant pieces of legislation. For instance, following the 1965–66 crisis, proposals for a directive on the free movement of capital in the EC were abandoned by the Commission for two decades. Similarly, unanimous voting has allowed Tory-led British governments to oppose the adoption of significant pieces of legislation in the social and fiscal fields.

Provisions on treaty reform

What is true for day-to-day EU policy-making also applies to major, history-making decisions on institutional reforms. Indeed, treaty provisions on the amendment of EU treaties (Article 48 of the Treaty on European Union (TEU)) foresee that, once member states have determined the amendments to be made to the treaties 'by common accord', 'the amendments shall enter into force after being ratified by all the Member States in accordance with their respective constitutional requirements'.

Certainly, the unanimity requirement (both for the adoption and for the ratification of amendments) may be considered as more democratic than the majority logic, at least for those who understand the EU primarily as a union of states. Furthermore, for pro-Europeans, the unanimity requirement may act as a safeguard against risks of institutional spillbacks, such as a situation in which a majority of governments would be willing to trim the powers of the Commission.

At the same time, requiring unanimity for the adoption of amendments allows one single government to block negotiations on treaty reform. As a consequence, Eurosceptic governments, or governments which are under pressure from Eurosceptics in the national arena, can block or delay significant reforms. For example, during the 1997 Amsterdam European Council, German Chancellor Helmut Kohl blocked the extension of the scope of QMV, which was supported by all other governments. Chancellor Kohl's attitude was mainly due to his weakened position in domestic politics on the eve of a crushing electoral defeat and to a growing Euroscepticism in some of the *Länder* (Peterson and Bromberg 1999:18). Another example relates to the negotiations on the Lisbon Treaty in June 2007, when the Polish government, led by Eurosceptic Prime Minister Jaroslaw Kaczyński, insisted on postponing the implementation of the new treaty provisions on double majority voting until 2014.

The unanimity requirement for the ratification of amendments also allows one country to block the entering into force of major treaty revisions. The failed ratification of the EU Constitutional Treaty is a good example of this. Following its rejection by the French and Dutch electorate, the ratification process was put on hold by the European Council in June 2005, at a time when eighteen member states, accounting for 56 per cent of the EU population, had ratified the treaty. Finally, the lack of a uniform procedure to ratify treaty reforms tends to bias the distribution of political clout among member states during IGCs, by strengthening the position of those member states where treaty revisions are to be ratified by referendum and where high levels of public Euroscepticism make this ratification uncertain. This was illustrated by negotiations on the Lisbon Treaty in 2007, as the UK (where Prime Minister Blair had committed himself to upholding a referendum on the EU Constitutional Treaty) relied on this argument in order to obtain significant opt-outs.

The mounting pressure for national referenda

The increasing use of referenda in relation to European integration in the course of the 1990s is illustrative of how Eurosceptics influence the agenda of mainstream parties on issues of integration. In fact, it is not the demand for referenda *per se* which can be analyzed as a Eurosceptic claim, but rather demands for referenda in an exclusively national context. Whether EU-wide (as opposed to national) referenda could contribute to a de-nationalization of domestic public debates on EU issues, as has been argued elsewhere (Habermas 2008:11), remains uncertain. However, the national context certainly biases the terms of the debate by obscuring the European dimension of the issues at stake in a referendum.

Between 1972 and 2009, 36 EC/EU-related referenda (half of which were accession referenda) were organized in current EU countries – the number rises to 43 if one adds non-EU countries (Norway, Greenland, Liechstenstein and Switzerland) and referenda on the European Economic Area (EEA). Accordingly, between a fifth and a third of referenda related to European integration have resulted in the rejection of major treaty changes, EU accession or participation in EMU (see Table 1.1).

Traditionally, advocates of further integration have been reluctant to promote direct democracy in an EU context. Beyond traditional arguments pointing to the limits of referenda in general (the low levels of information voters have on complex issues and the plebiscitary use of referenda, for example), those who oppose the use of referenda in relation to EU issues put forward three arguments. First, referenda on EU issues tend to be intrinsically biased in favour of 'No' campaigners. Indeed, arguing in favour of institutional deepening, monetary union or enlargement is especially difficult since gains are either long-term and/or abstract. As a consequence, the arguments of Yes campaigners are often either very general or negative (emphasizing, for instance, the consequences of a No). Secondly, EU citizens have very unequal voting rights in this respect, given the variety of national constitutional provisions on the use of referenda. Among the 36 referenda that have been organized in the EC/EU between 1972 and 2009, 40 per cent took place in only two countries (8 in Ireland and 6 in Denmark). Third, there is a discordance between the dimensions of integration that are affected by referenda outcomes and the willingness of voters to express their preferences on specific EU policies. Indeed, EU-related referenda concern the EU's 'constitutive issues' (Bartolini 2006:35), i.e., issues of membership and institutional reforms. However, large segments of voters defeat institutional reforms in order to express dissatisfaction with the content of EU policies or opposition to further EU enlargement. Hence, there is a risk that EU-related referenda raise expectations for policy change that are unlikely to be fulfilled, thus creating further frustrations

TABLE 1.1   *EC/EU-related referenda in EU countries. 1972–2009*

Subject	Year	Turnout(%)	% Yes	% No
Accessions				
Åland Islands	1994	49	73.60	26.40
Austria	1994	81.30	66.60	33.40
Czech Republic	2003	55.21	77.33	22.67
Denmark	1972	90.10	63.40	36.60
Estonia	2003	64.06	66.83	33.17
Finland	1994	74.00	56.90	43.10
France*	1972	60.24	68.32	31.68
Hungary	2003	45.62	83.76	16.24
Ireland	1972	70.90	83.10	16.90
Latvia	2003	72.53	67	32.30
Lithuania	2003	63.37	91.07	8.93
Malta	2003	91	53.65	46.35
Poland	2003	58.85	77.45	22.55
Slovakia	2003	52.15	92.46	6.20
Slovenia	2003	60.29	89.61	10.39
Sweden	1994	83.30	52.80	47.20
UK**	1975	64	67.20	32.80
Treaties				
SEA				
Denmark	1986	75.40	56.20	43.80
Ireland	1987	43.90	69.90	30.10
Maastricht				
Denmark	1992	83.10	49.30	50.70

* On whether Denmark. Ireland and the UK should join the EC.
** On continued membership of the EC.   →

about the EU. The 2005 French referendum illustrated this, as a large majority of voters voted against the alleged 'neo-liberal' bias of EU policies. In a similar vein, the 2001 Irish referendum on the Nice Treaty appeared to have been driven, to a significant extent, by hostility towards the coming EU enlargement.

Despite these reservations, since the beginning of the 1990s political elites have been under mounting pressure to hold referenda in order to legitimize major EC/EU institutional reforms. This can be attributed to several factors. To begin with, it is due to a global trend dating back to the 1970s, as Western democracies started

$\rightarrow$

Subject	Year	Turnout(%)	% Yes	% No
Denmark	1993	86.50	56.70	43.30
France	1992	69.70	51.05	48.95
Ireland	1992	57.30	69.10	30.90
Amsterdam				
Denmark	1998	76.20	55.10	44.90
Ireland	1998	56.20	61.70	38.30
Nice				
Ireland	2001	34.80	46.10	53.90
Ireland	2002	49.47	62.89	37.11
Constitutional Treaty				
France	2005	69.34	45.32	54.68
Luxembourg	2005	compulsory	56.52	43.48
Spain	2005	42.32	76.73	17.24
Netherlands	2005	63.30	38.50	61.50
Lisbon				
Ireland	2008	53.13	44.60	53.40
Ireland	2009	59	67.10	32.90
EMU				
Denmark	2000	87.60	46.80	53.20
Sweden	2003	82.60	42	55.90
Political union				
Italy***	1989	81	88.10	

*** On whether the EP should be given a mandate to draft a European constitution.

experiencing increasing demands for more direct and participatory democracy. Moreover, it results from EU-related developments. First, the Maastricht Treaty and its provisions on EMU have prompted the creation of single-issue parties, like the British Referendum Party and the German *Bund Freier Buerger*, which demanded referenda on EMU. Second, the acceleration and the widening of the scope of EU enlargement waves since 1994 have prompted calls for referenda on the accession of new countries to the EU. Third, the so-called 'constitutionalization' of the EU, with the drafting of the EU Charter of Fundamental Rights and the EU

Constitutional Treaty, conveyed the idea of a change in the nature of the integration process. Thus, even if it is somewhat improper in relation to the EU (Bartolini 2006:38; Dehousse 2005), the term 'Constitution' has added further pressure on European elites to hold referenda on the EU Constitutional Treaty in countries where it was not a constitutional requirement (as was the case in the four countries where referenda on the treaty were held in 2005). A good illustration of this is the case of the Netherlands, where Parliament has been pushing the agenda for referenda on EU enlargement and on the Constitutional Treaty since 2002 (Harmsen 2004:114–15).

Euroscepticism and the evolution of EU governance: towards a less supranational Union?

What is at stake in the debate between soft Eurosceptics and advocates of a tightly integrated Union is not the existence of the EU as such but the nature of the EU. As has been shown, hard Eurosceptics are lightweights in electoral terms (at least in most countries during national elections). Moreover, several crises in the course of the integration process have illustrated the robustness of EC institutions. President de Gaulle's failure to promote alternative institutions in the field of political cooperation, with the so-called Fouchet plan (1961–62), was a case in point. What is more, even in times of heightened tension with the EU, Eurosceptic governments do not question the legitimacy of the Union as such. A good example of this was the stance of the British Conservative government during the 1996 BSE crisis, when it made clear that it would only use legal means to contest the decision of the EU veterinary committee not to lift the ban on British beef. By doing so, John Major's government clearly stated that it accepted in advance the authority of the ECJ on this issue, even if it was under intense pressure from a vociferously anti-European tabloid press (Neyer and Wolf 2000:9). Regarding the nature of the Union, there are two conflicting views (with some intermediate positions between the two). Whereas most soft Eurosceptics wish the Union to operate more like an international organization (with unanimity-based decision-making and a streamlined Commission acting as secretariat, except in market-making policies), advocates of the EU as a political community think the underlying logic of the EU should be that of integration. While the EU certainly combines, in complex ways, both logics (interstate cooperation and integration), the dividing line between the two positions relates to the principle of supranationalism. To pro-integration advocates, the *sui generis* nature of the EU, as an original way of managing interdependence between countries, resides in the idea that a general interest can be defined that is more than the mere addition of national interests and more than the lowest common denominator between governments' positions. The definition of this general interest must be entrusted to supranational institutions (in this case the Commission), whose independence *vis-à-vis* the states should be safeguarded. By contrast, most Eurosceptics are highly sceptical of supranationalism and understand the EU's legitimacy as relying exclusively on the states.

In this respect, it is argued in this section that soft Eurosceptics have influenced the terms of the debate on the evolution of EU governance, as the decreased centrality of the Community method attests. Parallel to this, as changes in the balance of power inside the EU's institutional triangle have occurred, the European Commission has had increasing difficulties in defining and promoting the Union's general interest, a trend to which Euroscepticism at elite and public levels has contributed. Finally, it is argued that soft Eurosceptic ideas are more likely to be influential in a context where the EU lacks governmental leadership, as recent IGCs have illustrated.

The decreasing centrality of the Community method

The core positions of soft Eurosceptics on EU institutional issues were outlined in Margaret Thatcher's Bruges speech: opposition to a so-called 'European super-state' or 'federal Europe', a strict limitation of the Commission's powers, and an emphasis on the European Council as the overarching institution of the Union, seen as a way to trim the Commission's powers (1988:6–7). These core tenets of Thatcher's understanding of the EC have permeated successive reforms and evolutions of EU governance since the early 1990s, allowing, to some extent, for a 'Thatcherisation of the EU' (Usherwood 2004:15). The weakening of the historic Community method and the development of new forms of governance of an intergovernmental nature attest to this influence.

Historically, the Community method has been seen as a guarantee of supranationalism. It refers to a specific mode of governance, where all institutions jointly participate in the exercise of power. More specifically, it entrusts the Commission with a monopoly on legislative initiative, implies majority voting in the Council, the adoption of legislation under the co-decision procedure, and full powers of judicial review and legal adjudication for the ECJ. The Community method has been targeted by Eurosceptics since the early days of integration, notably because the Commission's monopoly on legislative initiative endows this institution with a clearly political role, that of the motor of integration. To Eurosceptics, however, the Commission is and should remain an 'appointed bureaucracy' (Thatcher 1988:7). Furthermore, the Community method implies a specific political culture – the constant search for compromises and the acceptance of 'dissymmetric concessions' between partners (at least in the short run), which presupposes a relatively high degree of trust between governments (Olivi 2001:111).

Eurosceptic leaders have contributed to undermining the political culture that underlies the Community method. Indeed, the first breach with the Community method was initiated by French President Charles de Gaulle, with the use of national veto power (in 1963, 1965 and 1967). De Gaulle's successive vetoes have had a lasting impact on the EC's predominant political culture. From that time on, member states were no longer prepared to postpone concessions. The Commission's political role was also affected, as it became clear, especially with the Empty Chair crisis (1965), that integration could only be furthered on the basis of *ad hoc* agreements between the most influential member states (Olivi 2001:111–5). Similarly, Margaret Thatcher's famous claim during the 1984 Fontainebleau European Council ('I want my money back') legitimized the logic of a 'fair return', versus the principle of 'dissymmetric concessions'. Certainly, governments' willingness to counter-balance the Community method was not limited to Eurosceptics. The formal creation of the European Council in 1974 could be analyzed, partly at least, from that angle. Indeed, the increasing coordinating role of the European Council has tended to develop at the expense of the Commission's power of initiative (Majone 2006:615). Negotiations on the Maastricht Treaty represented a landmark in this respect, as most governments rejected the Dutch presidency's proposal to generalize the Community method and opted for a pillar structure, with largely reduced powers for supranational institutions in the second and third pillars.

What is more, since the end of the 1990s, the decreasing centrality of the Community method was facilitated, in part, by the development of new forms of governance of an intergovernmental nature, such as the Open Method of Coordination (OMC). Presented as a 'third way' between harmonization and intergovernmental cooperation, the OMC, defined by one EU scholar as 'integration without law' (Dehousse 2004:166), is a lax coordination mechanism relying on soft law. It aims at fostering the diffusion of the 'best practices' in areas where the EU has no or little power (such as employment and social policies). Even if it gives the Commission the mission of defining guidelines for policy reform, the OMC clearly enhances the role of the European Council and completely bypasses the EP and the ECJ. The OMC is also emblematic of a specific type of discourse on EU governance, which tends to emphasize the intergovernmental dimension of the EU. For instance, advocates of the 'network Europe' metaphor call for the development of 'market-like relations' between the different components of the EU, laying greater emphasis on 'horizontal' (instead of 'top-down') relations and 'decentralisation' (Leonard 1999:9–12). In this respect, the ideological background of the OMC is very reminiscent of the ideas of Dutch soft Eurosceptics (such as former Secretary for European Affairs Dick Benschop and former EU Commissioner Frits Bolkestein), who also advocate a greater emphasis on interstate relations as an alternative to a strong Commission leadership, a greater reliance on soft law and a stricter respect of the subsidiarity principle. In line with Thatcher's views, they want the Commission to refocus on core tasks, such as completing the internal market and guaranteeing free competition (Harmsen 2004:101).

A weakened Commission

The ability of the Commission to demonstrate leadership skills has certainly always varied across policy areas and time. Moreover, the Commission may exercise different forms of leadership (Nugent 2001:217), so that the relative decline of one form of leadership may be compensated, at the same time, by increased opportunities to provide other forms of leadership. Keeping these nuances in mind, it seems that, in the course of the last decade, the Commission has shifted from a proactive leadership, seeking to expand the Union's powers, to a more defensive strategy, aiming first and foremost at strengthening its own legitimacy. Parallel to this, the role of the Commission as an agenda-setter, as the driving engine of the integration process, seems to have declined. This trend is due to multiple factors, and notably to the growing power and political clout of the EP, as was illustrated in 1999 by the collective resignation of the Commission's College under EP pressure. It is also due to increasing tensions between the Commission's multiple types of accountabilities, since reforms aimed at enhancing 'democratic accountability' (bringing the Commission closer to citizens) may diminish the Commission's ability to take national interests into account ('diplomatic accountability') (Christiansen 1997). Expressions of elite and public Euroscepticism have also contributed to the development of this more defensive strategy on the part of the Commission. In the course of the 1990s, 'Commission bashing' by national governments became quite frequent. An illustration of this was the 1998 joint Kohl–Chirac letter, in which the Commission was indirectly blamed for its alleged inappropriate interference in domestic affairs and its supposed remoteness from average citizens (quoted in Meyer 1999:634). Moreover, declining levels of public support for EU membership, as well as recent referenda, further restrained the Commission's room for manoeuvre in acting as promoter of the Community's general interest. This political context had a threefold impact on the Commission: on the reform of its governance and working methods, on its roles as initiator of legislative processes and guardian of the treaties, and, albeit indirectly, on re-nationalization tendencies inside the College of Commissioners.

Reform of the Commission's governance and working methods
The influence of Eurosceptic criticism on the reform of the Commission's work is illustrated by the fact that terms like 'centralism', 'red tape' and 'bureaucracy' have become common parlance in relation to the Commission, which increasingly has to justify its initiatives. In communicating on its proposals, the Commission increasingly articulates a self-justifying discourse, centred on notions of subsidiarity and impact assessment. Since the Maastricht Treaty has elevated subsidiarity to a core principle for the exercise of the EC's (non-exclusive) powers, the Commission has to justify its proposals with regard to this principle. In a similar vein, since 2002, the Commission has had to conduct a threefold impact assessment (economic, social, environmental) for each legislative proposal, an assessment which, since 2006, has included potential administrative costs. The introduction of systematic impact assessment illustrates a wider climate in which the Commission tries to respond to criticism over alleged red tape and bureaucracy. To this

end, it set up, in 2007, a high-level group on administrative burdens, chaired by former Bavarian Minister-President Edmund Stoiber (Euractiv 2007), who has long advocated a repatriation of the Union's powers to the regional level and regularly criticized the Commission's alleged regulation excesses (Leconte 2003:424–5).

A lower profile as agenda-setter and guardian of the treaty
Weak governmental enthusiasm for integration and recent referenda have also affected the Commission's key roles as agenda-setter (deriving from its monopoly on legislative initiative) and as guardian of the treaties (notably, the possibility of engaging in infringement procedures against member states failing to comply with EU law).

The 2005 referenda in France and the Netherlands and the 2008 referendum in Ireland illustrated how expressions of public Euroscepticism may affect the Commission's power of initiative. A good example of this is the Directive Proposal on Temporary Agency Workers, initially tabled in 2002, which aimed at guaranteeing better protection for temporary workers across the EU. This directive proposal was very controversial in some member states, especially in the UK, where a referendum on the EU Constitutional Treaty had been foreseen. In September 2005, a couple of months after the French and Dutch referenda, the Commission announced it would 'reconsider' the proposal, as part of a wider initiative on 'better legislation' (European Commission 2005a:4). Similarly, the results of the first Irish referendum on the Lisbon Treaty prompted the Commission to abstain from presenting a legislative proposal on a Common Corporate Consolidated Tax Base (CCCTB), as it had announced it would do in 2008 (European Commission 2007c:7). The need for a CCCTB had been stressed, however, by the Commission itself, as a way to eliminate tax base competition for corporate headquarters in the internal market. As concerns over a possible harmonization of corporate tax systems had been one of the core arguments of No campaigners during the referendum, the Commission's services did not wish to jeopardize the second Irish referendum on the Lisbon Treaty. This perspective also prevented the French presidency (in the second half of 2008) from taking bold initiatives in the areas of defence and tax harmonization (*The Irish Times* 2008a).

Moreover, concerns over risks of fanning Euroscepticism also influence the Commission's role as guardian of the treaties. This is especially likely in cases where specific EU legislation proves highly controversial at the domestic level. In the past, for instance, the Commission hesitated to start an infringement procedure against Germany for faulty compliance with the Packaging Directive (on waste recycling), taking into account 'the high level of political conflict such a step would have provoked in this sensitive regulatory area' (Haverland 2000:99). Recently, the prospect of a second Irish referendum on the Lisbon Treaty in October 2009 deterred the Commission's services from starting infringement procedures against Ireland. The financial crisis that broke out in 2008 reinforced this low-profile strategy. In October 2008, the Irish government reacted to the financial crisis by offering unlimited guarantees to citizens who deposited their savings in the biggest Irish banks. This decision could have been highly detrimental to free competition in the internal market, as there were serious risks of massive shifts of savings from non-Irish banks to Ireland. However, despite mounting pressure to act, the Commission did not start an inquiry into whether the Irish government had violated treaty provisions on state aid.

Re-nationalization tendencies
To the extent that Euroscepticism serves as a pretext for a more blunt articulation of national interests by member states (see the case of the IGCs below), it might have contributed to re-nationalization tendencies inside the Commission, among Commissioners' cabinets and the College of Commissioners.

Existing studies have refined the ideal-typical perception of the Commission as a purely supranational institution that is entirely detached from national influences and loyalties. For now, it seems that the Commission has developed neither a common identity nor a shared emotional commitment to further European integration (Cini 1996:223). Even among the Commission's civil servants, who are often assumed to be the forerunners of a new cosmopolitan identity, patterns of national identification and logics of solidarity among fellow nationals persist. This phenomenon is compounded by appointment procedures for top civil servants in the institution and by member states' attempts to enhance the influence of their nationals at the summit of the Commission's hierarchy (Meyer 1999:627; Bellier 2000:144–8). These practices may hamper the Commission's ability to act as the promoter of a general interest, thus possibly fostering public scepticism as to its legitimacy. Indeed, member states' interference within the Commission's organization makes it less transparent and less comprehensible to citizens.

Similarly, within the College of Commissioners, several factors have contributed, since the late 1990s, to a weakening of the principle of collegiality and to the reaffirmation of national logics (Jacqué 2008:459), notably the increasing political influence of Commissioners' cabinets inside the institution. In order to counter the tendency of member states to consider commissioners as representatives of national interests, the Lisbon Treaty foresaw a reduction in the size of the College (which would operate, from 2014 on, on the basis of equal rotation between member states), thus breaking with the current principle of 'one Commissioner per member state'. Such a reform was also deemed necessary in order to maintain the authority of the Commission's President over his team and allow a smaller team to focus on core priorities. However, the prospect of losing a Commissioner in the College raised concerns in smaller member states, notably in Ireland, where it was one of the reasons underlying the rejection of the Lisbon Treaty in 2008. Consequently, in order to secure Irish ratification of the same treaty in a second referendum, the European Council decided in June 2009 that 'the Commission shall continue to include one national of each Member State' (Council of the European Union 2009:2). Certainly, this decision does not question other Lisbon Treaty provisions aimed at enhancing the authority of the Commission's President over his team (for instance, by allowing him personally to remove individual Commissioners). However, this concession is likely to further the re-nationalization of the College and undermine attempts to reinforce the president's leadership capacities.

A lack of governmental leadership

This lack of leadership is not compensated for at the governmental level, as recent European Councils and the latest IGC have illustrated. During the last decade, the blunt articulation of national interests among heads of state and government was clearly perceptible at successive European Councils (notably in Berlin in 1999, Nice in 2000 and Brussels in 2005), marking 'the return to brutal periods of defence of the national interest' (Majone 2006:610). Certainly, European Councils in the past had also witnessed tough bargaining between member states (as was most famously the case in Fontainebleau in 1984). However, the increasing media coverage of

European Councils, as well as the discrepancy between discourses on the EU as a 'community of values' and hard interstate bargaining, can only foster scepticism among citizens. As media scholars have shown, this 'hard bargaining' image of European Councils conveys a negative view of the EU among the public, which may be conducive to Eurosceptic orientations (see p.199).

Negotiations on the Lisbon Treaty during the 2007 IGC were also a good example of this lack of governmental leadership. Certainly, for advocates of further integration, the Lisbon Treaty is a success, as it implies enhanced powers for the EP, an extended scope for majority voting, the principle of a double majority, and new powers for the EC. However, the 2007 IGC contrasted with previous exercises in crisis management in the life of the EC/EU. Previously, when a single country rejected a new amending treaty by referendum (as in the case of Denmark in 1992 and Ireland in 2001), governments did not re-open negotiations on the treaty but, instead, sought specific solutions (usually in the form of European Council resolutions) in order to accommodate the concerns voiced by national electorates. This time, governments decided to re-open negotiations on the EU Constitutional Treaty, a text they had signed in 2004. Furthermore, the Dutch and French 2005 referenda empowered Eurosceptic governments, such as the British and Polish ones, by reinforcing their demands for derogations (relating to the EU Charter of Fundamental Rights, as well as cooperation over police and criminal justice for the UK). The 2005 referendum also put considerable pressure on the Dutch government, which defended a tough line against the Union's symbols and the EU Charter of Fundamental Rights (Ziller 2008:24). This is due to the fact that concerns over national identity and a possible extension of the Union's powers had been key motivations underlying the Dutch No (see p.180). More generally, EP observers in the 2007 IGC deplored 'the wording of several passages of the Treaty ... entailing an unjustified shift to a negative tone, which gives an impression of mistrust vis-à-vis the Union and its institutions and thus sends a wrong signal to public opinion' (European Parliament 2007:9). Finally, during the 2007 IGC, few governments were willing to put forward initiatives to further integration. For instance, a proposal by the Italian delegation (led by former Commission President and Prime Minister Romano Prodi) to add a protocol on enhanced cooperation in monetary policy and macro-economic coordination to the Lisbon Treaty was only supported by a handful of delegations (notably the Belgian and Luxembourg ones).

Euroscepticism outside the EU: implications for international relations

At stake in the debate between soft Eurosceptics and advocates of a tightly integrated community is also the role that the EU is expected to play in international relations. Indeed, many Eurosceptics (from both right and left) argue that the EU is too 'inward-looking' (Thatcher 1988:10). While left-wing critics emphasize the impact of EU protectionism on developing countries, right-wing critics aim at making the EU a free trade area open to global trade. To (right-wing) Eurosceptics, the EU should drive the agenda for global trade, without developing a political self-understanding of its role in international relations. Such was the meaning, for instance, of Henry Kissinger's famous 'Year of Europe' speech, in which the Secretary of State declared that 'the United States has global interests and responsibilities. Our European allies have regional interests' (Kissinger 1973:594). This speech was (correctly) interpreted by many Europeans as a statement confining EC political cooperation to a merely regional scope.

By contrast, for advocates of a political union, the EU has a specific contribution to make in the stabilization of the international system – an idea that was first articulated in the Declaration on European Identity, adopted by the nine EC countries in reaction to Kissinger's speech (Council of the European Communities 1973). EU enlargement especially, it is argued, allows the EU to act as a 'transformative power' (Leonard 2005) by reinforcing processes of political and economic transition in candidate countries. Moreover, as the most regulated market in the world, the EU could drive the agenda for more regulations (environmental, social, financial, etc.) at a global level. This section highlights the stakes of the debate between these two different understandings of the EU's international role. It shows how expressions of Euroscepticism within and outside the EU might affect the EU's ability to enlarge further and drive the agenda for global governance.

Enlargement: the end of geographical spill-over?

Although opposition to further EU enlargement does not necessarily correspond to Euroscepticism, it might be developing into a significant dimension of Euroscepticism, both at elite and public levels. As was mentioned (p.7), hostility to further enlargement tends to be associated with hostility towards further integration among segments of domestic political elites. Similarly, it was a key dimension of the No vote during the 2001 (Ireland) and 2005 (France and the Netherlands) referenda (see pp.178–9). Furthermore, between 2002 and 2009, public support for further enlargement in the EU experienced a nine percentage point decline; in the older member states, there was a fourteen percentage point decline. In 2009, a relative majority of EU citizens were opposed to further EU enlargement – even more so in the older member states, where less than 40 per cent supported it (EB 71:159). In this context, the accession of new countries to the EU might be delayed or impeded, thus undermining the logic of 'geographical spill-over' identified by neo-Functionalists in the 1960s. Geographical spill-over refers to the soft power of the EU, or its capacity to attract neighbouring countries by making alternative forms of cooperation progressively irrelevant (as the case of the European Free Trade Area illustrated).

Pro-enlargement advocates argue that a halt to future EU enlargements, especially in the case of Turkey, might not only reduce the EU's influence in international relations; it might also endanger the stabilization and democratization processes of candidate countries. In the United States, in the aftermath of the 2005 Dutch and French referenda, this concern was voiced by members of the foreign policy establishment, as the debate on the future of transatlantic relations held by the US House of Representatives' Committee on International Relations illustrated. As one representative stated, 'I am particularly concerned that EU expansion will fall victim to the ongoing constitutional crisis. Halting the enlargement process is contrary to the interests of the European Union and, I would argue, the United States and sends the wrong political signal to those nations whose entire political, judicial and economic reform efforts are based on the possibility of accession' (United States House of Representatives 2005:11).

Moreover, perceptions of a widely reluctant public opinion in EU countries can increase opposition to EU accession in candidate countries, two of which (Croatia and, to a lesser extent, Turkey) display high levels of public Euroscepticism. In Turkey, public support for EU accession has been declining markedly since 2004. Since 2002, expressions of reluctance towards Turkey's accession within the EU might have contributed to this phenomenon. First, debates on the reference to Christianity in the preamble of the EU

Constitutional Treaty showed that large segments of political elites understand the EU as a community rooted in Christian values, a perception shared by a majority of Turkish citizens (Cautrès and Monceau 2008:586). Second, public opinion polls showing that opposition to Turkish accession was widespread in the EU, as well as the role this issue played in the 2005 referenda, may have fostered public Euroscepticism in Turkey.

Eurobarometer surveys highlight how Turkish Euroscepticism has evolved in parallel with scepticism towards Turkey's accession within the EU. They indicate a continuous decline in levels of support for EU accession in Turkey between 2004 and 2008, from 70 per cent to 40 per cent (CCEB 2004:7; EB 70:32). This is corroborated by polls published in the Turkish press, showing that the proportion of hard Eurosceptics (those who think their country should definitely stay out of the EU) increased threefold during that period, from 8 per cent to 25 per cent (*Milliyet* 2006).

Eurosceptic agendas outside the EU: hostility towards global governance

The outcome of the debate between advocates of a minimalist international role for the Union and those who support political union will also have global consequences. Certainly, the EU only accounts for eight per cent of the world's population, so its future influence at a global level should not be overestimated. However, its experience in conflict resolution through law and market regulation in a multinational context may serve as a role model for advocates of regional cooperation and a more regulated globalization in other parts of the world. The failure of political union in the case of the EU – the most successful form of interstate cooperation up till now – would send a signal to the rest of the world, increasing scepticism towards institutions of global governance.

This was illustrated by reactions to the 2005 and 2008 referenda in the United States among (neo-)conservative think-tanks such as the Heritage Foundation, the American Enterprise Institute or the Foreign Policy Research Institute. As explained below, their attempts to influence the debate on the future institutional and political development of the EU is part of a wider agenda, aimed at weakening institutions of global governance and preventing the emergence of regulatory authorities at regional and international levels.

In the discourse of the neo-conservatives, three motives underlie the hostility towards a more integrated EU. The first motive relates to the perception that the EU might develop policies that are at odds with what neo-conservatives identify as US national interests. Among those interests is the wish to prevent the setting up of regulations (either at EU or global levels) that might harm the interests of US companies (notably those operating in the EU, for example in Ireland). Similarly, there is a wish to prevent the development of a common EU foreign policy that might be at odds with perceived US interests. In that respect, the Lisbon Treaty entails reforms that contradict US interests, including the strengthening of the foreign and defence policies and the EP's new trade policy powers, which might reinforce the EU's defence of specific societal preferences (such as for Genetically Modified Organisms (GMOs)) in international trade negotiations. That is why, according to the Heritage Foundation, 'the re-emergence of the EU constitution [in the form of the Lisbon Treaty] represents a fundamental threat to American interests' (McNamara 2006:1). The second motive is a strong opposition to the strengthening of multilateralism and international organizations. Reactions of neo-conservative thinkers to the 2005 and 2008 failed referenda illustrate this. For instance, John Bolton, a former US ambassador to – and self-declared foe of – the United Nations, sees the EU's attempts to forge a common security and defence policy as a welcome pretext to withdraw US commitment to European security through NATO, if not to suppress NATO altogether (Bolton 2008:2). In a similar vein, contributors to the Heritage Foundation suggest that intra-EU cleavages between free-traders and allegedly protectionist governments should be exacerbated in order to undermine the EU common trade policy and create a coalition of free-trading nations around the US, as an alternative to the World Trade Organization. This would create a 'global free trade alliance', understood as an 'economic alliance of the willing, determined to liberalize trade among its members', which would offer free trade agreements 'between the US and any other country that has demonstrated a commitment to free trade and investment, minimal regulations and property rights' (Huisman 2005:2). The third motive relates to a form of value-based Euroscepticism (see p. 57 for a definition of the term). Neo-conservatives are indeed concerned that US society might be 'contaminated' by so-called European values (for instance, on the issue of the death penalty), notably through the internationalization of US federal law, via the case law of the Supreme Court (which has forged contacts with its EU counterpart, the ECJ) or via international, legally binding texts, which the EU could promote in international organizations (see McNamara 2006; Bolton 2008).

These think-tanks have tried to influence subsequent national public debates on the EU, as was the case in Ireland. For instance, the Foreign Policy Research Institute offered Declan Ganley, an Irish businessman and Eurosceptic political entrepreneur, a platform to publish his views on the EU Constitutional Treaty in 2003 (see Ganley 2003). During the referendum campaign on the ratification of the Lisbon Treaty in 2008, the Irish press widely reported on the No campaign's alleged use of US funds, prompting Irish authorities to set up an independent commission to investigate these allegations (European Parliament 2008). Furthermore, US Eurosceptic think-tanks have forged alliances with Eurosceptic groups in the EU in order to influence perceptions of the EU among the US foreign policy establishment (see Chamorel 2006:165; Vaïsse 2004:453) and to 'support the idea of a EU made up of sovereign nation-states' (McNamara 2006:6). An example of this is the Margaret Thatcher Center for Freedom, hosted by the Heritage Foundation.

Criticism of regional or global forms of governance, however, is not always rooted in anti-regulation concerns. It might also result from the perception that governance beyond the nation state also challenges modern understandings of democracy – that is, in the words of one EU scholar, 'the idea that some degree of coherence is necessary between cultural identities, socio-economic practices and rules/institutions' (Bartolini 2003:8).

Euroscepticism: a welcome thorn in the EU's side

By pinpointing how global forms of governance can put national democracies in question, Eurosceptics have made a crucial contribution to debates on the legitimacy of the EU. First, the main reforms that have helped democratize the EU were prompted, to a large extent, by Eurosceptic criticism. Second, in terms of policies, Eurosceptics have questioned inefficient status quos and raised the issue of the limits of integration. Third, Euroscepticism raises a key question for the EU: what should be the role of politics and political conflict in a political system that, in its very essence, relies on relatively de-politicized and consensual interactions? In that respect, Euroscepticism confronts the EU with an uncomfortable question: the impact of its own alleged democratic deficit on national democracy.

Eurosceptic criticism and the democratization of the EU

Many of the reforms that have contributed to democratizing EU institutions have indirectly resulted from Eurosceptic initiatives or challenges to EC institutional authority. For instance, President de Gaulle's 1961–62 Fouchet plan, which aimed at weakening EEC institutions through the creation of a (potentially rival) purely inter-governmental organization, with a powerless parliamentary assembly, spurred the determination of small member states and European parliamentarians to reinforce the legitimacy of the EP and push for its direct election by citizens (Wallace 1995). The most significant institutional development that occurred in the 1990s, the extension of the EP's powers, resulted from criticism over the EU's 'democratic deficit'. The development of ECJ case law can also be interpreted, in part, from that perspective. For instance, the challenge of some national constitutional courts regarding the primacy of EC law (as illustrated, for example, by the 'Solange I' ruling of the German constitutional court in 1974) prompted the ECJ to guarantee the protection of fundamental rights, by referring to the general principles of EC law and the European Convention for the Protection of Human Rights (ECHR) (Jacqué 2008:444).

What is more, Eurosceptic criticism has prompted the EU to adapt to new standards in terms of transparency, information and communication. Indeed, from the end of the 1970s on, public authorities in Western democracies have been confronted with demands emanating from civil society, asking for more transparency and more accountability. In the EU's case, the first moves in the setting up of an EU transparency initiative were initiated in 1993, following debates surrounding the ratification of the Maastricht Treaty, as were the first significant information programmes targeting the average citizen (the so-called Prince programmes). By the same token, the 2005 referenda led the European Commission to launch a more interactive EU communication strategy, aimed at 'listening' to citizens' concerns (European Commission 2006a). Like major international organizations, the EU reacted to public criticism by shifting from a rather passive information policy to a more proactive communication strategy.

Policy status quos and the limits of integration

EU policies have also evolved as a result of Eurosceptic criticism. For instance, the accession of countries whose governments were seen as Eurosceptic has led to significant policy developments. The UK's EEC accession prompted the crafting of the EEC's regional policy (with the creation of the European Fund for Regional Development). Moreover, Eurosceptic leaders have often contributed to debates about the evolution of EU policies, thus breaking the status quo on 'frozen' policy choices, as Margaret Thatcher did when she criticized the heavy focus of the EEC budget on the Common Agricultural Policy (CAP) (a claim taken over by Prime Minister Tony Blair when he held the EU presidency in 2005). In a similar vein, new forms of governance, such as the OMC, have prompted useful discussions on the limits of integration. Notwithstanding the fact that a majority of EU citizens do not want more EU power in fields such as social policy or taxation, attempts at harmonization in these policy areas might have adverse impacts on the competitiveness of European economies (Wyplosz 2005).

The lack of political conflict: the main cause of the 'democratic deficit'

Eurosceptics' main merit, nonetheless, is to have stressed the limits of a purely functionalist type of legitimacy, which has long been prevalent at the EC/EU level. President de Gaulle was among the first leaders to bluntly raise the issue of public consent when he offered to submit his intergovernmental vision of Europe to an EC-wide referendum (Wallace and Smith 1995). This clashed with the functionalist understanding of legitimacy that was predominant within EC institutions, and which assumed that popular consent would come gradually, as citizens realized that the EC fulfilled an expanding number of relevant functions. Since the 1985 Adonnino report on a 'citizens' Europe', this understanding of legitimacy has permeated every attempt by EC institutions to 'bring citizens closer to the EC'. To the extent that EC institutions have tried to promote the emergence of EC-level actors, these were assumed to be pro-European. This was the case, for instance, with Jacques Delors' concept of a European civil society, which sought to strengthen the Commission's legitimacy by forging a special relationship with interest groups, at the risk of empowering lobbies. In a similar vein, Article 191 TEC on European political parties provided that 'political parties at European level are important as a factor for integration within the Union. They contribute to forming a European awareness'. This article raised concerns that the EU might refuse funding for European political parties that were considered Eurosceptic or even, in an exaggerated version of the debate, that the ECJ might ban allegedly Eurosceptic parties (see the debate in the House of Commons 2001:39). Indeed, the provision referring to parties as a 'factor for integration' is suppressed in the Lisbon Treaty.

In a similar vein, recent contributions to academic debates on the legitimacy of the EU have emphasized the lack of political conflict within the EU political system as the main cause of the democratic deficit. The lack of a 'government–opposition nexus' at the EU level, the absence of an organized opposition and the predominant consensual political culture in the Council and in the EP lead, it is argued, to a 'waning of Opposition' at the EU level (Mair 2007:15). In a similar vein, other contributions (Lord and Magnette 2004) have argued that the existence of conflicting views about the sources of the EU's legitimacy (and how this legitimacy should be enhanced) should not be seen as a weakness of the EU political system. Rather, the open-ended, disputed nature of the EU, which has been subjected to permanent deliberation since the founding period of the EC, could enhance its legitimacy and facilitate its acceptance at member state level. Thus, what the EU needs is not less, but more political conflict.

The impact of integration on national democracy

In this respect, the phenomenon of Euroscepticism highlights the double-edged impact of European integration on national democracy. On the one hand, the EU played a key role in processes of democratic transition in southern and eastern Europe. It has made EU membership conditional upon the respect of democracy, the rule of law, and human rights, and has adopted significant pieces of legislation on non-discrimination. On the other hand, European integration might also have indirect adverse impacts on national democracy, by, for instance, contributing to the waning of opposition at the domestic level. Europeanization might indeed contribute to the disempowerment of democratic counter-weights, such as trade unions. The latter have not only been affected by wide-ranging mutations in labour markets, but also by processes of market integration. At the same time, no unified trade union movement has yet emerged at EU level. Consequently, the loss of power at one level has not been compensated at another. As far as political parties are concerned, integration contributes to reducing the range of policies available to governments, thus further blurring the difference between left and right and diminishing political competition between clearly discernible alternatives (Mair 2007:14). Wide-ranging market integration might thus reinforce public perceptions of the political elites' lack of manoeuvre, if not irrelevance, in the face of global challenges (Bartolini 1999). Moreover, while no robust European party system has yet emerged at EU level, at domestic level European integration exacerbates perceptions of a growing distance between party leaderships, intermediate levels and regional party organizations (Raunio 2002). That is why European integration might actually exacerbate the current lack of trust citizens have in political parties (in 2009, only 19 per cent of citizens in the EU trusted political parties (EB 71:15)).

In a similar vein, processes of Europeanization also challenge collective perceptions of national institutions. As the latter become increasingly interlinked with EU institutions and the administrations of other member states, a process of 'administrative fusion' (Wessels 1996) takes place, resulting in increasing complexity, less transparency and less accountability. This has significant consequences for state/society relations. Administrative fusion 'diffuses responsibilities and reduces transparency ... For the normal citizen, the "state" becomes less and less a clear object of "identification"' (Wessels 1996:100).

Finally, market integration also challenges mechanisms of redistribution and collective solidarity, as the free circulation of capital further reduces public decision-makers' room for manoeuvre, for example in taxation policy. It can also challenge national solidarity in more indirect ways. For instance, by favouring transnational cooperation between prosperous regions (a good example of this being Four Motors for Europe, a trans-regional cooperation between Baden-Würtemberg, Catalonia, Lombardy and Rhône-Alpes), European integration might indirectly contribute to a decreased sense of inter-regional solidarity within states (Judt 1992:114).

Conclusion

In analyzing developments in European governance, this chapter has shown how Euroscepticism, among other trends, has contributed to the decreasing centrality of key aspects of supranational decision-making, as it was understood in the foundational period of the EC. Moreover, it has highlighted the possible impact of Euroscepticism on processes of geographical spill-over and has shown how different expressions of Euroscepticism are intertwined with a more global competition between different views on international governance.

The impact of Eurosceptics, however, is by no means limited to attempts to block or paralyze the process of European integration. As the chapter argues, Eurosceptics have prompted attempts to make the EU more democratic and more efficient by exposing the limits of functional legitimacy and by questioning inefficient policy status quos. Furthermore, for scholars of democracy, the phenomenon of public Euroscepticism is also a warning. As analyzed later in the book, it is one of the many symptoms of the malaise of democracy and highlights how market integration processes at regional or global levels influence state/society relations and citizens' orientations towards institutions of representative democracy.

Chapter 2

Varieties of Euroscepticism

This chapter starts by outlining a broad historical overview of the emergence and evolution of Euroscepticism in the course of European integration, before putting forward a typology of different varieties of Euroscepticism, illustrating its changing nature over time.

Four different varieties of Euroscepticism are distinguished: utilitarian Euroscepticism, which expresses scepticism as to the gains derived from EU membership at individual or country level; political Euroscepticism, which illustrates concerns over the impact of European integration on national sovereignty and identity; value-based Euroscepticism, which denounces EU 'interference' in normative issues; and cultural anti-Europeanism, which is rooted in a broader hostility towards Europe as a continent and in distrust towards the societal models and institutions of European countries.

Euroscepticism across time: a historical overview

One can distinguish two stages in the development of Euroscepticism from the early days of European integration to the present day.

From the 1950s to the mid-1980s: the marginalization of Euroscepticism

To begin with, it should be noted that, contrary to widespread assumptions, Euroscepticism is first and foremost a phenomenon to be found among national political elites. In the early 1950s, political Euroscepticism – defined as opposition to the setting up of a supranational institutional system – was indeed a mainstream, if not predominant, view among western European political elites, even in continental Europe (see pp.102–3).

However, during the following decades (the 1960s and 1970s up until the mid-1980s), Euroscepticism was dampened by three

43

factors. First, the institutions of the EEC were less supranational than those of the European Coal and Steel Community (ECSC), which contributed to reducing opposition to supranationalism. Moreover, the authority of the European Commission was further circumscribed by President de Gaulle's nationalism during the so-called Empty Chair crisis of 1965. Second, this period was characterized by the absence of major institutional reforms, as integration progressed mainly through the less visible logic of the Europeanization of domestic law. Third, domestic party systems during that period were still relatively stable, as mainstream political parties were not challenged by 'new politics' parties articulating a Eurosceptic discourse.

The end of the 1980s: the real shift

The second period started after the signature of the Single European Act (SEA) in 1986. This period marked the beginning of the end of the hard-won, pro-integration consensus among national political elites. The SEA, which aimed at completing the common market by eliminating non-tariff barriers to free trade (thus creating the internal market), was indeed the last stage of the integration process which remained relatively consensual. At the same time, the SEA already entailed the seeds of future contestation: the extension of QMV in the Council of Ministers, the enlarged scope of the EEC's powers (in policy areas such as regional cohesion, health and safety at work, environmental protection, etc.) and the enhanced role for the Commission, implied by the highly ambitious goal of completing the common market. Soon after the signature of the SEA, a debate started emerging on the limits of European integration, as political elites divided over two core issues: the extent to which the internal market should be regulated (or remain a mere free-trade area with a common external tariff) and the transformation of the EEC into a political union. In that respect, Euroscepticism is first and foremost the consequence of a lack of consensus among elites on the goals of integration.

The famous 1988 Bruges speech by Margaret Thatcher was a landmark in that evolution. In this speech, the British Prime Minister clearly spelled out the concerns of those who did not want integration to go beyond the SEA, by rejecting any attempt at developing regulatory competences at EC level (beyond the area of competition policy) and by opposing any form of political union implying, for instance, a common foreign and defence policy. A milestone in the re-emergence of Euroscepticism in public debate on integration, the Bruges speech crystallized trends going far beyond the UK, as concerns were raised elsewhere in Europe over the extension of the EEC's powers. Indeed, at the same time a contentious debate on that issue emerged at a regional level in Germany. From the second half of the 1980s on, the German *Länder*, wary of a possible erosion of federalism and of their exclusive powers, started contesting the legitimacy of the EC's powers in fields such as occupational education, audiovisual services, environment, health, state aid, etc. The *Länder* succeeded in getting the subsidiarity principle inserted into the Treaty Establishing the EEC (TEC), through the SEA, with reference to environmental policy. That the subsidiarity principle was meant above all to limit the scope of the EEC's power was made clear by a resolution of the German *Bundesrat* in 1986, which specified that subsidiarity should not be used as a way to extend the EEC's powers.

These divisions culminated in controversies surrounding the Maastricht Treaty (1991). Indeed, the ratification of the Maastricht Treaty proved especially difficult, as the Danish and French referenda in 1992 illustrated (with 50.7 per cent of No votes in Denmark and a very narrow margin of 51 per cent in favour of the treaty in France). In the UK, ratification was only secured in July 1993, as only about a quarter of MPs in the House of Commons voted in favour of ratification. Although certainly not federalist in its essence, the Maastricht Treaty did entail several provisions that came to crystallize strong opposition at domestic level: the Economic and Monetary Union (EMU) (together with the contentious status of the European Central Bank (ECB)); a Common Foreign and Security Policy (CFSP); cooperation in Justice and Home Affairs (JHA); and EU citizenship. This, together with the symbolic transformation into a European Union, was rejected by those who advocated, and continue to advocate, a 'revisionist' position, namely going back to the previous stage of integration embodied by the SEA. Today, in fact, many among the Eurosceptics have never accepted the reforms entailed in Maastricht that, in their view, changed the nature of European integration by transforming it into an explicitly political project. At the same time, nevertheless, the Maastricht Treaty itself illustrated the reservations of a majority of governments towards a possible extension of the EU's power, as it elevated subsidiarity as the overarching principle delimiting the scope of the EU's competences. In that respect, the treaty itself was indicative of a mainstreaming of Eurosceptic discourses which, in the post-Maastricht era, started being articulated by traditionally pro-European actors – not the least of whom was former Chancellor Helmut Kohl, who, in the aftermath of the French referendum on the Maastricht Treaty, denounced what he saw as the 'regulation fury' (*Regulierungswut*) of the EC (*Le Monde* 1992). This mainstreaming of Euroscepticism was also facilitated by the emerging discourse on the democratic deficit of the EU, which made Euroscepticim intellectually acceptable. Finally, changes in the international context of European integration favoured the re-emergence of political Euroscepticism. The Cold War had been a decisive stimulus in favour of western European unification and had contributed to mute some of the Euroscepticism of national political elites, as the EEC was seen as a bulwark against communism. With the end of the Cold War, this rationale for closer integration disappeared. To some, like Margaret Thatcher, for instance, this was a key argument against the necessity of political integration.

Since Maastricht, two developments have exacerbated Eurosceptics' concerns. First, the treaties that followed entailed significant developments in policy areas tightly linked to national sovereignty: cooperation in internal affairs (police and justice) started being 'communautarized' with the Amsterdam Treaty (1997), while the CFSP created by the Maastricht Treaty was complemented by the setting up of a European Security and Defence Policy (ESDP) with the Nice Treaty (2001). Second, the 'constitutionalization process' of the EU proved highly divisive, as member states deeply disagreed on the content of the EU Charter of Fundamental Rights (drafted in 2000) and on the EU Constitutional Treaty (drafted by a convention between 2002 and 2003) which, by applying state-like concepts (such as constitution, laws, minister) to the EU, exacerbated concerns over the alleged transformation of the EU into a 'European super-state'.

This political Euroscepticism, however, is only one of the different varieties of Euroscepticism, as the following sections show.

Utilitarian Euroscepticism

Utilitarian Euroscepticism refers to scepticism about the gains derived from integration, or its distributional impacts, be it at an individual or collective level. This form of Euroscepticism was not very present between the 1960s and the late 1980s, as European integration coincided, on the whole, with a period of economic growth. From the beginning of the 1990s on, however, increasing utilitarian scepticism at the public opinion level was matched by a parallel development at the elite level, as governments explicitly articulated critical utilitarian assessments of the EU. This trend was compounded by two factors: EMU and EU enlargement to less developed countries. The costs of integration, calls for a re-nationalization of the EU's distributive policies, and backlashes of economic nationalism increasingly permeated domestic public debates as governing parties articulated a more blunt expression of national interests.

EMU: changing perceptions about mutual benefits

The aftermath of the Maastricht Treaty coincided with more negative assessments of benefits derived from EC/EU membership at the public opinion level (see p.174). Although certainly triggered by the economic recession of the early 1990s, this evolution was compounded, in the course of the 1990s, by the implementation of EMU. Indeed, in comparison to the EU distributive policies that already existed at the time of Maastricht (the CAP, social and regional cohesion), EMU changed cost/benefit evaluations both at individual and national levels. It contributed to changing perceptions about European integration as a mutually beneficial, win–win process.

With the need to meet the convergence criteria (including budgetary discipline, which is supervised by the European Commission), the EU became increasingly associated with public spending cutbacks. As Eichenberg and Dalton write, 'the Maastricht Treaty brought the EU into the area of *domestic* redistribution' (2007:132). As a consequence, the EU was increasingly associated with less protection in the eyes of many citizens, whereas member states remained the only providers of social welfare. Moreover, the introduction of the Euro contributed to more negative utilitarian appraisals of membership at the public opinion level, as it was associated with inflation. For example, before the 2005 Dutch referendum, more than 90 per cent of those polled thought that prices had gone up as a result of the introduction of the Euro (Aarts and van der Kolk 2006:244). Moreover, EMU clearly polarized domestic public debate on integration in some countries, while antagonizing large segments of public opinion. This was the case, for instance, in the UK, where debates on EMU during the 1997 general elections radicalized Euroscepticism among segments of the Conservative party, while roughly two-thirds of citizens were opposed to it (Alexandre-Collier 2000:136).

On a national level, EMU also contributed to changing perceptions about the 'winners' and 'losers' of integration, as some countries perceived themselves as being disadvantaged by EMU. This was most notably the case in Germany (at least for public opinion, which was strongly attached to the Deutsche Mark) but also, more recently, in the Netherlands. Indeed, during the campaign preceding the 2005 referendum, the widespread belief that the national currency (the guilder) had been undervalued during the shift to the Euro – and thus was 'sold' too cheaply – contributed to the idea that the country as a whole did not benefit largely from European integration (Aarts and van der Kolk 2006:244). The second impact of EMU on collective assessments of integration is linked to budgetary discipline, especially that deriving from the Stability and Growth Pact. According to the Pact, the Commission can recommend that the Council of Ministers give a warning (and possibly also financial sanctions) to a member state that does not respect the commonly agreed budgetary discipline. Even if only ministers can ultimately sanction another member state, the Commission's public warnings against national budgetary laxness have created an uproar in some member states. In 2001, for instance, the European Commission's criticism of Ireland's budgetary policy was harshly rebutted by then Finance Minister Charlie McCreevy (Kennedy and Sinnott 2007:67). Moreover, the inefficiency of the Stability and Growth Pact's sanctioning mechanism – especially the fact that large countries, like France and Germany, have not been sanctioned despite budgetary laxness – gave credence, especially in some smaller countries, to the idea that EMU implied an unequal distribution of efforts and costs among countries.

The costs of integration and calls for re-nationalization

Reforms conducted in order to respect the convergence criteria also exacerbated emerging debates on the costs of integration in some member states, especially among the strongest net contributors to the EU budget. Here, the 1984 quarrel over the EC budget, triggered by Margaret Thatcher, initiated a trend that would affect future negotiations on the EU budget by legitimizing the discourse on the fair returns that every country was entitled to expect from EC membership. This coincided with – and to some extent exacerbated – an emerging discussion in Germany, initiated in the first half of the 1980s, as Germany was increasingly portrayed as 'paymaster of the Community' in domestic public debate (Schild 2001:339). In the Netherlands, another big net contributor to the EU budget, debates on the costs of EU membership emerged in 1998–99, as the government announced that it hoped to secure a reduction of the Dutch contribution (Harmsen 2004:100). The same issue later became a cornerstone of public debate during the 2005 referendum.

These debates, which have to be analyzed in the context of EU enlargement, triggered calls for a re-nationalization of the EU's distributive policies. In the Netherlands, for instance, Frits Bolkestein (a leading figure of the liberal-conservative VVD (Volkspatij voor Vrijheid en Demokratie – People's Party for Freedom and Democracy) who later became EU Commissioner), from the early 1990s on asked for a fundamental reform of the CAP and the structural funds, while opposing the social chapter of the treaty; mechanisms of redistribution, in his view, should be limited to the national level (quoted in Harmsen 2004:105). In Germany, calls for a re-nationalization of the structural funds, which were first articulated by regional politicians, have been taken over at national level by the two main parties, the Christlich-Demokratische Union (CDU) and the Sozial-demokratische Partei Deutschlands (SPD), since the early 2000s (SPD 2001; CDU-CSU 2002).

Calls for a re-nationalization of the EU's distributive policies found much echo in the context of the 2004 enlargement. Indeed, at the turn of the twenty-first century, opposition to EU enlargement (and to the costs associated with it) was increasingly articulated by mainstream political parties, as was the case during the 2001 Irish referendum on the Nice Treaty, the Italian general elections that same year (as hostility to enlargement was articulated by Forza Italia) or in the Dutch general elections in 2002 (as some leaders from the liberal, governing party VVD questioned the economic benefits of enlargement (Van Ham 2002:3)). Other EU policies, which do not rely on a redistributive logic, continue to be perceived as entailing indirect and significant redistributive consequences at the expense of some member states. Such is the case with the Common Fisheries Policy (CFP) in the UK and the problem of quota-hopping by Spanish fishermen (who register their boats as

British in order to benefit from the fishing quotas allocated to the UK), at the expense of their British counterparts. The Factortame ruling of the ECJ (1991), which declared the national law that had been passed to prevent this practice as being incompatible with EU legislation, aroused Eurosceptic sentiments and prompted calls for a re-nationalization of the CFP in the UK.

Parallel to these developments, it became increasingly clear that market-making policies, such as competition, had far-reaching economic and political implications at the domestic level. Thus, the European Commission was increasingly confronted, in the course of the 1990s, with backlashes of economic nationalism, as governments tried to prevent the liberalizing impact of EU law on sensitive sectors, notably in the field of competition law and, especially, state aid. This issue became highly political in Germany, as the Commission started to scrutinize state aid to regional banks (*Landesbanken*), whose public service mission is to promote regional development but which, in practice, also compete with private banks (Smith 1999:40).

Bringing the national interest back in

In such a context, domestic public debates on integration became increasingly influenced by calls for a more explicit articulation of the 'national interest', notably in those founding countries of the EC where the pro-European consensus of political elites had been strong in previous decades. In the Netherlands, for instance, from the end of the 1990s on, mainstream politicians like Frits Bolkestein called for a reaffirmation of Dutch national interests in the EU (what he called a 'cultural break') (Harmsen 2004:107). In Italy, leaders of Forza Italia made similar statements (Leconte 2005:40).

Political Euroscepticism

Political Euroscepticism can be defined as principled opposition or defiance towards the setting up of a supranational institutional system, the delegation of powers to supranational institutions beyond a limited core of policies (internal market, competition policy) and to the principle of the pooling of sovereignties. As mentioned previously, this form of Euroscepticism underlay much of the opposition to the early stages of integration in the 1950s. However, from the mid-1960s until the end of the Eighties, it remained confined to minority groups; integration in that period was perceived as being essentially legal and economic. At the turn of the 1990s, however, and especially with the Maastricht Treaty, political Euroscepticism gained ground for several reasons.

EU citizenship: the spectre of double allegiance

One of the most controversial provisions of the Maastricht Treaty was the creation of EU citizenship. It was indeed the cornerstone of much of the anti-Maastricht opposition, especially in Denmark, France and the UK (precisely those countries where, two decades earlier, elites had been most opposed to the direct elections of MEPs).

Although certainly not revolutionary, since some of the rights it entails existed before the Maastricht Treaty, EU citizenship awoke a deep-rooted distrust towards 'double allegiance', that is, a fear that EU citizenship might compete with national citizenship and that citizens might give precedence to the former over the latter in cases of conflict between the two (Weiler 1995:22). Here again, Margaret Thatcher was among those who most clearly spelled out this concern when she declared, during the ratification debate on the Maastricht Treaty in the House of Lords in June 1993, that 'If there is a citizenship, you would all owe a duty of allegiance to the new Union ... There would be a duty to uphold its laws. What will happen if the allegiance to the Union comes into conflict with allegiance to our own country? How would the European Court find then? The Maastricht Treaty gives this new European Union all the attributes of a sovereign state' (quoted in Koslowski 1999:166). In Denmark also, the alleged infringement of EU citizenship on national sovereignty and identity contributed to the failure of the first referendum on the Maastricht Treaty. This is why, in December 1992, the European Council, in order to pave the way for a second referendum in Denmark, 'took cognizance' of a Danish declaration stating that 'citizenship of the Union is a political and legal concept which is entirely different' from national citizenship and does not aim to create 'a citizenship of the Union in the sense of citizenship of a nation-state' (Council of the European Union 1992).

In France, the symbolic threat posed by EU citizenship was compounded by additional concerns linked to the right to vote and be elected in municipal elections granted to non-national, EU residents. Things were made more complex by the fact that members of the upper house of the national parliament, the Senate, are elected by delegates of municipalities and by members of the lower house, the National Assembly. Consequently, non-French EU citizens, if elected mayors or deputy mayors, might have participated in the election of the members of one of the Parliament's two chambers. This led not only extreme right, but also mainstream politicians from the Gaullist party Rassemblement pour la République (RPR) (well-known figures such as Charles Pasqua and Alain Juppé, for instance), to reject EU citizenship as 'unacceptable' (quoted in Koslowski, 1999:167). Eventually, a bill excluding EU citizens from the functions of mayor and deputy mayor and from participation in senatorial elections was passed.

In 1997, the Amsterdam Treaty added a specification to provisions on EU citizenship, explicitly stating that 'citizenship of the Union shall complement and not replace national citizenship'. Moreover, during the 1997 IGC, audacious proposals aimed at extending EU citizenship rights, notably by the Austrian and Italian governments (such as a citizens' initiative and the 'right to receive an education taking account of the common heritage of European civilization') were rejected by other member states (Agence Europe 1986).

Against the flag: hostility to European identity and EU symbols

Underlying the hostility towards EU citizenship is indeed a deep reluctance towards concepts such as 'European identity' or European culture. The idea that European integration might imply the promotion of a shapeless and 'fake' European identity or culture underlies many Eurosceptic discourses. Here again, Margaret Thatcher's Euroscepticism clearly captured this feeling, as she declared in her 1988 Bruges speech: 'Europe will be stronger precisely because it has France as France, Spain as Spain, Britain as Britain, each with its customs, traditions and identity. It would be folly to try to fit them into some sort of identikit European personality' (1988:4). In this variant of Euroscepticism, European identity is often equated with a monstrous, shapeless mix where national identities get lost – a 'European conglomerate', in Thatcher's eyes, or 'a unitary, cultural and linguistic pulp that came out of Brussels bureaucrats' mincing machine', in those of former far-right leader Jörg Haider (quoted in Leconte 2003:157).

Indeed, since the second half of the 1980s, EC institutions have tried to promote a European cultural identity in order to boost popular support for integration and the common market. Parallel to this, efforts have been made to promote common EC/EU symbols aimed at fostering a common identity, such as the EU flag (which was hoisted for the first time as the Community flag in 1986), the European anthem (adopted in 1985), the European passport (introduced in 1985) and the selection of 9 May as commemoration day of the Schuman Declaration (since 1986). Such strategies aimed at coping with the deficit in common symbols that is often identified as one of the causes for the lack of public identification with the EU.

Nonetheless, these attempts have met with deep reluctance at member state level. As early as 1992, for instance, ministers of culture made it clear that EC actions in the sphere of culture should 'neither replace nor compete with' national and regional cultural policies (quoted in Pantel 1999:54). Reluctance towards EU action in the sphere of culture was also present during negotiations on the Amsterdam Treaty. An apparently minor change to Article 128 TEU specified that 'The Community shall take cultural aspects into account in its actions under the provisions of this Treaty, in particular *in order to respect* and promote the diversity of its cultures' (emphasis added).

EU symbols have induced a similar opposition. The 1996 British debate on ID cards, as the British government decided to combine new British identity cards with the new European driver's licence, was illustrative of this, as it provoked a fierce debate about which symbols should appear on the cards. It had been preceded a few years earlier by a controversy over the 1985 European passport, which had encountered much hostility, not the least because of the strong symbolic value attached to this symbol of national identity in the UK (Smith 2004:53). Such debates are indicative of a larger debate on the compatibility between European and national identities. Other attempts at creating EU symbols have met strong resistance among the member states. For instance, the Commission's proposal to let athletes from all member states appear as one delegation during the opening ceremony of the Olympic games in Barcelona and Albertville was rejected by governments (Smith 2004:53). More recently, the institutionalization of the EU symbols (flag, anthem, motto, currency and commemoration day), which was operated by the EU Constitutional Treaty (Article I-8), had to be abandoned in the Lisbon Treaty because some governments opposed it.

Finally, some ECJ rulings on prosaic issues have affected symbols of national identity and/or culture. For instance, in a 1987 ruling (*Commission versus the Federal Republic of Germany*), the ECJ declared a German law defining requirements for beer purity as incompatible with EC legislation on the free movement of goods. Another well-known example is the 2002 ruling by an English court (applying EU law) on the application of the metric system by British shopkeepers, which gave rise to the 'metric martyrs' saga in the UK.

The 'democratic deficit': a Eurosceptic shift of a pro-European notion

Opposition to state-like symbols included in the Constitutional Treaty, not to mention the term 'constitution' itself, might also be seen as the superficial expression of a more meaningful debate about the implications of European integration for national democracy and about the democratic nature of the EU.

Like the now famous 'subsidiarity' concept, which had initially been referred to in a pro-European context (the 1984 EP's project for a Constitution for Europe), the 'democratic deficit' is a notion forged by a pro-European author. In 1979, David Marquand, writing in the context of the first direction election of MEPs, warned against the emergence of a possible 'democratic deficit', whose origin he saw in the difficulty of applying accountability to decisions made at EC level. To prevent such a scenario, he advocated an extension of QMV in the Council of Ministers (thus preventing national governments from hiding behind the unanimity rule), as well as legislative powers for the EP. Without such reforms, he argued, transferring more powers to the EC would lead to a deficit in accountability (Marquand 1979). This represented the pro-European side of the democratic deficit debate.

Nonetheless, during debates surrounding the ratification of the Maastricht Treaty, the 'democratic deficit' became a rallying cry for Eurosceptic discourses of various sorts. As Yves Mény writes:

> We find a bit of everything in this mixed bag: academic 'learneds' who subscribe to this analysis; judges, indeed supreme courts, such as the German Constitutional Court, searching in vain for a European 'demos'; British tabloids of the so-called gutter press but also reputable newspapers noted for their seriousness; Europeans convinced that they want more and more from

Europe; Eurosceptics overpleased with the argument and unhesitating (like some Gaullists) to be content with a skimpy democracy at home ... and, last but not least, numerous European parliamentarians wishing to reinforce rightful parliamentary powers. (2004:186)

Here again, the tone had already been set by Margaret Thatcher in 1988, as she declared: 'Working more closely does not require power to be centralised in Brussels or decisions to be taken by an appointed bureaucracy ... We have not successfully rolled back the frontiers of the state in Britain, only to see them re-imposed at European level with a European super-state exercising a new dominance from Brussels' (1988:5).

This rhetoric illustrated concrete fears dating back to the SEA negotiations, as the extension of QMV in the Council of Ministers implied increasing difficulties for national parliaments in their ability to scrutinize the European legislative process. Seeing themselves as the losers of European integration, to the benefit of the executives, many national parliaments asked for constitutional reforms between 1985 and 1990 in order to enhance their ability to keep track of the EC legislative process. Many of these measures were reinforced in the aftermath of the Maastricht Treaty (Judge 1995). However, in some countries, like the UK, legitimate concerns over the erosion of the national parliament's power merged with less justified criticism against EU-level unelected institutions (the Commission and the ECB) in the Eurosceptic discourse, as code words such as 'unelected bureaucracy', 'European super-state' and 'Brussels dictatorship' became core concepts of the Eurosceptic jargon (Teubert 2001).

Of all countries, it was probably in Germany that the debate about the consequences of European integration for national democracy was deepest. Indeed, it took on a constitutional dimension with the German Constitutional Court's 12 October 1993 judgment about the Maastricht Treaty. Whereas the Court estimated that the Maastricht Treaty was compatible with the Basic Law (a case which had been challenged by the plaintiffs on the grounds that EMU and CFSP were not compatible with the Basic Law), it nevertheless reserved its right to determine the limits of the primacy of EU law over national constitutional provisions in case of conflict between the two. In the Court's view, it was legitimate to do so as long as the EU was not a state meeting the standards of national democracy, as there was neither an EU-level parliamentary democracy, nor an EU charter of fundamental rights. This judgment, which was welcomed by Eurosceptics across the EU, changed the scope of the democratic deficit discussion by launching a debate about the impact of European integration on national constitutions. In the German case, this issue added to concerns as to the possible erosion of federalism, as the latter has been seen as one of the fundamentals of democracy since 1949. As early as 1986, the debate in the German *Bundesrat* on the implications of the SEA for German federalism was indicative of concerns over the very principles underlying the national constitutional order, as was expressed by a Bavarian Minister: 'the *Länder* ... risk degenerat[ing] into mere administrative units depending upon Bonn and Brussels. This is our very constitutional order which is being questioned. The efforts to regulate more and more policy domains in a unified manner for the whole European Community fundamentally contradict the federal principle and the subsidiarity principle in the organisation of state and society. We are at a crossroads. Which path should the EC follow? Should it develop along a hierarchical, bureaucratic and centralist model or along a liberal, federalist model based on subsidiarity?' (quoted in Volmerange 1993:99).

The spill-over metaphor: an inescapable process?

As these concerns over the fundamentals of member states' constitutional orders illustrate, much of the democratic deficit discourse is rooted in the feeling that European integration is an inescapable process, potentially running out of the control of its constituent parts. This fear has been nurtured by the long-prevailing method of incremental integration in the absence of clarity over the EU's ultimate goals, by specific treaty provisions and by the communication style of EU institutions.

As early as 1965, French President Charles de Gaulle had provoked what became known as the Empty Chair crisis in order to contest the principle of an automatic extension of the scope of QMV voting, which was enshrined in the TEC. In a similar vein, the Maastricht provisions on EMU, which include a schedule in which the monetary union goes on automatically to the next stage, were criticized, notably by the British Parliament, on the grounds that this did not allow for an adequate oversight of the process by national legislators. In a similar vein, the silence of the treaties on the much-debated question of the right to secession, i.e. whether a member state can legally leave the European Union, has long underlain Eurosceptic discourses (a claim that the Lisbon Treaty counters by providing a legal basis for a member state to leave the Union).

Moreover, the communication style of EU institutions has contributed to ingraining the perception that integration is an irreversible and inescapable process. For instance, analyses of the European Commission's communication documents during the Delors presidency have highlighted the neo-functionalist, spill-over-oriented and deductive style of the Commission's discourse. Based on precise deadlines, and on the 'motor' or 'engine' metaphor used to depict European integration, they seemed to try to convince European citizens of the ineluctable character of European integration, thus heightening concerns about the process possibly spiralling out of control.

Value-based Euroscepticism

Value-based Euroscepticism (Madeley and Sitter 2005:13) refers to the perception that EU institutions unduly interfere in matters where not only strongly held collective and societal preferences, but, more fundamentally, value systems, are at stake (for instance, issues such as abortion, divorce, minorities' rights, the balance between individual liberties and public order, and so on). This form of resentment towards the EU originates in the idea that, as the integration process spills over into new policy domains, the EU is exerting a growing and allegedly illegitimate influence on issues that are 'socially constructed and culturally bound' (Weiler 1995:7). These concerns are compounded by the extension of the scope of QMV, which awakens fears of being outvoted on highly symbolic and deeply polarizing normative issues. Although some of these issues do not belong to the scope of the EU's powers (such as abortion), the implementation of EU law, under the supervision of the ECJ, can indirectly impact them. Like other forms of Euroscepticism, value-based Euroscepticism was always present in debates on integration but has been gaining in relevance along with three developments.

Developments in normative integration

The first development relates to the completion of the internal market, as the case law of the ECJ has progressively clarified the far-reaching consequences of the implementation of the four free-doms of circulation (goods, capital, workers and services) for a range of issues which, albeit not pertaining to the scope of the EU's powers, are affected by the principle of free circulation. A good example of this is the 1991 ECJ ruling in the *Society for the Protection of Unborn Children (Ireland) Ltd.* v. *Grogan and Others* case, in which the ECJ stated that an abortion performed according to the law of the member state in which it is performed constituted a service within the meaning of Article 50 of the TEC. This ruling triggered a vociferous debate in Ireland, as some saw it as an infringement of domestic legislation on abortion. Another striking example is that of the 1997 ECJ ruling on Swedish legislation on the sale of alcohol, as the ECJ stated that, although a state monopoly on the sale of alcohol could be justified to protect public health, the restriction of alcohol imports to a limited number of licenced importers violated the rules of the internal market.

Second, value-based Euroscepticism has gained ground following the mainstreaming of human rights in several EU policies. Significant legislative and policy innovations have occurred, especially since the mid-1990s, in a variety of policy areas that have strong implications in terms of ethics, including the fight against racism, anti-discrimination, the mainstreaming of human rights in Justice and Home Affairs. This evolution was reflected in the treaty itself (with Article 13 TEC on non-discrimination) and in ensuing secondary EU law (with directives aimed at combating different forms of discrimination). It has been embodied, notably, by the drafting of the EU Charter of Fundamental Rights, whose scope and legal status have been highly debated among governments. Among its most contested provisions, the Charter includes provisions on non-discrimination, social rights (which were the most contentious, notably the right to work) and minimum requirements in criminal law (concerning, for example, defendants' rights). Here again, some ECJ rulings clarifying the reach of EU legislation, notably on non-discrimination, have spurred criticism that the EU is overstepping the scope of its powers and unduly questioning long-established norms or *acquis,* which often have historical significance in national contexts. Examples include a 2000 ruling in which the ECJ declared that the prohibition on women serving in the German army from engaging in combat operations (a prohibition which was enshrined in the Basic Law) violated EU legislation on non-discrimination. This ruling was harshly criticized by the Bavarian CSU on the grounds that 'this question ... is a political, societal choice which should be decided only by German constitutional organs entitled with democratic legitimacy. It is unacceptable that the EU takes this decision out of the hands of national organs.' In the eyes of the CSU, this represented a drift of the EU away from its original design: 'EU law is intruding more and more in lifestyle choices, thus affecting sectors that are not purely economic' (Bocklet 2000).

Third, developments in the fields of criminal and, to a lesser extent, civil justice cooperation have also contributed to value-based Euroscepticism. Here, the Amsterdam Treaty represents a watershed in three respects. First, it not only foresees closer cooperation in criminal matters, but also the harmonization of member states' criminal law, when necessary. Second, it endows the ECJ, for the first time, with interpretative powers in the field of cooperation in criminal matters. Third, it aims at enhancing the mutual recognition of judicial decisions. As Ingolf Pernice states, in view of future developments foreseen in the Lisbon Treaty on police cooperation and the setting up of a EU public prosecutor office: 'Since the Amsterdam Treaty the EU changes its face. It becomes a political union in a new sense ... Will this eventually lead to the loss of the monopoly on the legitimate use of force hereto enjoyed by the member states?' (2005:6). Such developments have come up against strong resistance at the domestic level. For instance, the reluctance of member states' governments to approximate legislations in criminal law, in the name of national sovereignty, has long impeded important legislative proposals, such as the Council framework decisions on combating racism and xenophobia and on the procedural rights of defendants in criminal proceedings.

Opposition to the EU Charter of Fundamental Rights

The adoption of the EU Charter of Fundamental Rights, especially, has been met with strong resistance at the domestic level, triggering reactions inside both governments and political parties.

To begin with, fierce opposition to the Charter (either by opposition parties, in the case of the UK, or by incumbent parties, in the Polish case) has prompted the British and Polish governments to negotiate a derogatory status regarding the Charter. A protocol agreed upon at the Brussels European Council of 21–22 June 2007, which was annexed to the Lisbon Treaty, states that neither the ECJ, nor national courts in the UK, will be able to declare 'national laws, regulations or administrative provisions, practices or actions' as being incompatible with the Charter (Council of the European Union 2007:25). In the case of the Polish delegation, the centrality of normative concerns clearly appears in the unilateral declaration granted to the Polish government by the European Council, which states that 'the Charter does not affect the right of Member States to legislate in the spheres of public morality, family law as well as the protection of human dignity and respect for human physical and moral integrity' (p. 25). In a similar logic, following the 1991 disputed ECJ ruling related to abortion, the Irish government succeeded in getting a protocol annexed to the treaties (Protocol No. 7 to the TEU and TEC), stating that 'nothing [in the treaties] shall affect the application in Ireland of Article 40.3.3. of the Constitution of Ireland' (which acknowledges 'the right to life of the unborn').

At party level, both non-mainstream and mainstream political parties in several member states campaigned against the ratification of the Lisbon Treaty, notably in opposition to the Charter. The core of the argument was that, by giving legally binding force to the Charter, whose implementation could be submitted to the jurisdiction of the ECJ, the Constitutional Treaty would allow the Union to challenge domestic legislation on family and matrimonial matters, sexual minorities' and immigrants' rights, and in criminal law. This gave rise to two sorts of value-based Eurosceptic discourses. Among radical right-wing parties (such as the League of Polish Families, the Italian Northern League, and the United Kingdom Independence Party (UKIP)), the EU Charter was portrayed as entailing a risk of 'moral corruption' by allegedly empowering sexual or religious minorities. Among mainstream political parties, opposition to the Charter originated in two concerns: first, that social rights included in the Charter might harm the competitiveness of European companies; second, that provisions on non-discrimination and defendants' rights would threaten national self-determination in the fields of immigration and criminal justice, as was argued, for instance, by the British Conservatives.

Finally, value-based Euroscepticism is also present in some segments of public opinion, especially in countries where national legislation on such issues as abortion is rather restrictive. For instance, during the first Irish referendum on the Nice Treaty, the perception that EU law might affect domestic legislation on divorce and abortion in Ireland not only affected turnout by motivating people (either pro- or anti-abortion) to turn out to vote, it also induced some voters, notably women, to vote against the treaty (Sinnott 2001:19).

Cultural anti-Europeanism

The last form of Euroscepticism originates in scepticism towards 'Europe' as a civilization, as a historical and cultural entity. Here, EU scepticism is rooted in a deeper, cultural scepticism towards Europe in a broader sense, which can be defined as 'anti-Europeanism'.

There are two variants of this form of scepticism. In the first variant, 'Europe', as such, does not exist. By trying to bring closer peoples that neither share a common history, nor a political culture, proponents of European integration wrongly presuppose that there is something called 'Europe'. In the absence of a shared ethnic identity between the peoples of Europe, integration beyond a mere free trade area does not make sense. In the second variant, 'Europe' – or rather continental Europe – is portrayed as an entity with homogeneous values, norms and preferences that are deemed incompatible with national preferences and traditions. From this perspective, European integration is but one expression of wider processes of Europeanization/homogenization/globalization that are to be rejected because they could prove corrosive to national values.

Scepticism towards Europe as a historical and cultural entity

A first variant of this anti-Europeanism consists in saying that 'Europe' as a concept lacks complete historical and/or cultural validity. Lacking a consensus as to its geographical limits, the meaning of 'Europe' has varied so much across time and space that one can question its validity. Moreover, Europe as a civilization, if it ever existed, has always been intermeshed with other civilizations and/or cultures, be they Arabic, Turkish or Asian. As a consequence, Europe does not have a common past, nor is a history of Europe conceivable.

This kind of scepticism, which has been called 'historiographic Euroscepticism' (Carbonell 1999:1), also leads to scepticism towards European integration as it materialized in the course of the 1950s, with the ECSC and later the EEC. Indeed, from that perspective,

'Europe' was nothing more than successive failed attempts at its unification and the then integration through the EEC would not escape that fate. A 1967 essay by a French journalist about the history of Europe clearly captures this argument by stating: 'The account of European history is easy to do: there was never something called Europe ... It is now up to the present bureaucratic Europe to try and do better than assemble bits of a continent ... Three thousand years have not been long enough to unify the continent. Secular and religious princes, conquerors and dreamers have failed. Bureaucracy can only sketch out caricatures of Europe' (Sédillot 1967, quoted in Carbonell 1999:15).

This argument about an inescapable diversity is often present in today's Eurosceptic discourses. It was articulated, for instance, by advocates of the Mediterranean Union Project, who rebutted the criticism the German government levelled at the project; the latter expressed concerns that it would split the EU. The strongly Eurosceptic French website Voxlatina was one of them, as it stated: 'By imposing her views of a downgraded Mediterranean project, the German Chancellor has shown an obsessive denial of reality, namely division ... Indeed, whether one likes it or not, Europe is (already) divided! Just as there are still two Germanys cohabiting side by side despite reunification, divided by differences of mentality and economic development, there are at least two Europe(s). Everyone knows the dividing lines between those two Europe(s): the division, dating back two thousand years, between Romanic peoples and non-Romanic ones and, later, the division between Protestants and Catholics' (Mignot 2008).

In the eyes of some Eurosceptics, it is precisely this lack of shared history, together with the more general absence of a shared ethnic identity, that prevents the EU from becoming a democratic, political union.

Scepticism towards a European political identity

Indeed, scepticism towards Europe as a cultural entity underlies much of the scepticism and the hostility towards a possible European political identity. Much of this intellectual resistance towards the possibility of a democracy at a European level was fostered by two elements in the Maastricht period: the creation of an EU citizenship and the 12 October 1993 'Maastricht judgment' of the German Constitutional Court. This kind of scepticism has also been expressed in reaction to the writings of Jürgen Habermas, who, as early as 1992, argued that the formation of a European political identity based on a European equivalent of 'constitutional patriotism' was both possible and desirable. Besides, Habermas argued, a democracy at a European level was conceivable if a European public sphere and a unified party system emerged (Habermas 1992). Since the Maastricht developments, this thesis has been contradicted by intellectuals and politicians on two grounds.

The first argument consists in saying that cultural homogeneity is a pre-condition for the emergence of a common political identity and a democracy at EU level. In the absence of a shared ethnic identity (embodied in history, mythology, language, religion, social traditions, etc.), such developments are not possible. Even the definition of shared fundamental rights can be a conflict-ridden process, as the understanding of those rights might vary from one country to another (for example, the right to free speech). Moreover, since elements of ethnicity are deemed necessary for the development of democracy, a democracy at the EU level is allegedly not conceivable. An offshoot of that argument is the so-called 'no-demos thesis', i.e. the idea that a European demos is not conceivable in the absence of a shared ethnic identity. This argument underlay the German Constitutional Court's judgment on Maastricht (see pp.155–6).

The second argument consists in saying that, as the emergence of democracy and the construction of the nation are tightly interlinked historically, they cannot be dissociated. Thus, legal or constitutional patriotism cannot take root in a non-national context. In France, for instance, this critique is articulated, often with strong Eurosceptic undertones, by republican, left-wing essayists and politicians such as Jean-Pierre Chevènement (for an overview of this literature, see Lacroix 2005). However, it is also articulated by right-wing, liberal politicians, for example the late Lord Dahrendorf, member of the British House of Lords. As he declared, 'Democracy is tightly linked to the nation-state. The nation-state is the only context in which representative, parliamentary democracy, based on debate, can work. Europe is not democratic. The European Parliament does not produce democracy. We have no European public sphere in which we can seriously debate in a democratic way' (quoted in Leconte 2003:455).

The rejection of wider processes of Europeanization

Cultural anti-Europeanism also expresses itself through the rejection of wider processes of Europeanization that are not linked directly to the implementation of EU law but to broader, long-term sociological transformations affecting national societies. From this perspective, European integration is seen as one trend among others, which facilitates the circulation of debates, ideas, and practices across borders, thus fostering societal change. Increasingly, indeed, domestic public debates on issues such as welfare state reform or ethical issues such as euthanasia, stem cell research and drug policy are influenced by references to other national models and/or legislation, both within and outside the EU (for instance, Switzerland on the issue of euthanasia). Further on, the emergence of a deliberative space in the EU, for instance in the EP, enhances such a development. This was the case, for instance, for debates on reproductive rights (European Parliament 2002a) and discussions relating to the financing of stem cell research with EU funds in 2006.

These issues are not decided at an EU level but have been fiercely debated in the EP. This is why, to some Eurosceptics, European integration is seen as entailing a risk of degeneration (moral, cultural, political) of national societies, infusing them with corrosive values. This discourse partly overlaps the rhetoric articulated both by radical right- and left-wing parties, which presents Europeanization and European integration as forms of 'Americanization' and/or globalization. Similarly, in the eyes of Eurosceptics, the EU (and the ECJ) and the Council of Europe (and the European Court of Human Rights) both contribute to unwanted processes of Europeanization of national law and societies and are equally disliked as unwanted infringements of national sovereignty, notably on high-profile human rights issues. As one observer of British debate on European integration observed, 'These two Europe[s] have sometimes tended to become conflated in Eurosceptic discourse' (Drewry 2007:102), a phenomenon which is compounded by existing cooperation between the two organizations.

Distrust of European countries

A founding father of the Eurobarometer, Jacques-René Rabier, has emphasized the significance of mutual trust in the process of integration, as a form of social or 'horizontal' integration (Rabier 1977). This dimension of integration becomes increasingly relevant, for instance, with the creation of a European judicial area, which implies mutual trust in national judicial systems. Eurobarometer surveys investigating citizens' preferences indicate that there is relatively widespread distrust of other countries' judicial systems among EU citizens, which might affect cooperation in civil justice in the EU (SEB 292:29). This distrust can be equated with another form of anti-Europeanism originating in the depreciation of other countries' institutions and political systems.

As we shall see in the next chapter, this type of anti-Europeanism is especially present in British Eurosceptic discourses, which are often underlain by deep mistrust towards continental European countries' welfare states and institutions. This type of anti-Europeanism is also widespread among Eurosceptics in the United States. In his study on Euroscepticism in the United States, for instance, Chamorel shows that Euroscepticism (defined as hostility towards the EU or its main policies) is rooted in a deeper hostility towards European politics, diplomacy, culture and economics (which he calls 'anti-Europeanism') (2006: 166–7). The idea that the EU is built on continental European values alien to US traditions permeates, for instance, the hostility of neo-conservatives towards the EU Charter of Fundamental Rights, which is accused of 'greatly expanding the scope of state power' (McNamara 2006:5). Moreover, in the case of neo-conservatives, Euroscepticism is linked to the historical legacy of the 'Munich syndrome' (referring to European democracies' appeasement diplomacy towards Nazi Germany in the 1930s) (Vaïsse 2004:453). This stereotypical view of Europe's alleged moral laxness and cowardice towards dictators resurfaced during the 2003 military intervention in Iraq, as this comment illustrates: 'Americans just don't trust Europe's political judgment. Appeasement is its second nature. Europeans have never met a leader, Hitler, Mussolini, Stalin, Quaddafi, Khomeini, Saddam, they didn't think could be softened up by concessions' (Mead 2002).

This form of anti-Europeanism is not limited to English-speaking countries, however. It is also present in the discourse of Dutch soft Eurosceptics, like Frits Bolkestein, who argued that the '[Dutch] individualistic and open, democratised culture shares greater similarities with Canada than with Italy' (quoted in Harmsen 2004:10).

Ethnocentrism and xenophobia

In some cases, this type of anti-Europeanism amounts to sheer ethnocentrism, even xenophobia. This is the case, for example, in the strident Germanophobia (and Francophobia) underlying British tabloids' Euroscepticism. In a similar vein, Germanophobia also underlay early French opposition to the ECSC and the European Defence Community (EDC), just as it underlies Euroscepticism among the French extreme right or among some left-wing 'national-Republican' intellectuals. Examples include, for instance, Emmanuel Todd, who equated Maastricht Yes voters with heirs to the Vichy regime, obsessed with the 'German model' (quoted in Lacroix 2005:5). In a more mundane way, issues such as foreign land ownership (which can no longer be restricted as a result of the implementation of EU law) have also crystallized fears about a possible 'invasion' by foreign EU citizens in some countries. Examples include the French referendum campaign on Maastricht, as extreme-right politicians warned against a possible 'British invasion' of southern France (quoted in Koslowski 1999:167).

This ethnocentric Euroscepticism is also expressed in the idea that European integration amounts to imposing a specific national 'counter-model' on other countries. A widespread version is expressed in the (wrong) belief that the convergence criteria of EMU were imposed by the German government on other member states. A more radical version is articulated, for instance, by those who predict that the EU will experience a 'Belgian scenario' of communautarian fragmentation and dissolution, as separate cultural entities are forced to unite under the motto of an 'ever closer union'. This thesis has been put forward in a book by a Belgian journalist who claims to explain how 'Belgian political attitudes have infected those of the EU' (Belien 2005). Lord Ralph Harris, a British Conservative politician, praised this 'penetrating historical analysis [that] warns that the EU is heading the way of Belgium – towards a corrupt, corporatist, coercive construct devoid of national consciousness or cohesion' (Belien 2005). This idea is also present in the discourse of radical right-wing politicians in Austria who refer to inter-community tensions in Belgium in order to disparage the idea of closer union among the peoples of the EU (Leconte 2003:388).

Conclusion

As this chapter has shown, Euroscepticism is a highly diverse, multi-faceted phenomenon. Rather than one single Euroscepticism, there are indeed several forms, and although distinct, these varieties of Euroscepticim interact. At an individual level for instance, as we shall see later (see pp.237–8), scepticism regarding the distributional impact of a specific EU policy or legislation can easily spill over into a more principled opposition to a further delegation of powers to the EU.

Nevertheless, the likelihood of dissatisfaction with specific EU policies transforming into principled opposition also depends on pre-existing perceptions of European integration. In that respect, this chapter has highlighted the fact that different varieties of Euroscepticism reflect reservations about integration that are more or less deeply ingrained. As has been argued elsewhere in the case of French anti-Americanism (Roger 2002), disapproval of specific policies is sometimes rooted in a broader cultural and/or ideological hostility towards the United States as a model of society. Similarly, EU scepticism is often rooted in deeply ingrained perceptions resulting from collective processes of socialization over the long term. Indeed, the possibility that Eurosceptic discourses might resonate with broader perceptions of Europe as 'the other' is influenced to a great extent by the country context, as the next chapter explains.

Chapter 3

A Geography of Euroscepticism

Initially created by advocates of European unification, with a clearly political objective (to foster the emergence of a European public opinion) (Baisnée 2007), Eurobarometer surveys try to measure levels of public Euroscepticism by assessing citizens' support for their country's EU membership (i.e. whether they see it as a good thing or not) and by inquiring into citizens' utilitarian evaluations of membership (i.e. whether they think their country has benefited from membership or not). The resulting countries' rankings in terms of levels of pro-Europeanism can in fact be misleading. First of all, they can easily foster stereotypical views of countries, by classifying them into simplistic categories (for instance, Europhile versus Eurosceptic countries). Moreover, high levels of support for EU membership can coincide with widespread hostility to further integration, as was illustrated during the 2005 and 2008 referenda in the Netherlands and Ireland. In that respect, Eurobarometer rankings can obscure the existence of relatively widespread Eurosceptic orientations in apparently Europhile countries. For instance, a recent survey showed that in Belgium, a Europhile country by all Eurobarometer standards, one-fifth of citizens thought that European integration had already gone too far (Abts *et al.* 2009:9). In Spain, the very high abstention rate in the 2005 referendum, 57.7 per cent (FEB168:6) and the widespread indifference towards the EU (in 2001, 59 per cent would feel indifferent if the EU was scrapped (EB 55:33)) nuance the perception of a largely Europhile country. This shows that levels of membership support alone do not give an accurate picture of where national public opinion stands on European integration. This chapter aims to shed some light on the complex set of factors underlying collective perceptions of European integration, while explaining why countries differ in this regard.

Cross-country differences in relation to Euroscepticism are twofold. First, countries differ in terms of levels of Euroscepticism, be it party-based or popular Euroscepticism. Second, differences apply to predominant varieties of Euroscepticism. For instance, cultural anti-Europeanism is a key dimension of Euroscepticism in the UK. In a similar vein, it has been argued that countries like Denmark and France are especially prone to political Euroscepticism; since there is a strong overlap between state and nation in these countries, any step towards political integration at EU level tends to be perceived as a challenge to both state and nation (Hansen and Waever 2002). Value-based Euroscepticism is more likely to be relevant in countries where domestic legislation on ethical issues is either rather conservative (such as Ireland, Malta, and Poland) or rather permissive (such as the Netherlands). In both cases, European integration might be perceived as challenging collective preferences, either in a too liberal or in a too conservative direction.

The chapter starts by showing how the national context affects levels and forms of Euroscepticism. It then analyzes five types of variables accounting for these cross-country differences: the context, timetable and modalities of countries' accession processes to the EU; collective utilitarian assessments of countries' EU membership; the perceived fit or misfit between the EU and national institutions; references to 'Europe' in nation-building processes; and, finally, understandings of national identity. The chapter ends by showing how these variables can be transposed to the regional level of analysis, in order to explain cross-regional variations in levels of Euroscepticism within countries.

Different countries, different Euroscepticism(s)

Nationality is the most relevant factor influencing individuals' attitudes towards the EU, ahead of transnational factors such as level of education or occupation, according to several recent studies (Brinegar and Jolly 2005; Voessing 2005). For instance, the level of support for EU membership among Dutch workers is on average 20 percentage points higher than among their British counterparts. By the same token, Dutch and Irish manual workers display higher levels of EU support than executives in many countries, a fact which contradicts the core assumptions of the utilitarian theory (Brinegar and Jolly 2005). Leaving aside sociological factors, a British or an Austrian citizen, for instance, is twice as unlikely as an Irish or a Dutch one to be in favour of European integration (Baisnée *et al.* 2006:85).

Cross-country differences in membership support

To sketch a broad picture of cross-country variations, one can distinguish between three groups of countries on the basis of the Eurobarometer surveys, keeping in mind that these are ideal-typical categories. A first group of countries, including the Benelux countries, Spain and Ireland (and, more recently, Denmark, Poland and Romania), repeatedly displays the highest levels of membership support, with 60 to 80 per cent of citizens qualifying their country's EU membership as a good thing. A second group of countries at the opposite end of the pro-/anti-integration cleavage, comprising the UK, Austria and Hungary, recurrently appears as the most Eurosceptic, with less than 40 per cent of citizens evaluating EU membership positively. Other countries (Latvia and, to a lesser extent, Sweden and Finland) can, to some extent, be grouped together with this Eurosceptic group, as levels of membership approval in these countries often drop below 50 per cent. A third group, the intermediate category, is composed of countries such as Germany and France, where levels of support tend to vary around 50 per cent.

Certainly, this broad sketch implies neither that national attitudes to EU membership are homogeneous, nor that they are fixed. Indeed, some countries have experienced quite significant evolutions in public opinion trends over the long run (see Figure 3.1). In Denmark, for instance, public opinion since EC accession has evolved from being quite sceptical into being one of the most Europhile in the EU. Some countries, however, have experienced an opposite scenario. This was the case, for example, for Italian and, to a lesser extent, French public opinion. After experiencing a phenomenon of pro-European convergence with the most Europhile nations (the Benelux countries and Germany) in the 1970s and 1980s, public opinion in these countries turned less supportive of the EU, a phenomenon which was most striking in Italy (with barely 40 per cent of the public evaluating EU membership positively in the last couple of years).

However, for those countries located at each end of the pro-/anti-integration cleavage, the predominant scenario is that of relatively stable patterns of public opinion over the long term. As early as the late 1940s, for instance, public opinion in the Nordic countries (Norway and Sweden) was rather sceptical towards the idea of 'the United States of Europe', whereas such an idea was strongly supported by public opinion in the Benelux countries (Rabier 1989).

FIGURE 3.1 *Evolution of public support for EC/EU membership by country, 1957–2007*

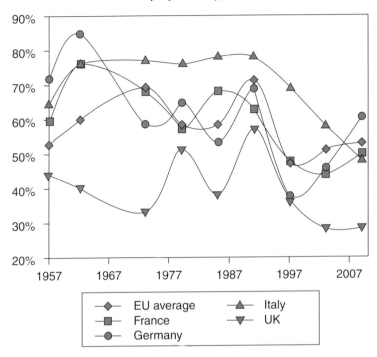

Source: data from various issues of Eurobarometer.

In the same period, British public opinion was largely undecided in that respect. Whereas it had started to converge towards the pro-European orientations of continental countries in the course of the 1950s, it departed from the pattern of the six founding EEC countries by the beginning of the 1960s. Moreover, these cross-country differences also applied to attitudes towards political integration. For instance, opposition to the creation of a European army in 1948 was strongest in the UK, Sweden and Switzerland, where a majority of citizens opposed this scenario. Finally, levels of information about concrete developments in European integration clearly set the UK apart from other countries participating in those developments. In 1957, whereas two-thirds of EEC citizens knew about the creation of the common market, less than 40 per cent of British citizens were aware of it (Rabier 1989).

Policy-based Euroscepticism and cross-country differences

The influence of the country context on attitudes towards the EU is not limited to general perceptions about EU membership, however. It also applies to citizens' preferences as to the desired scope of the EU's power. For instance, citizens in the UK and Denmark seem to be the most willing to restrict the scope of the EU's power in general (Voesssing 2005). Besides, the national variable also influences citizens' preferences as to the Europeanization of specific policies. Indeed, policy-specific Euroscepticism varies across countries. In the Nordic countries, much of the opposition to a further extension of the EU's power concerns welfare issues, environmental protection, defence and police cooperation, while much British Euroscepticism is focused on EMU (Lubbers and Scheepers 2005:228). These differences between countries are reflected in public opinion patterns. For example, public support for a common EU immigration policy ranges from 10 per cent in Finland to 70 per cent in the Netherlands, while opposition to it is strongest in the UK, Finland, Sweden and Austria (Luedtke 2005). The case of EMU also highlights these national patterns of support. In 2002, as the Euro was being introduced, German public opinion systematically displayed the most negative evaluation of the Euro, according to several indicators (FEB 139:59–60).

The country context mediating transnational variables

What is more, the country context also influences perceptions of integration indirectly, as it determines the respective relevance of specific, transnational factors in shaping individual perceptions of the EU. For instance, demographic factors, such as gender, are more or less influential in shaping an individual's views on the EU, depending on his/her nationality. Indeed, probably the most powerful transnational variable influencing individuals' opinions on the EU, namely attitudes towards minorities, still has a highly differentiated impact across countries, depending on the relevance of immigration issues in a given country (McLaren 2006). Finally, nationality also influences the parameters according to which individuals evaluate EU institutions. Depending on an individual's nationality, for instance, the input legitimacy of EU-level decision-making will be accorded more or less relevance in general evaluations of the EU.

Certainly, there are country-specific issues that come to crystallize Eurosceptic feelings: the issue of truck traffic in the Austrian Alps, concerns over EU legislation on state aid and its possible impact on the wine sector in Malta, and scepticism towards the common EU fishery policy in potential EU members such as Iceland and Norway, for instance. Beyond this diversity, however, there are similar types of variables that influence collective perceptions of the EU. These are indeed the consequence of different temporalities: the short-term time-span of accession processes and the long-term effects of century-old processes of nation-building and political socialization in a national context.

Accession processes and seniority as an EU member

To begin with, national perceptions of the EU are shaped by accession processes: the context in which a given country joins the EU, as well as the length and modalities of the accession process. Moreover, it has been argued that EU membership induces a process of socialization; citizens allegedly become more supportive of the EU as societies Europeanize.

Context of the accession process

The context in which a country joins the EU is especially relevant. In some cases, for instance, EC/EU accession has been closely connected with processes of democratic transition and/or consolidation, as was the case for Greece, Portugal and Spain. In the Spanish case, for instance, the link between EEC accession and democratic transition (which was definitively secured in 1981–82) explains the high level of support for EU membership in Spanish public opinion (Diez-Medrano 2003). Nonetheless, perceptions of a clear association between EU accession and democratic transition also depend on the timetable of accession. In cases where accession processes are especially lengthy, the perception of a link between the two processes can be eroded. Such an argument has been put forward in the case of the eastern and central European (ECE) countries that joined the EU in 2004. Certainly, their accession process did not last significantly longer than for southern countries: ten years for those that applied in 1994, which is comparable to the Spanish case. However, the lapse of time between the return to democracy and EU accession was significantly longer for the ECE countries than for Spain (five years in the case of Spain, compared with fifteen years in the case of ECE countries). This implied a significant political cost for the EU in terms of symbols. The perceived link between the return to Europe and the return to democracy was eroded, if not disrupted, as was the idea of joining the EU as a community of values. Both receded as the accession talks focused on highly technical issues (Rupnik 2004:16). The inability of elites in the EU to convey the normative significance of accession to publics in member and non-member states has allegedly damaged the understanding of the EU as a political community.

Besides, accession processes in the case of the ECE countries have coincided with swift and more or less radical processes of economic transition, with big redistributive consequences. In some countries, the economic transition has been especially abrupt. This factor has been put forward to account for different levels of support for EU accession among ECE countries during the 2003 referenda. A good example of this is Estonia, whose electorate was the least supportive of EU accession (see Table 1.1, p.22). This has been attributed, notably, to the especially swift and radical economic transition which transformed the Estonian economy into the most liberal and open one among the new member states (Vetik, Nimmerfelt and Taru 2006:1082). In another context, it could be hypothesized that the economic terms under which the UK joined the EC in 1973 might have had long-lasting consequences for popular evaluations of EC/EU membership. The bad economic situation of the country, coupled with the perception that the structure of the EEC budget, with its heavy emphasis on the CAP, did not benefit the UK, might explain that, already at the time of accession, a majority of British citizens thought that the economic interests of their country were not well served in the EC (Inglehart and Reif 1991:9).

Probabilities and modalities of accession

In addition to the context in which accession takes places, potential difficulties linked to the accession process might spill over into negative perceptions of the EU. Accession processes indeed shed light on countries' unequal probability of joining the EU, thus giving rise to perceptions of unequal treatment by EU institutions and EU member states.

To begin with, support for accession in non-member countries can depend on the probability of their joining the EU. Countries in which public opinion is confident about the probability of a smooth and rapid accession tend to display higher levels of Euroscepticism (Krastev 2004:294). Once EU accession is perceived as granted, it becomes less valued and critical voices about the EU are more likely to be raised. This argument could be put forward to explain the relatively more critical tone of domestic public debate on accession in the Czech Republic (which, as a country located at the geographical centre of Europe, saw accession as a long overdue return to Europe), Hungary and Estonia (where comparatively good economic performances secured a place in the first accession wave). This contrasted sharply with a country like Slovakia, where accession had been jeopardized by the anti-democratic tendencies of the Meciar government and where support for EU accession in 2003 was highest among all accession countries (see Table 1.1, p.22).

Moreover, the way accession is presented in political elites' discourses also plays a role in shaping perceptions of the EU. The predominance of expressions conveying the idea of domestic backwardness versus EU modernity (heavily centred on notions of adaptation, harmonization, screening, etc.) might trigger, as a reaction, the development of a 'reactive' identity defining itself in opposition to the EU (Vetik 2006:1086). In that respect, a parallel can be drawn between EU enlargement to the ECE countries and German reunification. In both cases, official discourses and rationale underlying the reunification process failed to include the specific experiences of new democracies as being meaningful for both parties.

Seniority as an EU member: testing the socialization hypothesis

A last variable linked to accession processes relates to the length of a country's membership of the EU. It has been hypothesized, indeed, that EU membership might imply, in the long run, a process of socialization whereby citizens gradually become more supportive of their country's EU membership. As citizens become accustomed to the EU, notably through its symbols, a sense of 'banal Europeanism' could develop (Cram 2001). Indeed, public opinion in the six founding countries experienced a process of pro-European convergence in the course of the 1970s; a similar process applied to Danish, Irish and, later, southern public opinion, which all converged towards a pro-EC orientation after their accession

(Inglehart and Reif 1991:9). Even British public opinion seemed to follow a similar path in the course of the 1980s, as support for EC membership rose from 50 per cent to nearly 80 per cent (Evans and Butt 2007:180).

This socialization hypothesis, however, was not validated by developments in the 1990s and in the first decade of the twenty-first century. As mentioned earlier, public opinion in some founding countries became less pro-European in the course of that decade, while support for the EU in the UK declined again. Moreover, citizens in the 1995 accession countries do not seem, as yet, to have become more pro-European since they joined the EU. Similarly, new member states that joined the EU in 2004 and 2007 are evenly distributed on the anti-/pro-integration cleavage, which suggests that seniority in the EU does not influence attitudes towards the EU. In that respect, one must distinguish between two processes: the Europeanization of state institutions and judicial and administrative practices on the one hand, and the Europeanization of national identity on the other. Whereas the former certainly advances along with seniority in the EU, the latter does not necessarily do so, as the British case best exemplifies.

As is evidenced in the next sections, collective perceptions of the EU at national level are shaped by several other factors, thus making any linear prediction of pro-European convergence among national publics rather risky.

Collective utilitarian assessment of EU membership

Euroscepticism can be attributed to collectively widespread negative evaluations of gains derived from integration and/or the costs implied by membership. Cost/gain evaluations of a country's membership of the EU influence one's support for that membership both directly and indirectly, since they also influence individuals' views as to how integration affects them. In other words, individuals in countries where positive evaluations of EU membership for one's country are below average are more likely to assess the impact of integration on their personal situation negatively (McLaren 2007:246). However, utilitarian assessments of a country's EU membership are not only shaped by economic and budgetary issues, they are also driven by perceptions about the political and security gains and/or costs associated with membership.

Economic cost/gain calculations

Collective, utilitarian assessments of a country's EU membership are quite influential in shaping national patterns of support for integration. For instance, economic growth linked to the increase in intra-EEC exports has been found to be closely correlated with increased support for European integration (Eichenberg and Dalton 2007:130). In a similar vein, support for EU membership often lies above the EU average in so-called cohesion countries that benefited most from the EU's structural funds (Ireland, Greece, Portugal and Spain for the old member states). Besides, citizens from countries that are net beneficiaries in relation to the EU budget are slightly more likely to think they have personally benefited from integration (McLaren 2007:249).

A contrario, countries where perceptions of being disadvantaged by core EU policies and/or of paying too much to the EU budget are widespread tend to display – with the exception of the Netherlands – comparatively low levels of support for integration. For instance, it has been mentioned that the context of British accession to the EC has been largely influenced by widespread reservations regarding the gains of accession. In a similar vein, among the five biggest net contributors to the EU budget, one finds three countries with high levels of public Euroscepticism (Austria, Sweden and the UK).

Cost/gain evaluations in terms of security

Utilitarian assessments of EU membership are not limited to economic cost/gain calculations, however. They are also affected by perceptions as to the benefits of integration in terms of geopolitical influence and military security. The EU is certainly not a military alliance. However, with the setting up of the European Security and Defence Policy (ESDP), the EU aims at developing capacities in terms of conflict prevention and crisis management, notably in neighbouring countries. Moreover, being a member of an organization in which 21 out of 27 countries are NATO members can be a political guarantee in terms of security. In this respect, cross-country differences in terms of benefits derived from EU membership can be rooted in different threat perceptions, a sense of vulnerability and varying needs for additional security resources.

To begin with, it should be remembered that support for integration among elites and in public opinion, even in the early decades of integration, was affected by periodic changes in the perception of external threats to national security. As mentioned previously, one of the instrumental rationales for supporting integration in the early years of the process was the perception of the EEC as a bulwark against communism. This was especially true in times of heightened tension with the Soviet Union, as was the case between 1947 and 1953. However, in periods of thaw, furthering integration appeared less as a priority to segments of elites and the public. The evolution of public debate on integration in France and Germany from 1953 on illustrates this. In the French case, for instance, perceptions of a less threatening Soviet Union, together with an increasing focus on decolonization wars, contributed to the failed ratification of the treaty establishing the European Defence Community in 1954. In West Germany, at the same time, public opinion was becoming less supportive of supranationalism and higher numbers of citizens ranked European integration as a secondary goal, far behind German reunification, global disarmament and economic recovery. This has been attributed, notably, to a much less acute perception of the Soviet threat and to West Germany's accession to NATO (Loth 1989:588–90).

In the present period, cross-country differences in the perception of a potential Russian threat might explain different levels of support for the EU among ECE countries. For instance, the more acute perception of a Russian threat in Poland could explain the much higher level of support for the EU in that country, compared with the Czech Republic. Moreover, support for the setting up of a common defence policy also depends on national military resources. The lower the degree of perceived threat and the greater the national military resources, the lower the support for a common European defence. For example, citizens in countries possessing nuclear weapons are less likely to support the setting up of a common foreign policy than those who live in countries that are not nuclear powers (Schoen 2008).

Nonetheless, the evaluation of gains derived from EU membership is not entirely based on rational calculations. Indeed, according to some surveys, the latter are secondary to other (political, cultural) country-level factors (McLaren 2007:249). In this respect, national institutions act as an especially powerful filter that mediates individuals' perceptions of the EU.

Degree of fit between the EU and national institutions

Institutions are not only state organs designed to perform specific tasks. In a broader sense, they refer to non-material notions like, for instance, the notion of the '*Rechtsstaat*' in Germany or the rule of law in the UK (Stone 1992:163–4). Following Peter Hall's definition, institutions can be understood as 'official and unofficial procedures, protocols, norms, conventions that underlie the organizational structure of the polity or of political economy' (Hall and Taylor 1997:471). In that sense, written and unwritten rules that govern relations between specific state institutions, between state organs and civil society and between civil society actors (like those rules that govern interactions between social partners) can be defined as institutions. Institutions as 'collective cognitive structures' refer to social practices to which specific meanings are attached. They embody collective identities, in the sense that they express 'the social consciousness of a given group' (Stone 1992:164). National institutions as understood in this section include state organs as well as non-material structures such as the welfare state or specific models of democracy (for example, 'consensual democracy').

The process of Europeanization implies wide-ranging consequences for national institutions (see pp.144–5). However, member states are not equal in their capacity to adapt to European integration. Not only do they have different administrative and financial resources but, more fundamentally, national institutional systems, policy-making styles, administrative practices and so on are more or less compatible with what the EU is and how it works. For instance, it has been argued that countries with a strong tradition of centralization (like France and the UK) are less likely than federal, decentralized countries (like Germany) to adapt to a polycentric organization like the EU. This also applies to social models or macro-economic preferences. This type of argument underlies the 'goodness of fit' theory. According to this theory, the level of pressure resulting from Europeanization depends on the degree of compatibility (fit) between EU institutions and domestic institutions. By challenging national institutions, European integration might even 'threaten deeply rooted collective understandings of national identity' (Green Cowles *et al.* 2001:7–8).

In such cases, the perceived misfit between European integration and national institutions can be a factor of Euroscepticism.

This section highlights this point with two examples: the influence of the type of welfare state and of the perceived democratic quality of national institutions on collective perceptions of European integration.

Type of welfare state

Esping-Andersen's (1990) famous typology of European welfare states, although much debated, has highlighted the fact that the welfare state historically developed in different ways across countries. According to this initial typology, three types of welfare state developed in western Europe after 1945: the liberal type (to be found in Ireland and the UK), the social-democratic type (in the Nordic countries) and the corporatist or conservative type (in France, Germany, the southern countries and in neo-corporatist systems like Austria or Belgium). As has been argued elsewhere (see Scharpf 1997), European integration entails significant challenges for national welfare states. While the free movement of capital constrains national elites' ability to pursue some welfare state policies, there is no consensus among member states on the development of welfare state policies at the EU level. Thus, in countries with the most generous welfare states (the social-democratic type), European integration is more likely to be perceived as a threat to national welfare. In fact, citizens in the largest welfare states, whatever their level of income, are more likely than others to fear a decrease in social spending as a consequence of European integration (Ray 2004).

Moreover, the national welfare state type can influence attitudes towards European integration in a threefold way. First, the size of the welfare state (measured by levels of social spending as a percentage of national GDP) influences individual preferences on the Europeanization of specific policies. Indeed, opposition to the extension of the EU's powers in issues such as social security, health and workers' rights increases with the size of the welfare state (Eichenberg and Dalton 2007:143 and 150).

Second, the type of welfare state influences individual perceptions of the EU indirectly. In fact, it mediates the influence of transnational variables that shape individual attitudes towards the EU, such as occupational status or political orientation. As regards occupation, workers in the most generous welfare states are more likely to equate integration with a 'race-to-the-bottom' that would erode the welfare state, while workers in the least generous welfare states can expect EU legislation to improve their situation, for instance on the issue of workers' rights (Brinegar and Jolly 2005). Furthermore, the type of welfare state mediates the influence of political orientations in shaping individual attitudes towards the EU. For instance, as identification with the right increases in a liberal welfare state, so does the likeliness of being Eurosceptic, because the EU tends to be equated with 'socialism through the back door'. Similarly, as identification with the left increases in social-democratic welfare states, so does the likelihood of being Eurosceptic, as the EU tends to be perceived as 'neo-liberalism through the back door' (Brinegar and Jolly 2005; Ray 2004).

Third, the type of welfare state shapes domestic public debate on EU issues. It influences the degree of politicization of EU issues and the extent to which they polarize public opinion and parties. It has been argued that EU issues are more likely to be politicized and have a polarizing impact in liberal and social-democratic welfare states (Brinegar *et al.* 2004). Since the EU's policy mix is a combination of liberal and social-democratic policies, it is more likely to be perceived as incompatible with national welfare preferences in these countries. The UK, a liberal welfare state according to Esping-Andersen's typology, is a good illustration of this hypothesis. Since the end of the 1980s, any attempt at developing the EC/EU's power in the social field has contributed to an intense politicization of EU issues and the latter has had a significant impact on inter-party competition. In a similar vein, domestic public debate on EU accession (and, later, on EMU) in a social-democratic welfare state like Sweden was deeply polarizing and had a highly divisive impact on mainstream political parties.

Perceived quality of domestic public governance

The role of national institutions in shaping individual perceptions of the EU is also linked to citizens' perception of the democratic quality of domestic governance. As for the welfare state, the EU tends to be evaluated according to the potential added value it might bring to the national situation: is it associated with better governance (greater transparency, less corruption, etc.) or with democratic standards that are perceived to be lower than domestic ones?

It has been argued that citizen support for further integration is influenced both by their perception of national institutions and by their evaluation of EU institutions (Sanchez-Cuenca 2000). According to this thesis, minimum support for further integration is to be found among those citizens who have a good opinion of national institutions and a poor opinion of EU institutions. Such a situation is to be found mainly in countries where corruption is perceived to be weak and where social expenditure as a percentage of GDP is high (two factors which enhance satisfaction with domestic institutions). This thesis sheds some light on the following statement: in most of the countries where trust in the national government is higher than the EU average, trust in EU institutions lies below the EU average (notably in the UK, Sweden, Finland and Austria). In a similar vein, of the ten countries where the perceived degree of national corruption is lowest, half tend to display comparatively high levels of popular Euroscepticism (Finland, Sweden, Austria and the UK) (SEB 291:4).

Nonetheless, this correlation does not always apply. In some countries, dissatisfaction with national institutions is coupled with comparatively low levels of satisfaction with EU membership, for example in Greece or Hungary. Moreover, at the individual level, dissatisfaction with domestic institutions often translates into negative evaluations of EU institutions. How can these apparently contradictory statements be reconciled? It might be hypothesized that there is a cumulative effect in dissatisfaction with public institutions at individual and country levels. This dissatisfaction might increase to the point where it transforms into general political cynicism and dissatisfaction with the way democracy works at the domestic level, or into feelings of disenfranchisement that are then projected onto any public institution, be it domestic or European.

Moreover, the thesis linking poor domestic governance and positive evaluations of EU institutions with higher support for further integration can be nuanced. Indeed, the degree of satisfaction with national institutions does not directly influence general support for integration. Rather, it might influence the relevance of the EU's perceived governance quality for citizens' general support for further integration. Consequently, the stronger the satisfaction with national institutions, the more likely that perceptions of a 'democratic deficit' at EU level will diminish support for further integration (Rohrschneider 2002).

Analyses of EU accession referenda as well as European election results seem to confirm this thesis. Evidence from the 1994 accession referenda is worth mentioning, since they took place in countries where satisfaction with domestic institutions is high. Concerns over the EU's alleged democratic deficit played a role in individual voting behaviour; in Sweden for instance, it was mentioned by 65 per cent of those who voted against accession (Kaiser 1995:5). In addition, the good electoral scores of single-issue parties campaigning for more transparency in the EU in the 2004 EP elections in Austria and the Netherlands seem to confirm that the national context influences the relevance of the EU's 'input legitimacy' for citizens. Indeed, these two countries rank among the less corrupted in the EU according to citizens' perceptions (SEB 291:4).

Reference to 'Europe' in nation-building processes

National institutions are the product of processes of social construction that have unfolded over the long run. In this respect, present cross-country differences in attitudes towards the EU are also the consequence of different nation-building processes, during which Europe as a continent, a civilization, a cultural and/or political entity, has been mobilized in struggles over the meaning of national identity. In specific instances, 'Europe' has been held up as a model to imitate, while in others it has been disparaged in order to define allegedly superior national values. This section shows how collective perceptions of Europe inherited from history influence current perceptions of the EU.

Five different factors are examined below: the chronology and timing of nation state development, centre–periphery relations and the issue of minorities, national identity framing in relation to Europe, the role of religion in influencing relationship to Europe and, finally, countries' heritage in terms of foreign policy.

Chronology of state formation

EU countries have different heritages in terms of their existence as independent nation states. In this respect, it can be hypothesized that countries that have had little experience as independent states and/or which recovered national sovereignty only recently are reluctant to pool national sovereignties in an EU context. For instance, it has been suggested that those countries that did not exist as independent states during the Cold War, like the Baltic countries or Slovenia, could be especially receptive to alleged threats of 'centralization'. More generally, the equation of the EU with a new kind of

Soviet Union is indeed a landmark of Eurosceptic discourse among right-wing parties in the new member states. In a similar vein, Malta, which became independent in 1964, displayed the lowest level of support for EU accession in 2003, along with Estonia (see Table 1.1, p.22).

Centre–periphery relations and the minorities issue

In countries which experienced late state formation processes and have a centralist tradition, European integration and its potential consequences for centre/peripheries relations can raise concerns over a possible weakening of the state. This is the case with the EU's regional policy, which implied, in some countries, the setting up of new levels of regional governance (as was the case in some ECE countries). In Turkey, a country that has a tradition of strong centralization, preparations for the future implementation of the EU's regional policy come up against strong resistance among segments of political elites who fear that this might undermine the integrity of the state. Such concerns find even more of an echo in cases where centre/periphery cleavages overlap with the presence of minorities. For instance, the hostility of the Austrian extreme right to the Alpe-Adria Euro-region, which includes the Austrian *Land* of Carinthia, Slovenia and the north-eastern part of Italy, is rooted in the belief that it could serve the interests of the Slovene minority in Carinthia (Leconte 2003:174). Similarly, in Turkey, hostility towards the strengthening of regional levels of government is rooted in the concern that this might empower the Kurdish minority, which is heavily concentrated in some regions of the country.

Indeed, in some countries, the idea that the implementation of the *acquis communautaire* (including provisions on non-discrimination) and the Copenhagen criteria (which imply the protection of minorities' rights) might empower ethnic minorities underlies some of the scepticism towards EU accession. This has been observed in ECE countries, where 'local elites were in principle supportive of introducing regional administrative boundary adjustments in order to facilitate accession to the EU except in those cases where the potential empowerment of ethnic minorities was an issue' (Hughes *et al.* 2002:335). Similarly, the significance of the Russian minorities' issue in Estonia and Latvia (where they make up respectively 25 and 29 per cent of the total population) has been put forward as a possible reason for comparatively low levels of support for EU accession in the 2003 referenda. That these two countries were submitted to a deliberate and massive strategy of 'Russification' during Soviet rule might contribute to heightened sensitivity towards some EU policies today. Hungary, which currently ranks among the most Eurosceptic member states, also highlights the significance of the minorities issue in relation to the EU. Indeed, the Hungarian status law of 2001, which granted special rights to Hungarian minorities living abroad, had to be withdrawn under EU pressure because it violated EU law provisions on non-discrimination.

Seeds of distrust: framing of the nation in relation to 'Europe'

Negative references to Europe and other European countries have often been used in order to define a national model of society deemed superior to European standards. This cultural anti-Europeanism, as defined in the previous chapter, illustrates how ingrained distrust towards other countries' societies and institutions affects current scepticism towards the EU. A recent study has indeed identified distrust towards EU citizens from other countries as the most important variable underlying Euroscepticism at individual level (Abts *et al.* 2009:16). Two examples of how this distrust affects current collective attitudes towards European integration are analyzed below.

British Euroscepticism is a case in point. It is embedded in a specific understanding of the British nation (itself rooted in the idea of a British exception) and in deep distrust towards continental European societies and political systems. The idea of a British exception emphasizes the civic component of British identity and its unique contribution to democracy and freedom in Europe: the UK as the cradle of parliamentary democracy, the rule of law, the Bill of Rights, Parliament as the embodiment of national sovereignty, and so on. British institutions are presented as the embodiment of freedom, an idea which was very present in Margaret Thatcher's Bruges speech, as she declared: 'we have pioneered and developed representative institutions to stand as bastions of freedom' (1988:2). Nonetheless, this civic component of identity is itself embedded in an ethnic understanding of the nation – the belief in the superiority of a specifically British/Anglo-Saxon character, rooted in the idea of a 'chosen people' (Smith 2005:8; Ichijo 2005:26–7; Flood 2000:190). What is more, this typically British character is being defined in opposition to continental Europe: British commonsense versus European doctrinal rigidity, moderation versus extremism, freedom versus despotism, courage versus cowardice, etc. (Smith 2005:3). Again, this idea permeated Mrs Thatcher's Bruges speech, as she outlined that the EC should not be submitted to 'the dictates of some abstract intellectual concept' (doctrinal rigidity) since it was 'a practical means' of achieving prosperity and security (1988:4).The Bruges speech echoed a deeply ingrained idea of British exception in relation to continental Europe, as it has been circulated in segments of the media, academia and the education system (Daddow 2006). This idea relies on a set of few but recurrent metaphors (the fortress/island story, continental Europe as 'other', the imperial vocation, the special relationship, etc.) and critical, historical junctures (the Magna Carta of 1215, the victory against the Great Armada in 1588, British resistance in World War II, etc.). Closely correlated with this idea of national exception is a deep distrust of continental European countries. This concerns not only their economies and welfare states (portrayed as over-regulated and uncompetitive) but also their political elites and institutions (presented as corrupt, profligate and lacking accountability) and their judicial systems (deemed to be submitted to political authority and where trial by jury is absent) (Teubert 2001:62–5). This distrust merges with EU scepticism, as the EU itself is believed to be modelled on continental European institutions. Not only does it try to impose this uniform model of society on the UK, for instance by submitting its economy to a new 'totalitarian' regime of regulations (Booker 1996:197). It also has a corrupting effect on the British political system and institutions, as British democracy risks being submerged by or sacrificed to EU dictatorship. These ideas make up the discursive core of British Euroscepticism, which relies on a few, inter-related catch words (for example, bureaucracy, centralism and lack of accountability) widely circulated on Eurosceptic websites (Teubert 2001).

Nordic Euroscepticism displays at least three similarities to British Euroscepticism: the belief in the superiority of especially Nordic values different from the rest of continental Europe, the role of Protestantism in shaping this belief and the existence of an alternative community with which to identify, in addition to the national and European levels. The belief in the superiority of a Nordic model of society is rooted in supposedly shared values such as good governance, gender equality, low wage inequalities, strong environmental protection, the social-democratic type of welfare state and strict supervision of the Church by the State (as opposed to southern Europe). These values are often articulated as especially Nordic, sometimes in opposition to other EU countries or to the EU as such (Hastings 2007). The belief in the existence of shared Nordic values is embodied in the concept of *Norden*. This concept, which dates back to the nineteenth century, as it was used by pan-Nordic movements, allows citizens to identify (even vaguely) with an 'imagined community' beyond the nation state, while keeping national sovereignty intact (Hansen and Waever 2002). Indeed, the structures embodying Nordic cooperation, such as the Nordic Council (set up in 1953), are only weakly institutionalized and do not imply a transfer or pooling of sovereignties. In that respect, the *Norden* performs a function similar to that of the Commonwealth in the UK. It allows the Nordics to identify with a vague form of internationalism beyond the nation state, thus serving as a substitute for a European identity, without challenging national sovereignty.

The role of religion in framing collective perceptions of Europe

Religion has played a role in the emergence of these beliefs about national identity and stereotypes about other European countries. To begin with, religion has been identified as a relevant factor influencing individual perceptions of European integration. Indeed, Protestants have long seemed to be less enthusiastic about European integration than Catholics or members of the Orthodox church (Nelsen and Guth 2003:90; Vignaux 2004). Today the relevant distinction does not separate Catholicism from Protestantism, rather, it separates mainstream Protestantism, as embodied by national Churches (whose followers display levels of EU support similar to those of Catholics) from evangelical Protestantism, as embodied by non-mainstream, sectarian groups, which predisposes to Euroscepticism (Nelsen and Guth 2003:92).

Moreover, religions have played a role in framing a specific understanding of the nation in relation to Europe. It has been argued, for instance, that beneath Euroscepticism in overwhelmingly Protestant countries lies the perception of European integration as being permeated by Catholic influences. Indeed, the idea of European unity dates back to the Middle Ages, as it embodied the unity of Christendom under the leadership of the Pope. Moreover, the 'founding fathers' of the EC were mainly Catholic. Four main parallels have more specifically been drawn between European integration and Catholicism (Smith 2005; Lacroix 2007; Vignaux 2004).

First, European integration is often portrayed by Eurosceptics as a new dogma, a transcendental cause akin to a religious belief, which is incompatible with Protestant pragmatism and free examination. In that respect, scepticism towards European integration is presented as a sound and healthy reaction against dogmatism. This critique is present among Eurosceptics from both left and right. For instance, some French left-wing essayists criticize European integration as a new cause replacing religion On the right of the political spectrum, Thatcher's statement that 'the EC is not an end in itself' conveyed a similar idea.

Second, supranationalism is perceived as a Catholic-inspired principle, as opposed to national sovereignty. Catholic scepticism towards the nation state as the 'natural' political unit and its insistence on universalism (as a vehicle for Papal influence) contrasts with Protestant 'aversion towards a supranational structure including all believers' (Vignaux 2004:99). Since the Reform and the fight against Papal hegemony, distrust towards Catholic universalism is indeed present in Protestant countries, where religious freedom is tightly linked to state formation and national sovereignty, be it in the UK or in the Nordic countries.

Third, the EU is often suspected of an inbuilt tendency to centralization, as is the Catholic Church. Indeed, Catholicism, both as a Church and as a doctrine, is highly centralized, whereas the absence of such a hierarchical structure in Protestantism has led to the emergence of many splinter tendencies or groups, some of which, namely the evangelical ones, often display a value-based form of Euroscepticism.

Fourth, European integration is sometimes associated with the moral conservatism supposedly inherited from Catholicism, as opposed to progressive values, a discourse sometimes articulated, for instance, by Nordic social democrats.

National diplomatic history and geopolitical heritage

Finally, the framing of the nation in relation to Europe has been highly influenced by each individual nation's diplomatic history and self-understanding of its role in international relations. Countries with a colonial past and neutral countries are two examples of how these variables affect current perceptions of European integration.

To begin with, it can be hypothesized that having an imperial past does not predispose a nation to pro-Europeanism. To substantiate that point, one can compare the different trajectories of three former imperial powers: Spain on the one hand, the UK and France on the other. In the Spanish case, the 1898 defeat against the United States clearly marked the end of any imperial aspirations among political elites, as well as the idea of being one of the great European powers (Jáuregui and Ruiz-Jiménez 2005:75). On the contrary, in France and the UK, the illusion of being a significant power in world affairs was dashed much later, with de-colonization wars after 1945 and the Suez crisis in 1956. Moreover, being a nuclear power as well as a permanent member, with veto power, of the United Nations Security Council, furthered the idea of having a significant role to play in international relations, thus reducing incentives for building a common foreign and defence policy. Furthermore, in both countries European integration was initially perceived as a threat to colonial influence, with concerns over a reduced influence in the overseas territories (for France) and a loosening of ties with the Commonwealth (for the UK). In the British case, it was argued that Euroscepticism became a way to reinvent British national identity in a post-imperial context, especially among right-wingers (Gifford 2008). Indeed, the opposition of a protectionist, inward-looking, parochial EEC to a free-trade oriented, outward-looking UK with a global outlook is a cornerstone of many Eurosceptic discourses. This idea was very well captured by Margaret Thatcher, as she declared: 'We [British] have looked also to wider horizons ... and thanks goodness for that, because Europe ... will never prosper as a narrow-minded, inward-looking club' (1988:3). In many Eurosceptic discourses, British membership of the EU is contrasted with its membership of other, more international organizations (such as the Commonwealth, NATO, the WTO and the G8), in order to illustrate the idea that, by reducing it to the 'province of a European superstate' (Teubert 2001:73), the EU would also doom the UK to a parochialism alien to British tradition.

As well as post-imperial status, neutrality can also be a cause for Euroscepticism, especially when it is seen as an essential component of national identity. To begin with, neutrality can weaken support for a common European defence policy. In his study of public support for the ESDP, Harald Schoen (2008) shows, for instance, that attachment to neutrality significantly reduces public support for a common European defence. In 2003, the year the ESDP was born, opposition to a common defence policy was strongest among the four neutral EU countries (whereas opposition was limited to 15 per cent in the EU on average, it reached almost 40 per cent in Finland and Sweden) (EB 59:13). Two elements must be taken into account when examining such opposition. First, opposition to the ESDP varies according to one's understanding of the EU's role in international relations. It should be noted that although identification with Europe increases support for the CFSP (the common diplomacy to which the ESDP is subordinate), it tends to diminish support for a European rapid reaction force. This suggests that a large proportion of EU citizens supports the CFSP and the ESDP insofar as they conform to their understanding of the EU as a civilian power (Schoen 2008). Second, opposition to the ESDP increases as soon as it implies a supranational outlook and the acceptance of common, binding decisions on defence issues. This holds for a majority of countries, neutral or not. However, opposition to supranational decision-making in defence issues is strongest in neutral countries. Whereas half of EU citizens support this option, it is opposed by two-thirds of Austrians and Irish, 77 per cent of Swedes and 90 per cent of Finns (EB 59:14). Finally, attachment to neutrality as a component of national identity can underlie a more general opposition to a country's accession to the EU, as in the Swiss case (Theiler 2004:645), or opposition to a deeper involvement with the EU, as in the Irish case. In Ireland, concerns over neutrality were the second strongest motivation underlying opposition in 2001 to the Nice Treaty (which set up the ESDP) (Sinnott 2001:2), and ranked third among the motivations of No voters during the 2008 referendum on the Lisbon Treaty (FEB 245:8).

Strength and sense of national identity

Finally, collective attitudes towards European integration are also influenced by the strength and sense of national identity. It was long held that European integration would allow for the development of smooth interactions between different levels of identification, as the proportion of citizens displaying an exclusive understanding of national identity seemed to be declining. This thesis is disputed, however. To begin with, countries differ widely as to the proportion of citizens who never feel European and/or feel exclusively national (see Figure 3.2). Besides, among researchers, the main debate focuses on how different territorial identities interact in the formation of

FIGURE 3.2   *Percentage of citizens that never feel European/feel only national, by country, 1985–2005*

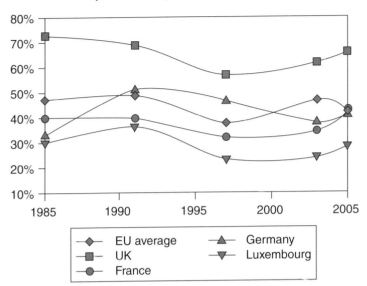

Source: data from various issues of Eurobarometer.

Eurosceptic attitudes. Do strong territorial (regional and/or national) attachments predispose a person to Euroscepticism or, on the contrary, does Euroscepticism originate in a lack of solidly rooted territorial identities?

There are, in fact, two variables relevant to this debate: the strength of national identity (measured, for instance, by one's level of pride in it) and the degree of inclusiveness (as opposed to exclusiveness) of national identity. There is no consensus on how these two variables influence each other. Not only do countries differ in terms of levels of national pride, but also in the way national pride influences the inclusiveness/exclusiveness of national identity.

Strong and multiple identities as safeguards against Euroscepticism

A common-sense view is that a strong national identity predisposes to Euroscepticism. Several elements can be put forward to substantiate that correlation. First, from the 1970s to the mid-1980s, there was a steep decline in national identity in two of the most pro-European countries, Belgium and Germany (in 1985, 30 per cent and 20 per cent of Belgian and West German citizens, respectively, were proud of their national identity) (Inglehart and Reif 1991:19). This suggests that strong attachment to Europe can be seen as a substitute for a weak national pride, whereas strong national pride might make identification with Europe less appealing. Second, weak national pride often correlates with a so-called 'post-materialist' value system, which supposedly predisposes to pro-Europeanism. Indeed, international surveys show that strong national pride tends to be associated with hostility to multilateralism, globalization and immigration (Smith and Seokho 2006:5). Since this hostility is strongly correlated with Euroscepticism (see p.180), one could conclude from this that countries where national pride is high are likely to display high levels of Euroscepticism. Indeed, according to international rankings, Austria (where popular Euroscepticism is high) and, to a lesser extent, Hungary (which is the most Eurosceptic of all the ECE countries) rank among those countries where national pride is strongest, whereas Bulgaria (one of the most Europhile countries) ranks last in terms of national pride.

Nonetheless, there are important limits to this hypothesis. First, the correlation between weak national identity, post-materialism and pro-Europeanism is at best spurious. Indeed, post-materialists are as likely to identify first with local or regional levels of political representation as with Europe, since they value direct democracy and public participation. Second, there is no systematic overlap between the strength of national pride and levels of Euroscepticism. Although there are EU countries where both national pride and popular Euroscepticism are high, Eurosceptic countries are also located at the bottom end of the international scale of national pride (notably Latvia, the Czech Republic, and the eastern part of Germany) (Smith and Seokho 2006:10). In summary, strong national identity *per se* does not necessarily imply Euroscepticism. In fact, it is only when strong national identity is simultaneously exclusive that it cultivates Euroscepticism.

Indeed, work on territorial identities suggests that a robust national identity rather incites pro-European orientations, whereas the probabilities of being Eurosceptic increase as attachment to region and nation decreases. According to Ronald Inglehart, 'those who say that they belong to their nation first of all are markedly more likely to identify with Europe or the world at large than those who feel closest to their town, province or region' (1977:337).This hypothesis has more recently been confirmed by several case studies. In the French case, for instance, as attachment to the nation decreases, so does attachment to Europe (Dargent 2001:791). A similar correlation has been observed in Belgium, where individuals identifying themselves exclusively as Europeans (and not as nationals) display higher levels of Euroscepticism than those who identify both with Belgium and Europe (Abts *et al.* 2009:16). Several arguments can be put forward in order to explain this correlation between lack of attachment to the nation and Euroscepticism. First, a weak collective identity can exacerbate fears of being 'diluted' in the process of European integration. In his analysis of Euroscepticism in the Swiss case, for instance, Tobias Theiler (2004) hypothesizes that the absence of a strong ethnic, Swiss identity heightens fears that EU accession might erode the civic pillars of Swiss identity, notably direct democracy and federalism. Second, the absence of attachment to the nation might be coupled with hostility to mechanisms of redistribution and collective solidarity, which in turn predisposes to Euroscepticism (Cautrès and Denni 2000:353).

The antagonistic relationship between national and European identities

Consequently, strong national identity might lead to pro-Europeanism. Nonetheless, there are instances where it might be coupled with an exclusive sense of national identity.

First, the activation of an exclusive sense of national identity might happen when citizens are asked to choose between national and European identities or when they feel they have to choose between the two (Dargent 2001:793). This might happen especially in instances of strong polarization on EU issues (for example, during EU-related referenda or European elections), which foster the perception of a rivalry between national and European identities, especially when political elites appear to be divided on the issue.

Second, the positive correlation between strong national identity and pro-Europeanism does not hold for all countries. In this respect, the question is whether European integration is seen as strengthening or weakening national identity. In some countries (such as the UK, Austria and Denmark) there appears to be, at the individual

level, a strong correlation between lack of support for EU membership and the perception that the EU is a threat to national identity
(McLaren 2006).

Euroscepticism at regional level

Collective attitudes towards European integration also vary across
regions. Euroscepticism at the regional level can be measured in
two ways: by comparing EU-related referenda results across
regions in a specific country and by analyzing European election
results at regional level. Referenda, especially, highlight significant
differences across regions in terms of levels of Euroscepticism. For
instance, the 2005 French referendum on the EU Constitutional
Treaty highlighted differences of up to 30 percentage points
between counties in terms of shares of No votes (Perrineau
2005:316). Similarly, during the 1994 accession referenda, inter-
regional differences in levels of support reached a 20 percentage
point difference in the Nordic countries (Kaiser 1995:6).
Moreover, successive EU referenda in some countries have highlighted the robustness of regional patterns of Euroscepticism over
time.

Certainly, region-specific issues might explain higher levels of
Euroscepticism in some regions, such as the transit issue in Tyrol,
opposition to the CAP and the Common Fisheries Policy (CFP) in
the most rural Norwegian regions, hostility to the CFP in some
French coastal regions (Landes), and dissatisfaction with the EU's
reform of the wine sector in the wine-producing regions of
Aquitaine, which voted markedly against the EU Constitutional
Treaty (Trouvé 2005:106), to name a few.

Nonetheless, beyond this issue-related Euroscepticism, structural
factors can be identified that account for relatively stable patterns of
Euroscepticism at regional level, four of which are analyzed below:
cost/gain evaluations of EU membership and the socio-economic
profile of a given region; centre–periphery relations and regional
identity; political culture; and geographical location.

Regional Euroscepticism: the mere reflection of socio-economic cleavages?

European integration entails different opportunities for different
regions across the EU. First, regional entities are unequally endowed

with resources in order to defend their interests in EU policy-making (for instance, poorer regions cannot always afford a permanent office in Brussels). Second, the implementation of the internal market has an indirect, redistributive impact on regions by exacerbating inter-regional competition. This is why the EU has set up a regional policy, endowed with structural funds, in order to help member states' poorer regions. In that context, perceived benefits and/or costs associated with European integration might explain some of the inter-regional differences in levels of Euroscepticism. For instance, the eastern Austrian region of Burgenland, which benefited most from EU structural funds, was the most supportive of accession in the 1994 referendum (74 per cent in favour compared with 66.6 per cent for the national average) (Österreichische Gesellschaft für Aussenpolitik 2008).

Moreover, as the utilitarian theory predicts, regions where macro-economic conditions lead to relatively high levels of socio-economic pessimism are more likely to display higher levels of Euroscepticism than the national average. In that respect, indeed, EU-related referenda have highlighted the significance of two cleavages: the cleavage between competitive regions benefiting from trade liberalization and post-industrial regions (where heavy industry has been declining), and the cleavage between urban and rural areas.

The first cleavage was especially relevant in the latest EU-related referenda, even in a prosperous country like Luxembourg. In this country, seven out of the nine constituencies in which the EU Constitutional Treaty was rejected by a majority of voters are located in the border region with France (Minette), where the iron and steel industries were predominantly located (Reichel 2006:80). Similarly, in France, the 1992 and 2005 referenda both highlighted the clear predominance of No votes in post-industrial regions, such as Nord Pas-de-Calais and Haute Normandie (Perrineau 2005:243). In fact, recent referenda highlight a cleavage in terms of income level and affluence. In France in 2005, predominantly working-class and less affluent constituencies tended to display higher levels of No votes (Fourquet *et al.* 2005:112). A similar cleavage was observed in Ireland in 2008. After rural constituencies, the highest share of No votes was found in the working class constituencies of Dublin South-West and Cork North Central (65 per cent and 64 per cent respectively, compared with 53 per cent for the national average) (Electionsireland 2009).

The second relevant cleavage in a utilitarian perspective is the urban/rural cleavage, as rural areas in all countries display significantly higher levels of Euroscepticism than urban ones. In France, for example, referenda in 1992 and 2005 illustrated the importance of the No vote in the most rural parts of Aquitaine (Dordogne and Lot-et-Garonne) and the Centre region (Perrineau 2005:316). Similarly, in Ireland, the highest shares of No votes during the 2008 referendum were reached in the rural regions of the north-east and south-east, where the No vote reached above two-thirds (Electionsireland 2009). This cleavage was also very significant in the 1994 accession referenda in the Nordic countries. Whereas capitals and/or big cities (such as Malmö in southern Sweden) displayed high levels of support for accession, rural areas voted overwhelmingly against it (Kaiser 1995:6).

Finally, town size (Boy and Chiche 2005:93), distance from city centres, and geographical isolation have all been found to be relevant factors explaining territorial variations. For instance, that geographical isolation is conducive to Euroscepticism was illustrated by the fact that in the same *département*, the most isolated areas are more prone to Euroscepticism than those that are better connected to transport and mass communication networks (Delbos 1994).

However, purely utilitarian accounts of Euroscepticism at regional level must be nuanced in two respects. First, the residual or spatial effect, well documented by spatial analyses of voting behaviour, indicates that the spatial context has an influence on voting, independently of the socio-economic profile of a given region or area. This residual effect was quite strong in France, for example, as some of the areas with the highest proportion of working-class voters (regions like Alsace, Choletais, and Vendée) voted, with a large majority, in favour of the EU Constitutional Treaty (Fourquet *et al.* 2005:116). Second, there is no significant correlation between instrumental support for EU membership and political support for integration at regional level. Indeed, some regions that score average or relatively high in terms of instrumental support (for example, the Spanish regions of Andalucia and Extremadura) score relatively high in terms of political Euroscepticism (Lubbers and Scheepers 2005:234). This suggests that public support for further integration at regional level cannot easily be secured through structural funds alone.

Centre–periphery relations and regional identity

Dating back to processes of state formation in the nineteenth century and earlier, the centre–periphery cleavage can be relevant to explain current attitudes towards European integration. In some countries, this cleavage has given rise to strong regional identities. Such a situation is double-edged for the EU. On the one hand, strong regional identities and historically conflicting centre/periphery relations can prevent the emergence of strong national sentiments potentially coupled with Euroscepticism, as in the Spanish case. By the same token, hostility to centralization at the national level can lead to pro-Europeanism, if the EU is seen as a way to circumvent or diminish the influence of central national authorities. For example, the rather high level of support for the Maastricht Treaty in the French Basque country has been analyzed from that angle (Trouvé 2005:104). On the other hand, regional nationalism is not necessarily conducive to pro-Europeanism, as dissenting, anti-centrist traditions can be projected onto the EU.

Several EU-related referenda illustrate the correlation between historically dissenting and/or strong regional identities and Euroscepticism. In the 2005 Spanish referendum on the EU Constitutional Treaty, for example, the percentage of No votes in the Basque country and Catalonia, with 33.6 per cent and 28 per cent respectively, was clearly above the national average of 17 per cent (FEB 168:16). This might be due, among other things, to an overlap between the referendum campaign and an ongoing, polarizing discussion on the reform of the status of autonomous communities, notably in Catalonia, where the nationalists of the Republican Left of Catalonia campaigned against the treaty, on the grounds that it did not respect regional identities. In Austria, the *Land* of Tyrol clearly displays the highest level of Euroscepticism. Not only did it register the lowest level of support for EU accession during the 1994 accession referendum, it has also systematically displayed the lowest turnout in every European election since 1996 (Österreichische Gesellschaft für Aussenpolitik 2008:7). Tyrol is an example of a historically dissenting regional identity that has expressed itself in opposition both to external threats (Bavaria and the 'Welsh' nations (France and Italy)) and to the liberal, centralizing forces that ruled in Vienna at the end of the nineteenth century. In Norway also, the region around Bergen, which was historically the cradle of anti-Swedish Norwegian nationalism, voted overwhelmingly against accession (Kaiser 1995:6).

Political culture, prevalent type of trade unionism and religion

Regions with a politically centrist tradition tend to display higher levels of support for European integration than regions where voting for relatively radical parties tends to be strong.

In France, for example, the 1992 and 2005 referenda highlight a clear cleavage between regions where voting for the centre right (notably the former Christian Democratic party Union pour la Démocratie française (UDF)) has traditionally been strong (such as in the north-west) and regions that are former communist strong-holds or where a radical, left-wing and protest-based tradition is well implanted (like Nord Pas-de-Calais, Midi, centre of Bretagne and Côtes d'Armor) (Boy and Chiche 2005:96).

Other factors, such as the historically prevalent type of trade unionism, combine in order to shape a specific regional political culture. In the north-western part of France, the influence of pro-European Christian Democracy has been compounded by the implantation of moderate Christian trade unionism. A similar logic holds for rural areas. For instance, the pro-Maastricht orientation of an otherwise strongly rural *département* like Aveyron has been attributed, to some extent, to the influence of relatively pro-European, traditional farmers' trade unions.

A third component of regional political culture is the prevalent religion. As already mentioned, the religion and degree of religiosity both play a role in shaping attitudes towards European integration and EU-related referenda have highlighted the relevance of that factor in explaining cross-regional differences in levels of Euroscepticism. In the case of Protestants, for instance, strong religiosity might be associated with lesser pro-Europeanism. This seems to be confirmed by the 2005 referendum results in the Netherlands, where the 'bible belt' (regions where religiosity is strong and where the influence of non-mainstream Protestant parties is significant) displayed higher levels of No votes than other parts of the country (*De Volkskrant* 2005). For instance, the region of Zeeland, where opposition to the treaty was strongest (with 67 per cent, together with Flevoland) also displayed the highest electoral scores for the two religious parties SPG and CU during the 2009 EP elections (17 per cent, against 7 per cent for the national average) (Netherlands elections 2009a, 2009b). In France, by contrast, the 1992 and 2005 referenda illustrate a striking permanence in the pro-European orientation of traditionally strongly Catholic regions, such as the north-western part of the country, Vendée, Alsace and the Basque country (Fourquet 2005:114).

Geographical location

Finally, geographical location might influence perceptions of European integration at regional level. For instance, it is often assumed that border regions tend to be relatively pro-European. French Alsace and the Austrian *Länder* of Burgenland and Salzburg, which display levels of support for European integration well above national averages, could be seen as good examples of this. However, the correlation does not hold systematically. Hostility towards EU enlargement might also lead to an increase in Euroscepticism in border regions, if it raises concerns over increased immigration and competition. This was the case, for instance, in French Aquitaine with the 1986 enlargement to Portugal and Spain (Trouvé 2005:101). Furthermore, for geographically peripheral regions, the fear of being further marginalized as a consequence of enlargement might also foster Euroscepticism, as was argued, again, in the case of Aquitaine, in order to explain high levels of opposition to the EU Constitutional Treaty in that region in 2005.

Conclusion

National and territorial cleavages are highly relevant when analyzing the phenomenon of Euroscepticism. In that respect, different temporalities must be taken into account: the chronology of accession processes but also national history and processes of state and nation building. This section shows, as has been argued for some time by some EU scholars (Bartolini 2001), that the study of European integration cannot be dissociated from classical theories of social and political cleavages. They inform collective perceptions of Europe which reverberate onto the current EU.

Chapter 4

Political Elites

European integration is often described as an 'elite-led' project, where political elites especially have played a crucial role as driving forces. In fact, it has been convincingly argued that the main European party families (Christian Democrats, Liberals and Socialists, together with most Greens), accounting for roughly two-thirds of the European electorate, have progressively converged towards a pro-European position in the course of European integration, thus reaching almost complete convergence by the end of the 1980s and early 1990s. Faced with more volatile public support for the EU in the post-Maastricht period, these elites, it is argued, have coalesced in order to take EU issues out of electoral competition, and thus preserve this pro-European consensus (Hix 1999:89). This has been corroborated by later studies, which have shown Europhile orientations to be a majority view among national MNPs and a clearly predominant view among MEPs (Ray 2007; Katz 2002). However, the predominantly pro-EU views of most mainstream parties' leaderships (at least in continental Europe) should not obscure the fact that Euroscepticism is alive and well in domestic party systems, including inside mainstream parties. By the end of the 1990s, roughly one-third of all Eurosceptics in national parliaments belonged to either Christian Democratic or Social Democratic parties (Katz 2002:8).

This chapter argues that, although relevant for mainstream party leaderships at national and European levels, the 'pro-European convergence theory' must be nuanced in several respects. First, a historical overview of political elites' positioning towards the EC/EU shows that political elites' 'conversion' to supranational integration was largely utilitarian in nature. Second, after introducing the main theories accounting for the phenomenon of party-based Euroscepticism (in the second section) the chapter argues (in the third section) that, in the contemporary period, Eurosceptic positions have been gaining ground inside mainstream political parties, as intra-party divisions on EU

100

issues have increased. Finally, while debunking myths about an increase of Eurosceptic forces in the EP, the fourth section refines the widespread assumption that MEPs are clearly more pro-European than their national counterparts.

Elites' conversion to 'Europe': 'limited, short-ranged and tactical' (Haas 1958)

The idea that political elites enthusiastically supported European integration from the beginning must be nuanced. In order to assess political elites' current attitudes towards the EU, it is essential to fully grasp the built-in ambiguities of their initial commitment to European integration. As is shown below, in the face of widespread resistance to supranational forms of integration in the early days of integration (the 1950s), proponents of the ECSC and the EEC had to appeal to self-interest and cost/gain calculations in order to rally support for their supranational designs. As for public opinion, support for intra-European cooperation at elite level must thus be carefully distinguished from support for strong supranational institutions.

Limited support for supranationalism

In fact, commitment to European unity in the form of a federal Europe was a minority view among Resistance movements during the Second World War and its aftermath. Soon after the war, it became obvious that 'federalists had deceived themselves with regard to the speed with which the resistance of national traditions could be overcome' (Spinelli 1967:328). In fact, throughout the 1950s, reluctance towards supranational integration was widespread in western European party systems.

Certainly, outright hostility was first and foremost expressed by the usual suspects – Communist parties (in France, Italy and the Benelux countries), nationalist parties (such as French Gaullists), as well as a few marginal parties (such as Dutch religious parties) – either because European integration was regarded as a capitalist project supported by the US, and/or because it was seen as being incompatible with national sovereignty. Until the late 1960s/early 1970s, communists (who accounted for about 10 per cent of the EEC electorate by the mid-1960s due to their strong appeal in France and Italy), expressed their opposition by refusing to send delegates to the EP, as they did not recognize EEC institutions as legitimate.

Beyond this hard core of Eurosceptics, however, reservations towards European integration were largely present among more mainstream political parties. To begin with, neither the ECSC nor the EEC elicited much enthusiasm among socialist parties. The German SPD eventually supported the ratification of the Rome treaties only after much hesitation and after having voted successively against the ECSC and the EDC, out of concern that western European integration would contribute to perpetuating the division of Europe and of Germany. While the Italian Socialists abstained during the vote on the ratification of the Rome treaties, their French counterparts also proved largely sceptic: only a sixth and half of them voted for the ECSC and the EDC respectively (Parsons 2006:111). In addition, while being predominantly opposed to the EEC, many of them voted for ratification to avoid disowning the Socialist Prime Minister Guy Mollet. Even in an overall pro-European country like Belgium, the leader of the Socialist party (who was Prime Minister at the time) opposed the ratification of the Rome treaties.

Furthermore, significant segments of centre-right, liberal and Christian Democratic parties had reservations towards the ECSC and the EEC. In France, only one-third of the centre-right and Christian Democratic parliamentary majority supported the Schuman plan and hostility towards the EEC predominated among these parties (Parsons 2006). In Germany, concerns over the supra-national nature of the ECSC were expressed by segments of the CDU. Whereas the party largely endorsed the ratification of the Rome treaties, parts of the CDU (around Finance Minister Ludwig Erhard, who favoured an OEEC type of cooperation) had initially expressed scepticism towards what they saw as the protectionist bias of the common market. Moreover, the liberals of the Freiheitliche Deutsche Partei (FDP) voted against the Rome treaties, out of concern that European integration in a divided Europe would prevent German unification in the future, as well as out of opposition to protectionism (Loth 1989). This concern was shared by Dutch liberals, who also opposed the ratification of the Rome treaties (Zellentin 1967:421).

Such lack of enthusiasm was mirrored in the tedious support for strong supranational institutions among national leaders. During negotiations on the ECSC and the EEC, even leaders of the Benelux countries had reservations towards strong national institutions (Milward 1992:434), such as Dutch Prime Minister Willem Drees during negotiations on the EEC. German Chancellor Konrad Adenauer himself was reluctant towards a too far-reaching supranationalism, as he opposed a further extension of the High Authority's range of power and expressed reservations about a strongly supranational EEC (Küsters 1989:498,501). Strongly supranational views were held by a minority of political entrepreneurs, who managed to commit their compatriots to the ECSC and the EEC by making connections with other issues and by presenting European integration as a tool for the realization of national goals. For instance, support for the ratification of the Rome treaties among sceptical French MPs of the right was secured, notably, by the CAP (Parsons 2006:124). In a similar vein, Social Democratic support for ratification in Germany was eventually won once guarantees were given that German division would not be furthered by European integration (as it was agreed that the customs union would not apply to East Germany) (Loth 1989:598). Thus Wilfried Loth's description of the pro-EEC consensus of the German political class in 1957 as 'rather superficial' could apply to other countries.

Utilitarian conversion to European integration

In this context, how can elites' enduring support for integration beyond its early years be explained? Revisionist accounts of the history of European integration put forward interesting theories in this respect, by highlighting the utilitarian dimension of elites' commitment to European integration. They argue that, in a context where the idea of European unity had been misused by fascist ideology, European integration initially developed on the basis of narrow, materialist, even nationalist motives (see notably Judt 1996:9). Three different types of motives can be identified: short- and medium-term geopolitical, political and economic gains for the country as a whole; long-term gains related to the rehabilitation and strengthening of the nation state; and gains related to party strategies in the context of domestic, inter-party competition. They explain why commitment to Europe among mainstream political elites has long been seen as compatible with the strengthening of national identity and of elites' own power. As is evidenced below, such strategic calculations also explain later conversions to European integration by parties who had remained Eurosceptic in the early decades of the EEC.

Short-term gains deriving from participation in the EEC include geopolitical benefits (the bulwark effect of the EEC against communism), diplomatic and political benefits (the rehabilitation effect for countries such as Germany and Italy) and economic benefits (gains in productivity and GDP growth induced by the common market) (Milward 1992). Such considerations also explain the pro-European conversion of formerly Eurosceptic parties in countries that joined later on. A good example is the Greek socialist party PASOK which, once it accessed government in 1981, shed its anti-EC rhetoric, in view of the considerable financial benefits linked to accession and in view of the political ascendancy that EC membership gave Greece in relation to Turkey (Hersant 2008:642).

Besides these short-term gains, European integration offered one significant advantage in the eyes of national political elites: its contribution to the reconstruction and even strengthening of the (western European) nation state in the post-war era. This contribution is multi-faceted. First of all, European integration facilitated processes of identity (re)building at the domestic level. It was part of a meta-narrative on a resistant, anti-fascist Europe, and as such contributed to national myth-making in societies where only a minority of citizens had taken part in the Resistance. To some extent, identification with Europe whitewashed national identities and facilitated the 'collective amnesia' of the post-war period (Judt 1992:95). In some countries, identification with Europe was an ersatz for weak national identities (as in Belgium and Germany). Moreover, European integration facilitated internal political integration. By enhancing national prosperity, it contributed to the development of the welfare state, which in turn secured loyalty to and identification with the nation state (Milward 1992). Europe's contribution to internal political integration also resided in its role of strengthening democratization processes in the post-war period (notably in Italy, where it was seen by elites as a bulwark against communism at the domestic level) and, later on, in southern (1980s) and eastern countries (1990s). Furthermore, in countries with strong regional identities (Belgium, Italy, and Spain), European integration could be seen by central elites as a counter-weight to claims for independence (Bruneteau 2000). Indeed, it has been argued that the EU's regional policy (which has alleviated the costs of redistribution for richer regions) and/or new institutional opportunities for political representation at the EU level may have contributed to a shift away from secessionist claims for some regionalist parties, such as moderate nationalists in Catalonia and the Scottish National Party (Keating 2003).

Finally, commitment to European integration can be a useful rhetorical resource in party strategies in the domestic arena. In fact, the plasticity of the idea of European unity allows all major mainstream party families to identify with it (Bruneteau 2000). Moreover, commitment to European integration can serve at least two types of strategic purposes: it signals ideological compatibility with governmental participation and fulfils a legitimizing function, and it can also be used as an ideological identikit, filling in gaps in party programmes and re-shaping a party's identity.

On the right of the political spectrum, a good illustration of this is the evolution of the EC policy of the Gaullist RPR party under Jacques Chirac's leadership. Before the end of the 1980s, the RPR and its leader had a fairly good record of strongly Eurosceptic statements, rooted in traditional Gaullist nationalism, preference for protectionism (in view of the party's rural constituency) and anti-Americanism. All these grievances were condensed in the famous 'Cochin call' of 1978, on the eve of the first direct EP elections, in which Chirac opposed a federal Europe and an extension of the EP's powers, accused the EEC of being responsible for unemployment, and opposed the accessions of Spain and Portugal (out of fear of increased competition for French farmers) (Chirac 1978). A decade later, during the campaign for the 1988 presidential elections (when candidate Chirac needed the support of the pro-European Christian Democrats), the RPR leader, in a reference to the deadline set by the SEA for the completion of the internal market, presented himself as 'the candidate of the 1992 objective', thus trying to link his image with the dynamism and modernization associated with the internal market (Dasseto and Dumoulin 1992). In that case, conversion to 'Europe' was part of a wider modernization of the party's identity. In other cases, commitment to Europe also served legitimizing purposes, notably for parties that wanted to break with an ideologically uncomfortable past. For instance, the Spanish People's Party actively sought membership of the European People's Party (EPP) in the late 1980s, in order to signal its definitive dissociation from Franco's heritage. In a similar vein, the Italian Alleanza Nazionale shifted from a Eurosceptic to a pro-European position in 1994–95, as it transformed itself from a neo-fascist movement into a mainstream Conservative party (Quaglia 2003:18).

On the left, several Social Democratic parties have shed Eurosceptic rhetoric and adopted a pro-European stance in order to strengthen their legitimacy as government parties. Such was the case, for example, of the German SPD, as it made its acceptance of the EEC official in the party's 1959 Bad Godesberg programme (SPD 1959), a move that went hand in hand with the party's disso-ciation from Marxism (Loth 1989). Thirty years later, a similar logic lay beneath the British Labour party's evolution towards a pro-EEC stance between 1984 and 1988. Whereas the party still advocated a withdrawal from the EEC in its 1983 programme, notably because EEC membership was incompatible with 'radical socialist policies' (Labour Party 1983), a crushing electoral defeat in 1987 allowed Labour leader Neil Kinnock to convert the party to a pro-EEC stance, as part of a wider re-shaping of its identity. As Daniels (1998) writes: 'The Europeanization of the Labour party may be seen as a response to its long exclusion from national office and as a key element of a broader electoral strategy designed to convey the image of a party which is modern, credible and fit to govern.'

While there has been a pro-European convergence of the main party families in the course of integration, this support was and is partly of a utilitarian nature. Thus the question is, whether this support is likely to endure in a changed context.

Explaining party-based Euroscepticism

This section introduces the main theories explaining why parties are, or become, Eurosceptic, before explaining how the national context influences levels of party-based Euroscepticism in domestic party systems.

The two dimensions of party-based Euroscepticism

Two broad types of factors can be put forward to account for parties' attitudes towards European integration: their strategies in relation to government, and their general ideology. Whereas the first type of factor explains party-based Euroscepticism as a result of strategic calculations, the second type of factor relates Euroscepticism to a party's identity and *Weltanschauung*.

Euroscepticism as a strategy
To begin with, parties' stances on European integration depend on their relationship to executive power and government. Indeed, it is widely assumed that government participation is barely compatible

with anti-EU positions or even strong Euroscepticism. Given the huge exit costs associated with a country's withdrawal from the EU, even mild Euro-enthusiasts have to deal with the reality of EU membership once they are in office. Moreover, day-to-day participation in EU decision-making and contact with EU officials and other governments may have a 'socializing effect' on government officials, which tends to mitigate strongly Eurosceptic positions. Besides, Eurosceptic parties participating in coalition governments with pro-European parties may have to avoid or mitigate Euroscepticism. Conversely, parties that are not in office or do not wish to access it are not constrained by the imperatives of 'Euro-compatibility' and can give free rein to their Eurosceptic orientations. Beyond this general pattern, the explanation can be refined by classifying parties according to three distinctions: parties of government versus protest-based, anti-establishment parties; incumbent parties versus opposition parties; and office-seeking parties versus vote-seeking and policy-seeking parties.

As regards the first distinction, parties of government tend to be Europhile, while protest-based parties tend to be Eurosceptic. Indeed, protest-based Euroscepticism has been found to be 'the most pervasive form of party-based Euroscepticism in Western Europe' (Taggart 1998:372). For protest-based parties, Euroscepticism is a useful strategic resource in their anti-system opposition to the political establishment, as they denounce the pro-European bias of mainstream elites and try to tap into the electoral niche of Eurosceptic voters, who do not feel represented by mainstream parties. As such, there is a strong correlation between the phenomenon of the 'cartel party', referring to the collusion of mainstream parties sharing the resources of the state 'to ensure their collective survival' (Katz and Mair 1995) and Euroscepticism. Indeed, parties mobilizing against the alleged collusion of mainstream parties at the domestic level also disparage the EU as being dominated by the cartel of the three biggest party families (the centre right, social democrats and liberals). Consequently, as parties choose to engage in a protest-based type of strategy, they tend to break with previous pro-European commitments. The Austrian Freedom party (FPÖ), which shifted to an anti-EU course in 1991–92, as negotiations on EC accession started, and the Italian Lega Nord, which operated a similar change in 1998, in order to counter its electoral decline, are very good illustrations of this (Leconte 2003; Quaglia 2003).

The incumbent/opposition distinction only partly overlaps with the government/protest-based distinction. It also relates Euroscepticism to oppositional status and analyzes Euroscepticism as 'the politics of opposition' (Sitter 2001). However, compared with the first distinction, it also accounts for softer forms of Euroscepticism inside mainstream political parties, once they are in opposition. In this respect, strongly pro-European parties can be expected to become slightly less pro-European when they are in opposition. For instance, it has been shown that the Spanish Socialist party, which is strongly pro-European, became slightly less pro-European when it was in opposition between 1996 and 2004 (Ruiz Jiménez and Egea de Haro 2004).

With the third distinction, parties' attitudes towards the EU are analyzed according to Strøm and Mueller's typology (1999), which distinguishes between office-seeking, vote-seeking and policy-seeking parties. When faced with dilemmas, parties give priority to one of these three goals: access to government, electoral success or influence on policy. Prioritizing one goal over another has repercussions on parties' stances towards the EU. It is generally expected that smaller, office-seeking parties tend to moderate Euroscepticism in order to be considered as reliable coalition partners, as did several Green parties (notably the German and French ones). By contrast, parties seeking first and foremost to maintain or increase their electoral share may use Euroscepticism in order to tap into electoral niches. Similarly, if Eurosceptic, policy-seeking parties are able to influence the government's EU policy without accessing office, they will have few incentives to moderate their Euroscepticism, as has been argued in the case of Eurosceptic parties in Denmark and Sweden (Raunio 2007).

Euroscepticism as an ideology
Despite being strongly relevant, analyses of parties' attitudes towards the EU in terms of strategies and calculations must be combined with another type of factor: party ideology. Four types of cleavages are relevant here: centrist ideology versus ideological extremism; the left/right cleavage; the state/church cleavage; and the parties' positions on the 'new politics cleavage'.

First of all, a centrist ideology predisposes to pro-Europeanism, while an extremist ideology predisposes to Euroscepticism. Indeed, the strongly consensual nature of the EU necessarily produces centrist policy outcomes. Moreover, while extreme right parties project their nationalism and their anti-immigration stance on to the EU, radical left-wing parties are prompt to denounce the EU as a neo-liberal, capitalist project responsible for the erosion of the welfare state and detrimental to developing countries' growth (notably because of the CAP). In both cases, anti-Americanism often lies beneath anti-Europeanism or strong Euroscepticim. The correlation between ideological extremism *per se* and Euroscepticism has been confirmed by recent studies (Hooghe *et al.* 2002:971; Ray 2007:164). As a party's distance from the centre of the political spectrum grows, so does its likelihood of being Eurosceptic. However, parties located on the ideological margins of domestic party systems display different degrees of Euroscepticism. Among the radical left, some parties (such as the Dutch Socialist Party or the German Left Party) strongly criticize the EU (viewed as neo-liberal and democratically deficient), without advocating a withdrawal from the EU, while others (such as the Communist Revolutionary League in France) express hard Euroscepticism. Similarly, among radical right-wing parties, some support EU membership and the internal market (such as the Danish People's Party, the Flemish Vlaams Belang, and the Austrian and Dutch Freedom parties), while others (like the French National Front) stand for a withdrawal from the EU and can thus be qualified as anti-European parties.

Second, a party's attitudes towards European integration could theoretically be influenced by its position on the left/right cleavage. In that respect, it has been argued elsewhere that left/right positions towards the EU have been reversed in the course of the 1990s. Centre-right parties were historically more supportive of European integration, while socialist and social democratic parties, concerned about increased economic competition, were rather reserved towards the EC (albeit with cross-national differences). With the development of market-correcting policies at the EU level in the course of the 1990s, centre-right, conservative and liberal parties may have become less committed to integration (by articulating an anti-regulation discourse), while social democratic ones may have become more supportive of further integration (Gabel and Hix 2002:951). However, recent studies suggest that right-wing parties are slightly more pro-European than left-wing ones (Marks and Steenbergen 2004). In fact, there is no clear correlation between left/right positioning and general stances towards European integration (Hooghe *et al.* 2002:972). Recent works suggest two things in that respect. First, the impact of left/right positioning on attitudes towards further integration varies across time and, above all, across sectors. For instance, there is much less support for further Europeanization in cohesion, employment and environmental policies among centre-right parties than among left-wing parties. Second, the impact of left/right positioning on attitudes towards the EU depends on the country context. In countries with generous welfare states, such as Sweden, party-based Euroscepticism is essentially a left-wing phenomenon (Aylott 2008:184). By the same token, the Danish Social Democratic party has been rated as one of the least pro-European parties among the social democratic party family (Hooghe *et al.* 2002:975). By a similar logic, it has been assumed that mainstream, party-based Euroscepticism in the new member states is more likely to be a right-wing phenomenon, given that mainstream right-wing parties in post-communist countries seem to be more economically liberal, socially conservative and more prone to defend sovereignty than their counterparts in the older member states. Examples include soft Eurosceptic parties like the Czech Civic Union and the Hungarian Fidesz, which both project their anti-regulation discourse onto the EU.

A third ideological determinant of a party's position on EU issues relates to religion. Two aspects must be considered: the religion and the degree of religiosity. As regards the former, it has already been said (see p.87) that Protestantism used to be seen as one factor predisposing to Euroscepticism. As far as parties are concerned, it has been argued that, inside the Christian Democratic family (traditionally a staunch supporter of European integration), a distinction should be made between Catholic (and mainly Continental) Christian Democracy and Protestant Christian Democracy (notably in parts of Germany and the Nordic countries). For instance, all Nordic Christian Democratic parties have either adopted a Eurosceptic stance in the past or are currently soft Eurosceptics (with the exception of the Swedish Christian Democrats, who are divided on the issue). This can be attributed notably to the fact that 'Protestant Christian Democracy ... has tended to be ambivalent about European integration', mainly out of 'value-based Euroscepticism' (Madeley and Sitter 2005). This holds even more so for deeply religious Protestant parties, such as the two Christian parties in the Netherlands (Political Reformed party (SGP) and Christian Union (CU)), which campaigned against the EU Constitutional Treaty.

The fourth and final relevant aspect of ideology in relation to the

EU relates to the party's position on what is known as the new politics cleavage. 'New politics' is a phenomenon deriving from the politicization of 'new' issues, that is, new societal issues that appeared on the agenda of Western democracies (starting with the USA) from the mid-1960s on: inter-ethnic relations and immigration, gender equality, the rights of sexual minorities, reproductive rights (e.g. abortion), civil liberties and environmental protection. The politicization of these issues gave rise to cleavages opposing citizens with diverging value priorities. Consequently, although traditional class cleavages still dominate the politics of Western democracies, they increasingly coexist with new value cleavages (Inglehart 1977). Thus, at the level of party politics, the old politics cleavage now coexists with the new politics cleavage (Dalton 1996:153). Several studies show that a party's position on the new politics cleavage significantly influences its general stance towards European integration: the more parties hold conservative and/or authoritarian views on the new issues, the more they are predisposed to Euroscepticism (Hooghe *et al.* 2002:985; Kriesi 2007:94). This holds for extreme right parties (such as the Lega Nord, UKIP, and the League of Polish Families) but also for conservative parties (such as the Czech Civic Union, the Polish Law and Justice Party, the Italian Alleanza Nazionale and, to some extent, the British Tories and Forza Italia), as well as for Christian Democratic parties (the Bavarian CSU and the Slovak Christian Democratic party) (see Leconte 2008). At the opposite end of the new politics cleavage, parties holding libertarian views, such as the Greens, have become rather supportive of European integration, albeit with some nuances (see for instance their criticism of the EU immigration policy) and exceptions (the Swedish Greens, for instance, have remained Eurosceptic).

In fact, both types of variables (party strategies and party ideologies) should be combined in order to account for a party's position on European integration. Moreover, as has been shown with the left/right cleavage, the influence of these variables is mediated by the national context.

Cross-country differences in levels of party-based Euroscepticism

A comparative perspective highlights significant cross-country differences in levels of party-based Euroscepticism. Countries differ as to the extent of intra-party divisions on EU issues and as to the electoral weight of non-mainstream Eurosceptic parties. Countries such as Austria, France, Poland, the UK and Sweden display high levels of party-based Euroscepticism, whereas countries such as Belgium, Finland, Germany, Portugal and Spain display low levels (Ray 2007:42). How can these cross-country differences be explained? Three types of factors can be put forward: national political culture, institutional opportunities at the domestic level and the level of popular Euroscepticism.

First, political culture plays a significant role in shaping a party's identity and constraining the options available to it. To begin with, political history and the relative strength of political extremisms certainly influence a party's position towards integration. In France, for instance, where the communists and, later, the radical left have traditionally been strong, the Socialist party has had difficulties transforming into a reformist, social democratic party fully embracing the free market principle, which explains its current ambiguity towards the EU. A comparison between the EC/EU policy of the French PS and the German SPD shows that whereas the latter officially renounced Marxism in 1959, large sections of the former are still influenced by a form of 'social nationalism' coupled with Eurosceptic orientations. Furthermore, collective perceptions of nationalism are also relevant. In countries where nationalism is associated with past experiences of dictatorship and largely considered as illegitimate, as is the case in Spain, mainstream parties are less likely to indulge in Euroscepticism.

Second, levels of party-based Euroscepticism are also influenced by the existence or the lack of institutional incentives for Eurosceptic parties. Three institutional factors are relevant in that respect: the type of electoral system, the use of referenda, and decision-making processes in relation to EU policy. Regarding electoral systems, it has been argued that the majority system gives disproportionate influence to Eurosceptic factions inside mainstream parties, which need large support in their own camp in order to govern (as is the case in the UK), whereas the proportional system allows parties to set up large government coalitions across the board with other pro-European parties, thus marginalizing Eurosceptic factions in their own ranks (as is the case in Germany). As for direct democracy, the frequent use of referenda in relation to EU issues (be it due to constitutional provisions or not) represents a significant institutional opportunity for Eurosceptic parties, as is shown in the next section. The third institutional factor relates to decision-making processes in relation to EU issues and national coordination processes, as governments define the official position to be defended in the EU Council. Depending on the country, these processes are more or less centralized, top–down oriented and hierarchical. Furthermore, they vary as to the extent of the national parliament's ability to influence them. It has been argued, for instance, that the more the national coordination mechanisms are open and inclusive (such as in Denmark and Sweden), the less likely parties are to pursue an 'office-seeking' strategy in order to influence decision-making processes. As a result, they are less motivated to mitigate Eurosceptic positions in order to access office (Raunio 2007).

Third, levels of party-based Euroscepticism could be correlated with levels of popular Euroscepticism in a given country. However, in some countries (such as Poland), levels of party-based Euroscepticism are higher than levels of popular Euroscepticism, while in other countries (such as Finland) the opposite is true. In fact, it is the degree of intra-elite division on European integration in a given country that is most likely to induce Eurosceptic orientations among voters. Recent EU referenda in 2005 and 2009, in which overwhelmingly pro-EU political establishments were defeated by Eurosceptic voters, illustrate the very limited relevance of the so-called 'cueing theory', according to which voters simply follow party lines on EU issues. In fact, the more political elites appear divided on issues of European integration, the more likely voters are to reject further integration (Hooghe and Marks 2005:430). In that respect, there is a clear correlation, at the domestic level, between levels of popular Euroscepticism and levels of intra-party division on the EU. Countries ranking among the most Eurosceptic in terms of public opinion are also countries where core parties are most divided on the EU: Austria, the UK, Sweden and Latvia (Ray 2007:170).

Indeed, intra-party divisions may be the most difficult challenge that mainstream political elites have to face as a consequence of European integration.

Parties of government: a mainstreaming of Euroscepticism?

Does the pro-European 'cartel' still hold today? It certainly does, to the extent that the leaderships of most mainstream parties remain committed to European integration. However, there is, at the same time, a mainstreaming of Eurosceptic positions inside government parties. The latter are becoming more divided on EU issues, as a result of EU-level developments and changes in domestic party systems.

Increasingly divided parties

Analyses of the evolution of party programmes present two interesting results.

First, there is a clear trend of increasing internal party dissent on EU issues over the long run. While dissent increased between 1988 and 1996 (notably as a result of increased integration with the Maastricht Treaty), it declined between 1996 and 1999, only to rise further from 1999 on (Hooghe and Marks 2006). This leads to two remarks. First, increased elite division on European integration preceded the relative decline in public support from 1991 on, thus confirming hypotheses linking public scepticism to intra-elite divisions. Second, the convergence of the party leaderships of the three main party families towards a pro-EU stance has been paralleled by increasing intra-party divergence on the EU. This illustrates the challenging impact of European integration on mainstream political parties. Not only do EU issues cut across traditional cleavages, thus provoking divisions inside mainstream parties (Mair 2000:36), European integration also tends to empower party leaderships (which are increasingly networking with their counterparts at the EU level), at the expense of mid- or intermediate-level party officials and national parliamentary groups (Raunio 2002). Thus the distance between a party's 'Europeanized' leadership and the rest of its apparatus increases. Consequently, European integration may produce both horizontal divisions between different currents inside a party and vertical divisions between different levels of party structures.

The second interesting finding derived from content analyses of party programmes is that references to European integration in national party manifestos declined from 1999 on (Hooghe and Marks 2006). This can be interpreted in different ways. First, this may indicate an increasing indifference towards European integration among national political elites. Party leaders such as Gordon Brown or Silvio Berlusconi illustrate this (see p.125). This may also be a strategy aimed at muting or mitigating intra-party divisions on the EU, in conformity with elites' attempts to de-politicize EU issues.

Whatever interpretation is retained, these two statements point to long-term changes in government parties' attitudes towards European integration.

Challenges to the pro-European consensus

The core idea underlying this section is that the strategy of 'selective Europeanization' developed by political elites has reached its limits. Selective Europeanization has two aspects. At the EU level, elites have sought to achieve market integration without political and social integration (Majone 2006:117). They have pushed for the completion of the internal market, while trying to insulate other policy fields from the impacts of European integration. This strategy is currently reaching its limits, as it is becoming obvious that a deeply integrated market has repercussions on social rights, normative issues and so on. At the domestic level, mainstream parties have tried to insulate domestic party systems from the divisive impacts of European integration, by 'taking Europe itself out of national competition' (Mair 2000:48). This other aspect of the strategy is also reaching its limits, as profound changes in domestic party systems challenge this tacit agreement.

EU-level developments

Recent developments in European integration have exacerbated the dilemmas faced by mainstream parties of the right and left in relation to European integration. For conservatives, 'normative integration' exacerbates the dilemma between their pro-market orientation and concerns over 'normative sovereignty' (see the section on 'value-based Euroscepticism', pp.57–61). The best example of this is the British Conservative party, where an individualist wing (pro-market oriented and pragmatic towards the EU) has long coexisted alongside a traditionalist wing (Flood 2000:188), articulating a value-based Euroscepticism. For Christian Democratic parties, traditional commitment to European identity is challenged by debates on the Christian identity of Europe. Indeed, the lack of reference to Christianity in the preamble of the TEU (as reformed by the Lisbon Treaty) challenges traditional Christian Democrat understandings of European integration. In its 2009 EP elections programme, for instance, the Bavarian CSU insisted that 'Europe must clearly commit itself to the values of Christianity' (notably on abortion and euthanasia) (CSU 2009:2). Similarly, its federal sister party, the

CDU, insisted that they want a reference to God in future EU treaties (CDU 2009:12). Moreover, this view of the EU as a Christian club is linked to a clear opposition to Turkish EU accession (CSU 2009:15; CDU 2009:13).

For social democratic parties, the completion of the internal market, particularly in the service sector, together with the latest enlargement waves, proves especially challenging. Here developments in European integration confront social democrats with their own contradictions. On the one hand, they theoretically support enlargement and the opening up of domestic labour markets to new member states' citizens in the name of solidarity. On the other hand, this stance risks pitting them against their core traditional constituencies as well as trade unions. Such was the case, for instance, for the British Labour Party in early 2009, as it was confronted with strikes linked to the implementation of the EU Directive on the transfer of foreign workers. Prime Minister Gordon Brown was then reminded of his speeches to the GMB (a union representing mainly employees of local government and the health service) and Labour conferences (in June and September 2007 respectively), when he pledged to 'create British jobs for British workers' – thus echoing Labour leaders of the early 1970s when they warned against an invasion of Italian strike breakers as a result of EC accession (Alexandre-Collier 2000:34).

Evolutions in domestic party systems
The fragmentation of domestic party systems with the emergence of 'new politics' parties, from the 1960s on, has resulted in increased electoral competition for mainstream parties and has led to a re-polarization of politics – two trends which, in turn, have influenced the stance of mainstream parties towards the EU.

Between the 1960s and the end of the 1990s, more than one hundred and forty new parties emerged in European party systems (Mair 2000:30), most of them as part of the 'new politics' phenomenon (Green, radical left-wing, radical right-wing, regionalist, and single-issue parties). With the exception of most Green parties, and (some) regionalists, these parties tend to be Eurosceptic.

The first consequence of this phenomenon was that parties from the mainstream right and left have been confronted with the electoral challenge of these new parties, which sometimes appealed to their core constituencies. Although electoral shifts from mainstream to extremist parties derive from multiple factors (such as political cynicism, anti-immigration views, or concerns over neo-liberal policies), Euroscepticism may contribute to electoral volatility. This is suggested by the fact that several mainstream parties lost votes to single-issue, anti-European parties, notably during European elections. For instance, the British Conservatives had to face the competition of UKIP and the British Referendum Party from 1993–94 on, as both parties attracted former conservative voters (Alexandre-Collier 2000:133). The Swedish social democrats were confronted with a similar challenge during the 2004 EP elections, as they lost votes to the Eurosceptic June List (a quarter of June List voters were former social democratic voters (Déloye 2005:640)).

Moreover, 'new politics' parties have been articulating claims for more confrontational politics, by denouncing the alleged political correctness, for example, on immigration, of mainstream political parties, the increasing ideological convergence of the right and the left, and the reduction of policy options presented to voters. They have contributed, to some extent, to a re-politicization of widely de-politicized political arenas. These mobilizations have also had an impact on public debates on the EU, as these parties sought to 'break the pro-European taboo' (Jörg Haider, quoted in Leconte 2003:170) of mainstream elites. The correlation between the two phenomena (the end of consensual politics and a challenge to the pro-EU cartel) makes sense since the process of European integration itself contributes to a phenomenon of de-politicization. By 'promoting a high degree of consensus among the mainstream' (Mair 2000:49), it further blurs the differences between the left and the right, thus reducing citizens' ability to make sense of politics. The difficulty most voters have making sense of politics in the EP highlights this, as consensual practices between the two main groups seem to make traditional cleavages irrelevant.

This twofold movement of increased political polarization and challenge to the pro-European consensus was most pronounced in so-called 'consociative democracies', that is, political systems where power was shared by grand coalitions or relied on tacit agreements between the main parties. In these countries, the populist backlash against consensual politics by 'new politics' parties (the FPÖ and the Greens in Austria, the Pym Fortuyn List and the Greens in the Netherlands, and Forza Italia in Italy) usually went hand in hand with a discourse challenging the pro-European consensus of elites. Indeed, the end of the 'grand coalition' in Austria in 2000, the end of the 'purple coalition' in the Netherlands in 2002, and the disappearance of the *Democrazia Christiana* in Italy in 1994, all coincided with a more polarized debate on EU issues, which became a stake in inter-party competition. In the Netherlands, for instance, there was a confluence of a couple of trends. The end of the 'purple' coalition in 2002 coincided with explicit inter-party divisions on the EU (as government parties like the liberal VVD articulated a more critical appraisal of the gains derived from integration) as well as with a wider conservative revolution (for instance, on issues such as patriotism, immigration and religious pluralism) (Van Ham 2002).

Furthermore, with the erosion of consensual politics, mainstream parties become less inhibited from reasserting national interests, notably in those countries, such as Germany and Italy, where the assertion of the national interest had been dampened in post-war decades. For instance, German Christian Democratic parties have become more sensitive to this issue, asking for a fairer representation of their country (CSU 2009:11) and for an enhanced status for the German language (CDU 2009:14) in the EU institutions.

Party responses: externalizing and toughening

Mainstream political parties have reacted to these challenges by engaging in two strategies. In some countries, they have tried to 'externalize' divisive EU issues from intra-party dissent by upholding referenda. In numerous cases, they have toughened their stance on the most politicized EU issues, such as the use of referenda and further EU enlargement.

The backfiring impacts of referenda

Governing parties may choose to uphold referenda on EU issues for several reasons. While the most obvious reason for doing so relates to the plebiscitary use of referenda, it is certainly not the only reason. When parties are deeply divided internally on the issue at stake, they may choose to externalize it by letting voters decide. Such was the case in the UK for the 1975 referendum. Similarly, in face of strong intra-party divisions on issues of EU accession (1994) and EMU (2003), the Swedish Social Democrats relied on a 'compartmentalization strategy' (Aylott 2008:198), consisting in shifting EU issues from intra-party dissent to public debate by upholding referenda (none of which was compulsory). Whether such strategies prove successful or not can be debated. On the one

TABLE 4.1 Electoral scores of single-issue, Eurocritical, Eurosceptic and anti-European parties in EP elections, 1994–2009

Election year	Austria	Denmark	France	Netherlands	UK	Sweden
1994		JM:15% PM: 10% Total: 25%	MPE:12.3%		UKIP:1.2%	
1999		JM: 16% PM: 7% Total: 23%	RPF: 13%		UKIP: 7%	
2004	HPM:14%	JM: 9% PM: 5% Total: 14%	MPF: 8.4%	ET: 7.3%	UKIP: 15.64%	JL:14.5%
2009	HPM:17.6%	JM:2.3% PM:7% Total: 9.3%	Libertas: 4.6%		UKIP: 16%	JL:3.5%

ET*: Europe Transparent
HPM*: Dr Hans-Peter Martin List
JM**: June Movement
JL**: June List
MPE***: Majorité pour l'autre Europe
MPF***: Mouvement pour la France

PM***: People's Movement against the EU
RPF***: Rassemblement pour la France
UKIP***: United Kingdom Independence Party

* Eurocritical
** Eurosceptic
*** Anti-European

Source: data obtained from European Parliament sources.

hand, it has been argued that referenda have allowed elites to keep Euroscepticism 'out of the political party mainstream' (Ray 2007:42). On the other hand, in some cases, strongly polarized referenda can increase general levels of party Euroscepticism across the party system, as has been argued in the case of Sweden in the wake of the 2003 referendum.

Furthermore, referenda have had two damaging consequences for the pro-European party leaderships of mainstream political parties. First of all, they have opened windows of opportunity for the creation of single-issue, anti-EU parties or strongly Eurosceptic parties: the anti-EU Danish People's Movement against the EC (1972), the strongly Eurosceptic June Movements in Denmark (1992) and Sweden (1994), and the anti-EMU Swedish June List (in 2003). These parties have occasionally had good electoral scores at EP elections (see Table 4.1). Second, EU-related referenda have exacerbated intra-party dissent by encouraging Eurosceptic faction-alism, or the secession of Eurosceptic entrepreneurs who created their own Eurosceptic movements. France is a case in point, as the three main political parties experienced strong intra-party dissent during the 1992 and 2005 referenda. The 1992 referendum on the Maastricht Treaty proved especially challenging for intra-party cohesion for all parties. The Socialists suffered from the defection of 'national-republican' Jean-Pierre Chevènement (who created the Eurosceptic Citizens' Movement in 1992), the Christian Democrats from the secession of the ultra-Catholic Philippe de Villiers (who created the Eurosceptic Union for French Democracy in 1994) and the Gaullists from the anti-Maastricht stance of Charles Pasqua (who in 1999, together with de Villiers, set up the Rassemblement pour la France). In 2005, the EU Constitutional Treaty proved espe-cially challenging for the Socialist party, as the most left-wing currents in the party (accounting for roughly 40 per cent of Socialist MPs), led by well-known leaders such as former Prime Minister Laurent Fabius, campaigned against a treaty regarded as neo-liberal. Even though the conservative Union pour la Majorité Présidentielle (UMP) managed to maintain a more united, pro-treaty stance, it still had to face the dissenting views of some MPs, such as Nicolas Dupont-Aignant, a Eurosceptic Gaullist, who created the Committee for the No to the Constitution. In the Swedish case, referenda contributed to the institutionalization of Eurosceptic factions inside the Swedish Social Democratic party, with the setting up of the Social Democrats against the EC in 1993 and of the Social Democrats against EMU in 2002 (Aylott 2008:184).

Toughening stances on EU issues
Furthermore, mainstream parties have reacted to the challenge of Eurosceptic, non-mainstream parties by toughening their stance on the most politicized EU issues. Two recent examples illustrate this: calls for EU-related referenda and parties' positioning on EU enlargement (especially on Turkey's EU accession).

In 2008–09, several mainstream parties across the political spectrum made calls for national referenda on all future treaty changes and EU enlargements: Tory leader David Cameron and the Bavarian CSU during the 2009 EP elections (Cameron 2009; CSU 2009:2), the Austrian Social Democrats (in an open letter published in the tabloid *Neue Kronenzeitung* on 26 June 2008) and the Greek Socialists of PASOK (via Greek President George Papandreou) in 2008 (ALDE 2008).

The issue of Turkey's EU accession entered widespread public debate from 2002 on (as discussions over the Christian identity of Europe erupted in the convention on the EU Constitutional Treaty), and it played an increasingly significant role in recent (2004 and 2009) EP election campaigns. In 2009, this was especially the case in countries with the largest populations of Turkish origin (Germany, Austria, France and the Netherlands), where (except for the Netherlands) more than two-thirds of public opinion is opposed to further EU enlargement (EB 71:160). In these countries, as well as in Denmark and Italy, the extreme right has tried to capitalize on this issue. Conservative parties have reacted by making their opposition to Turkish EU accession official, as did the French UMP and the German CDU during the 2004 EP elections campaign, while the liberal Dutch VVD had already shifted to an anti-Turkey course before the 2002 elections. Several social democratic parties have reacted similarly. For instance, while the Danish Social Democrats have expressed principled opposition to Turkey's accession, the French Socialist party, again divided on the issue, has expressed only conditional support for this accession. Certainly, pro-Europeans can oppose further enlargement because they see it as a threat to deepened integration (the 'enlarging versus deepening' dilemma). However, a study suggests that, while this might be true for MEPs, it does not hold for MNPs. Among the latter, there is 'a positive relationship between Euroscepticism and hostility to the introduction of new members to the EU' (Katz 2002:19).

Beyond these common trends, there are differences between the mainstream left and the mainstream right as far as changes in attitudes towards the EU are concerned. While social democratic parties, facing similar challenges, display increasingly divergent trajectories in that respect, the mainstream right, with the growing influence of conservative parties, is becoming more receptive to soft forms of Euroscepticism.

Social Democrats: similar challenges, diverging trajectories

For social democratic parties in general, further integration is all the more challenging since left-wing voters are slightly less supportive of the EU than right-wing voters, especially in countries with large welfare states (Brineggar and Jolly 2005). The typical example is the Swedish Social Democratic party, whose natural constituencies (members of the working class, public sector employees and women) display above-average levels of Euroscepticism (Aylott 2008:196). Moreover, the stronger the links between parties and the trade unions (such as in Austria, Sweden and the UK), the more likely social democratic parties will be to perceive further economic integration as a threat. This is becoming more likely as trade unions' attitudes towards the EU are changing (see p.231). In such a context, it might well be that factions of social democratic parties break with previous pro-EU commitments and start articulating an 'anti-system' type of opposition to an EU where conservative and centre-right parties are likely to remain the dominant political force in the future (notably in view of demographic projections). Such a scenario was partly highlighted by the TV election broadcasts of the French Socialist Party during the campaign for the 2004 EP elections, where images of a post-industrial France, affected by massive unemployment and outsourcing, were presented as the likely consequence of 'a EU governed by the Right' (Maarek and Bras 2005:60).

Beyond these similar challenges, a comparison of the evolution of the EU policies of social democratic parties in the three largest countries shows diverging trajectories. While the German SPD remains a staunch supporter of further integration, the British Labour and French PS clearly display forms of soft Euroscepticism, albeit for opposite reasons. In terms of left/right positioning and attitudes towards the EU, the evolution of these parties illustrates three different scenarios: that of an inversion of left/right preferences on integration, that of increasing convergence between right and left and that of increasing polarization between left and right.

The case of the German SPD perfectly fits Gabel and Hix's theory about the inversion of left/right preferences on issues of European integration (2002:196). The party certainly calls for a slightly more 'social' EU implying, for instance, some degree of tax harmonization (SPD 2007:29). However, it clearly stands for a federal EU, with an EU executive (the Commission) elected by Parliament, extended powers for the EP and an EU Constitution. What is more, it argues, if necessary, in favour of the setting up of a hard core of integrationist countries leading the way – an idea clearly reminiscent of the CDU's own concept of *Kerneuropa*. In fact, the SPD has taken over the very positions previously defended by the CDU, when that party was still a staunch supporter of a federal Europe.

By contrast, the case of the British Labour Party illustrates a phenomenon of (partial) left/right convergence towards the EU. Certainly, there are some differences between Labour and the Conservatives on the EU. For instance, only 5 per cent of Labour MPs voted against the Lisbon Treaty during its ratification by the House of Commons in March 2008 (House of Commons 2008:71). Moreover, Labour stresses some of the advantages of EU membership, for example the protection of consumer rights and the environment. However, on the core issue of the nature of the EU, its role and missions, differences between the two parties are small. First of all, Labour does not stand for an institutionally deepened EU, but rather for a 'streamlined EU' (Labour Party 2009). Gordon Brown's statement that the EU should move away 'from inward-looking institutional questions' (Cabinet Office 2007:2) clearly echoes Margaret Thatcher's wish to end 'internal disputes or arcane institutional debates' (1988:4). Similarly, Thatcher's plea for a Europe 'open to the world', breaking with protectionism and driving the global agenda for free trade, perfectly fits Brown's view of a 'global Europe', which he sees as a tool to adapt to globalization, rather than as a unified, political regional bloc trying to shape the modalities of globalization. In this respect, the concept of 'global Europe' can be misleading. It does not so much refer to the EU as a political, international actor, but rather as a form of 'open regionalism', paving the way for global free trade (Chaouad 2008). Like the Conservatives, Labour does not stand for a political Union, but for an (enlarged) EU re-focused on limited, specific tasks: world trade liberalization, the fight against illegal immigration and against climate change (Labour Party 2009). In this respect, Labour's agenda for the EU is very similar to that of Conservative leader David Cameron's Movement for European Reform. Finally, confronted with the Conservatives' vocal Euroscepticism, Labour has been articulating a strong defence of the national interest, captured by Brown's concept of 'pro-European realism' (Brown 2005), which echoes some conservative, soft Eurosceptic views (see, for instance, the Czech ODS' *Manifesto for Eurorealism*).

The third scenario is illustrated by the French Socialist Party. Faced with deep internal divisions on institutional as well as enlargement issues, the French PS toughened its stance towards the EU while trying to play down the EU issue as much as possible. For instance, the party's 2007 programme dedicates very little space (only half a page) to Europe. At the same time, it resembles some of the criticism of the radical left, by calling for a re-orientation of the EU along more interventionist lines, asking for the setting up of an EU 'economic government', and requesting a re-definition of the ECB's tasks so as to include growth and the fight against unemployment. As for institutional issues, the party's soft Euroscepticism was expressed in its call for a referendum on the Lisbon Treaty, in order to make the EU 'more democratic' (Parti Socialiste 2007:3). French socialists thus depart from their German counterparts by being clearly less pro-European, and from their British counterparts by projecting a strongly polarized left/right cleavage on EU issues.

The divergences illustrated by these three cases show both the weight of the country's context on a party's position and the cross-cutting impact of integration issues on parties and party families. However, while European social democracy is clearly affected by this divisive impact, the mainstream right seems to be gaining in intra-family convergence, while at the same time becoming more receptive to Euroscepticism.

The mainstream right: more conservative and Eurosceptic?

From the early decades of integration until the 1990s, Christian Democracy was the core force underlying the pro-European consensus among continental party elites. This is changing as a result of two trends. First, Christian Democracy tends to move away from some of its core tenets (social market economy and European federalism) as it moves towards more conservative positions (when it has not been simply absorbed by conservative parties). A very good illustration of this is the Dutch Christian Democratic party, traditionally a strong supporter of supranational integration, which has recently renamed itself a 'Euro-realist' party, in a context of increasing competition among Dutch parties on EU issues (*Elsevier* 2009). Second, successive EU enlargements have weakened the influence of Christian Democrats at the EU level, with the arrival of Protestant Christian Democratic parties and conservative parties (especially with the 1973, 1995 and 2004 enlargements). This tilting of the balance in favour of conservatives has significant implications for the evolution of the mainstream right on EU issues. Whereas Christian Democrats were traditionally fervent supporters of European integration in a supranational form, conservatives always favoured intergovernmental cooperation where national allegiance should not be superseded by a supranational interest (Hix and Lord 1997:32). More specifically, it is argued that the mainstream right in the EU has become more Eurosceptic as a result of three trends: the erosion or implosion of Christian Democracy in some countries, which has benefited soft Eurosceptic conservatives; the relative decline of pro-Europeanism among former federalist Christian Democrats in other countries; and the radicalization of Eurosceptic orientations among some conservative parties.

The first scenario applies to countries such as Italy and France. In France, the former pro-European UDF has been marginalized by the conservative UMP, which, albeit much more pro-European than its Gaullist ancestor, neither favours strong supranational institutions, nor unequivocally embraces the free circulation of services or the independence of the ECB from the UDF's protectionist and interventionist traditions. In Italy, the implosion of the pro-European Christian Democracy in 1994 has made way for Forza Italia, whose stance on European integration is eclectic and hardly predictable. Beyond the widely reported Eurosceptic statements of some Forza Italia ministers against the Euro and EU enlargement (Leconte 2003:471), two elements predispose this party to soft Euroscepticism. First, Berlusconi's own views (his admiration for Margaret Thatcher and his anti-regulation stance, as expressed in his hostility to the Kyoto protocol) and the party's hostility to multiculturalism (as expressed in the defence of a 'Christian society' (Hooghe *et al.* 2002:981)), predispose it to soft Euroscepticism. Second, and above all, Berlusconi's stance towards the EU is made up of indifference and parochialism. The EU is seen as the prolongation of domestic politics and of the party's vocal fight against the left (for instance, its criticism of the Euro was due to the fact that Italian participation in EMU is largely considered an achievement of previous centre-left governments) (Quaglia 2002:20).

The second scenario is that of the German CDU-CSU. In the early decades of European integration, it defended a clearly federalist stance. Federal Europe was an explicit goal of party programmes throughout the 1960s and 1970s for the CDU, as well as for its Bavarian sister party, the CSU (CDU 1968, 1978; CSU 1968, 1976). The CDU especially supported a federal Europe with a constitution, extended powers for the Commission and for the EP, a direct election of the Commission by the EP, and a fully-fledged foreign and defence policy. Thirty years later, the CDU has become less enthusiastic about European integration, while the CSU has shifted to a clearly Eurosceptic position. Not only has the reference to federal Europe been abandoned, but the CDU is calling for a strict application of the subsidiairty principle and advocates the repatriation of some EU powers to the national level (CDU 2009). Certainly, it still supports the long-term goal of an EU constitution but its support for the Lisbon Treaty is less than enthusiastic, as it relies primarily on the enhanced role of national parliaments (not of the European Parliament) as a way to 'prevent European centralism'. In the CSU's case, the Eurosceptic shift was already discernible in the 1993 programme, drafted under the influence of former party leader Edmund Stoiber (CSU 1993). Its 2009 EP elections programme is permeated throughout by hostility towards deeper integration. Not only does the CSU call for a strict application of the subsidiarity principle, but in a clear challenge to the ECJ, it designates the German Constitutional Court as responsible for ensuring that the EU does not overstep its powers (CSU 2009). Furthermore, the overall tone of the programme is clearly critical *vis-à-vis* the EU, which is equated with 'foreign rule' (*Fremdbestimmung*). In this respect, the CSU's stance towards the EU increasingly resembles that of the British Conservatives, which illustrate the third type of scenario.

Several factors explain the increased Euroscepticism of the British Conservative party in the course of the 1990s, and especially in the post-John Major era (from 1997 on): the increasing polarization of the British debate on the EU (notably with EMU), the challenge of the hard Eurosceptic far right, and the growing conservatism inside the party on social issues and immigration, among others. In this respect, the development of integration in 'normative issues' has been colliding with a growing conservatism among the Tories, as the party has been increasingly influenced by its US Republican counterparts on socio-economic issues (Flood 2000:199). These trends have been exacerbated by a generational change inside the party. As a result of these developments, the most pro-European wing in the party has been marginalized, while Eurosceptics have gained the upper hand. During Margaret Thatcher's leadership, for instance, it was estimated that one-third of the party was made up of pro-Europeans, who had voted in favour of continued British membership in 1975 and were open to some forms of 'regulated capitalism'. The rest of the party was made up of a majority of Euro-pragmatists who approved of the completion of the internal market (but not of EMU) and a minority of nationalists, who stayed principally hostile to British EU membership (Flood 2000:188–9). Moreover, at that time, Thatcher's toughening stance towards the EC was counter-balanced by the influence of pro-European heavyweights in the party (such as Michael Heseltine, Edward Heath and Lord Henry Plumb) and in her own government (such as Foreign Secretary Geoffrey Howe and Chancellor of the Exchequer Nigel Lawson). By comparison, the current Conservative shadow cabinet barely includes one pro-European heavyweight. The ratification vote on the Lisbon Treaty in the House of Commons highlights the extent of the Conservatives' hostility towards further integration, as only three Conservative MPs (out of 193) broke with their party's line and voted for ratification (House of Commons 2008). Evolutions in conservative voters' views on the EU have been mirroring those at party level. Indeed, from 1997 on, Conservative voters have become less supportive of EU membership than voters of the two other main parties (Labour and the Liberal Democrats) (Evans and Butt 2007).

At the European level, the growing influence of conservatism in the Christian Democratic party family is illustrated by changes in the membership of the European People's Party (EPP), which has welcomed conservative parties such as the Spanish People's Party (in 1991) and Forza Italia (in 1999), which do not share the federalist stance of the EPP. Is the pro-European consensus of mainstream elites also challenged at the European level?

Political elites in the European Parliament: enthusiastic Europeans?

Contrary to widespread belief, the weight of Eurosceptics in the EP has not been strengthened in the last couple of elections, as the latter benefit both strongly Eurosceptic and unequivocally pro-European parties. Furthermore, the actual influence of self-declared Eurosceptics in the EP is very limited. At the same time, however, MEPs are not significantly more pro-European than MNPs.

European elections: privileged channels for Eurosceptic votes?

It has been argued that EP elections have allowed mainstream parties to 'channel Eurosceptic voting into EP rather than national elections' (Ray 2007:42). Underlying this theory is the assumption that EP elections represent a privileged electoral arena for Eurosceptic parties. Certainly, dynamics underlying voting behaviour in European elections differ from national ones. However, as is shown below, recent quantitative surveys offer a more nuanced picture of the dynamics underlying EP elections. The latter can be analyzed from two different theoretical perspectives.

For the first theory, EP elections are second-order elections. Seeing little at stake in elections which do not result in the selection of a new executive, voters tend to select a party closest to their preferences on a specific issue (immigration or the environment, for instance) or vote in order to sanction incumbent governments, if they are dissatisfied with their policies. Consequently, it is argued that EP elections offer 'brighter prospects for small and new political parties', without, however, expressing voters' views on the EU. The second theory refines the first one by assuming that EP elections are increasingly about Europe. In that context, parties that give much salience to EU issues, and that have a clear and united position on them (be they pro-European or Eurosceptic), are likely to fare better than parties that give low salience to these issues and that are highly divided (which is a sign of second order elections progressively transforming into first order elections) (Reif and Schmitt 1980). The 2004 EP elections in the UK, for example, seem to fit this scenario, as they resulted in good electoral scores both for the anti-EU UKIP and for the pro-European Liberal Democrats.

Quantitative surveys testing these theories have led to a twofold conclusion. To begin with, the first theory remains the most relevant in explaining differences between the national and European electoral arenas. The sanction effect, combined with party size, remains predominant, as large governing parties tend to lose, while smaller parties (whether in opposition or not) tend to gain votes (Hix and Marsh 2005:19). However, the 'second order' theory must be combined with the 'EU matters' theory in order to fully capture the dynamics underlying EP elections. If a party focuses strongly on EU issues, it increases its votes in EP elections, a fact which benefits both strongly Eurosceptic and clearly pro-European parties. This is why single-issue Eurosceptic parties of the soft and hard type (see Table 4.1) and Green parties tend to have good electoral results in European elections. Of course, EP elections do not display one single pattern across countries. For instance, while anti-EU parties had good electoral results in the 2009 EP elections in Austria and the UK (with 18 per cent and 17 per cent respectively), they scored quite poorly in Denmark and Sweden. Similarly, Green parties recorded significant gains in France, Sweden and Luxembourg, but not in Germany. Furthermore, contrary to another widespread assumption, EP elections from 1979 to 2004 display no systematic patterns of electoral gains for extreme right or extreme left parties. The most recent 2009 EP elections illustrated this. While extreme right parties strengthened their electoral weight in Austria, Denmark, Hungary and the Netherlands (with 15 to 20 per cent of the vote) and experienced electoral breakthroughs in the UK and Finland (with 7 per cent and 10 per cent respectively), they scored rather poorly in Belgium and France compared with the last EP election. Consequently, average electoral results for Eurosceptics at EP elections do not exceed those of national elections. Whatever the electoral arena, they gather a maximum of roughly one-fifth of the vote.

Eurosceptics in the EP: steady numbers and limited influence

In a similar vein, the common-sense view that the representation of Eurosceptic forces in the EP has increased over the years does not hold. Even if new parties have gained access to the European assembly since the 1970s, and despite successive EU enlargements, the total share of self-declared Eurosceptic MEPs has not increased.

In the first European legislatures, Eurosceptics were mainly represented by nationalists like the French Gaullists (later joined by the Irish Fianna Fail), some liberal parties (the Dutch and German ones) and, to some extent, by the French radical-socialists (Zellentin 1967). At that time, Eurosceptic forces in the EP were under-represented compared with their electoral weight in the national arenas, since the communists did not want to send delegates to the EP. This also fitted the views of pro-European elites, as it was feared that the direct election of MEPs would be a privileged channel for Eurosceptic votes. Later on, Eurosceptic parties gained access to the EP in three waves: communists and conservatives (from the 1973 accession countries) in the 1970s, right-extremists beginning in the second half of the 1980s, and single-issue, anti-European parties especially since the 1994 election. Contrary to initial concerns, however, the direct election of MEPs did not result in a clear increase of the proportion of self-declared Eurosceptics in the EP, as a comparison between legislatures in the 1960s, 1980s and 2000s illustrates.

In the mid-1960s (after the 1966 EP elections), strong Eurosceptics in the EP (which included Gaullists and independents) represented 13.5 per cent of the total number of MEPs, without taking into account Eurosceptic segments among the liberals and the socialists (who accounted for a fifth and a quarter of the EP respectively) (Zellentin 1967). Fourteen years later, in 1979, Eurosceptics accounted for 19 per cent of parliamentarians in the first assembly to be directly elected (a share which included communists, the far left, Gaullists and Fianna Fail, as well as the independents) (Reif and Schmitt 1980). A quarter of a century later, in 2004, the share of the Eurosceptic hard core in the EP had not increased much. Eurosceptics from the nationalist group UEN (Union for a Europe of Nations), anti-European parties from the IND-DEM (Independence and Democracy) group, the Eurosceptic communist and far-left group GUE-NGL (Group of the United European Left-Nordic Green Left) and the independents represented 17 per cent of the assembly. However, what *had* changed was the increased Euroscepticism of British conservatives and the accession of Eurosceptic conservatives from the new member states, notably the Czech ODS. By adding these Eurosceptic conservatives belonging to the former ED (European Democrats) faction of the EPP-ED group, the total share of Eurosceptics rose to a quarter of the assembly. After the recent 2009 European elections, self-declared Eurosceptics now make up 21 per cent of the assembly, including the newly-created European Conservatives and Reformists' (ECR) Group (made up of the former Eurosceptic ED faction of the EPP-ED and the Polish Law and Justice Party), the United European Left, the single-issue anti-Europeans of the Europe of Freedom and Democracy's Group (former IND-DEM group) and the extreme right MEPs sitting as independents. In conclusion, the hard core of Eurosceptics has not increased much (around 15 to 20 per cent of the assembly) over the last thirty years.

Moreover, Eurosceptic forces have had little practical impact on the agenda of the EP and on its legislative record. This is due to two factors. First, Eurosceptic forces, being made up mainly of nationalists, have experienced considerable difficulties in trying to organize as transnational parliamentary groups or parties (for an overview of Eurosceptics' troubled history of cooperation, see Hanley 2008). Often, contentious relationships between two nationalist delegations hampered this cooperation. For instance, the ITS (Identity, Tradition, Sovereignty) group set up in 2007, made up of extreme right parties of several old and new member states, eventually dissolved because of clashes between the Italian and Romanian representatives. Attempts to set up transnational parties failed for similar reasons. For instance, the Euronat, created in 2007 and which aims at rallying nationalists across the EU, is only a loose coordination platform without the participation of nationalist heavyweights such as the Austrian FPÖ and the Flemish Vlaams Belang (Hanley 2008:198). Moreover, it is also out of hostility towards the principle of transnational cooperation that some of these parties have refused to join multinational parliamentary groups. As was already noticed in the 1960s, there is, indeed, a correlation between hostility towards a closer union and the degree of organization/institutionalization of parties at the EU level (Zellentin 1967). More recently, for instance, anti-European members of the IND-DEM group tried to oppose the adoption of the 2003 Regulation setting up a statute for European parties for that reason (Hanley 2008:187). This situation sometimes results in Eurosceptics ending up as independents, with all the disadvantages linked to this status (in terms of resources, staff, positions in committees, etc.). Furthermore, Eurosceptic groups in the EP are characterized by comparatively low levels of internal cohesion, while other groups benefit from a relatively strong internal unity during votes (see p.14).

The second reason for Eurosceptics' limited influence is that, in cases where they have managed to set up parliamentary groups, they are scattered across smaller fringe groups. Politics in the EP (for the allocation of influential committee positions as well as for legislative decision-making) is still dominated by grand coalition agreements between the two main groups, with the liberals as the potential pivotal party. In that respect, the absence of Eurosceptics in the large mainstream groups is also the result of external constraints, as the latter have been cautious not to include party delegations with dubious ideological credentials. This explains, for instance, why member delegations from the nationalist group UEN, such as Alleanza Nazionale, could not join the EPP. The only exception to this exclusion from the core of EP politics were the British and Danish Conservatives (joined by their Czech counterparts in 2004), who sat in the ED sub-group of the EPP from 1992 to 2009. This exception to the rule, due to the EPP's strategy of quantitative expansion, was detrimental to the cohesion of the group on EU issues. This was most evident from 2003 on, as members of the ED were explicitly allowed to depart from the group's line on crucial issues (see, for instance, the British Conservatives' campaign against the EU Constitutional Treaty). Beyond this exception, however, Eurosceptics' practical influence has remained marginal. Above all, they have not been able to make the integration/independence cleavage a salient dimension of inter-party competition in the EP.

Are EP elites more pro-European?

Nonetheless, the widespread assumption that MEPs are more pro-European than their national counterparts does not hold. This alleged pro-European bias has been attributed, notably, to socialization processes. As MEPs become accustomed to the day-to-day workings of EU institutions, they become more supportive of further integration, advocating extended powers for the EP and an enlarged scope of the co-decision procedure. However, such assumptions are not corroborated by facts.

First, MEPs, while being predominantly in favour of European integration, have been found to be only slightly more pro-European than MNPs (Katz 2002). What is more, existing studies comparing MNPs and MEPs could not take into account the impact of the 2004 enlargement on the EP. In fact, a survey of MEPs from the 2004 accession countries found that they were slightly less supportive of European integration and less favourable to an extension of the EP's powers than their counterparts from the older member states (Farrel *et al.* 2006).

Second, the assumption that experience as an MEP has a pro-European, socialization impact has not been validated. Whereas the length of experience as an MNP tends to increase hostility towards an extension of the EP's powers, the length of experience as an MEP neither enhances general support for integration, nor increases support for a more powerful EP (Scully 2005). In fact, it seems that the main variables influencing the general attitude of MEPs and MNPs towards European integration differ. While an MEP's attitude is primarily influenced by his/her level of satisfaction with the way democracy works in the EU, an MNP's attitude is predominantly influenced by his/her sense (or lack) of European identity (Katz 2002). This suggests that an MNP's orientations towards the EU might be less likely to evolve than those of an MEP.

While the EP remains a predominantly pro-European-oriented assembly, several factors may influence the representation of Eurosceptic forces in this arena in the future: future EU enlargements, changes in the dynamics underlying EP elections, and, above all, the evolution of turnout for EP elections. Certainly, the continuous decline in turnout observed since 1979 should not be automatically interpreted as the expression of Eurosceptic orientations among voters. However, critics of the EP might point it out as a valid reason for questioning the legitimacy of the European assembly. The German Constitutional Court's ruling on the Lisbon Treaty, which clearly questions the representative capacity of the EP (Federal Constitutional Court 2009: consideration no. 1) shows that such criticism can be voiced by key mainstream actors in national political systems.

Conclusion

Party-based Euroscepticism may be losing its characteristic as a phenomenon mainly located at the fringes of domestic party systems. As political elites are confronted with the limits of their selective Europeanization strategies, the in-built ambiguity of their support for European integration becomes apparent. The latter now reveals itself as a double-edged project for elites. On the one hand, it increases the executive's autonomy towards parliaments and offers party elites the opportunity to network at the EU level, while occasionally playing the blame game at the expense of the EU. On the other hand, European integration challenges intra-party cohesion and makes national political parties increasingly irrelevant in the eyes of voters, as they appear less and less able to shape macro-economic conditions in a purely national context. In a similar vein, national political elites have been reluctant to set up robust European parties in order to maintain themselves as 'gate-keepers' of the European electoral arena (Mair 2000). This may also backfire on them, as decreasing voter interest in EP elections risks empowering those who question the legitimacy of the EP.

Chapter 5

National Institutions

With the extension of the scope of QMV, member states are more likely to have to implement EU legislation that they initially opposed. In this context, there is a tendency for member states to 'react to the intensifying integration process with a strategy of selective and recalcitrant compliance with European regulations' (Neyer and Wolf 2000). However, compliance involves not only central governments, but also national parliaments and administrations (which adopt the national transposition laws and measures necessary to implement EU legislation), regional levels of governance or authorities (which supervise the implementation of EU legislation at the local or regional level), and domestic courts (which incorporate EU legislation into their case law and can refer to the ECJ via the preliminary ruling procedure, in order to interpret EU treaties). Having a reduced administration, no police and no power over the use of force, the EU actually relies on these national institutions for the effective implementation of EU law at the domestic level.

The uniform implementation of Union law across member states is crucial for the EU. First of all, it is a necessary precondition for the smooth functioning of the internal market, as economic actors have to benefit from similar conditions of market access and distribution across the EU. Moreover, the lack of or incorrect implementation of EU law can deprive citizens of their rights. Furthermore, non-uniform implementation of Union law or policies by member states can have discriminatory consequences for some actors. The case of the EU Common Fisheries Policy (CFP) is a good illustration of this, as insufficient supervision of quota limits by French and Spanish authorities leads to over-fishing at the expense of British and Irish fishermen (Majone 2006). Consequently, heterogeneity in implementation can affect the legitimacy and acceptance of Union law and policies.

The aim of this chapter is to analyze perceptions of the EU among national institutions, from the point of view of EU law implementation, compliance and enforcement. Compliance 'refers to the likelihood that members of a system will behave in conformity with decisions made by the political authorities and with the rules of the regime' (Easton 1974). While non-compliance does not necessarily express a lack of principled support for the regime, it may be an indicator of attitudes towards the latter, depending on the context and the motivations underlying non-compliance. This chapter puts forward three relevant arguments.

First of all, it is argued that, although non-compliance can be attributed to a variety of factors, faulty or non-compliance by member states may illustrate specific varieties of Euroscepticism, be they political (i.e. opposing a legislation extending the scope of EU action) or cultural (when, for instance, efficient implementation requires high levels of trust in other member states' institutions). Secondly, problems of compliance must be analyzed in the wider context of the Europeanization of national political systems, as European integration challenges organization, working habits and, above all, redistributes power inside and between national institutions. In this context, some national institutions (for instance national parliaments or national constitutional courts) may act as veto players in the implementation and/or enforcement of EU law in order to express dissatisfaction with the impact of integration on their own power. Thirdly, even institutions that seem to gain in influence as a result of European integration (intermediary national courts, for example) may engage in a strategy of selective enforcement of EU law, acting as gate-keepers of the state's core competences, especially in a context where EU-level developments in police cooperation and criminal justice activate concerns over a hollowing out of state power.

The chapter proceeds in three steps. First, after examining the different factors that may affect processes of EU law implementation, it assesses to what extent non-compliance can be conceptualized as an expression of Euroscepticism. In this manner, it explains why governments oppose the adoption of specific EU legislation in the first place. In a second step, it focuses on actors involved in the implementation and enforcement of EU law at the domestic level – domestic administrations, courts and parliaments – and shows how their perceptions of the EU affect their role as implementers. In a third step, it analyzes the relationship between member states, public opinion and the ECJ and shows how evolutions in ECJ case law and treaty reforms contribute to an increasingly tense relationship between the ECJ and (some) national constitutional courts.

The compliance problem: Euroscepticism through the back door?

The question of whether the EU suffers from a specific compliance problem is debatable (see Börzel 2001). Leaving aside this particular aspect of the debate, this section seeks to explain whether problems of implementation of EU law can be attributed to general attitudes towards European integration and, possibly, to Eurosceptic orientations among governments or parts of the state apparatus.

First of all, one must distinguish between implementation and compliance. In order to be transposed into national law, EU directives have to be implemented, either by legislative texts or administrative acts. Compliance relates to the extent to which member states abide by directives once they have been implemented or transposed. Making this distinction matters for the following reason: whereas official data from EU institutions attest to a high and rising directive transposition rate (almost 99 per cent on average in 2008 (European Commission 2009)), problems related to the implementation process are frequent. Often, member states either delay the implementation of directives, implement only parts of the text, or implement it in a way that is inconsistent with the directive's objectives. Indeed, the two most frequent problems are related to the delayed transposition of directives and to inadequate national measures of transposition. For instance, in the transport sector, where implementation problems are frequent, it is estimated that roughly 70 per cent of national transposition measures are inadequate to reach the directive's objectives (Kaeding 2008). Furthermore, member states also choose not to abide by the directive once it has been implemented, by failing to supervise and sanction cases of non-compliance (a problem which has recently made headlines in the case of the fishing quota supervision). Finally, even when member states are condemned by the ECJ in infringement cases, problems of compliance can persist. For instance, it has been shown in the German case that complete compliance as a result of an ECJ ruling (for EU legislation in the social and environmental fields) accounted for less than 50 per cent of cases. In another 40 per cent of cases, the German government continued its non-compliance, and in 10 per cent of cases, it chose only partial compliance (Panke 2007). Ultimately, only the prospect of financial sanctions (which can only be decided by the ECJ in a second ruling) can force reluctant member states to comply, and even then only if societal opposition (to the text) is weak.

Involuntary non-compliance: limited explanatory power

Cases of bad implementation, non-implementation or non-compliance can be interpreted from different points of view. To begin with, involuntary non-compliance must be distinguished from voluntary non-compliance.

Involuntary non-compliance can be due to two types of factors. First, it might simply be the result of a general lack of precision in the wording of directives, which deliberately leave member states some room for interpretation. Second, it might be due, in some member states, to the lack of administrative and/or financial resources (this might explain the poor performance of Greece, Luxembourg, Italy and Portugal regarding implementation).

However, existing research suggests that, even if sufficient administrative resources and good governance positively affect implementation and compliance, they are not crucial variables in explaining non-implementation or compliance failures. This holds for both new and old member states (Toshkov 2008; Falkner *et al.* 2005). Similarly, incorrect interpretation of directives has been found to have little explanatory power in the case of new member states as well as for the older ones. According to existing research, it can thus be assumed that most cases of non-compliance are voluntary.

Voluntary non-compliance at the regional level

Implementation and/or compliance problems might be due to a member state's specific institutional features and to 'the number of institutional veto points that central governments have to face when imposing European provisions on their constituencies' (Haverland 2000). In the case of federal states, for example, where the number of veto players is high, the implementation process can be affected by opposition to EU legislation at the regional level. Such an interpretation has been put forward to explain late implementation of the EU Packaging Directive in Germany, for example, where EU legislation was opposed by a coalition of hostile *Länder*. More generally, non-compliance can also be a way for regional levels of governance to oppose EU legislation that was adopted with the agreement of the central government. For instance, in the wake of the SEA, local authorities in some member states decided not to abide by the EU rules on public procurement. In this case, 'non-compliance represents a form of passive, unorganized resistance' (Smith 1999:36).

Voluntary non-compliance at the national level

There are several ways in which member states can limit the impact of undesired EU legislation at the domestic level. Before a directive is adopted, for instance, governments can still try to obtain derogations, opt-outs or limitations. Moreover, in principle, directives give member states a good deal of room for manoeuvre in choosing national instruments of transposition (even if the Commission checks the adequacy of these instruments). Furthermore, if the text has been adopted, governments can still challenge it before the ECJ, as the British government did on social legislation and the German government on the Tobacco Advertisement Directive, for instance. In this context, non-compliance can be a form of last resort, *ex post* 'opposition through the back door' to unwanted EU legislation (Falkner *et al.* 2005).

Why states oppose EU legislation: reasons unrelated to the EU

To scholars of Euroscepticism, the crucial question is: does non-compliance express general negative attitudes towards European integration or are the two issues disconnected? In fact, there are many cases where failure to implement and/or comply does not relate to general attitudes towards European integration.

First of all, in line with the 'goodness of fit' argument (see p.79), specific pieces of EU legislation might imply changes in policy-making and regulatory styles that are completely alien to a domestic administration's traditions and practices. For example, the discordance between regulation instruments underlying parts of EU environmental protection legislation and the prevalent regulation mode in Germany has been put forward as a relevant factor explaining implementation problems in Germany (Knill and Lenschow 2000). Second, attempts to delay implementation can be due to an overlap (or linkage) between the EU and national agendas. If the content of a specific piece of legislation becomes a focal point for intense conflict at the domestic level, especially in pre-electoral periods, the probability that implementation will be postponed is high. Here, the domestic issue linkage variable comes into play. Indeed, the implementation process can be affected by linkages made with other issues on the national agenda. For example, researchers have found that the implementation of social EU legislation in France (notably in the case of the Working Time Directive) was affected by controversies in the domestic arena on the reduction of statutory weekly working hours (Falkner *et al.* 2005). Third, difficulties in the implementation process can also be due to the mobilization of powerful interest groups who expect disadvantages or costs as a result of specific legislation, as was the case in the German tobacco industry with the tobacco directive. Fourth, non-implementation or non-compliance can also derive from ideological preferences in terms of the left/right cleavage, as was the case with the British Tory government's hostility towards EU social legislation.

Implementation problems and attitudes towards the EU

At first sight, implementation and compliance problems do not seem to correlate with general attitudes towards European integration. Indeed, some of the best performers in terms of directive implementation, such as Finland, Sweden, Austria and the UK, are countries where levels of Euroscepticism are high. Conversely, the worst performers in terms of implementation are countries where levels of Euroscepticism are lower, such as Belgium, Luxembourg, Greece, Portugal and Italy. However, there might be some correlation between non-implementation and Euroscepticism in the new member states as well as in the older ones.

In the case of the new member states, it has been shown, indeed, that implementation performance is closely correlated with the government's general attitude towards European integration. Timely transposition of a directive especially is tightly linked to levels of support for integration inside governments: '[T]he less supportive of integration that ECE governments have been, the fewer efforts and resources they seem to have put into meeting the transposition requirements' (Toshkov 2008). Hence the governments that were the least supportive of European integration among central and eastern European countries (for example, the Hungarian government under Prime Minister Viktor Orban between 1998 and 2002) transposed EU directives at a slower pace than other, more pro-European governments.

In the older member states, failure to implement and/or comply can also be due to general reservations towards some aspects of European integration. Three cases are examined below: general reluctance towards a possible extension of EU power, concerns over specific dimensions of national identity, and finally, distrust of other member states' institutions.

First of all, hostility towards a specific piece of legislation might express broader concerns over a possible extension of the scope of the EU's power. A good illustration of this was the opposition of successive German governments to the Tobacco Advertising Directive, adopted in 2003, which bans tobacco advertising in the media (except for TV) and forbids tobacco sponsorship of events with trans-border effects. Besides opposition from the tobacco and advertising industries, another reason for opposing the directive was the ongoing German debate (notably at the regional level) on the scope of the EU's power. Indeed, the federal government challenged the directive before the ECJ, on the grounds that the EU's power should not extend to public health (*Deutsche Welle* 2006).

Furthermore, the perceived discordance between specific EU legislation and national traditions, practices, preferences, etc., can be so strong as to be perceived as a challenge to national identity. In that case, opposition to EU legislation can originate in the willing-ness to 'protect national institutions' (Falkner *et al.* 2005), which are broadly defined so as to encompass norms, conventions and values (see p.79). As scholars of the Europeanization process argue, 'If adaptational pressures are very high, European institutions seri-ously challenge the identity, constitutive principles, core structures and practices of national institutions. [In such cases] we expect some sort of stalemate between EU institutions and domestic institutions resulting in severe implementation deficits' (Green Cowles *et al.* 2001:8). A good illustration of this was opposition to the Working Time Directive in France, where the directive was seen as challeng-ing one of the core principles of the 'social *acquis*', namely the prohi-bition of night work for blue collar women (Falkner *et al.* 2005).

In other instances, EU legislation is seen as a direct challenge to long-predominant understandings of national identity. Such is the case for EU citizenship, which contributes to the detachment of citi-zenship from nationality. As we have seen (p.51), EU citizenship was much contested in some countries, notably in France where it challenged deeply ingrained, 'Jacobin [and] centralized notions of state and citizenship' (Ladrech 1994). These reservations largely affected the implementation of EU citizenship rights by member states, who tried to limit their scope as much as possible. The prob-lem was especially related to Directive 94/80/CE, which aims at implementing voting and eligibility rights for non-national EU residents in municipal elections. During negotiations on the text, member states tried to minimize its scope. In addition to specific derogations for Belgium and Luxembourg (where over 20 per cent of the voting population in some municipalities is made up of non-national EU residents), the directive contains limitations that are open to all member states: specific functions (such as mayor or deputy mayor) can be reserved for nationals, while national authorities can exclude non-national EU residents from participation in the election of parliamentary assemblies. These limitations were a significant departure from the general philosophy underlying EU citizenship (namely detaching citizenship from nationality) and clearly discriminated against non-national EU citizens. In fact, many member states made extensive use of these limitations when implementing the directive (Fabry 2005:229–30). Furthermore, the implementation of the directive was largely delayed in several member states. Despite the 1996 transposition deadline, it was only in 1999 that all member states had communicated their transposition measures to the Commission. The two most serious latecomers, Belgium and France, first made use of the directive in 2000 and 2001 respectively.

In a similar vein, member states tend to oppose EU legislation when it constrains their ability to restrict the free movement of persons, which is often linked to concerns over national identity or security. In that respect, an interesting example of non-compliance is related to the implementation of EU legislation on the free circulation of people in Greece. Limitations to the principle of the free movement of persons and to the acquisition of property have long been imposed by Greek authorities on inhabitants of Western Thrace, a border region with Turkey mainly populated by the Muslim minority. Condemned by the ECJ in 1989 for violating EU legislation on the free movement of persons, Greek authorities complied reluctantly by limiting the impact of the EU legislation as much as possible (Hersant 2008:645–6).

Finally, incorrect implementation or non-compliance can also express distrust towards the institutions of other EU countries. A good illustration of this is the implementation of the European Arrest Warrant (EAW). Instituted by the Council Framework Decision of 13 June 2002, the EAW is a cornerstone of the emerging EU judicial area, aimed at facilitating extradition procedures between member states. The question of trust is crucial here since the EAW relies on the principle of mutual recognition of criminal justice decisions, and thus, ultimately, on trust in other member states' judicial systems. On the insistence of some governments – and the British government especially, as it is wary of the possible development of a 'European judicial superstate' (Sievers 2008:117) – member states have only agreed on common, general guidelines (entailed in the framework decision), leaving a great deal of leeway to national parliaments, which adopted laws to implement the framework decision. These laws often illustrate a clear willingness to limit the scope of the EAW, as well as widespread distrust of other member states' judicial systems. In fact, numerous national parliaments have adopted laws giving national courts additional reasons for refusing a warrant issued by another member state. In some cases, they have laid down additional conditions for executing an extradition (for instance, in the British, German and Italian laws), which completely contradicts the EAW's main goal to make extradition procedures easier and faster. As debates in the British and German Parliaments revealed, opposition to the framework decision at the national level was rooted in a deep-seated distrust of other countries' judicial systems. In the UK especially, parliamentary debates on the implementation law (the so-called Extradition Act) illustrated 'major distrust' of criminal justice systems in Continental Europe, which were qualified by one Tory MP as being incompatible with the principle of the presumption of innocence (Sievers 2008).

Administrations, courts and parliaments: loyal applicants of EU law?

Some accounts of European integration tend to analyze the EU as one emerging, multi-level political system, where national and EU institutions are increasingly enmeshed (the so-called fusion thesis). This image can convey the misleading impression that the whole system relies on smooth cooperation between national and EU institutions. Certainly, those segments of national institutions that benefit from participation in the EU's decision-making process are likely to actively contribute to the penetration of EU law into national legal systems. However, purely utilitarian accounts of support for the EU do not capture the ambiguity of these actors' attitudes towards the EU. This section demonstrates this point by focusing on the three actors that are primarily responsible for implementing EU law and ensuring it is complied with: national administrations, courts, and parliaments.

The Europeanization process: challenges for national political systems

Attitudes towards the EU among national institutions must be analyzed in the context of the far-reaching changes that European integration implies for national political systems. Three types of impact can be identified: a redistribution of influence between executive, legislative and judicial powers; changes in the balance of power between different levels of government; and a general adaptational pressure on national political systems.

First of all, Europeanization contributes to changes in the balance of power between the different branches of government. That it tends to reduce the influence of national parliaments, to the benefit of executives, has often been noted. It also tends to strengthen the role of the judicial power *vis-à-vis* the executive and legislative powers, notably in countries like the UK (Drewry 2007:114). Specific EU legislation can also alter the balance of power between the executive and judges, as does the framework decision setting up the EAW. Compared with traditional extradition procedures, the framework decision seriously reduces the role of Justice Ministries (and hence risks of political interference), which are only endowed with (optional) coordination and administrative support tasks. By comparison, it endows judges with the key decision-making authority in the process. This issue proved highly political in Italy, for instance, where it touched on the very sensitive issue of the relationship between politicians and judges. This is probably why the national law implementing the framework directive on the EAW, which, according to one law expert, 'negates the Framework Decision rather than implements it' (Impalà 2005:56), entails numerous legal and administrative hurdles to effective cooperation and reinstates the Justice Ministry as a gate-keeper filtering communication between judges.

Second, European integration entails significant implications for the relationship between central and regional levels of governance. In countries like Germany, it has raised concerns over a possible erosion of federalism, which has been conceived as a cornerstone of the democratic order of the Federal Republic since 1949.

Third, the Europeanization process, and the implementation of EU law especially, exert strong pressure on administrations and judicial systems to adapt. In that respect, 'there is still a significant gap between the productive capacity of the Union, which generates new rules on an almost daily basis, and the capacity for assimilation of national legal systems and cultures' (Impalà 2005:61).

Civil servants and judges: utilitarian supporters of the EU?

According to utilitarian accounts of patterns of support for the EU, top national civil servants and judges benefit from interactions with EU and other member states' institutions. They are therefore likely to be supportive of European integration and to promote the Europeanization process, via the implementation and enforcement of EU law.

As far as national administrations are concerned, they are tightly associated with the elaboration of EU legislation through the Commission. Furthermore, participating in the EU-level decision-making process is an advantage for national civil servants in several respects, namely 'by enlarging their administrative expertise, their factual knowledge and by increasing their weight inside their respective national networks' (Wessels and Rometsch 1996:78). Moreover, a large number of national civil servants regularly come in contact with the EU in the course of their career, which might induce a Europeanization or socialization effect. Even if such participation is not necessarily conducive to a shift in allegiance towards the EU, it might limit the diffusion of negative attitudes towards the EU among national civil servants. Such hypotheses are corroborated by surveys on senior national civil servants' attitudes towards the EU. For instance, a 1996 survey conducted among five different categories of top decision-makers across member states found that top civil servants were the strongest supporters of EU membership (with 96 per cent), ahead of politicians and business associations (Spence 1996).

There are similar assumptions regarding the overall pro-EU orientation of national courts, which may rely on both utilitarian and political/normative support. To begin with, the development of the EU judicial system and the possibility of referring to the ECJ via preliminary rulings has contributed to empowering lower national courts in the domestic arena, in their relation to governments and in the context of 'inter-court competition' between higher and lower national courts (Hix 2005:137). In countries where the power of courts was traditionally limited, such as the UK, EU membership has led to a general empowerment of judges *vis-à-vis* Parliament and government (Drewry 2007:114). In addition, in some countries, the

EU may be seen as an ally of judges in the fight for independence and/or against corruption. More generally, as one EU scholar argues, 'the ECJ and its rulings are used as instruments by national courts to promote the rule of law, judicial review and the protection of individual rights against the domestic state' (Hix 2005:137). An example of this is the 1996 Geneva call, launched by seven high-profile, anti-corruption magistrates (among whom were Baltasar Garzon Real and Renaud Van Ruymbeke), which called for the development of a EU judicial area. In line with this argument, a 2007 survey found that, of all national actors, the judiciary clearly displays the most positive perception of EU institutions (Koopmans *et al.* 2007:202).

National administrations: a limited allegiance to the EU

National administrations and courts are certainly not homogeneous in their attitudes towards European integration. One must distinguish between different types of actors and logics among them. To begin with, one must not forget that not all top civil servants were enthusiastic supporters of European integration in the early days of the EEC, notably in France and Germany. In France, for instance, hostility to the common market was strong among top civil servants, notably in the Finance Ministry, who opposed trade liberalization. Furthermore, top civil servants were concerned that the implementation of the common market in France's overseas territories would decrease French influence there, as a result of a diversification of trade links. Opposition to the common market was also strong in other ministries, such as agriculture, social affairs, transport and overseas territories (Parsons 2006:119–21). In Germany, the federal administration was not homogeneous, as the Foreign Ministry favoured strong supranational institutions and segments of the Finance Ministry favoured an OEEC type of cooperation (Küsters 1998:498). It has thus been argued that the acceptance of EC/EU law by national administrations was highly instrumental, as it was perceived as empowering existing administrations or, more generally, contributing to the development of the domestic 'regulatory state' (for instance, by contributing to the setting up of new regulatory agencies at the domestic level) (see Chalmers 2000).

What is more, one must also distinguish between different levels of governance, as utilitarian support for the EU does not necessarily apply to local and regional administrations. For instance, in the case of the ECE countries, scholars have identified 'hidden forms of incipient Euroscepticism [which] takes the form of non-compliance with EU-transposed directives' at local and regional levels (Hughes *et al.* 2002:335). More generally, European integration represents very different opportunity structures for actors, depending on their ability to access and mobilize the different levels of EU governance. For instance, scholars of EU governance have distinguished between 'multi-level players' (such as members of the Council's working groups and EU committees), who are able to mobilize across all levels and benefit from horizontal, transgovernmental cooperation, and 'national players' (such as parliaments), who 'are present during the preparation and implementation phases but not in the crucial arenas of EU joint decision-making' (Maurer *et al.* 2003:66–7). In fact, the socialization process in which civil servants interact with their counterparts from other member states and with EU civil servants on a regular basis only concerns limited segments of national administrations. Principally they include civil servants working in national Permanent Representations with the EU, those who are temporarily seconded within EU institutions, and experts from national administrations meeting in different types of committees. While it has been argued that these committees act as loci of a transnational socialization process, thus cross-cutting national identities (Joerges and Neyer 1997), this certainly does not hold true for the overwhelming majority of national civil servants.

More generally, Europeanization implies significant challenges for national administrations, albeit to various extents across countries. It creates pressure to adapt (for instance, by setting up or reshuffling departments to deal with EC/EU matters, when necessary) and entails corresponding costs, especially for the less effective administrations. For the latter especially, European integration is a further source of stress, as it implies both a 'compliance pressure' and a more informal 'peer pressure', as the EU context implies a constant comparison between the performance of the different member states in terms of good governance (Knill and Lenschow 2005). Furthermore, Europeanization can challenge deeply ingrained administrative cultures. The case of British public administration is a good illustration of this. It is permeated by 'a traditional antipathy towards legalism in public administration and public management' (i.e. a strong reliance on formal legal rules of procedures) and has been built on 'a non-legalistic, even an anti-legalistic, model' (Drewry 2007:113). British public administration was built partly in opposition to the French administrative model, which relies heavily on administrative codes and legal rules. This echoes the cultural, anti-European variant of British Euroscepticism rooted in concerns over a possible contamination of British institutions by the bureaucratic traditions of continental countries.

Lower and intermediate courts: gate-keepers of state power?

Conventional academic wisdom holds that lower and intermediate courts are most likely to promote the penetration of EU law into national judicial systems and develop a cooperative relationship with the ECJ, as it empowers them in the domestic arena. There are, however, some limits to this theory.

First, even if national courts are key actors in the enforcement of EU law, they often act without referring to the case law of the ECJ or to the ECJ itself (except when this is compulsory, for instance in the case of appellate courts). Hence, there are possibilities that national rulings implying EU law might depart from the ECJ interpretation of that same law. Moreover, knowledge of EU law (including awareness of directives that have not been transposed on time by national authorities) is rather heterogeneous within national judiciaries, as past surveys by the Commission have shown (Conant 2002:81).

Second, the willingness of national courts to refer to EU law, and, when relevant, to the ECJ or its case law, varies according to policy fields and issues. In some cases, non-reference to the ECJ is due to courts' wish to contain the potential impact of ECJ rulings in specific policy areas and isolate some domestic norms from the impact of EU law. For instance, it has been argued in the case of British courts that references to EC law and/or to the ECJ are less successful when EC law is perceived as a potential challenge to state institutions' ability to ensure societal conformity (for instance, through the application of criminal law) and to promote 'collective boundaries' (for instance, by restricting the free movement of people in the name of national security) (Chalmers 2000). Whereas references to EC law or the ECJ are welcome as long as they contribute to strengthening the state's monopoly on the legal use of force (for instance, by imposing sanctions either in criminal matters or in more mundane issues, such as fisheries or the environment), 'there is, however, an extremely resistant approach to EC law and the Court of Justice where ... EC law hinders the capacity to impose not just sanction, but collective ties' (Chalmers 2000). As an illustration of this, Chalmers found, for instance, that British courts were less receptive to requests for preliminary references by defendants in criminal proceedings than in civil proceedings. This might be illustrative of a wider ambiguity, on the part of some national courts, towards the development of integration in criminal law (see below). In terms of citizens' rights under EU law, it has been argued, also in the case of the UK, that EU law provisions on non-discrimination are more likely to be applied than provisions on the free circulation of people that affect national security and collective bonds. Moreover, the behaviour of national judges sometimes corroborates the 'justice contained' thesis. In the UK, for instance, it has been found that courts apply EU law provisions without addressing the issue of the possible suspension of incompatible national provisions (Conant 2002:90). Like their constitutional counterparts, lower courts can thus also act as gatekeepers of state authority and collective identity.

Third, national judges may also act as gatekeepers of national legal systems. First accounts of the implementation of the EAW by national courts exemplify this. In countries like the UK and Ireland, proceedings are especially long and cumbersome, a fact which British judges attribute to the poor quality of incoming requests, which are sometimes based on practices alien to national traditions (for instance, EAWs are issued at an early stage in the procedure, which, according to British judges, might harm a defendant's rights). This brings us back to the issue of trust. As Sievers explains, 'national judges sometimes distrust foreign legal systems and regard the national system as superior in quality ... They may act as gatekeepers of the national legal system, using their leeway to reject an EAW if it diverges too much from well-known national standards' (2008:126).

National parliaments: utilitarian or identity-related scepticism

In almost all countries, European integration has tended to empower executives at the expense of parliaments, which are usually qualified as 'losers' of the integration process. Whereas national parliaments have hitherto reacted to this reduced influence by pushing for incremental institutional reforms (at EU and domestic levels) to enhance their influence in the EU decision-making process, recent developments might suggest that they could increasingly use their role in the implementation of EU law to voice their dissatisfaction with what they see as insufficient participation rights.

Indeed, in all countries but Denmark, parliaments cannot legally constrain governments to take their views into account when adopting legislative proposals in the Council. Even if parliaments are given a minimum six-week delay to deliver opinions on a Commission's proposal, they will not be binding on ministers in the Council. Consequently, parliaments have a limited ability to make ministers accountable for decisions made by the Council. Moreover, the sheer rhythm of EU law production, as well as the parliamentary workload, makes it difficult for parliamentarians to adequately scrutinize EU legislative proposals. Hence, in most cases, their role has been reduced to that of registering chambers. They are competent to ratify EU treaties and to adopt legislation that transposes (some) directives into EU law. According to utilitarian theories, parliaments should thus have developed a hostile attitude towards European integration. Yet this does not seem to be the case. Indeed, studies have shown that MNPs are not likely to be significantly less supportive of European integration than MEPs (see p.132).

However, recent developments in the integration process might contribute to a more assertive attitude on the part of national parliaments, as they imply an inroad into their core historic role as the proponents and guardians of fundamental rights. The development of EU-level cooperation and approximation of national law in criminal justice lies, again, at the core of this debate. As EU law ventures into criminal justice, it might indeed affect fundamental rights. Several national parliaments have thus used debates on the EAW to express their dissatisfaction with what they see as their insufficient involvement in EU decision-making, notably in view of the safeguard of fundamental rights. That this was forcefully expressed by members of the British Parliament is not surprising. However, even traditionally 'Euro-supportive' parliaments (such as the German and Italian ones) expressed much discontent during debates on the adoption of national transposition laws. While MPs from otherwise pro-EU parties, like the CDU, expressed concerns about the German Parliament being increasingly 'by-passed' in EU issues (Sievers 2008:115), the framework decision on the EAW received a 'frosty welcome' in the Italian parliament (Impalà 2005:57).

Member states and the European Court of Justice: towards a more tense relationship

Ultimately, the credibility of EU law and its uniform application across the EU relies on the authority of the ECJ, which has acted as the proponent and guardian of the primacy principle – the idea that EU law supersedes national law, including national constitutions. As such, the ECJ is the cornerstone of the EU as a community of law, and its contribution to the process of European integration has even been compared to the role of the US Federal Supreme Court in the development of federalism. Often suspected of pursuing a federalist hidden agenda, the ECJ elicits complex feelings among domestic institutions. Long underestimated as a core actor of European integration, the ECJ and its case law are increasingly submitted to political debate and media attention. Moreover, developments in integration and in ECJ case law have led to a more tense relationship between some national constitutional courts and the ECJ.

Patterns of support for the ECJ: governments and public opinion

According to mainstream realist understandings of international relations, acceptance by national authorities of the primacy of EU law and of the authority of the ECJ is puzzling. Why would states accept the authority of a supranational judiciary over national norms, and even constitutions? Even in the case of the United States, the legitimacy of the Federal Supreme Court's decisions was contested well into the 1960s. In post-war western Europe, the extent of the authority of the European Court of Human Rights (of the Council of Europe) was debated, as some wanted to limit its ability to condemn states and thus limit the possibility for individuals to initiate an action before the Court. Consequently, the decision of whether to allow individuals to bring actions before the Court was initially left to the states. Similar reservations prevailed at the time of the drafting of the Rome treaties. Contrary to the Court of Justice of the ECSC, individuals do not have the ability to initiate an action before the ECJ against member states that have violated EU law. They can only bring actions against decisions of EU institutions that are of direct concern to them. Legal action against EU law violations by member states can only be introduced before the ECJ by the Commission or by another member state. This is illustrative of the change in mood that occurred among governments in the period between the drafting of the Paris Treaty (which set up the ECSC) and the drafting of the Rome treaties, as reservations towards strong supranational institutions were more widespread. As a result, senior civil servants in charge of drafting the Rome treaties tried to limit cases of direct, individual actions before the ECJ (Dehousse 2002:32). As a consequence, individuals can only lodge complaints with the European Commission against member states who fail to comply with EU law.

Setting aside these limitations, there are several reasons for member states' acceptance of the ECJ's authority. For instance, it has been argued that the ECJ has long avoided overly intense politicization and media coverage because it first asserted its authority on mundane, prosaic issues (such as the famous Cassis de Dijon ruling) which did not trigger debates beyond limited groups of lawyers and private interests. Even now, unlike its American counterpart, the ECJ has no competence to rule on the most divisive issues, such as abortion. Moreover, the ECJ has limited its alleged activism on highly sensitive issues at times when a political backlash against its authority was likely to occur. For instance, its timorous 1997 ruling on alcohol sales in Sweden was partly politically motivated, as the Court wanted to avoid massive 'EU-bashing' in its very first judgment involving Sweden, following a previous statement from the Commission on the issue which had caused an uproar in the country (Bromberg and Peterson 1999:67). Finally, national governments have a strong incentive not to jeopardize the credibility of the ECJ since it is the key actor which prevents free-riding behaviours by other member states or companies. Without its authority, the internal market and, eventually, the entire EU would derail.

While government acceptance of the ECJ's authority is mainly utilitarian, the latter has come under criticism from a growing number of actors (among political parties and civil society) as a result of an increasing number of high-profile rulings, which were directly or indirectly related to symbols of national identity, normative issues (see p.58) and trade union rights (see p.230). In fact, the ECJ is faced with a more and more acute dilemma. On the one hand, it has been endowed with the task of being the jurisdictional guardian of EU treaties. As such, it has to interpret existing treaties in the light of their main constitutive goal – free circulation in the internal market. On the other hand, by performing this task, the ECJ is increasingly perceived as indirectly interfering in non-economic issues (such as abortion or trade union rights) and is accused of ignoring non-economic values (such as social rights or public security). This situation is all the more difficult for the ECJ since its rulings often correspond to 'anti-majoritarian views' in the domestic arena (for instance, on minorities' rights or on the free circulation of people, services, etc.). Moreover, the ECJ cannot count on the utilitarian support of those groups who have strongly benefited from its case law. For instance, an analysis of patterns of public support for the ECJ found that women, while being clear beneficiaries of ECJ case law (on issues such as equal pay and maternity leave), are less supportive of the ECJ than men. Furthermore, patterns of support also depend on the nature of the issues that will be affected by ECJ rulings. In fact, legitimacy becomes crucial once rulings affect issues on which most citizens have clearly formed opinions. As scholars of judicial politics point out: 'It is the highly visible disputes of Union law – whether the right to travel includes the right to travel with the purpose of having an abortion; whether one can shop on Sundays – that evoke potential opposition and non-compliance and raise the important issues of acceptance and compliance' (Caldeira and Gibson 1995a,1995b). As ECJ rulings (directly or indirectly) affect high intensity issues (issues on which citizens have strong preferences), its authority is likely to be increasingly challenged.

Finally, criticism of the ECJ goes hand in hand with a more usual and classically populist denunciation of judges in general, whom populists pit against the 'people's will' or Parliament's sovereignty. Criticism of the ECJ and attacks on national judges become conflated in the same discourse for two reasons. First, the cooperation between national courts and the ECJ (via preliminary references) becomes more visible. In the UK, for instance, the famous 1991 Factortame ruling (on fishing quota 'hopping' by Spanish fishermen), which resulted from a British court's preliminary reference to the ECJ, highlighted the role of national courts as agents of EU law enforcement. '[T]he [Factortame] case remains as a black mark in the ledger of Eurosceptic grievances – marking the point at which the courts suddenly entered public and political consciousness as the allies of Brussels' (Drewry 2007:107). Second, in countries like the UK where parliamentary sovereignty was paramount, European integration (together with the implementation of the European Convention of Human Rights) has contributed both to the empowerment of courts (*vis-à-vis* parliament and government) and to a wider process of 'juridification' of the political system. In this context, it is logical for Eurosceptics to conflate criticism of the EU/ECJ with criticism of allegedly all-powerful judges. Statements from British Conservative leader David Cameron during the 2009 EP elections campaign were a case in point in that respect, as he proclaimed that 'The EU and the judges – neither of them accountable to British citizens – have taken too much power over issues that are contested aspects of public policy ... [We want to] redistribute power from the EU to Britain and from the judges to the people' (Cameron 2009). This echoes the discourse of right-wing Eurosceptics in Italy, such as the former Justice minister Roberto Castelli, of the anti-European Lega Nord, who opposed the adoption of the EAW, which, in his opinion, represented the emergence of 'a Europe of judges', who would abolish free speech in the name of 'political correctness' (quoted in Leconte 2003:475).

National constitutional courts and the ECJ

In their rulings on the compatibility of EU treaties with national constitutions, constitutional courts have usually been cautious not to derail the integration process. In this respect, all Eurosceptic attempts to use constitutional review in order to prevent the ratification of major EU treaties have failed. (Recent examples relating to the Lisbon Treaty include a coalition of Eurosceptics comprising a Bavarian CSU MP, members from the radical left-wing party Die Linke in Germany, and senators from the Eurosceptic ODS in the Czech Republic). At the same time, the highest courts have no utilitarian incentive to support the ECJ. As gatekeepers of national constitutional law, constitutional courts in particular might perceive the ECJ as a rival, especially since the EU has developed a 'constitutional order' of its own (Dehousse 2002:24–6). Can this reluctance be equated with Euroscepticism? It can in some cases, and for two reasons. First, national constitutional courts' self-understanding as gatekeepers of constitutional law can be permeated by nationalist beliefs in the superiority of national norms, leading to an exclusive understanding of national constitutional identities. Second, some recent rulings on EU treaties express principled reservations towards further integration, as was shown by recent controversies over the primacy principle.

National constitutional identities or 'constitutional nationalism'?
Some law scholars have pointed to the 'Euroscepticism of constitutional law' (Favoreu 2006) or to the 'constitutional nationalism' (Weiler 2002) underlying collective understandings of national constitutions as being paramount. Underlying these expressions is the idea that there is some sort of consubstantial Euroscepticism in the uppermost value placed on national constitutions.

The primacy of EU law over national constitutional provisions can certainly sometimes challenge constitutional provisions endowed with strong historical legitimacy. The 2002 ECJ ruling on the status of women in the German army is a very good illustration of this (see p.58). A similar logic applied to the EAW, whose implementation could, in some member states, challenge constitutional provisions prohibiting the extradition of nationals. For instance, in the Czech case, the Charter of Fundamental Rights, drafted after the fall of communism, included a provision according to which no Czech citizen shall be removed from his/her homeland. This provision was added in view of human rights violations by the communist regime, which used to remove political opponents from the country (Pollicino 2008:1336).

However, to law scholar Joseph Weiler, the argument relying on the preservation of national values enshrined in constitutions misunderstands what European integration is about, as a 'melting pot' of different legal and political legacies. According to Weiler, beneath this argument against the primacy of EU law over national constitutions lies an implicit nationalism, relying on the illusion of allegedly unique, if not superior, national values: 'The defence of the constitutional integrity of member states is nothing less than the visible expression of self-celebration, which endows constitutions with an unbelievably strong normative authority ... This constitutional ethos ... glorifies, even implicitly, a (allegedly unique) moral identity; it glorifies the wisdom, even the superiority of the Constitution's fathers, of the people, of the constitutional *demos*' (2002:169).

The idea that there can be no European equivalent of the national demos underlies much of the German Constitutional Court's scepticism towards further integration. It was mentioned as a justification for challenging the principle of EU law primacy over national constitutions in its 1993 Maastricht ruling. It was also present in the Court's 2009 ruling on the Lisbon Treaty, as the Court stated that public opinion remained 'connected to a considerable extent to patterns of identification which are related to the nation state, language, history and culture' (BVerfGE 2009:s.251). This latter statement corroborates Weiler's thesis that, in its stance towards the EU, the German Constitutional Court displays an ethnic understanding of the demos, which contradicts the ethos of European integration. In the Court's 1993 ruling, the demos – defined in the words of Justice Kirchhof as a shared ethnic identity, religion, language, history and culture – was seen a homogeneous collective actor which does not correspond to the society's actual pluralism (Weiler 1996:95–102). In the Court's 2009 ruling on the Lisbon Treaty, a similar understanding of collective identity is put forward in order to oppose a further extension of the EU's power, notably in criminal law. Regarding the latter, the Court reminds us indeed that 'the administration of criminal law depends on cultural processes of previous understanding that are historically grown and also determined by language' (BVerfGE 2009:s.253). It produces a similar argument for education or family law – areas which reflect values supposedly 'rooted in specific historical traditions and experiences' (s.260). More generally, in the Court's view, there should be no extension of the EU's power in 'political decisions that particularly depend on previous understandings as regards culture, history and language' (s.249).

As well as this ethnic understanding of collective identity, the Court's recent rulings are also permeated by concerns that further integration might loosen the relationship between the state and citizens, which is conceived as being exclusive, especially in the areas of criminal law and social security and, more generally, in 'areas which shape the citizens' circumstances of life' (s.249). The Court's concerns relating to developments in criminal law were illustrated in its 2005 ruling on the national law that implemented the EAW framework decision which, in the Court's view, offered insufficient guarantees for the protection of German citizens' fundamental rights in case of extradition. In that case, the Court expressed an 'ill-concealed distrust in the legal systems of other member states as to the safeguarding of the accused person', as it stated, for instance, that the 'trust of German citizens in their own legal order shall be protected' (quoted in Pollicino 2008). More generally, concerns over national identity were evidenced in point 77 of the ruling, stressing the need to 'preserve national identity and statehood in the uniform European legal area'. In its 2009 ruling on the Lisbon Treaty, the Court clearly rejected additional EU influence in 'identity-building' policies that command citizens' loyalty towards the state, such as social policy and education. It argued that 'the essential decisions' in social policy must remain with the member states. The distrustful tone towards EU institutions was explicit here, as the Court observed that 'the Basic Law ... safeguards social tasks for the German state union against supranational demands in a defensive manner' (BVerfGE 2009:s.258).

The primacy principle: an old conflict in new clothes
As has been illustrated, 'constitutional nationalism' can express a form of value-based Euroscepticism that is rooted in an ethnic understanding of collective identity. It can also express a political type of Euroscepticism, illustrated in the defence of national sovereignty against EU law primacy and ECJ authority. While reservations towards the primacy of EU law over national constitutions were already expressed by some constitutional courts in the 1970s, two recent developments have exacerbated (some) courts' concerns in this respect: the increasing authority of the ECJ in police and criminal justice cooperation, and the explicit recognition of the primacy principle in the EU Constitutional Treaty.

In the 1970s, some constitutional courts were already challenging the principle of the primacy of EC law on the grounds that, in the absence of sufficient fundamental rights protection at the EC level, it could violate the fundamental rights of citizens as enshrined in national constitutions. For example, in the 1974 Solange I ruling, the German Constitutional Court made the primacy principle conditional upon its conformity with the fundamental rights entailed in the Basic Law. The Italian Constitutional Court delivered a ruling based on a similar argument in 1973. The fact that these rulings were delivered only a couple of years after the ECJ made its strongest affirmation of the principle of EC law supremacy over national constitutions (the 1970 *Internationale Handelsgesellschaft* ruling) is certainly not a coincidence. In the 1990s, notably in the context of the Maastricht Treaty ratification process, the arguments of national constitutional courts focused more markedly on the issues of sovereignty and transfer of power to the EU, as the 1993 Maastricht ruling of the German Constitutional Court attests. As regards the French Constitutional Court, it clearly acknowledged the primacy of EU law over national legislation in a 2004 ruling, but, according to the Court, this principle does not apply to some constitutional provisions (those which are peculiar to the French constitution). In addition to constitutional courts, some of the highest administrative courts have also been reluctant to recognize the principle of primacy. This is the case, for example, with the French highest administrative court, which resisted recognizing the primacy of EC law over national law until 1989 – a resistance which has been qualified as 'one of the longest-standing cases of national judicial intransigence' (Conant 2002:92).

In the last couple of years, conflicts over the scope of the primacy principle have been heightened by EU-level developments in criminal justice cooperation. While the authority of the ECJ in third pillar issues has long been limited, it has been enhanced by recent institutional reforms. For the first time, the Amsterdam Treaty conferred interpretative powers in third pillar issues on the ECJ. Moreover, recent ECJ case law has raised concerns that the ECJ might use its newly acquired powers in an extensive way. For instance, the 2005 Pupino ruling (relating to the application, by member states, of the 2001 framework decision on the role of victims in criminal proceedings) implied that national courts must interpret framework decisions in a spirit closer to that of directives (Pollicino 2008:1325). This interpretation reduces the leeway of national authorities and courts when implementing and enforcing framework decisions. In fact, this ruling exacerbated existing concerns that policy issues hitherto decided on an intergovernmental basis might be progressively 'communautarized', due to the alleged activism of the ECJ. This is especially true for issues relating to the state's power to sanction and to make decisions about the use of force, both inside and outside its borders. In this respect, the 2005 ruling of the German Constitutional Court on the national law implementing the EAW illustrates some courts' reluctance towards increased integration in third pillar issues. While evoking the strictly intergovernmental character of third pillar issues, the Court stressed, indeed, that cooperation in criminal justice 'does not presuppose general harmonization of the criminal laws of the member states' (quoted in Pollicino 2008:1329). More generally, this debate illustrates a broader concern among segments of the state apparatus that member states might end up losing their monopoly of the use of force. Here again, the 2009 ruling of the German Constitutional Court on the Lisbon Treaty is indicative of EU-wide trends, as the Court warned against further integration in third pillar issues and military defence (ESDP): 'What has always been deemed especially sensitive for the ability of a constitutional state to democratically shape itself are decisions on substantive and formal criminal law, on the disposition of the police monopoly on the use of force towards the interior and of the military monopoly over the use of force towards the exterior' (BVerfGE 2009:s.253). Regarding military interventions in the context of the emerging ESDP, the Court warned against any application of the supranational logic, which would be 'inadmissible in this area' (s.255). The 2008 Irish referendum, where No campaigners argued that Ireland could be forced to commit troops to EU military missions, showed that such concerns are not limited to the Karlsruhe judges.

The other development that raised concerns among some constitutional courts was the institutionalization of the principle of EU law primacy in the EU Constitutional Treaty. Certainly, as already mentioned, the ECJ established the principle of primacy, including primacy over national constitutions, in the 1960s. However, this primacy was neither explicitly stated in EC/EU treaties, nor recognized (as far as primacy over constitutions is concerned) by all constitutional courts. The EU Constitutional Treaty broke with the status quo by including a new article (I-6) that explicitly stated the primacy principle, as highlighted in the ECJ's case law (that is, as also applying to national constitutions). This provision furthered concerns about the development of an EU federal super-state, because it echoed similar provisions in the German and American federal constitutions. Failed referenda in 2005 empowered opponents of an explicit reference to the primacy principle, notably among the British and Dutch governments (Ziller 2007:103). As a consequence, it was decided that the Lisbon Treaty would not include such an article. A reference to the primacy principle, as well as to ECJ case law, was removed from the treaty and placed in a declaration annexed to it.

As regards constitutional courts, the explicit affirmation of primacy in the EU Constitutional Treaty has induced mitigated judgments, notably by the French Constitutional Court. In its 2004 decision on the EU Constitutional Treaty, the Court stated that the national constitution remained the supreme norm within the domestic hierarchy of norms. Its argument relied notably on two articles of the Constitutional Treaty, which have been added to the TEU by the Lisbon Treaty: Article 4 TEU on the need for the Union to respect member states' 'national identities, inherent in their fundamental structures, political and constitutional', and Article 50 TEU on membership termination by a member state, which clearly distinguishes the EU from a federal state (Priollaud and Siritzky 2005:45–6).

For its part, the ruling delivered by the German Constitutional

Court on the Lisbon Treaty, qualified by a German newspaper as 'a declaration of war against the ECJ' (*Der Spiegel* 2009) can be seen as a clear challenge to the authority of the ECJ. While evoking its understanding of the EU as 'an association of sovereign states' and of its own role as gatekeepers of 'constitutional identity', the Karlsruhe judges argued that they would perform, from then on, a double review of EU legislation, comprising an '*ultra vires*' review (to check whether the EU has overstepped its bounds) and an 'identity review' (to check whether the EU's 'legal instruments' respect 'the constitutional identity' of the Basic Law) (Federal Constitutional Court 2009:s.2(e)). In the words of the Court's own president, 'existing anxieties towards European harmonizers (*Gleichmacher*) have erupted' (Papier 2006:1).

Conclusion

National institutions have a complex relationship with the EU. On the one hand, segments of national institutions are increasingly enmeshed in the EU political system. On the other, European integration implies significant challenges for national institutions, by creating strong pressures to adapt, challenging deeply ingrained norms and redistributing power between and within national institutions. In some cases, states tend to react to this situation by limiting the impact of EU law on public policies and administrative practices, thus endangering the uniform application of Union law across the EU.

This becomes even more visible as the integration process touches upon core powers of the state, as is the case with criminal justice cooperation. In this context, even those national institutions that theoretically benefit from European integration – like lower and intermediate courts – can act as gatekeepers of state power by circumscribing the scope of EU-level legislation and cooperation. Moreover, for those institutions which have historically been hostile to the principle of EU law primacy (like some constitutional courts), the acceleration of integration – notably in areas related to the power to sanction and the use of force – exacerbates concerns over a hollowing out of state (and their own) authority. When the authority of the ECJ is challenged, it is, ultimately, the very nature of the EU as a community of law that might be weakened. This is all the more true since recent high-profile ECJ rulings have fanned Euroscepticism in sections of the public and civil society.

Chapter 6

Popular Euroscepticism

Popular Euroscepticism refers to scepticism towards European integration in public opinion. In the mid-1990s, Eurobarometer surveys highlighted an apparent gap between top decision-makers and the general public in terms of attitudes towards the EU: in 1996, the former were twice as supportive (94 per cent) of EU membership as the latter (48 per cent) (Spence 1996). More recently, referenda on major institutional reforms illustrated this gap. Albeit supported by the overwhelming majority of political elites, major treaty changes were rejected by large majorities of electorates in three countries in 2005 and 2008.

However, the mere existence of popular Euroscepticism is debated. First, levels of information about the EU among citizens are quite low. Second, issues that matter most to citizens are dealt with primarily at the domestic level. In 2009, of the six main concerns of citizens, (including macro-economic conditions, employment and public health), only one directly concerned the EU (the fight against inflation, which is the core mission of the ECB) (EB 71:22). Consequently, some observers have argued that there is no public opinion on European integration. It is argued that popular Euroscepticism (as it might be reflected in low levels of support for EU membership, votes for Eurosceptic parties or opposition to further integration during referenda) merely reflects citizens' appraisal of a domestic government's performance, or even a distrust of national elites (Anderson 1998). Early interpretations of European elections (see p.128) and of EU-related referenda (Franklin *et al.* 1995) have defended this thesis. Hence the following question: does popular Euroscepticism exist at all?

As will be argued in this chapter, popular support for European integration must in fact be broken down into several dimensions: support for the general idea of European unification, support for the EU membership of one's country, and finally, support for a tightly integrated, supranational institutional system. As defended on the basis of this distinction, popular Euroscepticism does not, in most cases, equate to principled opposition to the unification of Europe. However, it does reflect scepticism towards EU institutions and policies, as well as concerns over wider evolutions (such as economic globalization and immigration), of which European integration is a catalyst.

The chapter starts by analyzing popular Euroscepticism in the pre-Maastricht period, highlighting the difference between support for western European unification during the Cold War and support for the first concrete stages of integration, in the form of the ECSC and the EEC. It argues that public opinion was always ambiguous towards European integration and that, consequently, the idea of a post-Maastricht Eurosceptic shift must be refined. The following sections address the apparent increase in popular Euroscepticism after the signature of the Maastricht Treaty by proposing several explanations. The second section emphasizes the role of attitudes towards domestic politics, linking Euroscepticism with increasing levels of political cynicism and economic pessimism in the context of a growing malaise affecting representative democracy. The third, fourth and fifth sections emphasize the role of concerns relative to changes in the nature of the EU since Maastricht and in the wider context of integration since the end of the Cold War. In that respect, popular Euroscepticism is indicative of utilitarian concerns over the redistributive impacts of integration and of identity-based concerns, often rooted in exclusive understandings of national identity.

Patterns of support before Maastricht: an ambiguous public opinion

The 'permissive consensus': indifference rather than support

The widespread idea that, before the Maastricht Treaty, public opinion was strongly supportive of European integration often relies on an incorrect interpretation of the famous 'permissive consensus' theory, initially applied to European integration by neo-functionalist authors. In the writings of these authors, the notion of permissive consensus in fact referred to the indifference of public opinion towards European integration, rather than to enthusiastic support for supranational integration (Lindbergh and Scheingold 1970:41). The passivity of the west European public, it was argued, allowed elites to push through their pro-integration agenda, without encountering popular resistance. Writing at the end of De Gaulle's presidency, which had highlighted the permanence of nationalism in one of the EC's founding countries, Ernst Haas defined pro-Europeanism as 'tolerance and unstructured sympathy for a united Europe', or as 'merely a mood, an *ambiance* that remains compatible with the attenuated national consciousness that now prevails' (1968:xxix). The idea of a highly supportive opinion in the early decades of integration must in fact be nuanced. While affective support for the idea of west European unification remained strong throughout the Cold War, support for the first European Communities and for continued EC membership proved less robust and more volatile. What is more, strong affective support for unification did not equate with comparable levels of support for political integration and for strong supranational institutions.

Affective support for the unification of Europe

During the Cold War, support for the unification of western Europe was strong. In 1952, for instance, between 60 and 70 per cent of citizens were in favour of European unification; only a small minority (between 10 and 15 per cent across countries) opposed it (Rabier 1989). Moreover, in the following decades, this support rose in all countries involved in the early stages of European integration, the European Coal and Steel Community (ECSC) and the European Defence Community (EDC). Between the mid-1950s and the mid-1970s, the number of opponents of European unification halved, as large segments of previously sceptical communist voters in France and Italy converged towards the pro-European stance of other voters. Western publics reached almost full convergence by the mid-1970s (Inglehart and Reif 1991:3), the only exception to this trend being British public opinion (Rabier 1989:567). Thus, at the end of the 1980s, average support for unification in EC countries reached 80 per cent (see Figure 6.1).

Support for the early stages of integration

However, from the beginning, support for a country's participation in core projects was often less robust than general support for the unification of Europe. This was already the case for the ECSC and the EDC in the early 1950s. In countries like France and Germany,

FIGURE 6.1 *Support versus opposition in EC/EU countries: EC/EU membership and the unification of Europe, 1953–2009*

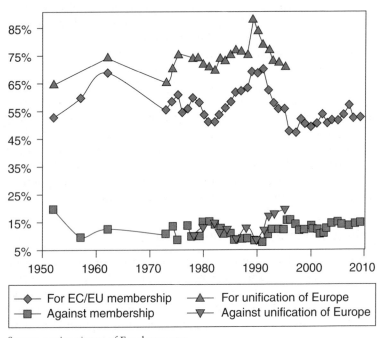

Source: various issues of Eurobarometer.

for instance, popular support for the ECSC was lower than support for the unification of Europe, as larger segments opposed it (roughly one-fifth in France and Germany). This was most clearly the case in Germany, where support for the Schuman plan was 20 percentage points lower than support for the unification of Europe. As regards the EDC, supporters of a common defence certainly outnumbered opponents in all countries, including the UK. Nonetheless, those who were opposed to the EDC were twice as numerous as those who opposed the unification of Europe) (Rabier 1989).

Certainly, a few years later, levels of support for the common market were comparable to support for European unification. In 1957, roughly two-thirds of citizens in the countries concerned supported it, while opponents did not exceed 10 per cent. However, this support must be examined more closely, given the high numbers of undecided (ranging from one-fifth in Germany to one-third in France and Italy) and uninformed citizens (in Germany, for instance, over half of those polled were unaware of their country's participation in the common market) (Rabier 1989; Loth 1989).

Support for EC membership

A similar logic held for support for EC membership. Although high in the early stages of integration, it proved less robust than affective support for the unification of Europe. Certainly, as early as 1962, an average of more than 70 per cent of citizens in the six founding countries supported their country's membership of the EC. This support rose sharply in the 1980s, as net support for membership in the nine EC countries experienced a 30 percentage point increase (Eichenberg and Dalton 2007:129) and as public opinion in the 1973 accession states (including the UK) converged towards the pro-European orientation of the original Six (Evans and Butt 2007:180).

However, this general pattern of strong and rising membership support must be nuanced in several respects. First, levels of information about the EC, what it does and how it works, have always been very low. This was already the case at the beginning of the 1960s, as a poll conducted in the six founding countries showed that less than one-fifth of the general public was well informed about the EC. Second, support for EC membership was more volatile than affective support for unification. It was more affected by periods of recession, as fluctuations in the 1970s indicated. Indeed, during that decade, it experienced relatively large fluctuations in the aftermath of the two oil shocks: a 10 point decline after the first oil shock (1974), and a 15 point decline after the second (1979). Third, even as levels of membership support rose, large numbers of citizens (about one-fifth on average) remained indifferent towards the EC (Janssen 1991; Rabier 1989).

Support for political integration and supranationalism

Finally, political integration enjoyed less popular support than economic integration, while support for supranationalism remained fragile. A majority of Europeans supported the two major steps in economic integration represented by the creation of the common market (see above) and the completion of the internal market (supported by more than half of European citizens at the end of the 1980s (EB 29:28)). However, projects of a political nature, such as a common defence, elicited less support. In that respect, a comparison between popular support for the ECSC and popular support for the EDC is particularly revealing. In 1952, roughly one-third of citizens opposed the creation of a common European defence, while only 15 to 20 per cent opposed the creation of a common market for coal and steel. In addition, contrary to what happened for the ECSC, support for the EDC tended to decline as citizens were informed of the concrete the implications of the project (Rabier 1989).

Moreover, support for deeply integrated, supranational institutions became much less clear-cut once citizens were informed of the potential consequences for national sovereignty. Polls conducted in West Germany before the signature of the Rome treaties, for instance, illustrated this ambivalence. Whereas 75 per cent declared themselves in favour of the United States of Europe, a relative majority thought that the decisions of the future European Parliament affecting Germany should be binding for their country only if the German government agreed to it, and that, in case of conflict between the German Parliament and the European assembly, the former should prevail. Only a quarter of those polled were ready to accept the legitimacy of a European decision that would have been opposed by their national government (Loth 1989).

In a similar vein, support for a European government was lower than general support for the unification of Europe. For instance, at the beginning of the 1980s, the latter reached 80 per cent on average in the EC, while the formation of a European government accountable to the European Parliament was supported by less than half of EC citizens. Moreover, this statement also held for the most pro-European countries. Support for a unified European government was twice as weak as support for the unification of Europe in the Netherlands, for instance (Inglehart and Reif 1991:10).

There never was a permissive consensus in the sense of overwhelming and unconditional public support for a strongly supranational and explicitly political form of integration. Furthermore, viewed within a broad time span, the high and continuously rising levels of support for EC membership in the 1980s appear as an exception rather than a rule. In that respect, changes in the post-Maastricht period relate to two elements: the speed of the decline in membership support, which was 'unprecedented in the history of the Eurobarometer surveys' (Eichenberg and Dalton 2007:131) and the fact that this decline continued after the economic recession of the early 1990s, making public opinion's fluctuations harder to explain.

The Maastricht Treaty: an elite/public opinion gap?

Contrary to what is often assumed, the decline in public support for EC/EU membership started before the debates surrounding the ratification of the Maastricht Treaty. In fact, the decline began in late 1991 as European leaders were negotiating the treaty. Support started declining between autumn 1991 and summer 1992 (Danish referendum), as both specific and affective support decreased in almost all countries (Niedermayer and Sinnott 1995:64). Between these two dates, average net support experienced a 10 point decline. This evolution accelerated in 1991–94, with a 20 point decline in net support and an 18 point decline in membership support between 1991 and 1994 (Eichenberg and Dalton 2007; Gamble 1995). By 1997, net support had dropped to 39 per cent. Overall, it is estimated that the average level of public support in the twelve EC countries that participated in the Maastricht negotiations experienced a 17 percentage point decline during the 1990s (Mair 2007:2) (see Figure 6.1).

In this context, the ratification process of the Maastricht Treaty seemed to highlight the emergence of a gap between public opinion and political elites. While overwhelming majorities in most national parliaments supported the ratification of the treaty, ratification by referendum proved very difficult in Denmark and France, where large segments of undecided voters (roughly one-third in both countries in the summer of 1992) swung against the treaty.

What are the elements of the post-Maastricht context that might account for this evolution? A first type of explanation relates this evolution to changes independent of the integration process. The early 1990s were characterized by rising levels of political cynicism and an economic recession that was harder than those of the 1970s. As the next section argues, this might well have affected popular support for the EU.

Post-Maastricht Euroscepticism: symptom of a national democratic malaise

A commonly-held assumption is that citizens' views on integration simply reflect their degree of satisfaction with incumbent governments and general economic conditions. From this perspective, popular Euroscepticism must be analyzed as a protest-based vote and an expression of the voters' desire to sanction unpopular executives and/or voice their anxiety over economic prospects at the individual and/or collective levels.

In relation to that debate, it is contended that, although European elections and EU referenda often illustrate the relevance of the 'sanction effect', they highlight, above all, how wider forms of political cynicism are projected on to integration, in a context where low trust in national, executive and legislative institutions negatively affects perceptions of EU institutions. In this respect, popular Euroscepticism can be analyzed as a form of political cynicism, rooted first and foremost in a national democratic malaise.

The sanction effect

Whereas day-to-day evaluations of EU membership are not significantly influenced by levels of support for incumbent governments, the sanction effect certainly influences voting behaviours during European elections and EU-related referenda. This is most evident during European elections. During the first direct elections to the EP, the sanction effect was already being played out in eight out of nine countries (Reif and Schmitt 1980). A quarter of a century later, the 2004 European elections confirmed the continuing relevance of the sanction effect, especially in countries where the executives had been in place for a longtime, as was the case, for instance, in the three biggest member states (Perrineau 2005:13).

By the same token, the sanction effect also plays a role during EU-related referenda. This was the case for referenda on the ratification of the Maastricht Treaty, which 'succeeded' where the executive was popular (Ireland) but failed where it was unpopular (Denmark and France, to the extent that approval for the treaty by the French electorate was secured by a very narrow margin). Besides, voters who were dissatisfied with government performance were more likely to vote against ratification than those who were not (Franklin *et al.* 1995). A similar logic applied to recent EU-related referenda. Not only did referenda held by unpopular executives fail (France, the Netherlands), while those organized by popular governments succeeded (Spain, Luxembourg), in all countries, voters from opposition parties were more likely to vote No than voters of incumbent political parties.

Euroscepticism as a protest-based phenomenon

Nonetheless, the analysis must go beyond the sanction effect, by highlighting how anti-elitist attitudes and alienation from politics affect views of the EU. Indeed, decreasing levels of EU membership support since the early 1990s coincide with increasing distrust of political parties in western democracies.

Day-to-day evaluations of the EU (as measured by levels of membership support) depend to a great extent on citizens' attitudes towards politics, specifically on their level of information and on their interest in politics (Inglehart 1977). More crucially, they are highly influenced by their perception of the domestic political system. Indeed, as an individual's sense of disenfranchisement towards politics increases, his/her positive orientation towards European integration tends to decline sharply (Cautrès 2000). Thus, dissatisfaction with politics influences voting behaviours during European elections and EU-related referenda.

First, it affects voter turnout and party choice during European elections. As regards turnout, it has often been argued that relatively low turnout at European elections (as compared to general national elections) confirms the relevance of the 'second order theory'. Indeed, with the exception of countries that apply compulsory voting, average turnout is much higher at national than at EP elections (with mean differences reaching up to 47 and 36 percentage points in Sweden and in the UK over the period 1979–2004) (Steinbrecher and Rattinger 2007:12). Moreover, EP elections are much more strongly affected by declining turnout levels than national elections (see Figure 6.2). However, low turnout at EP elections cannot be explained by the 'second order theory' alone. It is also an expression of dissatisfaction with politics. Indeed, dissatisfaction with politics was the first spontaneous response of non-voters when asked about their reasons for not participating in the 2004 European elections (FEB 162:17). As far as party choice is concerned, protest-based parties often display good electoral results at European elections (for instance, they accounted for 15 per cent of the votes in the 2004 European elections). Indeed, some of the most radical, non-mainstream parties in Europe experienced their first electoral breakthrough in European elections, as was the case for the extreme right (for instance, the French National Front in 1984 and the Belgian Vlaams Blok in 1989). The French case is particularly revealing in this respect, as the score of protest-based

FIGURE 6.2   *Evolution of turnout for EP elections (EU average), 1979–2009*

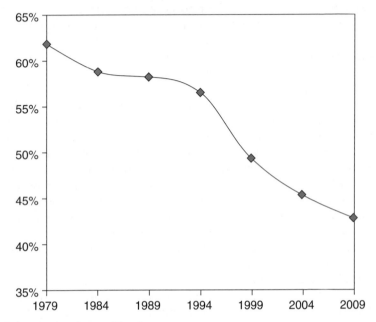

Source: various issues of Eurobarometer.

parties from the radical right and radical left amounted to 40 per cent in 1994 and 1999 and 30 per cent in the 2004 European elections (Perrineau 2005:15).

In the same vein, the 2005 and 2008 referenda highlighted the overlap between the electorate of protest-based parties and the Eurosceptic vote (see Table 6.1). In all countries, the proportion of No voters was highest among the electorates of anti-establishment parties (Aarts and van der Kolk 2006; Perrineau 2005; Milward Brown 2008). In France and the Netherlands especially, the 2005 referenda coincided with long-term trends such as the rise of protest-based politics. This was highlighted by the high electoral scores of extreme-right, anti-European parties in the French 2002 presidential elections (about 20 per cent of the vote in the first round) and in the Dutch national elections that same year (17 per cent for the Pim Fortuyn List), whose electorates are characterized by a strong cynicism towards the political system.

TABLE 6.1 Shares of No voters among parties' electorates during EU referenda

Party proximity	France (2005)	Netherlands (2005)	Luxembourg (2005)	Spain (2005)	Ireland (2008)
Mainstream right	20% (UMP) 24% (UDF)	47% (CDA)	21% (CSV-PCS)	19% (PP)	40% (FF) 49% (FG)
Mainstream left	56% (PS)	63% (PvdA)	49% (LSAP-POL)	4% (PSOE)	55% (LP)
Liberals		51% (VVD)	42% (DP-PD)		
Greens	61% (les Verts)	45% (Groen Links)	49% (DG)		57% (GP)
Radical right	95% (FN + MNR)	86% (LPF)	77% (ADR)		
Communist and radical left	98% (PCF) 94% (rad. Left)	87% (SP)	86% (DL)	61% (IU)	
Religious parties		75% (CU) 100% (SGP)			
Moderate nationalists				19% (CiU) 57% (PNV)	
Pro-independence nationalist parties				87% (ERC) 61% (EA) 77% (BNG)	95% (SF)

Sources: data from Eurobarometer surveys; Perrineau 2005; Aaarts and van der Kolk 2006.

Lack of trust in national institutions

Furthermore, popular Euroscepticism is closely correlated with broader attitudes towards the institutions of representative democracy. In this respect, scepticism is actually widespread in the EU. In 2009, only 32 per cent of EU citizens trusted their national government and their national parliament (EB 71:73–4). However, higher levels of trust in the European Commission and the EP (with 44 per cent and 48 per cent respectively) are little cause for comfort for EU institutions. Indeed, lack of trust in national elected institutions has been identified as one of the most powerful variables underlying perceptions of the EU.

Low trust in national institutions diminishes trust in EU institutions, which in turn is conducive to lower levels of support for EU membership (McLaren 2006:249). This factor clearly played a role in the 2005 and 2008 referenda. In the Netherlands, for instance, the degree of trust in national institutions (notably Parliament) has been found to be the most significant variable underlying voting behaviours, ahead of identity-related factors (Lubbers 2008). In the Irish case, the referendum unfolded in a context of growing malaise towards the political establishment, which shed suspicion on the pro-treaty position advocated by the three main political parties (Milward Brown 2008).

In addition, sceptical evaluations of democracy negatively influence perceptions of European integration (Grunberg and Schweisguth 2002) and of core policies of the EU, such as EMU (Gabel and Hix 2005). Those citizens who are dissatisfied with the way democracy works in their own country are more likely to oppose further integration or the common currency. The French referendum, for example, confirmed this correlation. Voters who thought democracy was not working well in France were more likely to vote No than others (Cautrès 2005:148).

Economic pessimism

The impact of this political cynicism can be compounded by economic pessimism. Indeed, it has long been argued that popular support for integration was linked to perceptions of macroeconomic conditions (in terms of growth, employment rate and price stability). In fact, the aftermath of the Maastricht Treaty coincided with the economic recession affecting EU countries, albeit to different rhythms, from 1991 on. Starting in 1990–91 in the UK, and in 1993 in other EU countries, this recession was worse than those of the 1970s, with a bigger GDP contraction and a stronger rise in unemployment. It was compounded, in the UK and Germany respectively, by the 1992 crisis of the European Monetary System and by the costs of reunification. Between 1991 and 1994, there was a clear chronological parallelism between the exacerbation of the economic crisis and the decline in popular support for EU membership (Gamble 1995).

Recent EU-related referenda corroborate this thesis. No voters in all countries were characterized by comparatively high levels of socio-economic pessimism. For instance, in France, a pre-referendum survey showed that, among those who intended to vote No, 75 per cent were concerned about the evolution of their standard of living, a share that was halved among those who intended to vote Yes (Brouard and Sauger 2005:129). In Ireland, a general feeling of pessimism about present and short-term economic prospects, in a context of declining consumer confidence and a tightening job market, significantly contributed to the No vote (Milward and Brown 2008:12).

The filters of domestic politics and macroeconomic conditions thus certainly play a role in popular Euroscepticism, through the interplay between evaluations of domestic political systems, trust in national institutions, and perceptions of the EU. However, popular Euroscepticism also has to do with the EU as such. For instance, the fact that voters tend to sanction the incumbent government in European elections is also indicative of their attitudes towards the EU. Indeed, those voters who think that integration goes too fast are more likely to sanction incumbent governments than those who do not (Schmitt 2004). In a similar vein, in recent EU referenda, the desire to sanction incumbent parties was clearly second to other factors, such as concerns over employment in France (Brouard and Sauger 2005), and distrust of Parliament coupled with concerns over national identity in the Netherlands (Lubbers 2008). Indeed, as the following sections make clear, evaluations of the EU *per se*, of its current direction and its core policies, are crucial dimensions of popular Euroscepticism.

Utilitarian scepticism and concerns over the redistributive consequences of integration

To begin with, popular Euroscepticism expresses concerns over the socio-economic consequences of integration. In that respect, what has changed in the post-Maastricht era is the way integration is perceived to influence an individual's and a country's economic situation and prospects. Previously, attitudes towards the EC were influenced by general perceptions of macro-economic conditions, but the EC was thought to be neutral as far as the allocation of resources between countries and individuals was concerned. With the implementation of EMU and the EU enlargement to poorer countries, the EU is increasingly perceived as influencing the allocation of resources between individuals and countries (Eichenberg and Dalton 2007:132).

This seems to corroborate utilitarian accounts of popular Euroscepticism. The core assumption of the utilitarian theory is, indeed, that people's views of the EU depend on a cost/benefit analysis of the socio-economic consequences of integration for them and for their country as a whole. This cost/gains analysis exerts a strong influence on attitudes towards EU membership, EU institutions and the Europeanization of specific policies (McLaren 2007:244).

In assessing the relevance of this theory, this section identifies factors that might explain the more negative appraisals of the EU in the post-Maastricht era and shows how the utilitarian theory accounts for differentiated levels of Euroscepticism across social groups. It argues that, contrary to utilitarian assumptions, recent EU referenda suggest that Eurosceptic attitudes tend to spread beyond the most economically fragile strata of society and point to a widening of the socio-economic basis of popular Euroscepticism.

Post-Maastricht utilitarian scepticism

To begin with, it can be hypothesized that the economic recession of the early 1990s led to a more critical appraisal of the benefits derived from integration. The immediate aftermath of the signature of the Maastricht Treaty is characterized by a clear decline in utilitarian support for the EU. Indeed, between 1991 and 1994, the number of citizens who thought that their country had benefited from EU membership experienced an almost 20 per cent decline (Gamble 1995).

This more negative appraisal of the benefits of integration against the background of economic recession might have been compounded by the progressive implementation of EMU criteria (notably implying reduced public spending), precisely at the time when EU countries were affected by the crisis. That this activated public concerns over the socio-economic consequences of integration was highlighted by the fact that, from 1989 until the early 2000s, the policy areas where preferences for further integration declined most were monetary policy, public health and social security (Eichenberg and Dalton 2007:142). The latter are tightly associated with the welfare state, which suggests that economic and monetary integration raised fears about a possible erosion of national welfare states.

Nonetheless, these concerns are not evenly distributed across socio-economic groups. Indeed, this more negative appraisal of the benefits of integration clearly distinguishes average citizens from top decision-makers. By the mid-1990s, the former were twice as unlikely as the latter to have a positive evaluation of their country's membership of the EU. The utilitarian theory seeks to explain this gap.

Eurosceptic citizens: 'losers' of globalization?

According to this theory, those citizens who are supposed to benefit the least from the opportunities created by the internal market (increased mobility, free circulation of capital, etc.) are more likely to be sceptical towards integration. This presupposes that those who do not possess the necessary skills and/or resources (e.g. capital) allowing them to benefit from these opportunities are more likely to be sceptical towards the EU. In the early 1990s, the prospect of the single market, although welcomed by a majority of Europeans, was already raising fears among significant segments of voters. In 1991, it was associated with fear by more than a third of citizens in France and Germany, and by a quarter in the UK (EB 36:24). Today, Eurobarometer surveys highlight an average 20 point difference in levels of membership support between the better educated and/or skilled (who are more supportive) and those who are less educated and/or less skilled (who are less supportive).

In this respect, the socio-economic profile of the average No voter in recent referenda has corroborated the assumptions of the utilitarian theory. In each country, manual workers and less educated citizens were over-represented among No voters (see Table 6.2). For instance, the difference between workers and managers in terms of the share of No voters in those categories represented a 40 point gap in France (Perrineau 2005:243) and in Ireland. Workers' voting behaviour also departed significantly from the national average, with

TABLE 6.2   *Socio-demographic factors and voting behaviour during EU referenda**

Socio-demographic variables	Percentage of No voters in corresponding category	Percentage of No voters – national average
Education (ceased at the age of 15 or younger)		
France	67%	54.7%
Netherlands	67%	61.6%
Luxembourg	49%	42%
Ireland	58%	53%
Spain	11%	17%
Sweden	67%	56%
Occupation (manual workers)		
France	66%	54.7%
Netherlands	78%	61.6%
Luxembourg	67%	42%
Ireland	74%	53%
Spain	26%	17%
Sweden	70%	56%
Age (18–24 years old)		
France	59%	54.7%
Netherlands	74%	61.6%
Luxembourg	62%	42%
Ireland	65%	53%
Spain	38%	17%
Sweden	60%	56%

*   The 2005 referenda for France, the Netherlands, Luxembourg and Spain; the 2008 referendum for Ireland; the 2003 referendum for Sweden.

Source: various issues of Eurobarometer.

a difference of 15 to 20 percentage points in every country. A similar, albeit clearly smaller, difference is to be found between the share of No voters among the less educated and the most educated, with a 10 to 15 point difference in each country. By the same token, the vote on the EU Constitutional Treaty also crystallized cleavages in terms of income. In France, for instance, the No vote was highest in the less affluent municipalities (Laurent and Sauger 2005:101).

In addition, utilitarian assumptions might also explain the gender dimension of popular Euroscepticism and the over-representation of Eurosceptic orientations among women. In terms of membership support, Eurobarometer surveys usually indicate a 10 point difference between male and female respondents, with the latter being less supportive of membership. Although this gender gap was not apparent in the Dutch and French referenda in 2005, other EU-related referenda have highlighted its relevance, especially the 1994 accession referenda (in the four countries concerned, support for EU accession was roughly 10 points lower among women (Kaiser 1995:7)), the 2001 Irish referendum on the Nice Treaty (Sinnott 2001:20) and the 2003 Swedish referendum on the Euro (FEB 149:11). Although the utilitarian theory does not capture all dimensions of female Euroscepticism, it partly explains it. Indeed, not only do women tend to be over-represented in lower skilled, lower paid and/or precarious jobs (and in low-skill jobs in the public sector), they also display higher levels of economic pessimism than men and are more likely to doubt their ability to adapt to an increasingly competitive environment (Nelsen and Guth 2000:281). Consequently, they might be more prone to utilitarian Euroscepticism than men.

A widening of the social basis of popular Euroscepticism

However, this first look at the sociological profile of Eurosceptic voters should not obscure the fact that the No/Yes cleavage in recent referenda did not simply overlap a cleavage between integration's 'winners' and 'losers'. Several elements can be put forward to substantiate that point, especially in the Dutch and French cases.

To begin with, the No vote reached into the middle classes in both countries. In the Netherlands, for instance, albeit more marked in the workers' category, the No vote reached nearly two-thirds among the self-employed (EB 172:11). Furthermore, socio-economic concerns were quite evenly distributed among the electorate, so they did not distinguish the No voters from the others (Lubbers 2008). In France, several studies have pointed to the widening of the socio-economic basis of the No vote, when compared with the referendum on the Maastricht Treaty in 1992. In 2005, the No vote reached into sections of the electorate (mainly middle-class voters) who are traditionally in favour of European integration, especially civil servants (64 per cent of No votes, with a

15 point increase over 1992) and employees (60 per cent of No votes, which represented a 11 point increase since 1992) (Cautrès 2005:154).

To continue, the 2005 and 2008 referenda show that the Eurosceptic voting behaviour of the less educated voters does not distinguish them so clearly from the electorate as a whole. Indeed, in each country, there was only about a 5 point difference between the share of No voters among the less educated and the share of No voters in the electorate as a whole. The French case, for example, illustrates to what extent the No vote reached the more educated segments of the electorate. Compared with 1992, it increased significantly among the better educated groups: a 20 point increase among those who graduated from high school and, more surprisingly from a utilitarian perspective, a 14 point increase among those holding university-level degrees (Perrineau 2005:242–3).

In the same vein, as explained below, the over-representation of younger voters (including students) among No voters seriously nuances the utilitarian thesis (see Table 6.2). Indeed, according to this theory, students should be among the groups that are most supportive of European integration. However, in Ireland, for instance, 72 per cent of students voted against the Lisbon Treaty (FEB 245:6). This seems to confirm previous findings that, contrary to widespread assumptions, student status is not necessarily conducive to strong support for integration (Nelsen and Guth 2003:101).

Finally, socio-economic concerns linked to European integration have been exacerbated by two interlinked developments: EU enlargement to poorer countries (in the wake of the 2004 and 2007 accessions) and economic globalization.

Concerns over EU enlargement

There are three types of socio-economic fears linked to EU enlargement: fears of increased competition for domestic labour markets, concerns over reduced comparative advantages for one's country, and concerns over the redistributive consequences of a new country's accession to the EU. Recent EU referenda have highlighted the relevance of these concerns among many No voters.

The first type of fear was predominant in France and Luxembourg, where debates over EU legislation aimed at completing the internal market (the Services directive) raised concerns over the possible competition from temporarily seconded workers from the new member states and over a race-to-the-bottom affecting working conditions and wages. As mentioned previously, concerns over the possible impact of further integration on employment was the main motivation of No voters in both countries. Even in the Netherlands, where employment was not a major issue in the campaign, more than 90 per cent of the electorate thought that, as a consequence of enlargement, 'jobs would be relocated to countries where production is cheaper' (Aarts and van der Kolk 2006:245).

These concerns were exacerbated, in 2007 and 2008, by a series of rulings by the ECJ aimed at securing the principle of the free circulation of services in the internal market (see p.230). In this context, the referenda illustrated many citizens' scepticism about the ability of the EU to secure workers' and trade unions' rights. In France, for instance, roughly 80 per cent of No voters thought that the EU did not secure social rights (Brouard and Sauger 2005:134). Similarly, in Ireland, 43 per cent thought that the Lisbon Treaty did not secure workers' rights (poll published in the *Sunday Business Post*, 29 June 2008).

In addition, the accession of new countries also raises concerns over reduced comparative advantages for the economies of old member states. Such concerns were very present during the campaign preceding the first Irish referendum on the Nice Treaty, as it was feared that Ireland's low corporation tax rate would have to compete with lower rates in some of the new member states. Similarly, the concern that further integration (tax harmonization) and/or enlargement might end Ireland's comparative advantage, as well as the desire to protect the national tax system, ranked sixth among the motivations of Irish No voters in 2008 (FEB 245:8). Moreover, enlargement crystallizes fears over its redistributive consequences: for the country's status in terms of EU budget contribution and for the subsidies it receives from the EU. For instance, the issue of national contribution to the EU budget played a significant role in the Netherlands in 2005. The belief that EU membership was too expensive ranked fourth in the motivations of No voters (FEB 172:15).

Scepticism towards trade liberalization

Finally, the socio-economic dimension of popular Euroscepticism is closely correlated with perceptions of global processes of trade liberalization. A year before the Irish referendum on the Lisbon Treaty, for instance, studies had shown that a majority of Irish citizens (52 per cent) perceived globalization as a threat to employment (Kennedy and Sinnott 2007). Those who feared globalization were more likely to assess Ireland's EU membership negatively than those who had a positive perception of this phenomenon. In France, two years after the 2005 referendum, a poll showed that 72 per cent of citizens perceived globalization as a threat rather than as an opportunity (poll published in *Le Monde*, 22 November 2007). These studies certainly do not point to a clearly discernible correlation between citizens' views of globalization and their vote on specific EU treaties. Indeed, attitudes towards globalization influence opinions on EU membership rather than opinions on a European constitution (Kennedy and Sinnott 2007:74). However, it is obvious that recent referenda unfolded in a context where significant segments of electorates were anxious about the implications of globalization.

In parallel with the increasing role of concerns of a distributive nature in shaping orientations towards integration, the post-Maastricht era is also characterized by the increasing relevance of identity-related variables.

Identity-related concerns

Recent EU referenda have illustrated the significance of identity-related concerns as one of the core dimensions of popular Euroscepticim. In the Netherlands and Ireland, for instance, the concern that further integration might erode national identity was the second key motivation of No voters (after a lack of understanding of the treaties). It remains to be seen, however, which specific dimensions of national identity are thought to be affected by European integration.

As shown below, some identity-based concerns are directly related to developments in European integration, namely the extension of EU power in identity-related policy areas and individual countries' decreasing ability to influence EU decision-making. At the same time, other identity-related concerns, such as those related to Turkey's EU accession, are linked to global social trends (such as immigration and increasing religious pluralism) for which European integration is a catalyst.

Decreasing support for the Europeanization of identity-related policies

The analysis of domestic public debates on European integration (see pp.52–4) has highlighted the fact that, since the second half of the 1980s, the extension of the EU's activities in fields such as culture and audiovisual services has triggered growing contestations at national level. This was compounded by some of the provisions of the Maastricht Treaty, such as EU citizenship.

This evolution of public debate was mirrored in the evolution of public opinion in the post-Maastricht era. Together with policy domains linked to the welfare state, policies linked to national identity (such as education, culture, and the regulation of audiovisual services) are those that experienced the strongest decline in support for further integration from 1991 on. These policy fields (especially education) were those where net support for an extension of the EU's influence was the weakest between 1989 and 2002 (Eichenberg and Dalton 2007).

Such reluctance towards a possible increase of EU authority in those fields is matched by parallel concerns over the ability of one's country to influence EU decision-making, and notably fears of being overruled in a number of identity-related issues.

National sovereignty and representation in the EU

The scepticism discussed above is strongest in smaller member states, where enlargement conjures up perceptions of being marginalized. This largely explains why concerns over a loss of national sovereignty ranked second in the motivations of No voters in the Irish (2001 and 2008) and Dutch referenda. In the first Irish referendum on the Nice Treaty, scepticism as to the fair representation of small countries in the EU and dissatisfaction with the way decisions are made at the EU level have already been identified as the most significant variables underlying the No vote (Sinnott 2001:5). Similarly, shortly before the 2005 referendum in the Netherlands, 83 per cent thought that small member states would lose influence as a consequence of further integration (Aarts and van der Kolk 2006:245). Not only reduced voting power in the Council, but also the prospect of losing a Commissioner in the College of the Commission crystallized such fears, as was the case in Ireland, where, in 2008, this concern ranked fifth in the motivations of No voters (FEB 245:8).

Further enlargement and Turkey's EU accession

Anxieties over the evolution of national representation in the EU are also exacerbated by the prospect of Turkish accession to the EU. This issue crystallizes some of the fears linked to enlargement in general, but also, to a significant extent, fears related to identity and culture. In this respect, opposition to the possible accession of Turkey to the EU lay beneath some of the Euroscepticism that came to the fore during the 2005 referenda.

To begin with, these referenda unfolded, in some countries, in a context of overwhelming opposition to possible Turkish accession. In France and Luxembourg, for instance, such opposition reached more than two-thirds (EB 63:162). In the Netherlands, this issue was one of the focal points of the referendum campaign (Aarts and Van der Kolk 2006:245). Opposition to Turkish accession influenced the voting behavior of sections of No voters. This was most evident in Luxembourg, where it was mentioned by 16 per cent of No voters as being key to their vote (FEB 173:12). In France and the Netherlands, it played a similar role for some conservative and Christian Democrat voters (voters of parties whose leaderships were divided on that issue). In France, out of the 20 per cent of conservative and centre-right voters (UMP and UDF) who voted No, 16 per cent did so to express their opposition to Turkey's admission to the EU (FEB 171:18). In the Netherlands, it was the case for 10 per cent of the voters of the liberal-conservative VVD who voted No (FEB 172:16). This hints at a possible future disaffection with an EU enlarged to Turkey among segments of conservative voters.

Moreover, the issue of Turkish membership sheds some light on the role of religion in shaping attitudes towards European integration. It has long been shown that mainstream faith and religious practice, especially among Catholics, are positively correlated with support for European integration, whereas atheism predisposes towards Euroscepticism (Nelsen and Guth 2003:99). The 2005 French referendum, for instance, confirmed the continuing relevance of this correlation. There was a 12 point difference in levels of support for the treaty between those who identified themselves as Catholics and those who identified themselves as atheists. However, the issue of Turkish membership blurs the correlation between Catholicism and pro-Europeanism, as Catholics are especially opposed to Turkish membership (73 per cent oppose it, compared with 63 per cent for the national average). This stands in sharp

contrast to French Muslims, of whom only 30 per cent are opposed
to Turkish accession, a fact that might explain the relatively strong
endorsement of the Constitutional Treaty by practising Muslims (60
per cent) (Brouard and Tiberj 2005). Hence, the prospect of a possible Turkish accession might foster identification with the EU among
some groups of citizens (for example, French practising Muslims)
and erode that same identification among segments of traditionally
pro-European groups (such as Catholics, Christian Democrat and
centre-right voters). The relevance of the issue of Turkey's EU accession in recent referenda must be seen in a wider context, where
public discussion on European integration at national level coincides with increasingly polarized debates on immigration, religious
pluralism and multiculturalism.

Immigration and multiculturalism

There are two ways to analyze links between attitudes towards
immigration and perceptions of European integration. First, hostility towards immigration can be analyzed as one element in a
broader value system (together with hostility towards minorities)
that predisposes to Euroscepticism (the post-Materalism theory; see
p.252). Second, hostility towards immigration can easily lead to
hostility towards European integration, as the latter is associated
with increased immigration (the free circulation of people across
borders), reduced room for manoeuvre for national policies on
immigration (as immigration policy is progressively being communautarized), and the empowerment of minorities (see EU legislation
on non-discrimination).

Since the end of the 1990s, orientations towards immigration
have been identified as an especially relevant variable influencing
support for EU membership (Cautrès and Denni 2000; McLaren
2002) and voting behaviour during EU-related referenda (De Vreese
and Boomgarden 2005; Jupille and Leblang 2007). Whatever the
country context, as hostility towards immigration increases, so does
the likelihood of Euroscepticism. This was confirmed by recent EU-
related referenda, as No voters were largely over-represented among
those segments of the electorate who display the most negative
views of immigration and multiculturalism. In France, for instance,
67 per cent of voters who thought that 'there are too many foreign-
ers in France' rejected the EU Constitutional Treaty, compared with
54 per cent for the electorate as a whole (Perrineau 2005:241). In

the Netherlands, concerns over a possible cultural threat to the Dutch way of life was identified as one of the main factors underlying the No vote, especially among those who perceive ethnic minorities as a threat (Lubbers 2008). A similar correlation was identified in Ireland in 2008, where No voters displayed a more negative perception of the impact of immigration on Irish society than Yes voters (Milward Brown 2008:21). Furthermore, anti-immigration feelings predispose to hostility towards Turkey's admission to the EU. In France in 2005, support for Turkey's admission reached only 11 per cent among those who thought that 'there are too many immigrants in France', while it was five times higher among those who strongly reject that statement (Brouard and Tiberj 2005).

Moreover, increasingly polarized public debates on immigration tend to spill over into debates on European integration. In Denmark (2000) and the Netherlands (2005), for instance, EU referenda coincided with the emergence of a strongly polarized discussion on previous liberal immigration policies and multiculturalism. Especially in smaller member states, the extension of QMV at EU level creates fears of being overruled on highly sensitive issues, especially immigration policy. This is compounded by what is often seen as illegitimate EU interference in domestic debates on immigration. For instance, during the Danish referendum on EMU in 2000, EU-level criticism against the Danish government's plans to tighten immigration policy reinforced some voters' determination to vote against further involvement in the EU (Bering 2001:72).

These identity-related concerns might have given rise to perceptions of a more tense relationship between specific understandings of national identity and European identity, fostering the feeling, among some citizens, that national identity and identification with Europe are mutually exclusive.

Exclusive understandings of national identity

Is popular Euroscepticism a form of nationalism? A common-sense view is that popular Euroscepticism does not illustrate principled opposition towards integration. Relatively high levels of support for continuing EU membership in most countries (including those where recent treaty reforms were defeated by referendum) are put forward as evidence of this. Indeed, in 2008, citizens supporting EU membership outnumbered those who did not in all countries (EB 68:71). However, several elements point to the existence of principled opposition to integration among a significant segment of Eurosceptic citizens, which is rooted in a lack of identification with Europe and an exclusive sense of national identity.

Exclusive national identity

It has long been held that European integration would facilitate the emergence of multi-level identities among European citizens, as the latter would increasingly be able to accomodate diverse (regional, national, European) and mutually inclusive identities. European integration would give rise to a liberal, banal form of nationalism, compatible with an ever-closer union. However, it was also pointed out that, to the extent that pro-European elites have been able to convince public opinion of the benefits of unification, they did so by presenting European integration as a tool for the projection of national values (Banchoff 1999:184). Thus, popular endorsement of European integration was won over, to a large extent, on false premises. This holds especially for the principle of supranationalism, which, ultimately, presupposes that citizens prioritize their European identity over their national identity in the case of conflict between the two (Weiler 1996). As deeper integration progressively illustrated the implications of a closer union for national identity, this sense of compatibility between national and European identites might have started to erode.

First of all, the number of citizens who often or sometimes feel European has not increased over the years. Today, as in the early 1980s, a relative majority of 43 per cent never feel European, while a large minority of 41 per cent consider themselves exclusively as national (EB 62:96). In the case of France and Germany, it was even argued that the number of citizens displaying multiple identities declined in the course of the 1990s, with a slight decrease in France and a strong decline in Germany (Schild 2001:337).

Even among those citizens who see themselves exclusively as national, a majority does not want their country to withdraw from the EU. Indeed, it was estimated that, among the one-third of EU citizens who have reservations towards the EU, roughly 15 pe cent might be described as hard Eurosceptics who do not feel attached to Europe, who see themselves exclusively as national and wish either a pause or a complete halt to European integration (Wessels 2007:304). This percentage corresponds roughly to the proportion of strongly Eurosceptic and/or anti-European representatives in the

European Parliament (see p.129). However, even citizens identifying themselves both as national and European would tend to give precedence to their national identity over their European identity, in the case of a perceived conflict between the two. Moreover, senses of exclusive national identity can be easily activated in contexts where debates on EU issues are strongly polarized and when political elites appear to be divided.

Exclusive national identity clearly influences citizens' views on integration. It directly and negatively affects support for EU membership and support for further integration. Indeed, those who feel attached only to their nation are more likely than others to perceive EU membership negatively. They are also more likely to oppose further steps in integration (McLaren 2007:248), be it through institutional reforms or through the Europeanization of specific policy sectors (for a case study on immigration policy, see Luedtke 2005).

Concerning European elections, identity-based analyses tend to nuance the long dominant assumption that low turnout is simply a confirmation of the relevance of the second order theory. Indeed, as the lack of identification with Europe decreases, so does participation. Non-voters in the 2004 European elections, for instance, displayed lower levels of attachment and identification to Europe than those who voted: 77 per cent and 74 per cent of the latter felt attached to Europe and would identify themselves as a citizen of the EU, compared with 63 per cent and 59 per cent for the former (FEB 162:47). The correlation between exclusive national identity and Euroscepticism was also illustrated by recent referenda. In 2005, 63 per cent of French No voters thought that preserving national sovereignty (as opposed to extending EU powers) was the best way to cope with global challenges (Brouard and Sauger 2005:136).

Lack of attachment to 'Europe'

The widespread idea that popular Euroscepticism does not reflect principled opposition to European integration and simply expresses the wish of many for 'another Europe' must also be refined in view of the significant numbers of citizens who simply display no attachment to 'Europe'. The aftermath of the Maastricht Treaty coincided with the end of the Cold War, which brought about, for the first time, a clear decline of support for the unification of Europe among west Europeans (see Figure 6.1, p.164). Moreover, even if, today, a

FIGURE 6.3   *Percentage of citizens indifferent to the idea of scrapping the EC/EU by country, 1983–2003*

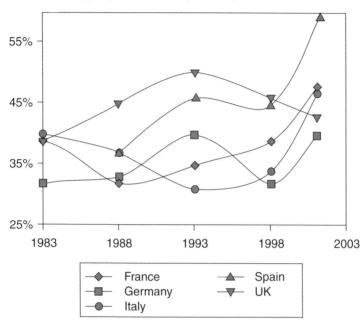

Source: various issues of Eurobarometer.

majority of citizens feel attached to the EU, the 1990s registered a decrease in the number of those who would feel very sorry if the EU was scrapped. Parallel to this, the number of those who would feel indifferent – which has always been quite high – increased, especially in largely Europhile countries (such as Belgium, Germany or Spain); in 2001, they represented a relative majority of 45 per cent (see Figure 6.3).

Recent referenda have also attested to the relevance of this dimension of Euroscepticism. Even in countries where social fears were predominant among No voters, a substantial segment of the latter displayed low levels of attachment to Europe. In France, shortly before the 2005 referendum, more than 80 per cent of those who intended to vote No displayed low levels of attachment to European integration. Only one-third of them could be described as Europhile in the sense that, albeit rejecting the treaty, they were attached to Europe and favoured an extension of the EU powers in order to cope with global challenges (Brouard and Sauger 2005:136).

These referenda also highlighted relatively low levels of attachment to Europe among large segments of young voters. First, these voters were overrepresented among No voters in all countries (see Table 6.2, p. 176). Indeed, the youngest age group (18–24) registered the highest number of No voters in Spain, Luxembourg and the Netherlands; it ranked second in France and in Ireland. Second, in three countries (France, Ireland and the Netherlands), a significant segment of younger voters displayed either comparatively low levels of attachment towards the EU or even principled opposition to integration. In France, at the time of the referendum, only 16 per cent of the youngest age group said they felt very attached to European integration, a share that doubled amongst the oldest age group (Brouard and Tiberj 2005). In the Netherlands, opposition to European integration as such was quoted by 16 per cent of the youngest No voters as being key to their vote. This clearly distinguished them from all other age groups, where such a motivation barely exceeded 8 per cent (FEB 172:16).

Distrust of EU institutions

Finally, exclusive national identity, together with distrust of national institutions, strongly predisposes to distrust of EU institutions (McLaren 2007). For instance, Dutch voters fearing that the EU might threaten national identity were more likely than others to distrust national and EU institutions (Lubbers 2008). This distrust, in turn, exercises a strong independent effect on attitudes towards integration.

First of all, a lack of trust in EU institutions decreases support for EU membership (McLaren 2007:249; Kennedy and Sinnott 2007:72). In this respect, there seems to be a link between the number of EU institutions that people trust and their support for membership. The fewer EU institutions they trust, the less they tend to support membership. Furthermore, this variable also affects participation in European elections. Indeed, those who abstained in the last European elections distrust EU institutions much more markedly than those who participated in the vote. Only 39 per cent of abstainers trust EU institutions, whereas 55 per cent of voters do so (FEB 162:47). Furthermore, lack of trust was a key aspect of the

No vote during recent referenda. In the Netherlands, perceptions of the EU as a threat to national identity, coupled with distrust in national *and* European institutions, have been identified as the most important variables underlying the rejection of the EU Constitutional Treaty (Lubbers 2008). In Ireland, two years before the rejection of the Lisbon Treaty, people's understanding of national identity and their perception of EU institutions were identified as the two most influential variables shaping their views on a European constitution. Those who saw themselves as exclusively Irish, as well as those who distrusted EU institutions, were more likely to oppose the adoption of a European constitution (Kennedy and Sinnott 2006:73–4).

This highlights the fact that scepticism towards EU institutions (not just scepticism towards national institutions) is a significant dimension of popular Euroscepticism. It has been shown, for instance, that support for further integration depends as much on citizens' utilitarian evaluation of the internal market as on their perception of the ability of EU institutions to represent them (Rohrschneider 2002). This variable plays a role during European elections, as non-voters are more likely than voters to have a negative perception of the EP's responsiveness to citizens' concerns. Indeed, in the 2004 European elections, only 39 per cent of non-voters thought that the EP took the concerns of European citizens into consideration, compared with 51 per cent of those who turned out to the polls (FEB 162:47).

Conclusion

The fact that a majority of citizens currently support their country's membership of the EU should not obscure two facts. First, popular Euroscepticism cannot be dismissed as a non-issue that merely expresses dissatisfaction with incumbent governments. On the contrary, it expresses a quite widespread malaise towards representative democracy at the national level. Moreover, it is underpinned, to a large extent, by precise concerns linked to current developments in the integration process. Second, a substantial segment of Eurosceptic citizens displays forms of principled opposition to European integration (hard Euroscepticism) or relatively low levels of attachment to the EU, notably among the youngest voters.

Today, as in the early decades of European integration, public opinion towards the EC/EU can be broken into three broad categories: a majority who are supportive of the unification of Europe in general but who are not well informed about its concrete implications; a large minority (about one-fifth) who are undecided and a small minority (between 10 and 15 per cent) who are principally opposed.

However, compared with the early decades of integration, when principled support for the unification of Europe was strong and on the rise, one element in recent EU-related referenda might point to a possible erosion of affective support for further integration: the declining role of general orientations towards the EU in the voting behaviour of the youngest voters. Indeed, recent EU referenda show that affective orientations towards integration have been less relevant for younger voters than for older voters as they cast their votes on major treaty reforms. In Luxembourg and Spain, for instance, general affective orientations towards the EU were less significant for younger voters than other factors, such as their opinion on the Constitutional Treaty, whereas a majority of older voters voted according to their general stance towards integration. A similar difference was observed in Sweden in 2003 where, unlike a large majority of voters, the youngest age group mentioned the Euro – as opposed to general feelings towards the EU – as key to their vote (FEB 149:20).

These findings do not mean that younger voters are more nationalist than older ones. They suggest that further integration can no longer be justified with general statements about the desirability of a closer union, and that variations in levels of specific support are increasingly unlikely to be dampened by unconditional, principled support for European unification on the part of citizens.

Chapter 7

The Media

As with party-based or popular Euroscepticism, levels of Euroscepticism in the media vary greatly from one member state to another. Several factors may account for these differences: the organization of the media system (notably the degree of media concentration on the domestic market), the relevance of the tabloid press (while being very influential in some countries, it is not in others), traditional expectations of the role of the media in public debate (in Germany, the media are primarily expected to give substantive information on a given issue, while in the UK they are primarily expected to foster public debate), the degree of politicization and partisanship of the media (for instance, the strongly politicized character of British media fosters polarization), and differences in terms of news framing, to name a few. Furthermore, levels of Euroscepticism in the domestic media might also reflect dominant perceptions of European integration in a given country. For instance, the German press seems to be characterized by a relatively strong pro-European consensus transcending political cleavages, reflecting the largely pro-European orientation of German political elites (Eilders and Volmers 2003).

Beyond national differences, varieties of Euroscepticism in the media are similar to those of other actors. Utilitarian Euroscepticism, for instance, can be due to concerns over the scope of the EU's powers in media regulation, as is highlighted in this chapter. Political Euroscepticism can result from proximity to a given party or from general political orientation, as is often argued in the case of the British press, of which large segments have espoused the Eurosceptic evolution of the Conservative party from the end of the 1980s on. More fundamentally, mass media played a key role in processes of nation building in nineteenth-century Europe, by contributing to the emergence of domestic public spheres and by diffusing stories and myths about national identity. They are thus tightly linked to the construction of the nation as an imagined community. Consequently, they are often suspected of parochialism, if not 'consubstantial Euroscepticism' (Cayla 2009).

Although such a generalization is exaggerated, remembering this historical role of mass media allows us to consider the issue of Euroscepticism from a wider perspective. Indeed, this chapter not only addresses explicit Euroscepticism in the media, as illustrated, for instance, in segments of the British press, it also addresses a broader, ongoing debate about the role of domestic mass media in the process of European integration. Can and should domestic mass media contribute to the emergence of a European public sphere? Are they rather likely to perpetuate national logics of opinion-making and identification?

This chapter begins by outlining the main trends affecting the changing relationship between the EU and the media (media coverage has increased and has become more critical with the development of EU-centred investigative journalism). It then analyzes EU coverage by the quality press, showing that, while being overwhelmingly pro-European, it tends to frame the EU in ways that might contribute to Euroscepticism. Furthermore, it shows how the pro-European consensus of established media is being challenged by the tabloid press and by the increasing relevance of new media in public debates on European integration. Finally, the chapter ends by showing how mass media perpetuate the segmentation of national public spheres and questions their ability to contribute to the development of a European public sphere.

The media and the EU: from pro-EC militancy to critical investigation

In the course of the 1990s, EU institutions had to cope with increasing media attention and with more critical coverage by the media. However, their ability to cope with this increasing media pressure has been limited, especially for the Commission. This has led some observers to identify the EU's 'communication deficit' in its relationship with the media as one of the core dimensions of the 'democratic deficit' (Meyer 1999).

The development of investigative journalism ...

In the course of the 1990s, EU institutions were exposed to rising media attention. For instance, the number of journalists accredited with the EU institutions doubled between 1986 (450) and 1999 (900), reaching 1200 press correspondents today, and as much as 2000 during European Councils, outnumbering the press corps accredited with the US White House or with the United Nations headquarters. On average, roughly 800 journalists attend the daily press conferences (Midday Express briefings) organized by the Commission.

EU institutions also had to cope with the rise of a more political and investigative journalism, which was furthered by two developments. First, the extension of the EP's powers in the nomination procedure of the College of the Commission, as well as its increasing political clout in relation to the EU's executive, have contributed to changing the perception of the European Commission given in the media. The Commission is increasingly 'banalized' in the sense that it is perceived as being equivalent to a national government, and is thus held accountable to the same standards. This might have contributed to a shift from a militant, decidedly pro-EU stance shared by most early Brussels-based correspondents to a more critical and incisive tone (Meyer 1999:621). During the key period of 1991–92, the image of the Commission in the media was already deteriorating. Between 1990 and 1992, favourable coverage decreased by 13 per cent while negative coverage increased by 10 per cent (according to citizens' evaluations of the media's stance) (EB 38:22). This 'banalization' of the Commission was most evident during the 1999 crisis, as the College of the Commission had to resign under pressure from the EP, due to allegations of nepotism and mismanagement. The inability of the Commission to articulate a political crisis communication strategy targeting the media, with its defensive and secretive attitude towards journalists, together with increasing media pressure, have been analyzed as the main factor behind the resignation of the College, which significantly weakened the Commission later on (Meyer 1999:635).

Second, the decision by EU institutions to adopt rules of transparency (for example, on access to documents), which were set up in 1993 and have been progressively updated ever since, also fostered this more incisive media coverage. This was compounded by the increasing political clout of the EP and its ability to set up ad hoc investigative commissions. Seizing the opportunities created by this new context, the Association of European Journalists decided, in 1998, to promote EU-level investigative journalism, as a way of enhancing the accountability of EU-level decision-makers. All this led to the uncovering of several scandals with large media coverage. For instance, during the BSE crisis (1996–97), investigations into the decisions of the veterinary committee uncovered severe short-comings in the management and control of EU experts' committees. In the '*Guardian* case', a British journalist, John Carvell, successfully challenged the Council's rules on confidentiality on decisions affecting individual liberties. More recently, in 2004, a former *Spiegel* journalist and elected MEP, Hans-Peter Martin, uncovered, together with the newspaper *Stern*, a scandal relating to MEPs' expenses, which made headlines in several member states.

... at the expense of the Commission

Assessing the impact of this trend on perceptions of the EU's legitimacy proves difficult. On the one hand, the development of investigative journalism improves the quality of democratic governance at the EU level. On the other, it might contribute to a biased perception of the EU (and thus, indirectly, to Euroscepticism) in a twofold way.

To begin with, it has been argued that, given the difficulties encountered by journalists when trying to convey a sense of the day-to-day politics of the EU, media coverage of the EU tends to focus more on crises and scandals than does media coverage of domestic politics. EU news coverage thus tends to be distorted by the tendency to focus more on 'affairs' (Kevin 2003).

Futhermore, it is mainly the Commission that has paid the price for the development of EU-level investigative journalism, while the other central executive actor, the Council, remained relatively spared by media criticism. This is due in particular to the division of tasks between EU institutions in terms of communication. Indeed, the communication of the Council in relation to the media is limited to three aspects: the post-Council meeting press conferences held by national ministers before the Brussels-based, national press corps, the communication policy of the rotating Council presidency, and communications on foreign policy and defence issues by Council civil servants. This situation 'allows national politicians to delegate communication accountability to the Commission and high civil servants' (Meyer 1999:633). Increasing coverage of EU institutions by domestic media contributes to this situation, as they focus overwhelmingly on the Commission, while giving the Council – and hence, national ministers – very little visibility (Meyer 1999; Koopmans 2007; Saurwein 2006).

The Europhilia of established media: some nuances

When trying to assess the distribution of Eurosceptic orientations across media types, researchers have found that the main cleavage relates neither to modes of ownership, (although public broadcasters have been found to be slightly more critical of the EU than private ones, according to one study (de Vreese *et al.* 2006)) nor to the type of media outlet. The most relevant cleavage in relation to Euroscepticism seems to pit established (the quality press) against non-established media (especially the tabloid press). Several authors have argued that the general stance of most quality newspapers is pro-EU. However, as this section argues, there are significant limitations to this statement. To begin with, the degree to which domestic mass media are Europeanized must be examined, as well as the idea that they are all enthusiastic advocates of further integration. Moreover, mainstream media often convey a biased image of EU institutions, which in turn might induce and/or reinforce Eurosceptic orientations. In fact, increased coverage of EU issues *per se* does not necessarily socialize EU citizens in a pro-European direction. Beyond uncertainties as to the impact of the media on public opinion, much also depends on the way the media frame the EU.

A limited Europeanization

It is often argued that domestic media contribute to popular Euroscepticism because they rarely report on EU institutions or EU issues. By giving no or little visibility to the EU, they allegedly contribute to citizens' lack of information and/or interest about the EU, thus indirectly fostering Eurosceptic orientations. Recently, this view has been challenged by studies attesting to an increasing coverage of EU issues by the media, especially the quality press. They argue that EU coverage by established domestic media has improved both quantitatively and qualitatively.

Quantitatively, EU issues are increasingly covered on a day-to-day basis, at least in the quality press. A comparative study of the quality press in five countries between 1982 and 2003 showed that the proportion of editorials in which the EU was the core theme rose from 2 to 9 per cent (Brüggeman *et al.* 2006). This coverage also tends to increase as does a country's seniority in the EU. For example, in the case of Austria, coverage of EU issues by the evening news programme of the main public TV channel and the quality press increased from less than 3 per cent at the time of accession to 10 per cent ten years later (Saurwein 2006). This trend is also discernible during European elections. For instance, a study comparing the coverage of the European election campaign by the main TV evening news programmes in several countries in 1999 and 2004 found that coverage had increased from 7 to almost 10 per cent (de Vreese *et al.* 2006). Parallel to this, some studies attest to increased qualitative coverage of EU issues in the sense that, instead of being referred to in purely descriptive, factual articles, they are increasingly present in opinion editorials and subject to political debates (see Trenz 2007:90–1; Pfetsch 2004:60).

However, general perceptions of increased Europeanization must be refined in a threefold way. First, even if it is on the rise, coverage of EU issues in domestic media remains limited, often not exceeding 10 per cent of media content on a day-to-day basis. In France for instance, the 2004 EP elections were covered less than regional elections that same year (Gerstlé 2006:4). Second, the extent to which EU issues are covered varies a lot across countries. While they are rather well covered in German news media, they are poorly covered in Italy (Kevin 2003). Third, EU news is rarely featured on the front page of newspapers and is seldom broadcast in prime time.

A pro-European permissive consensus?

It is often assumed that the established media display a pro-EU stance in their coverage of EU issues. In the 1960s, the majority of the press in the six founding countries was favourable to the EC (Ludlow 1998). More recent studies argue that this is still the case. For example, a 1996 survey on top decision-makers found that 91 per cent of decision-makers in the media sector were supportive of their country's EU membership (Spence 1996). According to one media scholar, 'quality newspapers raise the "European voice" against the undecided, hesitant and particularistic attitudes of the national governments and sometimes even against the Euroscepticism of their own readers' (Trenz 2007:90). Moreover, it is widely recognized that, especially during EU-related referendum campaigns, pro-European opinion-makers are over-represented in the established media. For example, during the 2005 referendum campaign in France, the evening news programmes of the two main TV channels allocated 85 per cent of the time devoted to the referendum to actors of the Yes campaign (Gerstlé 2006:11). Similar statements were made that same year for referendum campaigns in Spain and the Netherlands.

Nonetheless, the perception of a generally and unequivocally supportive established media must be examined more closely. First of all, several studies have challenged the idea that opinion-makers in the established media are necessarily highly supportive of integration. For example, although the survey of decision-makers cited above certainly showed that decision-makers in the media were highly supportive of EU membership in 1996, they ranked last (in terms of support) among the five categories of opinion leaders included in the survey (Spence 1996). A more recent study showed that the media are closer to other civil society actors than they are to government officials, political and trade union leaders as regards their evaluation of EU institutions. Indeed, when asked to evaluate EU institutions, 'media actors turn out to take a negative position, close to the average of non-media civil society actors' (Koopmans 2007:201).

Second, soft Euroscepticism proves rather frequent in the established media, even in the quality press. This 'banal Euroscepticism' usually consists in deploring the complexity of EU decision-making, the alleged irrelevance of the Monnet method, and a good measure of 'Commission-bashing' (Meyer 1999:621; Trenz 2007:99). By the same token, stereotypical references to the EU's alleged 'regulating fury' (*Die Zeit* 2009 a) or 'regulatory rage' (*Der Tagesspiegel* 2007) frequently appear in established pro-European newspapers.

Third, even in countries where the quality press is overwhelmingly favourable to European integration, there are of course nuances in degrees of support. In West Germany, for instance, in the late 1950s segments of the established media, such as *Der Spiegel* and its chief editor, Rudolf Augstein, were strongly sceptical of attempts to revitalize European integration via the common market. Augstein, who deplored that 'we [Germans] have let ourselves reduced to a European people' (quoted in Loth 1989:591), was also very critical of the common market, which he discarded as being merely an economic project. In a similar vein, the *Frankfurter Allgemeine Zeitung* was quite critical of the CDU's decidedly pro-European orientation during Kohl's leadership (Paterson 1996:65–68).

Fourth, there are cross-national differences, even in the quality press, regarding levels of support for EU institutions and for tighter integration. For instance, a comparative study on the media coverage of the 2004 EP elections in 25 countries suggested that the written press in old member states tended to be more critical of the EU than their colleagues in the new member states (de Vreese *et al.* 2006). Furthermore, domestic media, even if not homogeneous, might also reflect predominant national preferences on EU issues. This was highlighted by a comparative analysis of how the quality press of six countries covered the debate on the EU's future, a debate that had been launched in 2000 by the German Foreign Minister, Joschka Fischer (Fischer 2000). Editorials in the British and Spanish press were clearly less supportive of a federal option for the EU (which had been advocated by Fischer) and much less enthusiastic about revitalizing the Franco-German 'motor' than editorials in the German or French press (Trenz 2007:102).

Furthermore, while being pro-EU on the whole, the established media tend to frame the EU in ways that can bias perceptions of the Union, in at least a twofold way: they overwhelmingly focus on the intergovernmental aspects of the EU and they do not convey an accurate picture of the division of power among EU institutions.

An intergovernmental EU

To begin with, the overwhelming focus of the media on national governments and historic events, such as European Councils, conveys a mainly intergovernmental view of the EU and an essentially strategic image of the interactions between member states, at the expense of the community dimension of the EU.

In purely domestic debates, national executives (as opposed to opposition parties, civil society organizations, etc.) already tend to be the actors most quoted in the media (Koopmans 2007:193). This holds even more for media reports on debates with a European dimension. Several studies on the coverage of EU issues by domestic media attest to the overrepresentation of national governments, at the expense of EU institutions. This was the case, for instance, during the debate launched by Fischer in 2000. In the two main quality daily newspapers of six countries, national governments were by far the most quoted actors, accounting for more than 30 per cent of all quotations, while EU institutions and MEPs accounted for only 11 per cent (Trenz 2007:94). This was also the case during the 2003–04 debate on EU enlargement in Austria, where EU institutions only accounted for 13 per cent of all statements quoted by the quality newspaper *Der Standard* (Saurwein 2006:137), and for

TV coverage of the 2004 EP elections, where it was estimated that, across the 25 EU countries, only a quarter of all actors quoted could be defined as 'European' (including national candidates to EP seats) (de Vreese *et al.* 2006). In France in 2005, only 12 per cent of all those quoted or interviewed on the EU Constitutional Treaty in the two main evening news programmes could be described as supranational actors (Gerstlé 2006:8).

This intergovernmental bias in reporting is further exacerbated by domestic media's tendency to focus on high profile events such as European Councils, at the expense of a more extensive coverage of the day-to-day politics of the EU. Since European Councils tend to be about hard bargaining and classical diplomacy, they lend themselves easily to a strategic style of news reporting, thus conveying the idea that European integration is only about interstate bargaining and opaque deals between national heads of states and governments. This kind of reporting might contribute to the projection of political cynicism onto the EU (de Vreese 2007). Furthermore, by focusing disproportionately on the final stages in decision-making, the media fail to expose the close cooperation between national administrations and the Commission in the drafting of legislative proposals, as well as the multiple arenas where proposals are negotiated and compromises elaborated. This might reinforce the widespread perception that Brussels forces decisions upon member states, instead of presenting the EU as a constant search for compromises and consensus.

Finally, the image of the EU as an arena of power politics and interstate rivalries also results from the type of framing style journalists use when they report on the EU. Two framing styles can be distinguished: strategic game framing and thematic issue framing. Whereas game framing analyzes politics in terms of strategies and power politics, issue framing is more substantive and addresses the issues at stake in terms of public policy and problem solving. It has been argued that, given the complex, technical and allegedly boring character of most EU issues, journalists tend to rely predominantly on game framing when reporting on EU issues, even more so than for domestic issues. The 2005 referendum campaigns in France and the Netherlands illustrated this. During the Dutch campaign, the overwhelming majority of media coverage focused on the strategic aspects of the campaign (on the deficiencies of the Yes campaign, voting intentions, and the potential consequences of a No, among other topics). Only 16 per cent of all articles and TV programmes analyzed by researchers used an issue framing style highlighting the implications of the EU Constitutional Treaty (de Vreese and Schmuck 2006). Similarly, in France, 53 per cent of the broadcasting time spent on the campaign in the two most widely viewed evening news programmes used a game framing style, as opposed to 47 per cent for issue framing (Piar and Gerstlé 2005).

A Union dominated by the Commission

As well as the overwhelming focus on governmental actors and historic occasions, domestic media coverage of the EU is also characterized by a rather misleading representation of the distribution of power between EU institutions. Of all the EU institutions, the Commission is by far the most covered by the media, which gives the impression that the EU is dominated by an overarching executive power, when, in fact, it is a rather polycentric organization. Indeed, the visibility of the Council in the media is eclipsed by national governments, while the visibility of the EP varies greatly across time, with peaks in media coverage during EP elections. A comparative study of 28 newspapers from seven EU countries found that, in all articles referring to EU institutions, the Commission was by far the most quoted (in more than half of the cases), while the EP was quoted in barely a quarter of the cases (Koopmans 2007:194). Another study on the Austrian media found that, even during EP elections, the visibility of the Commission remained clearly stronger than that of the European Parliament, with almost 50 per cent (as a share of all references to EU institutions) for the former, compared to 30 per cent for the latter (Saurwein 2006). The overrepresentation in the media of the executive, at the expense of the legislature, certainly remains the rule in purely domestic debates. However, it has been argued that this overrepresentation is even stronger in media coverage of EU institutions (Koopmans 2007:194). As a consequence, the image that emerges in the media does not reflect the real distribution of power between EU institutions. The media failed, especially, to convey a sense of the increasing power and political clout of the EP in the course of the 1990s.

Finally, the image of the Commission is biased by the fact that domestic media tend to focus on the actions of nationals in the College of Commissioners, thus giving the impression that Commissioners represent national interests in Brussels and that the

Commission is a kind of replica of an intergovernmental body like the Council.

Certainly, this distorted view of the EU is not Euroscepticism *per se*. The established media remain pro-European on the whole. However, they are also increasingly challenged in their ability to frame domestic public debates on European integration by other types of media: the tabloid press and the internet.

The tabloid press and the new media

The increasing difficulty of the quality press in framing public debates on European integration was highlighted by the 2005 French and Dutch referenda on the EU Constitutional Treaty. The overwhelming presence of Yes campaigners in the established media and the latter's endorsement of the treaty did not prevent large majorities of voters from rejecting its ratification. In the French case, this has been attributed, among other things, to the key role played by the internet during the campaign – a medium that had been largely neglected by Yes campaigners. Similarly, a significant role in the rejection of the Lisbon Treaty by Irish voters in 2008 has been attributed to the tabloid press. In both cases, non-mainstream media offered a platform for Eurosceptics who challenged the overwhelmingly pro-EU stance of the established media and political elites. This section starts by highlighting the role of the tabloid press in domestic public debates on the EU, before addressing the issue of the new media.

Euroscepticism in the tabloid press: an anti-regulation concern?

An often-neglected dimension of Euroscepticism in the tabloid press is the potential role of the EU as a regulator of media ownership. The issue is crucial to the possibility of democratic public debate since media ownership concentration can endanger political and cultural pluralism. For instance, the overwhelmingly Eurosceptic orientation of a tabloid press almost entirely owned by one or two groups in the UK or Austria leads to an unbalanced distribution of views on the EU in domestic media. In Austria, for instance, it is estimated that the strongly Eurosceptic *Neue Kronen Zeitung* (owned by Mediaprint) has a readership of three million (out of a total population of eight million) and a 44 per cent market share of the daily written press. In the UK, several of the most widely circulated tabloid newspapers (*The Sun, The News of the World* and *The Sunday Times*) belong to Rupert Murdoch's News International group and accounted (together with *The Times*) for 75 per cent of the daily sales of the written press in 2002, with nine million copies sold (European Federation of Journalists 2002).

For the time being, the EU's ability to safeguard media pluralism is limited. It can only do so indirectly, by regulating media ownership when it applies competition law (for instance, by prohibiting mergers which would endanger competition). The definition of rules aimed at safeguarding media pluralism remains the exclusive right of member states and national regulators (as they define, for instance, rules on programme diversity, on the independence of journalists and programmers, on the transparency of owners' corporate or commercial interests and so on). Consequently, rules aimed at safeguarding media pluralism vary greatly across member states.

Faced with threats to media pluralism in the EU (which have also been pointed out by the Council of Europe's Committee of Experts on Media Concentrations and Pluralism), several actors have been asking for new EU powers to safeguard media pluralism, notably the EP (European Parliament 2002b) and the European Federation of Journalists, which pleads for stricter and harmonized EU rules on media ownership and for the adoption of EU legislation on editorial independence (European Federation of Journalists 2002:47–9). In 2009, all the main German newspapers drafted a European Charter on Freedom of the Press, which laid down a number of principles aimed at guaranteeing journalists' independence and was handed over to EU institutions (*Die Zeit* 2009b). Moreover, the EP has also denounced government attacks on journalists' editorial independence in some member states, such as Italy and the UK (European Parliament 2004).

Such attempts have come up against a coalition of powerful interests made up of broadcasters' and publishers' associations (the Association of Commercial Television, the European Radio Association, and the European Publishers' Council) as well as governments. For instance, the British and German governments vetoed a 1996 directive proposal on media pluralism (Klimkiewicz 2005:4). Although this resistance to EU-level regulation is not limited to the tabloid media, it may well be one of the rationales underlying Euroscepticism in the two countries where the tabloid press is the most concentrated and the most Eurosceptic, Austria and the UK.

The challenge of the tabloid press

The reach and influence of the tabloid press vary from one country to another. However, it does play a significant role in two of the countries where public support for EU membership is especially weak: Austria and the UK, and its significance is growing in Ireland. The tabloid press is certainly not a homogeneous mass in terms of attitudes towards the EU. Among the British tabloid press, for instance, *The Mirror* stuck to its pro-EC orientation from the 1960s to the 1990s. Moreover, attitudes towards European integration among the tabloid press have evolved greatly across time. For example, the British tabloid press (including *The Daily Herald*, the forerunner of *The Sun*) campaigned for continued British membership of the EC in the 1975 referendum and, later on, for the SEA. Since the end of the 1980s, however, as Tory policy towards the EC became much more Eurosceptic and commercial competition in the media sector became tougher, the overwhelming majority of the tabloid press shifted towards a Eurosceptic, if not anti-European, position (at least for the two hardest Eurosceptics, *The Sun* and *The Daily Mail*) (Alexandre-Collier 2000:62). Similarly, the main tabloid newspaper in Austria, the *Neue Kronen Zeitung*, campaigned for the country's accession to the EU during the 1994 referendum campaign, before turning Eurosceptic.

In other countries, the development of a Eurosceptic tabloid press is a more recent phenomenon. The 2008 referendum on the Lisbon Treaty in Ireland, for example, highlighted the emergence of a Eurosceptic tabloid press in the country, due to massive British newspaper imports, which already accounted for 30 per cent of daily newspaper sales in Ireland in 2000 (European Federation of Journalists 2002:22). During the referendum campaign, several British-inspired tabloids, such as *The Irish Daily Mail*, *The Irish Star*, and *The Sunday Times* (owned by Rupert Murdoch), campaigned against the Lisbon Treaty, and against the more pro-European stance of established titles such as *The Irish Times*, *The Irish Independent* and *The Irish Examiner* (*The Irish Times* 2009).

The tabloid press contributes to framing domestic public debates on the EU in a twofold way. First, it articulates a hard Eurosceptic discourse, diffusing rumours or 'Euro-myths' about the EU which find a large echo among its readership and even influence common discourse about the EU. Second, it acts as an agenda-setter, influencing the terms of domestic public debate on the EU. Thus, it also expresses serious popular concerns linked to European integration, which elites and the established media tend to downplay.

Euro-myths in the tabloid press

By spreading 'Euro-myths', the tabloid press in Austria and the UK has played a significant role in disparaging the EU as an over-regulating, or even absurd, form of totalitarian power threatening national ways of life and identity by trying to suppress national idiosyncrasies. In the UK, the completion of the internal market, which required the adoption of nearly 300 new directives and created a push for the approximation or mutual recognition of domestic legislation in a vast number of areas (such as food safety, sanitary and veterinary standards) gave a decisive boost to the diffusion of Euro-myths, as the head of the Commission's representation in the UK observed: 'The event which was singularly most generative of these Euromyths was the creation of the internal market ... Although much of the legislation merely reaffirmed national measures already in place, the misperception of the EU covertly pervading every aspect of everyday life was seized upon. The introduction of common marketing and labelling standards for foodstuff in particular ... proved a malleable source of misrepresentation' (Dougal 2003:2). The Austrian tabloid press played a similar role, for instance by feeding concerns over a possible 'selling away of Austrian drinking water' to other member states.

The propagation of Euro-myths by the tabloid press relies on a set of few, often interrelated key words or code words, which resonate strongly among its readership. For instance, the British Eurosceptic tabloid press regularly recur to notions such as 'federalism', 'superstate', 'dictatorship' or adjectives such as 'unelected', 'bureaucratic', or 'unaccountable', which have become code-words for 'Brussels' (Teubert 2001:55). Moreover, Oliver Daddow (2006) has shown how the two main Eurosceptic tabloids, *The Sun* and *The Daily Mail*, have been propagating a mythical view of Britain's history in order to buttress their main argument that Brussels acts against British interests, by presenting the UK as alien to European culture and history. In a similar logic, the tabloid press tries to rally its readership with key words such as 'independence', 'sovereignty', and 'British values', which are used as anti-EU mottos (Teubert

2001; Daddow 2006). Similarly, the Austrian tabloid press has popularized several negative key words in relation to the EU, such as *Vetokeule* (veto-hammer) or *Fremdbestimmung* (foreign rule), *Ausverkauf* (selling away) or 'EU juggernaut', which, in the *Kronen Zeitung*, have become common discourse when referring to the EU (Krejci 2004:13).

These code words can activate Eurosceptic orientations among readerships. In Austria for instance, periods when support for EU membership is lowest coincide with periods when Eurosceptic keywords appear with a higher frequency in the *Neue Kronen Zeitung* (Krejci 2004:17).

The tabloid press as agenda-setter

Furthermore, the tabloid press also acts as an agenda-setter, influencing the selection of the issues that are deemed relevant in relation to European integration. For instance, an Austrian study showed that the list of citizens' top concerns linked to the EU (in which the selling of drinking water ranked first) largely matched the list of themes most frequently mentioned in relation to the EU in the *Neue Kronen Zeitung*. More generally, the spreading of Euro-myths by the *Neue Kronen Zeitung* seems to have contributed to increased concerns over the impact of European integration on the Austrian way of life and national identity (Krecji 2004:5–6). The tabloid press has voiced concerns that are widespread among citizens, on issues such as the EU's transport policy (and its environmental impact in the Alps), the regulation of genetically modified organisms, or EU enlargement. Concerning enlargement, it has been shown that, of all the actors participating in public debates, the *Neue Kronen Zeitung* was by far the most hostile, along with the extreme right and the trade union confederation. Moreover, it has succeeded in framing the terms of the debate by, for instance, systematically linking the issue of the Czech Republic's EU accession to the problem of nuclear safety (Saurwein 2006). Thus, it has certainly contributed to the overwhelmingly negative stance of Austrian public opinion towards enlargement.

The impact on public opinion and politics

More generally, the concrete impact of the tabloid press can be twofold, as it influences the public's perceptions of the EU and the discourse political parties hold about the EU. As far as public opinion is concerned, there certainly is a mutually reinforcing dynamic between Eurosceptic readers and the Eurosceptic press. For instance, 52 per cent of Austrians who think EU membership is a bad thing quote the tabloid press (the *Neue Kronen Zeitung*) as their main source of information on the EU, whereas only a quarter of those who support EU membership do so (Krejci 2004:9). However, the relationship between the tabloid press and public opinion is, of course, not unidirectional. For instance, of all EU citizens, the British are the most dissatisfied with domestic media reporting on the EU, which they perceive as being too negative (36 per cent, compared to 13 per cent for the EU average) (EB 68:147).

As far as its impact on politics is concerned, the Eurosceptic tabloid press can, especially during election campaigns, contribute to a radicalization of party positions on specific EU issues, as was the case, for example, for EMU during the 1997 British election campaign (Alexandre-Collier 2000:136). Especially during IGCs, the tabloid press might exert pressure on governments by accusing them of selling away national sovereignty. For instance, before the June 2007 European Council (where negotiations on the Lisbon Treaty were on the agenda), *The Sun* published an editorial claiming that, due to the treaty's new provisions on foreign policy, the UK would lose its permanent seat on the UN Security Council. This prompted the Foreign Secretary, Margaret Beckett, to toughen the British government's line on the EU's External Action Service, which she attempted to veto (Grant 2009:4).

Euroscepticism on the Web

Over the years, the internet has become a significant source of information about the EU for an increasing number of EU citizens. This has been facilitated by the rapid spread of the internet in the EU. In 2008, nearly half of European households had internet access at home (SEB 293:54). In 1999, the internet ranked seventh among diverse sources of information about the EU (after TV, dailies and the radio, notably), and was mentioned by only 6 per cent of citizens as one of their sources of information (EB 52:17). In 2007, it ranked third (after television and the written press) in the list of the most favoured sources of information about the EU and was mentioned by 28 per cent as their main source of information (EB 67 2007:134). However, the impact of the internet on citizens' perceptions of the EU is difficult to assess. To begin with, the internet appears to be the least trusted medium among Europeans (EB

68:150). Moreover, the significance of the internet as the main source of information on the EU varies greatly from one country to another. It is quite strong in the Nordic countries and the Netherlands, but very low in Italy and Greece (EB 67:136).

Euroscepticism on the Web is certainly nothing new. Like the term Euroscepticism itself, it started developing mostly in the UK in the form of online extensions of the many groups, think-tanks and campaigns that sprang up in the wake of the debates on the Maastricht Treaty (Campaign for an Independent Britain, Free Britain!, Business for Sterling, etc.) (Daddow 2006). A study on Eurosceptic discourse on British websites found that these sites were usually well connected with each other and that, like the tabloid press, they share common Eurosceptic keywords constituting a common corpus (Teubert 2000). Moreover, British Eurosceptics have been the precursors of the development of Eurosceptic blogging, be it blogs written by Eurosceptic MEPs (such as Tory MEP Daniel Hannan), by pundits associated with think-tanks (for example, the blog *EU Referendum*, written by two contributors to the Bruges group, the *Open Europe Blog*, and *Through the EU Labyrinth*, the blog of the European Foundation), or by EU press correspondents for Eurosceptic journals (for example, the blog of *The Daily Telegraph*'s Brussels correspondent, Bruno Waterfield). In fact, Eurosceptics are using the internet just like any other medium, as pro-Europeans do. In the context of the 2009 EP elections, the Eurosceptic party Libertas used communication opportunities offered by the Web, such as Facebook and Twitter. Similarly, Eurosceptic MEP Daniel Hannan's YouTube video was viewed by more than two million visitors. In that respect, the internet has become a common tool of communication, both for Eurosceptics and pro-Europeans.

However, the internet displays specific features that make it especially attractive to non-elite actors willing to challenge the establishment. A largely unregulated, egalitarian medium that values any user's contribution, and where the distinction between public and personal information is largely blurred, it furthers participatory democracy but also facilitates the spread of rumours, fringe ideologies, and more. In that respect, it is certainly a double-edged phenomenon for public authorities, be they domestic or international. During the past decade, the internet has been used more and more by various actors in order to voice criticism of international organizations and call for a reform of international governance. For instance, it played a key role in the 1997–98 international campaign against the Multilateral Agreement on Investments (MAI), which was being negotiated in the framework of the OECD. The internet was used to raise public attention about the MAI and helped coordinate the international coalition of actors that mobilized against it. Eventually, negotiations on the text had to be abandoned, in part because of this mobilization.

In the EU context, the 2005 referendum campaign on the EU Constitutional Treaty in France highlighted the key role of Eurosceptic internet users in framing the terms of the debate and in shifting public opinion against the treaty. Not only were anti-treaty websites much more numerous than pro-treaty ones, but they were also much better interconnected (three times more) than pro-treaty websites, and were thus much more adapted to users' habits in terms of web-surfing (Thieulin and Senèze 2006). Moreover, anti-treaty websites were much better connected to community or NGOs' websites, while pro-treaty websites looked much more official and single issue (most of the time, they had been set up only for the campaign). In a similar vein, anti-treaty websites offered more opportunities in terms of participation and interactive debates (through forums, chats, blogs, etc.). The Yes campaign largely underestimated the significance of this medium. To the extent that Yes campaigners were present on the Web, they displayed a much more traditional, 'top–down' understanding of that medium, which fostered the perception that the Yes vote was mainly defended by the elites. Finally, No campaigners on the Web displayed a much more sophisticated use and better command of the latest internet techniques, such as hypertext cross-references and viral campaigning (Thieulin and Senèze 2006). As far as the content of the campaign was concerned, No campaigners on the Web largely managed to set the framing of the national public debate on the treaty. In that respect, the Web campaign highlighted the emergence of new opinion leaders who challenged the elites. These opinion leaders played a decisive role in framing the debate as a debate on employment and social rights. For instance, the controversy over the Services directive broke out on the website of a (widely unknown at the time) high school economics teacher, Etienne Chouard, who became one of the rallying figures of the No campaign. Mobilization against the Services directive (renamed the 'Bolkestein directive') was especially visible on the Web, as an online petition against the text was launched. More generally, surveys have found that the future of the

French 'social model', employment and liberalism in the EU ranked among the most popular issues debated by internet users (Thieulin and Senèze 2006:190). In fact, the internet set the terms of the debate which the established media took over later on.

National media versus European public sphere?

As the preceding sections suggest, increasing media coverage of EU news might be counter-productive for the EU, as long as debates remain confined to national public spheres, since an exclusively national perspective necessarily biases perceptions of the EU. This is why academics and EU institutions alike have come to advocate the emergence of a European public sphere as a way to respond to Eurosceptic criticism. However, in the absence of pan-European mass media, the assumption that domestic mass media can contribute to the development of a European public sphere is disputable.

The lack of a European public sphere: a root cause of Euroscepticism?

Unlike national governments, EU institutions cannot legitimize their decisions by referring to an existing EU-wide public sphere where significant issues are identified as public problems, different policy options are debated and policy proposals discussed. Indeed, there is a gap between widely Europeanized policy-making in an increasing number of policy areas, on the one hand, and public debates that remain confined to national public spheres on the other (Koopmans 2007:183). This poses a problem in terms of legitimacy, since there is a 'public opinion deficit' at the EU level (Gerhards 1993:107). Consequently, the absence of a European public sphere is regularly identified as one of the main causes of the democratic deficit and, indirectly, of Euroscepticism. This thesis has been adopted by EU institutions. For instance, following the Dutch and French referenda in 2005, the Commission came to the conclusion that one of the reasons for the citizens' disaffection with Brussels 'is the insufficient development of a "European public sphere" allowing for the development of a European debate' (European Commission 2006:5). For this European public sphere to emerge, however, there needs to be either pan-European media or connections between national public spheres.

The lack of pan-European media: a political resistance

It is often noted that existing pan-European media, such as *The Financial Times*, *Arte* or *Euronews*, are elitist media. In fact, in the course of European integration, there have been several attempts by EC/EU institutions to foster the emergence of pan-European mass media. Originally, the European Commission's plans for audiovisual media relied on the assumption that the free circulation of audiovisual products in the internal market would lead to the emergence of a European audiovisual space, which in turn would facilitate the development of pan-European audiovisual media (Schlesinger 1993). Such was the aim of the 1989 Television without Frontiers Directive, which implied the free circulation of television programmes in the internal market, while requiring broadcasters to keep the majority of broadcasting time for European programmes. In parallel, the Commission and Parliament have tried, since the 1950s, to promote the creation of a pan-European public TV channel, an idea which was recently reconsidered by the Commission's services (Vissol 2006:160–3).

However, these attempts have triggered three types of resistance. First, they had to overcome the initial reluctance of national public broadcasters, who feared increased competition in the domestic market. (In several member states, public broadcasters enjoyed a monopoly over the transmission of TV programmes well into the 1980s.) Second, any action of the EU in the field of audiovisual media raised fears of a possible encroachment on national or regional powers (as the case of the German *Länder* illustrates). As a matter of fact, the Television without Frontiers Directive is still not implemented in all member states. The UK, for instance, allows 40 cable and satellite channels to ignore its requirement on European programming (European Federation of Journalists 2002:14). Third, plans to create pan-European media raised concerns about identity. Indeed, communication specialists have shown that public television strongly contributed to strengthening national identities in the postwar period, by broadcasting a common national news agenda (Schlesinger 1993). These identity-related concerns were expressed in the Protocol on the system of public broadcasting in the member states, annexed to the Maastricht Treaty in 1997, which stressed the special status of public broadcasting as an element of national identity, by stating that 'the system of public broadcasting in the Member States is directly related to the democratic, social and cultural needs of each society'. This also explains why plans to create a European public TV channel within EBU (European Broadcasting Union, a network that brings together national public broadcasters) failed. Thus, eventually, bi-national or pan-European TV channels were created outside EBU (*Arte* in 1990 and *Euronews* in 1992) with no explicit relation to European integration.

National media as actors of a European public sphere?

As explained in previous chapters, exclusive national identity and distrust towards other countries are two variables that clearly influence Euroscepticism. In this respect, a pedagogical role is often attributed to the media. By reporting on other countries and cultures, they might open up domestic public spheres to outside influences and connect domestic public spheres to one another. The Commission's recent communication strategies have assigned a significant role to domestic media in that respect (European Commission 2007a: 11–12), while some media scholars see the domestic media as pioneers in the development of a European identity (Trenz 2007).

Such assumptions were shared by early European integration theorists, who hypothesized that the increasing exposure of western European citizens to mass communication flows would orient them towards a cosmopolitan identity. Indeed, one of the pioneers of the study of public opinion and the EC argued in 1977 that citizens' rising exposure to mass communication networks (via TV set ownership, for instance), even in a national context, would increase people's cognitive skills and develop their cosmopolitan orientations, thus benefiting European integration (Inglehart 1977:337).

For now, however, such hypotheses have not proved to be true. As explained below through the example of the French referendum campaign on the EU Constitutional Treaty, massive media coverage, coupled with an overwhelming national framing of the issue at stake, clearly favoured the No campaign. In fact, caution is appropriate when assessing the media's possible contribution to the development of a European public sphere. Certainly, a European public sphere does not imply one single public sphere on the model of national public spheres. Rather, it implies a twofold Europeanization of domestic public spheres: a 'vertical Europeanization', whereby EU issues are increasingly debated at the domestic level without being completely filtered by domestic lenses; and a 'horizontal

Europeanization', whereby domestic public spheres become increasingly interconnected (this distinction is borrowed from Koopmans 2007:186).

The question of whether domestic mass media can play a significant role in promoting these two types of Europeanization must be assessed critically, for three reasons. First, media reporting on EU issues is heavily filtered by domestic politics and by domestic news agendas, which limits vertical Europeanization. Second, domestic mass media display very low levels of horizontal Europeanization and thus perpetuate the relative parochialism of domestic public debates. Third, in times of crisis or tension, they may contribute to a re-nationalization of national public spheres.

The predominance of national frames of reference

As far as vertical Europeanization is concerned, the question is whether 'journalism for a Europe-wide public' (Schlesinger 2007:423) is likely to develop. For that to happen, there needs to be a common 'European news agenda' across domestic media and a '*common* "European" frame of reference' that transcend a purely national reporting and orient domestic audiences towards a European perspective (Schlesinger 1999:277). However, whereas researchers agree that there are signs of an emerging shared EU news agenda, the question of whether a common European frame of reference can develop is debatable. Some argue that this common European frame of reference does exist, at least in the quality press, and that it contributes to some sense of shared identity. For example, a comparative study of the coverage of the 'future of Europe' debate in 2000–01 in the opinion editorials of the quality press in six countries put forward a twofold conclusion. First, coverage attested to the emergence of a common EU news agenda, structured around the same sequence of events (Joschka Fischer's speech on the federal future of the EU, the drafting of the EU Charter of Fundamental Rights, negotiations on the Nice Treaty, etc.). Second, these 'op-eds' illustrated a common frame of reference in relation to European integration. Most of the time, they attested to a shared understanding of the EU as a supranational community in the making, rooted in a common understanding of European integration history (Trenz 2007:98–9).

However, presenting domestic mass media as the forerunners of a shared European identity is certainly too far-reaching. The deep-rooted habit of framing EU issues essentially through national lenses leads to an almost exclusive focus on national concerns, at the expense of EU-level issues. Certainly, it is inevitable and perfectly legitimate that reporting on the EU be influenced by national contexts. In this respect, it is perfectly normal for journalists to focus more, for instance, on the EU issues that are of special interest to their countries (for example, the CAP and the Common Fisheries Policy in Spain, the CAP and regional funds in Ireland, or the EU budget contribution in the Netherlands). The problem arises, however, when EU issues are almost exclusively covered through domestic lenses, thus obscuring their European dimension. This can happen in two different ways: by interpreting EU issues solely in terms of domestic politics and by letting the national news agenda completely obscure the European dimension of a specific issue.

By framing EU issues exclusively in terms of strategic reporting on domestic politics, the media may exacerbate the national bias induced by political elites' behaviour. The case of reporting on European elections illustrates this limited role of the domestic media as promoters of active European citizenship, as well as the collusion with political elites in the domestic framing of EU events. Of course, the degree of domestication of EP elections depends, among other things, on their timing and possible overlap with national electoral cycles. Media coverage of the 2004 EP elections in Spain illustrates this. As European elections were held only three months after crucial national elections, the three main dailies interpreted European elections in purely domestic political terms, according to their respective political orientations (Sàdaba 2006:124). Thus, to some extent, the domestic media perpetuate the national character of European elections. This also holds for the coverage and framing of EU-related referenda. For instance, a comparison between the framing of the 2004 EP elections and the framing of the 2005 referendum by the two main evening TV news programmes in France showed that national framing (as opposed to European framing) was even more pronounced in the case of the referendum. Whereas national framing (as opposed to a European framing) was used for 60 per cent of the broadcasting time allotted to the EP elections, it was used for 80 per cent of the broadcasting time allotted to the coverage of the referendum (Gerstlé 2006:10–11). This suggests that the higher the (perceived) stakes, the stronger the tendency to frame an issue in exclusively national terms. In terms of impact, this overwhelmingly national framing of the referendum might have reinforced the relevance of the domestic context among No voters, who were twice as likely as Yes voters to consider primarily the national context (as opposed to the European dimension of the issue) when casting their votes (Piar and Gerstlé 2005:60).

Besides the strategic framing in terms of domestic politics, the European dimension of a specific issue can be obscured by the content of the national news agenda. Again, the 2005 referendum campaign on the EU Constitutional Treaty in France is a case in point. At the time of the campaign, the national news agenda was overwhelmingly focused on social issues and concerns over unemployment and the decline of the French 'social model', among other things. As a result, media coverage of the campaign reduced the debate on the Constitutional Treaty to almost one single dimension: its potential impact on France's social system and its alleged neoliberal bias. A comparison between the media coverage of the Maastricht referendum campaign and that of the Constitutional Treaty referendum campaign is illuminating. Despite comparable unemployment rates in 1992 and 2005, the social framing of both treaties, and of the EU in general, was much more pronounced in 2005 than in 1992. Whereas, in 1992, less than 5 per cent of media coverage used a social framing, in 2005 a quarter of media coverage dealing with the Constitutional Treaty and the EU used a social framing (Piar and Gerstlé 2005:72). This might have contributed to the strong relevance of social concerns reported by left-wing No voters.

This domestic framing of EU issues is compounded by another factor: the lack of connection between domestic public spheres.

A limited 'horizontal Europeanization'

The horizontal Europeanization of domestic public spheres can be defined as 'increased attention for actors and institutions from other European countries in national news media' (Koopmans 2007:186). Why is horizontal Europeanization important for the EU as such? First, the lack of horizontal Europeanization might encourage a purely domestic view on EU issues. Second, debating EU issues without referring to other countries' preferences and perspectives does not allow citizens to understand the reality of European integration as a constant compromise between different political systems. A better understanding of other countries' preferences might facilitate the acceptance and legitimacy of majority decisions at the EU level. Third, a significant dimension of Euroscepticism has to do with mistrust of other countries' legal systems, institutions, etc. A more frequent coverage of other countries' politics and economics in the domestic media might help erode feelings of distrust. That is why promoting horizontal Europeanization was indeed one of the goals of the founding fathers of the Eurobarometer surveys. By familiarizing individuals with the opinions of their fellow European citizens on a variety of issues, Eurobarometer surveys contribute to 'de-nationalizing' national public opinion (Baisnée 2007).

In fact, as for now, domestic mass media have contributed very little to horizontal Europeanization. This can be assessed by quantifying the number of references to non-national actors from other EU countries in media reporting. Domestic media thus contribute to the 'nationalization' of domestic public debate, defined as 'a process whereby national news sources, perspectives and interests are privileged over others' (Downey and Koenig 2006:167). For instance, a comparative survey of the quality press in five countries over a 20 year period (1982–2003) concluded that there was no trend towards increased horizontal Europeanization in domestic media (Brueggeman *et al.* 2006:220). Other comparative surveys concluded that the degree of horizontal Europeanization of domestic media varied greatly from one country to another. While it is relatively strong in Germany, it is very weak in the UK (Kevin 2003) – a fact which might contribute to the distrust dimension underlying British Euroscepticism.

Moreover, horizontal Europeanization is also weak in media reporting on EU issues. For example, an Austrian study on media coverage of the 2004 enlargement found that, even in the quality press (in this case, the left-wing daily *Der Standard*), two-thirds of the actors quoted were nationals, whereas other EU non-nationals only accounted for 24 per cent of all actors quoted. More surprisingly, even among the latter category, only 10 per cent were actors from the candidate countries about to join the EU (Saurwein 2006:137). A similar statement applies to debates on the future of the EU, as was the case during the 2000 debate launched by Joschka Fischer. A study of the quality press in six EU countries found that, during that debate, actors from other European countries (with the exception of Fischer and Chirac, the debate's two main protagonists) only accounted for 15 per cent of the quotations, far behind domestic governments (Trenz 2007:94). It thus seems that other EU nationals are rarely considered as newsworthy sources in domestic mass media. In addition, to the extent that they are quoted, this largely applies to governmental actors and/or large countries' executives (Koopmans 2007; Trenz 2007), a fact which, in smaller and medium-sized countries, might reinforce widespread perceptions of the EU as being dominated by large countries.

The (re)nationalization of public opinion

Certainly, nationalism and even xenophobia are present in segments of the media, for instance in newspapers of the British tabloid press like *The Sun* or *The Daily Mail*. However, even established domestic media can, in some instances, reinforce patterns of national identification, at the expense of a European perspective. Three aspects of this phenomenon are examined below: rallying-round-the-flag reactions against the EU or other EU partners; the use of ethno-nationalist framings in the reporting on specific crises or events; and the use of framing devices that perpetuate national patterns of identification.

Rallying-round-the-flag reactions in domestic media can be either soft or hard. With regard to the soft type, some studies have shown that even the quality press tends to focus on issues where the national government's position is at odds with that of the EU or other EU partners. For instance, during its coverage of the work of the convention that drafted the EU Constitutional Treaty in 2002, the Dutch press focused on issues where the Dutch position was at odds with that of other governments (Crum 2007: 11). Similarly, from 2002 on, Dutch media have been reporting widely on clashes between Dutch finance ministers and their Euro-zone colleagues on the Stability and Growth Pact (Aarts and van der Kolk 2006:244). This might confirm perceptions that there is an in-built contradiction between integration and national interests. Furthermore, rallying-round-the-flag phenomena in the media can also give rise to jingoistic, even xenophobic, statements about the EU or other member states. For instance, the 1996 BSE crisis gave rise to an anti-EU – soon to become an anti-German – campaign in the British tabloid press, as newspapers such as *The Sun*, *The Daily Star* and *The Daily Mail* indulged in gross and radical rhetoric against the Commission and the German government, incorrectly presented as the main initiator of the decision to ban imports of British beef (Alexandre-Collier 2000:126).

However, there are more subtle ways in which media might contribute to a nationalization of domestic public debates since they use an ethno-culturalist framing in order to report on EU politics. The so-called Berlusconi-Schulz case in 2003 illustrates this. In 2003, Italian Prime Minister Silvio Berlusconi, at the time in charge of the EU Presidency, responded to criticism from Martin Schulz, the European Socialist leader in the EP, with a dubious remark bordering on anti-German xenophobia. EU-wide media coverage of the debate triggered by this incident certainly attested to the emergence of a common EU news agenda, but the framings most widely used in reporting did not reflect the emergence of a common European frame of reference. A comparative study of the media coverage of this incident in the quality press of six EU countries showed that it was mainly framed as an interstate dispute between Germany and Italy, rather than as a clash between left-wing and right-wing political leaders or as a clash between European values and jingoistic attitudes. In fact, both protagonists were widely portrayed by the press as 'representatives of ethnic nations' (Downey and Koenig 2006:184). In addition, stereotypical views about Italy and references to century-old antagonisms between European nations abounded in the articles. While two-thirds of them contained at least one ethno-nationalist framing of the incident, only one-tenth framed it as a clash between common EU values and xenophobic populism.

More generally, in day-to-day coverage of the news, domestic media tend to perpetuate patterns of national identification by using an unspecified 'we' to implicitly refer to the national community to which readers or audiences supposedly belong. Studies have shown that the use of this framing device is much more frequent in media reporting than the use of a 'we' referring to a shared European identity. What is more, this framing habit is frequent both in the tabloid and quality press. For instance, the study on the Berlusconi–Schulz debate showed that this form of 'banal nationalism' was present in a majority of articles in quality newspapers (Downey and Koenig 2006:176). Another study on the coverage of the 2004 EU enlargement by the Austrian press showed that references to an implicitly national 'we' were by far the most common framing of collective identity in the dailies. More surprisingly, references to an exclusively national framing of collective identity were as frequent in the Eurosceptic tabloid *Neue Kronen Zeitung* as in the quality newspaper *Der Standard* (Saurwein 2006:172).

Conclusion

Despite an increasing coverage of EU news, evidence that domestic mass media contribute to the emergence of a common European identity is scant. Even the quality press, which is globally supportive of European integration, might contribute to the diffusion of Eurosceptic orientations in different ways, by framing the EU as a purely intergovernmental organization dominated by an all-powerful EU executive or by obscuring the Europe-wide stakes of specific issues, for instance.

Moreover, despite the internationalization of TV and radio programming, news media largely remain consumed in a national context. Patterns of media consumption in some countries clearly reflect a lack of interest in European programming. For instance, large segments of national audiences in some countries (such as the UK, Finland and Sweden) would never watch a EU TV channel, even if it were broadcast in their own language (European Commission 2006b:36). This has implications in terms of attitudes towards the EU since an exclusively national perspective on EU issues may contribute to Euroscepticism. The media coverage of the French referendum campaign in 2005 perfectly illustrated this.

Finally, the issue of Euroscepticism in the media cannot be dissociated from global trends: the increasing parochialism of mass media, the growing relevance of highly specialized media, and a harder competition in media markets, to mention a few. New media in particular are a challenge for EU institutions and pro-EU governments in times of EU-related campaigns (referenda or EP elections). They allow for the emergence of new opinion leaders who capitalize on the gap between elites and citizens on issues of integration.

Chapter 8

Civil Society

This chapter analyzes various forms of Euroscepticism among civil society organizations and social movements. In a context where European integration has gained in relevance for a growing number of civil society actors, existing studies suggest that the latter tend to evaluate the EU more negatively than state actors and political elites. The most common hypothesis, in line with utilitarian theories, is that civil society actors tend to be disadvantaged in their ability to influence EU legislation and policies.

There are nonetheless, arguably, two limits to this hypothesis. First, European integration has a highly diverse impact on civil society actors' opportunity structures. Second, those civil society actors who benefit most from the opening up of new opportunity structures at the EU level are not more pro-European than others, and sometimes less so. This refines the common assumption that the (comparatively) more sceptical stance of (sections of) civil societies towards the EU is simply critical pro-Europeanism. As we shall see, contestation of specific EU legislation and policies may be embedded in a wider scepticism towards the perceived current direction of integration, leading some actors to ask for a general limitation of EU powers.

The chapter begins by presenting the main theories accounting for civil society actors' attitudes towards the EU, stressing the limits of a purely utilitarian perspective based on the opportunity structures theory. Three categories of civil society actors are then analyzed: churches, labour trade unions and social mobilizations (including protest by specific occupational categories and new social movements). While segments of the former (churches and unions, which are traditionally pro-European) are developing a more ambiguous relationship with the EU, it is argued that, contrary to widespread clichés, significant segments of the latter display forms of principled opposition to integration, instead of a simple alternative vision of the EU.

The EU: empowering or weakening civil society?

Compared with state actors and governing parties, 'most civil society actors display below average levels of support for European integration', as well as a more negative evaluation of EU institutions (which they evaluate as negatively as national institutions) (Koopmans 2007:203). How can this be explained? The most common explanation, in line with the utilitarian theory, attributes this comparatively lower support to the limited ability of civil society actors to influence EU-level decision-making processes and make their voice heard in public debates on EU issues, which tend to be dominated by state actors. This hypothesis corroborates intergovernmental theories arguing that European integration empowers national executives at the expense of civil societies, by enhancing a government's autonomy *vis-à-vis* 'particularistic social groups' and by legitimizing controversial policy choices (essentially market liberalization) (Moravcsik 1993:507).

In fact, this general hypothesis must be nuanced in two respects. First, the ability of civil society actors to influence decision-making processes depends on certain 'internal constraints' (Marks and McAdam 1996:258): their own degree of cohesion, and the intensity of their preferences and their resources (in terms of finances, staff, familiarity with decision-making processes, etc.). It could therefore indeed be assumed that European integration tends to empower 'the already powerful' – namely those actors who are able to organize mobilizations at diverse levels of decision-making. Nonetheless, other internal constraints are not related to actors' resources. For instance, the ability to set up transnational mobilizations depends on the social movement's heritage (in terms of ideology, relations with the state, and so on), on its type of organization and on its more or less marked national orientation.

Second, civil society's potential influence also depends on 'external constraints', notably on the characteristics of the issue considered. It is generally assumed that, in policy sectors where distributive costs are either absent or difficult to assess and where social or civic mobilizations find limited support (for instance, EU foreign policy, police and justice cooperation, and institutional reforms), governments enjoy greater leeway than in other sectors (like the CAP, for instance, where distributive consequences are easily assessed) (Moravcsik 1993:494). This potential influence also depends on the more or less transnational dimension of the issue and/or its degree of Europeanization. A high degree of Europeanization does not necessarily mean that it will be easy for outside actors to influence a specific policy. Some EU policies, such as the CAP, have generated robust and more or less exclusive policy networks, which make it difficult for new actors (such as alternative farmers' trade unions) to access decision-making and change the status quo. In that respect, the influence of civil society actors also depends on the receptiveness of EU institutions to their claims (Marks and McAdam 1996:258). This receptiveness, in turn, is partly influenced by the degree of openness of the corresponding Commission departments, which depends on the scope of the Commission's power in a specific field, the strength of political pressure emanating from governments and, consequently, the different needs for outside civil society support. In this context, EU institutions may try to manipulate their cooperation with civil society, by using it as a legitimizing rhetorical device (Eder and Trenz 2003:121).

Consequently, as has been argued elsewhere, European integration does not represent a 'uniform structure of political opportunity' for all civil society actors (Marks and McAdam 1996:258). It empowers some categories of actors, while contributing to the marginalization of others. 'Old' social movements, like labour trade unions, belong to the latter category. Their heterogeneity in terms of national background (for instance, the cleavage between poorer countries and richer countries) and ideological heritage (which is more or less reformist), together with the weak powers of the EU in social issues and the difficulty of transnationalizing traditional modes of mobilization, such as strikes, limit their ability to influence EU-level decision making. By comparison, some of the new social movements, such as the environmental movement, are among the winners of integration. The rather high degree of fit between their modes of action and EU governance, the lesser relevance of national cleavages, and the transnational character of the issues at stake have allowed the environmental movement to participate more easily in EU decision-making processes (Marks and McAdam 1996).

The question remains, however, whether the opportunity structure perspective really influences actors' attitudes towards European integration. If it were the case, trade unions would display a more negative attitude towards the EU than environmentalists or farmers. Existing studies show, however, that trade unions are much more supportive of integration than farmers and rather more supportive than environmentalists (Koopmans 2007; Bursens and Sinardet 2005). In fact, as we have seen in previous chapters, utilitarian theories must be combined with other types of variables in order to account for how civil society actors perceive the EU. Ideological and identity-related variables are also crucial here. As the case of churches illustrates, some EU policies or legislation can be seen as challenging deeply ingrained value systems or an actor's understandings of European identity. Similarly, EU policies can also challenge an actor's own understanding of his/her profession or role in society. For instance, the increasing influence of agro-business on the CAP challenges the status of farmers as well as traditional understandings of their role as the 'feeders' of society (Delorme 2002). Similarly, the EU wine policy – notably the Commission's plan to rely on the massive uprooting of vineyards to tackle production surpluses – has triggered strong resistance on the part of wine growers, partly because the Commission's services had not taken into account the strong symbolic and emotional impact that this decision would have among wine producers (Genieys and Smith 2000). Indeed, to be considered as legitimate, EU policies must also make sense and convey meaning.

The following sections apply this theoretical framework to diverse categories of actors, beginning with churches and labour trade unions. While churches progressively institutionalized their dialogue with the EC in the 1980s, with the creation of the Catholic COMECE (Commission of the Bishops' Conference of the European Community) in 1980, and that of the ecumenical CEC (Conference of European Churches) which brought together Protestants, Anglicans and members of the Orthodox church in 1989, labour trade unions were represented at the EC level as soon as 1973, with the creation of ETUC (European Trade Union Confederation). The EC remained relatively irrelevant to these actors' agendas in the early decades of integration, as they were either focused on national issues or on other European organizations (such as the Council of Europe). Progressively, the EU gained in relevance for these actors, as it undertook the completion of the common market and, later, developed a more political self-understanding, implying the definition of common values. During the Delors presidency of the European Commission, a weakly institutionalized dialogue started to develop with the trade unions (the European social dialogue) and with the churches (as an informal dialogue was established with the group of advisers to the

Commission's President). Churches and trade unions are thus examples of civil society actors who have been involved in a regular dialogue with EU institutions for two decades. Moreover they have been (or have become), on the whole, staunch supporters of European integration. However, as the two next sections argue, tensions are currently emerging between these actors and the EU, as the latter strives to define its normative identity and remains divided about the development of a social Europe.

Churches: a pro-European commitment under stress

Although European integration (in its EC form) was initially of limited interest to churches, the latter have always been largely supportive of the European project. The understanding of European integration as a project of peace was compatible with churches' concerns for fundamental rights and human dignity, and thus encouraged both Protestant and Catholic commitment to European integration. Moreover the prospect that European re-unification would occur under the aegis of the EC, and the fact that European integration would act as a bulwark against communism, were further motives for supporting integration, as Pope John Paul II illustrated in his 1988 speech in the EP. Protestantism has long been associated with lower levels of support for European integration at the societal level (see p.87). For instance, segments of Germany's Protestant liberal middle classes (including leading figures of the Protestant church, such as Pastor Martin Niemöller) were initially reluctant towards the EEC, which they saw as detrimental to future German reunification (Loth 1989:589). However, mainstream Protestant leaders, as well as their Catholic counterparts, were generally favourable to European integration. Both churches have, in some cases, officially supported EC/EU membership, such as the Church of England during the 1975 referendum (Alexandre Collier 2000:44) or the Catholic Church in Austria in the 1994 referendum. Recent trends in the integration process, however, are putting the relationship between churches and the EU under strain. They have highlighted three sources of tensions: concerns over the impact of EU law on the special status of churches in some member states, uncertainty as to the role of churches and religion in the integration process, and fears of a possible interference of EU institutions in deeply normative issues such as marriage, abortion or bioethics.

Concerns over the status of churches

To begin with, churches have expressed concerns relating to their participation in the integration process and over threats to their special (fiscal and/or political) status in some member states. In Italy, for instance, the privileged fiscal status of the Catholic Church has been challenged by the Commission as a consequence of the implementation of EU competition law. This triggered uproar among both left-wing and conservative politicians, who accused the Commission of anti-clericalism. In some countries, especially those where national identity is tightly linked to one predominant religion, a church's privileged relation to the state might be incompatible with requirements resulting from EU membership. Such was the case in Greece, in 2000–01, as the Socialist government decided to remove references to citizen's religious affiliation on identity cards, in order to conform with EU standards on privacy protection and civil rights. The Greek Orthodox Church opposed this change, calling it a 'national betrayal', and strongly protested against the decision. As the Archbishop of Athens declared: 'We are first and foremost Greek and Orthodox and only secondary Europeans' (quoted in Robinson 2001). This is why, on the insistence of churches, a Declaration on the status of Churches and non-confessional organizations was adopted at the Amsterdam European Council, stating that 'the EU respects and does not prejudice the status under national law of churches and religious associations or communities in the member states'.

Disillusionment with an 'atheist' Europe

Moreover, from 2002 on, during the convention for the drafting of the EU Constitutional Treaty, churches expressed deeper concerns about the future role of religion in the integration process. While the main organizations – such as the Catholic COMECE and the Protestant/Orthodox CEC – have officially welcomed the EU Constitutional and Lisbon Treaties, they have expressed reservations on two aspects. The first aspect relates to the lack of reference to Europe's Christian heritage in the preamble of the EU Constitutional Treaty, the second paragraph of which simply refers to 'Europe's cultural, spiritual and humanist' heritage. (The EU Constitutional Treaty's preamble will be added to the preamble of the TEU when the Lisbon Treaty comes into effect.) The second aspect relates to the EU Charter of Fundamental Rights which, while including provisions that have been welcomed by churches (such as the prohibition of the death penalty and of human cloning), is also permeated by a progressive philosophy which does not fit well with traditional understandings of society. This is the case with marriage, for instance. While Article 12 of the ECHR on the right to marry only applies to different-sex couples (according to the case law of the European Court of Human Rights), Article 9 of the EU Charter does not define marriage as the union between a man and a woman, leaving it to national legislators to decide. Similarly, the prohibition of any discrimination based on a person's sexual orientation (Article 21 of the EU Charter) does not fit with the conservative views of segments of the Catholic clergy.

As far as the lack of reference to Christianity is concerned, the most senior members of the Catholic clergy have expressed concerns over an EU that, in their view, negates its own identity. Pope Benedict XVI, in his speech on the fiftieth anniversary of the Rome treaties, compared the lack of reference to Christianity to a form of 'apostasy', adding that 'a community which intends to unite without respecting human dignity and which forgets that every human being is created after God's image will end up doing nobody any good' (Benedict XVI 2007). The main Brussels-based Catholic organization COMECE also deplored the lack of reference to Christianity in the preamble of the treaty (COMECE 2003). Although it did not call for an explicit reference to Christianity, the CEC, for its part, nevertheless warned against the degeneration of European integration into an increasingly soulless, materialistic project: 'What does the EU stand for today? Is it a community of values or a mere expanding market? Is it merely a club of rich people?' (CEC 2001:s.3.1)

National sovereignty on ethical issues

Alongside the debate on the reference to Christianity, large segments of the Catholic Church are increasingly worried about what they see as a potential violation of the subsidiarity principle, by EU institutions, on normative issues such as marriage, abortion and euthanasia. Although such issues do not come within the scope of EU powers, developments in normative integration, the drafting of the EU Charter of Fundamental Rights, and debates in the EP (on reproductive rights, homophobia, or stem cell research, for instance) have been conducive to various expressions of value-based Euroscepticism among segments of the Catholic Church. The EU Charter of Fundamental Rights especially crystallized concerns over a 'political instrumentalization' of EU antidiscrimination legislation in order to change domestic laws on issues such as marriage. Writing on the relationship between religions and the EU, the head of the Brussels-based Catholic European Study and Information Centre echoed these concerns: 'Religions worry about the carelessness and growing frequency with which non-discrimination is being referred to. Whereas a wide ranging implementation of the non-discrimination principle is certainly welcome, some of its uses lead to a disrespect for local and national cultures and violate subsidiarity' (de Charentay 2003:99). This concern has been expressed most clearly in the open letter published by Irish bishops during the 2008 referendum on the Lisbon Treaty, in which the bishops, warning against 'attempts to weaken the sense of subsidiarity', outlined their views of ethics and warned: 'Without doubts, challenges to this common vision will emerge in Ireland and from within the structures in the European Union. In a climate of legal positivism, attempts may well be to use traditional language concerning human dignity in ways which are contrary to traditional sense' (Catholic Bishops of Ireland 2008:5). In a similar vein, the COMECE declared that 'EU institutions should act within the remit of their competences and not encroach upon national competences. This is why we call upon member states to respect, in their respective legislation, the right to life from conception to its natural end and marriage as the union between a man and a woman' (COMECE 2007:s.4).

In 2006, controversies surrounding the EP's adoption of the EU's seventh Research Framework Programme, indirectly authorizing the use of EU funds to finance research on human embryonic stem cells (for therapeutic ends), are a case in point. According to the Secretary General of the COMECE, 'with this decision, the EU would interfere with the delicate national decisions made on this matter and would violate the principle of subsidiarity … Should this become the final decision, it would foster distrust towards the EU and its decision-making processes' (COMECE 2006). The official press organ of the Vatican, *L'Osservatore romano*, reacted by depicting the EU as stubbornly secular and hostile to religious values, as it 'united around a blind secularism' (*L'Osservatore romano* 16–17 June 2006).

Churches certainly remain globally supportive of European integration (indeed, despite its reservations, the COMECE had welcomed the signature of the EU Constitutional Treaty in 2004). However, leaving aside value-based Euroscepticism (which is mostly expressed by the Catholic clergy), church questioning about the role of religion in the integration process raises two important issues. First, they point to the risk that the EU may be increasingly perceived as a mere market (as is highlighted further below in the case of trade unions). Second, they raise the issue of a growing atheism and its impact on support for the integration process. Indeed, it has been found that, among younger Europeans especially, atheism is correlated with lower levels of support for European integration (Nelsen and Guth 2003:100). As most EU countries become increasingly secularized, uncertainties emerge as to how patterns of support for further integration will evolve in the future.

Trade unions: disillusionment with 'social Europe'

Like churches, labour trade unions are generally supportive of European integration. In a move similar to that of mainstream political parties, most trade unions in EU countries converged towards a pro-European position by the end of the 1980s. However, in the last couple of years, this pro-European commitment has been put under strain. As disillusionment with the prospect of a 'social Europe' grows among unions, the completion of the internal market and the two latest enlargement waves have enhanced the perception of increased competitiveness in domestic labour markets. Controversial ECJ rulings in 2007–08 – essentially on the free circulation of services – have come to crystallize these anxieties. As a consequence, tensions are emerging between the EU and trade unions, in a context aggravated by the financial and economic crisis that broke out at the end of 2008. This is happening in a context of declining union density in Europe. In the course of the 1990s, all but seven of the Union's 27 countries experienced a decline in union density. For instance, the powerful German confederation DGB (*Deutscher Gewerkschaftsbund*) lost 43 per cent of its membership between 1991 and 2007. Furthermore, the current average density of 25 per cent in the EU hides large cross-country differences, ranging from 70 per cent in Finland to 8 per cent in France (Fulton 2007).

Recent referenda in France (2005) and Ireland (2008) especially illustrated how widespread concerns over workers' and trade unions' rights are in an enlarged EU. In France, the referendum split the trade unions, as the hard-line CGT (*Confédération Générale du Travail*) and FO (*Force Ouvrière*) campaigned for the No, against the reformist CFDT (*Confédération Française Démocratique du Travail*) and CFTC (*Confédération Française des Travailleurs Chrétiens*). In Ireland, the pro-treaty consensus of trade unions was challenged by the largest craftsmen's union, the TEEU (Technical Engineering and Electrical Union). The TEEU's shift against the Lisbon Treaty followed the controversial ECJ rulings that had been perceived as encroaching on unions' rights (see below) (*The Irish Times* 2008b). The relevance of these concerns was further illustrated by the Conclusions of the European Council in June 2009, which aimed at accommodating Irish voters' concerns at the prospect of a second referendum on the Lisbon Treaty. At the insistence of the Irish government, a 'solemn Declaration on workers' rights and social policy' was adopted, in which the EU proclaims its attachment to the 'protection of workers' rights' (Council of the European Union 2009:Section D).

Concerns on the part of unions are documented by several studies reaching similar conclusions. On the one hand, labour unions remain supportive of the process of European integration; they are even almost as supportive as business associations. On the other hand, they are less positive than the latter in their evaluation of EU institutions, which suggests that they are less satisfied with the current direction of the integration process (Koopmans 2007:204). Indeed, it has been shown that unionists display a rather high affective support for the idea of European integration (higher than anti-globalization activists or environmentalists, for instance), while being both less satisfied and more undecided about the way it is currently proceeding (Bursens and Sinardet 2005:17).

Unions' conversion to 'Europe'

In fact, the pro-European convergence of mainstream trade unions from the end of the 1980s on can be attributed in part to two types of tactical considerations: the hope of counter-balancing neo-liberal policies at the domestic level, and the need to compensate for declining influence in the national arena. By the end of the 1980s, most governments had indeed converted to neo-liberal economic policies (albeit to various degrees), while, at the same time, the EC appeared as a possible new level of (re-)regulation. Indeed, when Jacques Delors (himself a former trade unionist) became President of the European Commission, he attempted to strengthen the social dimension of European integration, with the adoption of the 1989 Community Charter of the Fundamental Social Rights of Workers and the setting up of the European social dialogue. In that respect, Delors' speech before the British Trades Union Congress (TUC) on 8 September 1988, in which he emphasized his vision of a 'social Europe', was key to the pro-EC shift of the TUC. Whereas the TUC had become Eurosceptic during the 1970s, when the EC was suspected of being used by Margaret Thatcher as a vehicle for the reform of British society (which included cracking down on the trade unions) (Fetzer 2007), the pro-EC shift of 1988 relied on the opposite logic: seeing the EC as a counter-weight to radical, neo-liberal reforms in the UK.

Another motivation for trade unions' conversion to European integration was the new structures of opportunity offered by the EC in terms of representation. It has been argued, for instance, that the German trade union confederation's (the DGB) early conversion to the ECSC was due, in part, to the appointment of unionists to the High Authority (Hyman 2001:8). In France, the only union that has been consistently pro-European since the late 1980s, the CFDT (a union belonging to the Christian wing of trade unionism), became strongly involved in European social dialogue and in the ETUC, as part of its pro-EC conversion (Milner 2004). More generally, as trade union membership and influence began to decline in most countries, the conversion to a 'social Europe' could be seen both as a compensation for weakened influence at the national level and, in a manner similar to that of political parties, as a motto filling the 'vacuum of inspirational ideology' (Hyman 2001:4). In that respect, the pro-European convergence of unions was of course facilitated by a general ideological trend in favour of reformist options, of which the French CGT, traditionally close to the Communist party, was the last illustration, as it joined ETUC in 1999. This explains why, in several countries, the shift of mainstream trade unions to a pro-EC course occurred before that of social democratic parties, as was the case in the UK, France (at least for the CFDT), Germany and even Sweden, where the main trade union confederation LO (*Landesorganisationen i Sverige*) campaigned for accession. However, this pro-EC conversion created divisions between trade union leaderships and union rank-and-file members, of which some segments remained hostile towards European integration (Hyman 2001:2).

The challenge of recent ECJ rulings

In the enlarged EU, several factors challenge the pro-European commitment of mainstream union leaderships. By far the most important one results from the combination of the 2004 and 2007 enlargements and the implementation of internal market legislation, as it was interpreted in recent ECJ rulings in 2007–08. To begin with, the enlargement of the EU to (mostly) poorer countries in 2004 and 2007 provides workers from the new member states free access to the domestic labour markets of the older member states. Moreover, the TEC provides for the free movement of workers (art. 39 TEC) and services (art. 49 TCE) within the internal market. These principles were subsequently strengthened by secondary EU legislation, such as the 1996 Directive on the secondment of workers (specifying the working conditions of staff seconded for temporary projects in another member state) and the 2006 Services Directive (which aims at eliminating the remaining obstacles to the free provision of services within the internal market).

Within the last couple of years, the ECJ has had to interpret these provisions in several high-profile cases: the Laval and Viking rulings (2007) and the Rüffert and Commission versus Luxembourg rulings (2008). These cases raised the issue of 'social dumping' in the enlarged EU, as they involved (for two of them) detached, low-wage workers from the new member states working in Sweden and Germany (the Laval and Rüffert cases). Although the Posted Workers Directive states that firms seconding workers in another member state have to abide by the host country's conditions in terms of the minimum legal wage and working time limits, the ECJ declared that this principle only held if the minimum wage applicable was defined by the host country's legislation or by a collective bargain of general, national coverage, which was not applicable in the cases concerned. The Laval and Viking cases especially touched upon union rights. In both cases, Swedish and Finnish unions (in the construction and transport sector respectively) had taken action against the companies involved (the Latvian construction firm Laval which seconded workers in Sweden, and the Finnish shipping company Viking which wanted to hire lower-paid Estonian workers); the unions were subsequently sued by those companies. The

ECJ, while recognizing a union's right to take industrial action, stated that this right could be limited by the employer's right of establishment in order to provide services (in the Viking case) and that the blockade of a construction site by unions (as in the Laval case) violated EU legislation on the freedom to provide services.

Certainly (as the ECJ pointed out in its Laval ruling), national authorities could have implemented the Posted Workers Directive in a more protective way (e.g. by referring to provisions enabling them, in the absence of collective agreements of general coverage, to extend existing agreements to all similar companies working in the same sector). However, the ECJ was seen (partly unjustly so) as preventing public authorities (for instance in the Commission versus Luxembourg case) or unions from fighting against social dumping and as prioritizing market integration over workers' and unions' rights. In fact, blaming the ECJ itself for the weakness of a 'social Europe' makes little sense as governments (especially the British one) have consistently delayed or blocked the development of social legislation at the EU level. As is explained below, this policy is certainly responsible for unions' current perplexity towards the EU.

Changing attitudes towards the EU?

These developments may erode the pro-EU consensus of main-stream unions, notably in those countries (for example, France and the UK) where trade unions underwent a comparatively late conversion to European integration.

In the UK, the pro-European leadership of the TUC is under mounting pressure to manage internal divisions on EU policy. These divisions started emerging with debates on EMU in 2002, as some unions (such as Amicus, the second largest union in the private sector at the time) started distancing themselves from the TUC's pro-EMU line. Furthermore, the TUC's endorsement of the Lisbon Treaty places it in a dilemma since the Labour government has negotiated an opt-out from the EU Charter of Fundamental Rights (which includes social rights). These tensions were exacerbated in early 2009 by controversies surrounding the Posted Workers Directive, as an Italian subcontractor working for Total seconded Italian and Portuguese construction workers to work at the Lindsey oil refinery plant in the UK, triggering several workers' strikes in the country (*The Economist* 27 February 2009). Furthermore, as different sectors of the economy are affected by these trends in different ways, divisions may emerge between unions. Indeed, recent ECJ cases have mainly affected the construction and transport sectors. Transport workers' unions in particular have been concerned by the Viking case and by the 2005 case of an Irish shipping company (Irish Ferries), which replaced Irish staff with low-paid workers from eastern Europe. Both cases triggered the involvement of the International Transport Workers Federation and of national transport workers' unions. This, together with the EU-induced liberalization of freight and passenger railway transport, might be a reason for stronger scepticism towards the EU among those unions and may explain why, at the 2005 annual TUC conference, the National Union of Rail, Maritime and Transport Workers (NURMTW) put forward a motion (which was defeated) against the EU Constitutional Treaty. As a result, the TUC leadership's position in favour of the Lisbon Treaty has been increasingly challenged by sceptical union members, such as the NURMTW and the GMB, as recent annual congresses have shown. In 2007, delegates passed a resolution calling for a referendum to be held on the Lisbon Treaty (TUC 2007:19), reiterating the call in 2008. In addition, a harshly critical resolution (sponsored by the NURMTW) was passed following recent ECJ rulings, which were defined as 'a fundamental attack' on union rights (TUC 2008:8). That this perception might spill over into outright opposition against the Lisbon Treaty was illustrated by the following statement: 'The unelected judges of the EU, using the "free movement" provisions, have disembowelled the concept of social Europe ... The Lisbon Treaty could exacerbate these attacks by handing greater power to the ECJ.'

In the French case, strong internal divisions between decidedly pro-EU and Eurosceptic trade unions remain. For instance, the traditionally pro-European CFDT supported ratification of the EU Constitutional Treaty during the 2005 referendum, while the more sceptical CGT and FO campaigned against it. At the same time, however, disillusionment about the lack of a 'social Europe', notably following the Nice 2001 European Council, when the British government reiterated its opposition to QMV on social legislation, led the CFDT to be more critical of the EU. It joined forces with the CGT and FO during the European Council's alternative summits, in the name of 'another Europe' (Milner 2002). Moreover, mainstream French unions have faced new competition since more hardline confederations, such as SUD (*Solidaires,*

Unitaires, Démocratiques), have emerged. Such competition was clearly seen in the farming sector, as the traditional, Euro-pragmatic FNSEA (*Fédération Nationale des Syndicats d'Exploitants Agricoles*) was challenged, from the second half of the 1990s onwards, by the left-wing *Confédération paysanne* (led by anti-globalization leader José Bové), and by the right-wing *Coordination rurale*, created in 1992 with the aim of opposing reform of the CAP. The latter attracted 18% of the votes in the 2007 elections to the chambers of agriculture. The fact that these unions hold opposing views on the EU was illustrated by the 2005 referendum, when the FNSEA supported the Constitutional Treaty while the *Confédération paysanne* and *Coordination rurale* opposed it.

In countries where trade unions had apparently been less divided on European integration, recent developments related to EU enlargement and to ECJ case law have led to more criticism. In Austria and Germany, trade union confederation leaderships from the ÖGB (*Österreichischer Gewerkschaftsbund*) and DGB have officially been supportive of EU enlargement, at the price, however, of restrictions on eastern European workers' access to domestic labour markets. Out of the seven older member states that had applied transitional limitations on labour market access between 2006 and 2009, only Austria and Germany decided to maintain these restrictions beyond May 2009 (they will have to be lifted between 2011 and 2014). The Austrian authorities have added restrictions on the temporary secondment of foreign workers in some sectors. This explains the officially pro-enlargement stance of both confederation leaderships, despite widespread hostility within union ranks. For instance, an opinion poll in Austria on the 2004 EU enlargement found that unionists were among the most hostile towards enlargement, together with the extreme right party FPÖ (Saurwein 2006:150). In this context, recent ECJ case law has provoked harsh criticism from the traditionally strongly pro-European German confederation DGB. Commenting on the four ECJ rulings concerned, the DGB declared that 'the predominance of the EU Internal Market, which is perceptible in these rulings, is unacceptable. The DGB asks that priority be given to fundamental social rights over the four freedoms of the Internal Market' (DGB 2008:2). The DGB has asked that a social chapter stating this principle be inserted in the EU treaties and that the Posted Workers Directive and other pieces of legislation (for example, on public procurement rules) be reformulated, in order to better protect workers' rights.

The dilemmas of ETUC

For ETUC, whose leadership remains strongly in favour of further integration (as its successive endorsements of the Constitutional and Lisbon Treaties have shown), these evolutions represent a significant challenge. First of all, it is likely to increasingly be faced with internal divisions between national union members. Its vote on the EU Constitutional Treaty in 2004 (which was unanimously approved by the executive committee) was a first sign of this, as some member unions from France, Sweden and Portugal abstained during the vote (the French FO (*Force Ouvrière*) being the only union to vote against it). These divisions might also be heightened by the accession of new union members as a result of enlargement. Whereas new union members are supportive of further integration (they all voted in favour of the Constitutional Treaty), there are differences between (some) older members and new members on socio-economic issues, notably on the free movement of workers. ETUC also faces the problem of divisions between sectors. For instance, the European Federation of Transport (an ETUC member) abstained during the vote on the Constitutional Treaty.

Second, ETUC finds itself in a difficult situation as it may be perceived as being 'out of sync' with its members on EU issues. For instance, its very moderate criticism of the ECJ Laval ruling (which it qualified as 'disappointing') contrasted with some union members' strong reactions against recent ECJ case law. This was the case, for instance, in the *Commission* v. *Luxembourg* ruling, which triggered a large demonstration in Luxembourg in 2008, when unions from several countries (including Belgium, France, Germany (with the heavyweight DGB) and Switzerland) rallied with their Luxembourg counterparts.

In 2009, ETUC reacted to its members' unease about recent ECJ rulings by calling on governments to include a 'social protocol' in EU treaties and to reform the Posted Workers Directive (ETUC 2009). However, these attempts to influence the debate on 'social Europe' should not detract from the fact that ETUC's capacity for action is limited by two factors. First, there are serious obstacles to the development of social Europe, notably the lack of union cohesion and the absence of governmental consensus in favour of this concept. Second, ETUC's ability to respond to union concerns is limited by its own institutionalized position within the EU political system. As noted by specialists in social mobilization: 'ETUC's conundrum is that to the extent that it has adopted the logic of lobbying that links it to EU officialdom, it is unable to draw upon the tactic of mobilization that is the most familiar and powerful weapon its constituents possess on the national level' (Tarrow and Imig 1999:250).

Social mobilizations and new social movements: alter- or anti-European?

There is much debate about whether social protest against specific EU policies and dimensions of European integration is a form of Euroscepticism. It has been argued that, to the extent that these mobilizations are Europeanized (that is, organized on a transnational basis) and/or that they do not reject the idea of a European identity (but mobilize instead for 'another Europe'), they contribute to the formation of 'European collective identities', through interactions among 'ordinary Europeans' (Tarrow and Imig 1999:22). Conflicts over EU policies and over the current trajectory of the integration process would thus lead to 'Europeanization by contestation' (Della Porta 2006:19). Moreover, the growing number of claims addressed to the EU indicates that the latter is increasingly perceived as 'a relevant level of governance', as the emerging European dimension of the alter-globalization movement in recent years indicates (for a definition of this term, see p.239). This has implications in terms of legitimacy, as 'the EU is indirectly legitimized by social movement organizations that recognize its competences, by addressing at the European level claims of various types' (Della Porta 2006).

It is argued here that these theses must be refined in three respects. First, opposition to specific EU policies, as in the case of social mobilizations led by occupational groups, is often correlated with a more principled opposition to further integration. Second, levels of attachment to Europe or to the EU among social protesters and alter-globalization activists are relatively low. Third, 'Europeanized' protest represents only a small part of global social protest in Europe. This is illustrated below by two examples: social mobilization in the form of specific occupational protest, and the alter-globalization movement.

Transnational social protest

Early opposition to European integration in the 1950s was intense among specific social groups, notably among those who today are staunch supporters of the EU, such as business associations. In France, for instance, protectionist-minded business representatives were hostile towards trade liberalization in an EEC context, fearing that it would be faster and more far-reaching than in a looser organization like the OEEC (Parsons 2006:118). Their German counterparts also favoured an OEEC option, but for opposing reasons. They wanted a big free trade area instead of a protectionist common market (Loth 1989:595). In both countries, farmers' associations were strongly hostile to the setting up of the EEC. While French farmers thought the common market would be too small for French exports, while also fearing competition from their Dutch and Italian counterparts (Parsons 2006:118), German farmers were concerned about competition from Dutch and French farmers and strongly opposed the common market (Loth 1989:597). Later on, while hostility towards integration had given way to strong support among business associations (although the situation was much more complex in the post-SEA phase, at least in the UK), the violent reaction of French farmers in the wake of Spain's EC accession sparked occasional protests, particularly in southern France. It is essentially in the post-SEA era that social protest against EU policies increased. The share of protest directed against EU policies (as a proportion of all registered social protest) in the course of the 1990s rose from less than 5 per cent in the early 1990s to almost 10 per cent by the end of the decade (Imig 2002:923).

However, the overwhelming majority of all social protest in Europe is not 'Europeanized'. For instance, Douglas Imig (2002) found that 95 per cent of protest in western Europe at the end of the 1990s concerned purely domestic issues. As far as transnational protests are concerned, it has been argued that in 80 per cent of cases, social mobilizations were conducted in a purely national context (Chabanet 2002). Of course, there are instances of successful transnational European protest. A good example of this was the 2006 mobilization of dockworkers against the liberalization of port services (known as the Port Package II Directive, which would have allowed private service providers to load and unload freight without employing the port's affiliated workers). Partly coordinated by the European Federation of Transport Workers, the demonstration in front of the EP in Strasburg, which brought together dock workers from sixteen EU countries, went hand in hand with parallel strikes in several European ports and led to the withdrawal of the directive proposal in March 2006. Other examples include coordinated action by truck drivers or farmers. However, this type of transnational action still represents a small proportion of all social protest in Europe and overwhelmingly concerns few occupational categories: farmers, who accounted for half of all EU-generated protest at the end of the 1990s, followed by fishermen, construction workers and mine workers (Imig 2002:924). For the time being at least, this redefines the idea that Europeanized social protest may pave the way for Europeanized collective identities on a significant scale.

Moreover, the idea that these protests simply express opposition to specific EU policies, without expressing a wider resentment towards the EU as such, must be examined in closer detail. In fact, the very characteristics of the EU political system – the lack of a government/opposition logic, of alternative political majorities and of an identifiable opposition at the EU level – foster a form of spill-over from opposition to specific policies to opposition to the EU as such. As citizens are unable to protest against unpopular EU policies by changing the EU's executive via elections, they tend to direct their dissatisfaction against the EU. As Neunreither describes it: 'policy-oriented opposition tends to change into another category: into politics or into systemic opposition' (1998:437).

In fact the opposition of specific social groups to trade liberalization in the context of the common market was already underlain by hostility towards supranationalism *per se* in the 1950s. For example, the hostility of French farmers towards the EEC was due not only to protectionist considerations, but also to a political hostility towards supranationalism along the lines of the ECSC, which was perceived as being bureaucratic, *dirigiste* and biased in favour of consumer interests (Parsons 2006). In Germany, opposition to the EEC among economists and the founding fathers of the German model of a social market economy lay not only in their preferences for international free trade, but also in deep scepticism towards a possible spill-over from economic to political integration. In the words of one of these economists, Alfred Müller-Armack: 'The more national interests are subjected to a complex form of dirigisme ... the more states are compelled to do things they would not do in the interest of partner countries, [and] the more a Common Market is bound to produce antagonism' (quoted in Loth 1989:595).

As regards social protest against EU policies in the 1990s, it has been shown that 'the great majority of European protests have advanced Left political economic demands [i.e. for more protectionism] and called for greater national sovereignty' (Imig 2002:928).

In fact, dissatisfaction with specific policies does not necessarily lead to demands for increased EC regulatory powers but is often coupled with demands for more state protection and independence. Besides, the pro-/anti-integration dimension of social protest became more significant in the course of the 1990s. While it was almost absent in 1990, it was present in half the protests at the end of the decade. This suggests that in the course of the 1990s European integration became more clearly linked, in collective perceptions, to redistributive impacts and economic liberalization.

The correlation between opposition to specific EU policies and principled opposition to further integration is well illustrated by the example of farmers. Compared to a broad range of civil society actors (trade unions, media, etc.), farmers display the most negative evaluation of EU institutions (with the exception of consumers). Together with national media, they are the only category of actors to evaluate EU institutions more negatively than national ones (Koopmans 2007). EU-related referenda provide some information on the attitude of farmers towards further integration. During the French referendum on the Maastricht Treaty, farmers overwhelmingly voted No (up to 70 per cent) (Perrineau 2005). While they were not considered a separate category during the 2005 referendum, the predominance of the No vote in rural areas (Boy and Chiche 2005) suggests that a large majority of them may have voted against the treaty. In the Irish case, farmers voted marginally in favour of the Lisbon Treaty, although they also recorded 'a strong No vote' (Milward and Brown 2008).

While Euro-protests are largely of an occupational nature, scholars studying social mobilization in Europe have pointed to a new trend: the emergence of non-occupational mobilization mainly addressing 'post-materialist' claims (migrant rights, environmental protection, anti-racism, etc.) to EU institutions (Imig 2002). The recent projection of the alter-globalization movement onto the EU level is one manifestation of this trend.

The alter-globalization movement

The alter-globalization movement is a good example of a movement to which the EU has recently become relevant. This sub-section will set the movement in a broader historical context and sketch its development in relation to the EU. The idea of simple 'alter-Europeanism' will be examined: first, by showing that although it was once limited to specific policies, alter-globalist criticism has grown into a wider criticism of EU institutions and the prevailing logic of integration; and second, by analyzing the results of qualitative surveys that suggest that diffuse support for the EU is rather low in the European alter-globalization movement, which remains deeply divided between a reformist approach and anti-system opposition to the EU.

Taken from the French, the term 'alter-globalizers' theoretically refers to activists who, contrary to 'anti-globalizers', do not oppose a free market economy and international cooperation as such but rather, the perceived direction of economic globalization and its potentially damaging social and environmental consequences. Instead of advocating a return to protectionist options, they intend to put forward alternatives to unregulated free trade (for example, fair trade) and wish to refom the agenda of organizations like the WTO accordingly. The alter-globalization movement was initially focused on institutions of global governance. The first milestone in its development was the 1996–98 international campaign against the Multilateral Agreement on Investment (MAI), negotiated within the OECD, which, according to its opponents, risked driving down social and environmental standards globally by exacerbating competition between countries in order to attract foreign investment. Initially started in Australia and the US (where the NGO Public Citizens Global Trade Watch was especially active against the MAI), the movement triggered the formation of a broad-based coalition of consumer associations, environmentalists, labour and human rights activists and trade unions. Soon, the alter-globalization movement extended its scope to other international organizations, such as the WTO – notably during the Seattle Ministerial Conference of 1999 (which brought together at least 40,000 activists) – and the G8 (notably during the 2001 Genoa summit).

The emergence of the alter-globalization movement at EU level results from the confluence of several trends. The European Marches against unemployment, job insecurity and social exclusion were first launched at the 1997 Amsterdam European Council (where they brought together around 50,000 protesters) and have been perpetuated annually ever since. Although these marches did not articulate alter-globalist claims *per se*, they overlapped partly with the alter-globalization movement, notably at the 2001 Laeken summit (which united about 80,000 unionists and 20,000 alter-globalists). The most significant milestone showing that the EU had definitively acquired relevance for the alter-globalization movement was the organization of the first European Social Forum in Florence in 2002, which reunited 60,000 activists and which is now an annual event. The EU's external relations and inter-regional cooperation with other trade blocks have also come under attack from alter-globalists. A good illustration of this is the ASEM (Asia–Europe Meeting) process, an informal forum of cooperation between the EU and sixteen Asian countries, which has become a focal point for alter-globalization protests since its third summit in Seoul in 2000. NGOs denounce ASEM's predominant focus on trade issues, the role of big corporations in the process (in particular via the Asia–Europe Business Forum), and the poor representation of civil society. ASEM is seen by alter-globalists as a vehicle for deregulation and global trade liberalization. What is more, NGOs that were initially focused on the EU's internal issues, such as improving transparency and the regulation of lobbying activities at the EU level, have started denouncing the 'corporate bias' of ASEM (CEO 2002) as part of a wider attempt to regulate and limit the role of corporations in the integration process. This is, for example, the case with the Corporate Europe Observatory (CEO), an association created in 1997 which prompted the creation, in 2005, of ALTER-EU, a coalition of 140 civil society organizations campaigning for more transparency in EU decision-making. In parallel to this, European offshoots of the international alter-globalization movement have been created, such as the European ATTAC Network or the coordination platform 'From Seattle to Brussels', which coordinates the EU-level activities of NGOs belonging to the alter-globalization movement.

The alter-globalization movement is distinctly heterogeneous, including as it does environmental NGOs (Friends of the Earth, Greenpeace), NGOs working in the field of development cooperation and north/south relations (Oxfam), human rights NGOs (Amnesty International), non-mainstream farmer associations (Via Campesina), organizations initially focused on opposition to international trade liberalization (Globalise Resistance, ATTAC), and many others. These organizations do not all share the same views of the EU, and some of them remain focused on the policies that are of specific interest to them, such as the CAP and decisions on GMOs for Via Campesina. Nonetheless, some organizations, such as ATTAC and the organizers of the European Social Forum, have come to articulate a wider criticism of the EU, bordering on principled opposition to integration.

ATTAC (Association for the Taxation of financial Transactions and for Civic Action) was initially created in 1998 with the purpose of campaigning for the implementation of the so-called Tobin tax on financial transactions. It started mobilizing at the EU level in 2000, at the time of the Nice European Council. The core of its criticism against the EU, which ATTAC describes as 'undemocratic and antisocial' (ATTAC 2009), targets the EU's alleged neo-liberal bias, its emphasis on free competition, its trade liberalization policy and the ECB's exclusive focus on price stability. Beyond this core of traditional alter-globalist arguments, ATTAC has broadened its criticism in two directions: EU institutional issues and the EU's external relations. Regarding the former, ATTAC disparages the EU for its 'deep democratic deficit', which it attributes to an unclear division of powers, to the Commission's monopoly over legislative initiative (in the first pillar) and to the fact that the EP has too little power in some policy areas. Furthermore, it accuses the ECJ of exceeding its remit by acting 'as a de facto legislator' (2009). It also strongly criticized the EU Charter of Fundamental Rights (which it considered gave insufficient protection to social and women's rights) (ATTAC 2007). Consequently, it was a key actor of the No campaign against the EU Constitutional Treaty in the 2005 French referendum and opposed the ratification of the Lisbon Treaty. Regarding the EU's external relations, ATTAC seeks a stronger emphasis on the EU's independence of NATO and deplores the alleged 'militarization' of the EU through the ESDP (2009).

As far as the European Social Forum is concerned, its agenda seems to be heavily influenced by that of ATTAC. It articulates similar criticisms, for instance on the division of powers in the EU, albeit in a more radical tone. Denouncing what it sees as 'the failure of Europe's neo-liberal, anti-democratic and patriarchal construction', it disparages the EU as being exclusively a union of states and governments, to be replaced with a 'Europe of the peoples', where social rights would be guaranteed and the issue of the relationship with NATO 'resolved' through the latter's dissolution (ESF 2008).

Despite such criticisms, the position of organizations like ATTAC on the future of the EU remains unclear. This exposes the strong internal divisions of the alter-globalization movement. To begin with, it is not clear whether ATTAC views its criticism of the EU as part of a reformist strategy or as an anti-system, principled opposition, implying that the EU should be replaced by another type of organization. For instance, the European ATTAC Network's report on the future of the EU advocates the drafting of a new founding treaty, resulting from a directly elected convention, while at the same time advocating an extension of the current EP's power (ATTAC 2009). What is more, ATTAC does not define the type of institutional model it wants for the Union (federation, confederation, or other). The fact that it has no official position on some of the Lisbon Treaty's main institutional reforms (the election of a permanent European Council President, the shift to double majority voting in the Council, or the setting up of a High Representative for foreign and security policy) is indicative of these divisions (ATTAC 2007). As ATTAC's co-founder, Bertrand Cassen, recognized, the organization is divided between federalists (who criticize the EU for being too intergovernmental) and advocates of a 'Europe of nations' model (who criticize the EU for being too deeply integrated) (Cassen 2005). The case of ATTAC illustrates the deep ambiguity of the alter-globalization movement towards institutions of global governance. On one hand, these institutions are currently the only vehicles for some form of (re-) regulation at the regional or global level; on the other, they rely on a policy mix of both regulatory and liberalization logics.

This ambiguity extends to alter-globalization activists' perception of the EU. Indeed, a survey of protesters at the 2001 Laeken summit showed that alterglobalists (compared with trade unionists and environmentalists) were the most divided on the issue of European identity and identification with Europe independently of the EU (Bursens and Sinardet 2005). Alter-globalization activists seemed divided between a reformist stance and a principled opposition to the EU. On the one hand, they displayed low levels of trust in and attachment to EU institutions. A survey conducted at the 2002 European Social Forum in Florence showed that half of them did not trust the EU at all. In the same vein, the majority of respondents (52.5 per cent) at the Florence summit displayed little or no attachment to Europe in its current (EU) form (Della Porta 2006). On the other hand, they remain ambiguous as to whether existing organizations, including the EU, should be abolished or strengthened. In fact, while a relative majority of roughly 40 per cent of alter-globalist protesters in Laeken opposed EU membership, they were almost evenly split on the issue (Bursens and Sinardet 2005). Similarly, while advocates for the abolition of other organizations (such as the WTO) are clearly over-represented among alter-globalists (compared with environmentalists, for instance), they appear to be split on the issue of whether to extend the powers of organizations of regional or global governance (Della Porta 2006; Bursens and Sinardet 2005). What is more, national differences in perceptions of the EU remain strong among participants, as was the case with the Florence protesters. Regarding the attachment to Europe, there is an almost 20 percentage point difference between Germans and Britons. Similarly, while almost half of French protesters were in favour of extending the EU's power to face global challenges (which reflects French preferences for strong public authorities), 85 per cent of their British counterparts were strongly opposed to it (Della Porta 2006).

Finally, what emerges is a picture which refines the thesis of alter-globalists as forerunners of an alternative European identity: first, because attachment to the idea of European identity is not an overwhelmingly predominant orientation among organizations and protesters; second, because organizations and individual activists seem to be remaining deeply divided over the alternatives of strengthening or abolishing existing institutions of regional and global governance. Ironically, the latter option is favoured by alter-globalists' ideological foes, the ultra-liberals.

The ultra-liberals: fighting EU-level regulations

Indeed, the focus on left-wing organizations of the alter-globalization movement should not detract from the fact that other civil society actors are hostile to the EU for opposite reasons, as they see the EU's regulatory agenda as incompatible with their vision of a largely unregulated economy. Among those actors are think-tanks in the United States and the UK articulating a right-wing neo-liberal type of Euroscepticism, such as, for example, the Heritage Foundation, which is concerned about the interests of US companies possibly being harmed by EU regulations and competition law: 'The EU is acting as the world's greatest regulator ... [It] is now exporting its growth-sapping formula to the rest of the world ... [It] now determines the antitrust regime for big American companies' (McNamara 2008:9). The Heritage Foundation, which hosts the Margaret Thatcher Centre for Freedom, largely shares Thatcher's hostility towards regional or global regulations. Thatcher's view that the Rome treaties should be a 'Charter of economic liberty' (1988:6) would not be rebutted by the Foundation, which advocates the replacement of the WTO with an alliance of free-trading nations, sharing 'a commitment to free trade and minimum regulation' (Huisman 2005).

In the UK, similarly-minded think-tanks include the Bruges group, created in 1989 and named after Thatcher's 1988 speech, which has a clearly neo-liberal agenda (Usherwood 2004:10) and other anti-EMU think-tanks, such as Open Europe (led by businessmen opposed to EMU) and the European Foundation (which was financed by Lord Goldsmith and advocates a re-negotiation of all EU treaties since Maastricht). Although these groups claim that they are not in favour of abolishing the EU (or withdrawing from it), they advocate a radical reform of the Union, which would be stripped of most of its power apart from market-making legislation. Some anti-EMU parties, such as the Referendum Party in the UK (founded by Lord Goldsmith) and the Swedish June list (founded by two formerly social democratic economists), hold similar liberal views. In the UK, this coincides with the Eurosceptic shift of certain business sectors. During the last decade the City has become more receptive to stances opposing EU regulations (Grant 2008:6). The Confederation of British Industry has mustered a strong opposition against the EU Charter of Fundamental Rights, which entails principles such as the right to work, prompting the Labour government to negotiate an optout.

Conclusion

In its 2001 White Paper on European governance, the European Commission advocated stronger involvement of civil society in EU decision-making as a way of tackling Euroscepticism and citizens' lack of trust in EU institutions. The aim was to offer civil society organizations a 'structured channel for feedback, criticism and protest'. Such an argument is in line with the opportunity structure theory, suggesting that opposition can be defused by participation. However, this strategy was based on the premise that 'civil society increasingly sees Europe as offering a good platform to change policy orientations and society' (European Commission 2001).

That this is the case remains to be seen, however. Certainly, there are examples of successful mobilizations by civil society organizations that have had a real impact on the EU's agenda. A good illustration of this relates to the police and justice cooperation agenda (formerly called Justice and Home Affairs or JHA), which, NGOs argued, was biased in favour of a law and order approach. In this case, the mobilization of critical civic rights organizations (such as Statewatch), prompted governments to enlarge the JHA agenda in order to include issues such as the fight against xenophobia and the rights of immigrants and asylum-seekers (under the new heading of Justice, Liberty, Security) (Eder and Trenz 2003).

However, in some cases, European integration is perceived as further disempowering civil society actors and contributing to the weakening of counter-forces that are crucial for the safeguarding of democracy, such as labour trade unions. As the reactions to recent ECJ case law suggest, the EU might increasingly be perceived as a purely economic project eliciting little affective support. Dissatisfaction with specific EU policies can thus easily translate into systemic opposition against the EU as such. In the absence of an alternative model defended by 'European civil society', advocates of the anti-regulation discourse may well win the battle over the evolution of the European project.

Chapter 9

Understanding Euroscepticism

This chapter assesses, based on the book's main findings, how valuable different theories can be in enhancing our understanding of Euroscepticism.

The first section considers the nature and dimensions of Euroscepticism: to what extent does Euroscepticism relate to the EU as such? Does Euroscepticism only express dissatisfaction with specific EU policies or does it also relate to the political system of the EU (institutions, modes of decision-making, etc.)? It is argued that, while Euroscepticism is not exclusively EU-scepticism, it nevertheless expresses dissatisfaction with the EU as such, with its policies as well as with its institutions.

Drawing on theories of political support, the second section introduces the distinction between specific and diffuse support. It examines their interaction in the EU context, by stressing differences between patterns of support at national and EU levels. It explains why diffuse support for the EU is less robust than diffuse support for national political systems, and why lack of specific support is more likely to affect diffuse support in the case of the EU.

The third section deals with the rationale underlying Eurosceptic orientations. It evaluates the respective relevance of utilitarian, normative and identity-based theories in accounting for Euroscepticism at individual and collective levels.

The fourth section assesses how findings from research on Euroscepticism can be expanded to enhance our understanding of patterns of support for international governance.

The dimensions of Euroscepticism: scepticism about the EU

As we have seen, perceptions of the EU are largely influenced by issues apparently unrelated to European integration, such as citizens' perception of national democracy, immigration, multiculturalism and so on. At the same time, several chapters have emphasized the fact that Euroscepticism is also about the EU, its policies and its institutions.

Scepticism about national democracy and the EU

First of all, Euroscepticism is scepticism 'towards our own national institutions and modes of governance'; it expresses scepticism 'about how we are governed' (Mair 2007:16). Indeed, as we have seen, there is a close correlation between public distrust of (elected) national institutions, dissatisfaction with the way democracy works at the national level and defiance towards EU institutions. There is also strong interdependence between EU institutions and the member states, and expressions of political cynicism and distrust are likely to spill over from one level to another.

At the same time, however, this book challenges assumptions about Euroscepticism as an epiphenomenon that simply reflects attitudes towards domestic politics or national macro-economic perspectives. The so-called proxies theory, for instance, argues that citizens' attitudes towards EU issues are in fact 'proxies' for their opinions on domestic politics (in particular their satisfaction with incumbent governments and their support for the national political system) (Anderson 1998). However, recent EP election trends suggest that turnout and party choice in European elections are increasingly (albeit not predominantly) influenced by attitudes towards the EU (see p.129). Similarly, recent EU-related referenda reflected widespread concerns about the (perceived) current direction of the integration process.

Scepticism about policies and institutions

These concerns do not only relate to specific EU policies. An important question concerns the kind of political objects through which citizens perceive the EU. Do they view it mainly through the outputs or do they also apprehend it through its inputs? While the outputs of a political system refer to the policies and general performance of political authorities, the inputs refer to the 'basic political arrangements' (Easton 1975:437) underlying the political system (underlying values, distribution of powers between institutions, decision-making processes, etc.).

Policies and general performance: a more complex pattern of support

To begin with, patterns of support for EU policy outputs are becoming more complex. Until the end of the 1980s, support for integration was closely correlated with growth in intra-EC trade and with general perceptions of macro-economic conditions (Eichenberg and Dalton 2007:131). This changed as a result of three trends: the expansion of the number of EU policies, which automatically increased the probability that citizens might disagree with one or several policies; increasing concerns over EU policies (such as EMU or enlargement) that are perceived as having redistributive effects, within and between countries; and the extension of EU powers or the indirect impact of integration on non-economic, normative and cultural issues.

Moreover, regarding the perceived general performance of the EU, one of the main problems in the post-Maastricht era relates to the increasing number of tasks allocated to the EU, without corresponding means to deliver on these policies – the so-called capabilities–expectations gap. This problem is exacerbated by citizens' lack of information on the actual scope of EU powers. The fight against unemployment is a good example. Although the Amsterdam Treaty inserted a new title on employment in the TEC, the EU only has loose coordination powers in this policy area. Furthermore, contrary to widespread assumptions, citizens are able to evaluate the EU's performance, even in foreign policy issues. The EC's failure in former Yugoslavia is a case in point. In the autumn of 1991, a majority of EC citizens (and nearly 70 per cent in Germany) thought that EC initiatives in Yugoslavia had not been useful (EB 36:40).

Institutions matter: the growing relevance of inputs

Patterns of support for the EU are also becoming more complex because general attitudes towards the EU are increasingly influenced by perceptions of the inputs of the EU political system. Variables such as satisfaction with the way democracy works in the EU are more or less relevant to the formation of general attitudes towards the EU according to country context and type of actor. While it is largely relevant in countries where citizens are satisfied with national democracy, it is much less relevant in others (see p.82). Similarly, while it has been identified as the main factor influencing MEPs' general attitude towards the EU, it has been found to be almost irrelevant for their national counterparts (see p.133).

Nonetheless, public perceptions regarding the perceived responsiveness and trustworthiness of EU institutions play a significant role in voting behaviour during EP elections and EU-related referenda (see p.188). Indeed, recent research shows that distrust of EU institutions is an important dimension of Euroscepticism and has a direct impact on support, independently of other variables (McLaren 2007; Abts *et al.* 2009). There appears to be a correlation between perceived evolutions of EU policies and the growing relevance of inputs. The more policies crystallize redistributive and/or normative concerns, the more institutional issues such as the extension of QMV and related fears of being outvoted, or the prospect of 'losing' a Commissioner, become significant.

Contrary to widespread views, one of the main conclusions of this book is that Euroscepticism does not merely express dissatisfaction with specific EU policies or with the EU's perceived general performance. It also expresses scepticism towards the political system of the EU as such. At this point, classical theories of political support, and especially David Easton's distinction between specific support and diffuse support, can shed light on this aspect of the debate.

Specific or diffuse: what kind of support for the EU?

Specific and diffuse support

According to David Easton, political regimes can elicit two types of support: specific support and diffuse support. Whereas specific support refers to satisfaction with specific policies or with the general performance of incumbent governments (the outputs of the system), diffuse support relates to general support for the political regime. Diffuse support, especially, is crucial to the endurance of a regime since it constitutes 'a reservoir of favourable attitudes ... that helps members to accept or tolerate outputs to which they are opposed'. When diffuse support is secured, significant variations in specific support can occur, without endangering general attachment to the political system. Conversely, in the absence of diffuse support, positive outputs or performance will not easily translate into increased support for the political regime. Can the EU rely on a 'reserve of goodwill' (Easton 1975) robust enough to endure, even when citizens strongly disagree with specific policies or evaluate the EU's general performance negatively?

The EU's problem: a lack of diffuse support

First of all, diffuse support for the EU political system (i.e. support for EU membership) is rather fragile because it is not rooted in the most common source from which it usually arises in a national context – political socialization. In a national context, people are socialized into supporting national institutions by being exposed to 'rituals surrounding the selection' of office holders, 'official ceremonies on formal political occasions, the symbols of office, the affirmation of faith on patriotic days', and so on. (Easton 1975:446). This symbolic dimension of power, which sustains support for the political regime, is almost absent at the EU level. The EU suffers from a 'symbols deficit' which flag and anthem alone cannot tackle.

What is more, scholars of comparative politics have emphasized the fact that specific features of the EU political system are likely to erode existing diffuse support. The lack of a government/opposition dynamic and the lack of strong, EU-level counter-weights (such as fully-fledged European parties, a unified trade union movement and a European public sphere) generate frustrations about citizens' ability to bring about policy change.

The limited effect of cumulative specific support

The other possible source of diffuse support for the political regime is experience. As citizens accumulate specific support over the years, they may develop diffuse support for the political regime (Easton 1975). This was the main assumption of the neo-functionalist theory, proponents of which were well aware of the instrumental dimension of support for EEC institutions among national political elites (Haas 1968). Moreover, they had foreseen the possibility of setbacks or stagnation in the integration process. Nonetheless, the neo-functionalists' core assumption was that, at some point in the integration process, the sum of expectations and allegiances directed towards EC institutions would supersede those placed with the nation state, thus eventually producing a massive re-orientation of citizens' allegiance from the nation state towards EC institutions (a process described as 'political spill-over'). As EC institutions would satisfy an increasing number of needs, cumulative utilitarian support would spill over into affective support for the EC.

In fact, several neo-functionalist postulates have been proved wrong. First of all, the EC has been allocated very limited redistributive powers. As the satisfaction of fundamental social needs remained associated with the state, utilitarian support for the EU was bound to remain limited. At the same time, the assumption that acceptance of further integration would endure because European integration was perceived as a 'zero-sum game' (Haas 1968) was contradicted by developments in the 1990s, as it became clear that market integration and EMU implied redistributive consequences within and between states. Secondly, the assumption that socialization processes in institutions like the Council would Europeanize national political elites proved wrong. The Council remained the core institution of the representation of national interests and served to perpetuate patterns of public opinion formation. Ministerial press conferences after Council meetings, held in front of national press correspondents based in Brussels, are a good illustration of this. Similarly, the assumption that 'national consciousness would remain weak' (Haas 1968) also proved wrong, as did predictions that a transnational civil society would emerge at the EU level (see p.237).

The shift from specific to diffuse support has thus remained limited in the case of the EU. Certainly, it can be hypothesized that cumulative specific support has led to an 'integration threshold' (Haas 1968). Indeed, a majority of citizens do not want their country to withdraw from the EU. However, as the evolution of public opinion in the post-Maastricht period has illustrated, diffuse support remains volatile. Moreover, even those groups who strongly benefit from EU policies, EU legislation or the ECJ's case law do not necessarily develop forms of diffuse support for the EU. This is the case for environmentalists (who, while being rather satisfied with EU policies in the environmental field, display comparatively low levels of affective support for the EU) and women (who display comparatively higher levels of Euroscepticism, while being clear beneficiaries of EU legislation and ECJ case law on gender equality).

Utilitarian, normative and identity-based scepticism

Questions about different forms of support for the EU also relate to the debate about the respective relevance of utilitarian versus value- or identity-based theories to the formation of preferences regarding European integration. While utilitarian theories, based on interests, dominated the field in the 1980s and 1990s, a new interest in identity- and value-based theories has emerged since the end of the 1990s, thus mirroring the parallel developments of the integration process. This book's findings allow us to draw some conclusions about the respective relevance of these theories in explaining Euroscepticism.

Post-materialism: political union as a result of value change

The post-materialist theory is one of the earliest theories to have studied patterns of public opinion formation in relation to the EC. Initially developed by Ronald Inglehart in the late 1970s, this theory relies on a core distinction between two value systems: materialism and post-materialism. Whereas the former emphasizes 'conservative' values such as public order, physical security and economic growth, the latter prioritizes non-conformist values, such as self-expression and individual freedom, participative democracy and quality of life (Inglehart 1977). As the post-war era brought about economic growth and relative physical security, individuals who were politically socialized during that period tend to develop post-materialist value systems, while the war generation tends to display a materialist value system. Inglehart argues that post-materialists tend to be more supportive of European integration than materialists, because they are less anxious about the preservation of those materialist values (physical security, public order, economic stability) that were hitherto associated with the nation state. This change in value priorities among the post-war generation is indeed associated, from the 1970s on and throughout the 1980s, with a decline in nationalist orientations, as post-materialists are much less likely than materialists to be proud of their national identity (Inglehart and Reif 1991). Furthermore, this process is facilitated by rising levels of 'cognitive skills' (level of information and interest in politics, exposure to mass communication flows) among the post-war generation, which makes it more likely to develop feelings of solidarity beyond the nation state (Inglehart 1977). These changes in value priorities and levels of cognitive skills, it is argued, favour the development of a cosmopolitan (as opposed to a parochial) identity, which tends to be associated with support for European integration.

On the eve of the signature of the Maastricht Treaty, proponents of the post-materialist theory predicted that, if the decline in nationalist orientations continued, the political unification of Europe could be completed by the beginning of the twenty-first century (Inglehart and Reif 1991). As we have seen, evolutions among political elites and public opinion in the 1990s have not corroborated this assumption. Several limits of the post-materialist theory can be identified. First, there are several potential contradictions between post-materialism and European integration. Not only can post-materialist values be conducive to a re-orientation of identities and allegiances towards the regional level (as post-materialists value direct and participative democracy), but European integration as such embodies materialist values. It was, indeed, associated with a period of rapid economic growth and mass consumption until the late 1980s. Similarly, the post-materialist aversion to war does not fit well with the recent development of the ESDP. Secondly, high cognitive skills are not necessarily conducive to higher levels of support for the EU. In some countries, for instance, relatively high levels of information about the EU coincide with higher probabilities of being Eurosceptic. Third, hypotheses about a possible continued erosion of nationalism have been refuted by the perpetuation of patriotic orientations by national institutions and segments of the mass media.

The utilitarian theory: relevance and possible misunderstandings

In the late 1980s, the completion of the internal market highlighted the fact that the process of market integration benefited individuals, social movements, regions, etc. unequally. Consequently, the utilitarian theory, relating citizens' support for integration 'to the level of economic benefits they expect from European integration' (Gabel 1995) has been predominant in academic research in the post-SEA phase.

Nonetheless, this theory has to be refined in several respects. The first limitation relates to the 'cognitive incapacity objection' (Easton 1975). Indeed, it is difficult for citizens to have an accurate perception of how integration affects them. This cognitive incapacity objection has been highlighted in the case of European integration. Whereas managers and large numbers of individuals in the higher income categories think they have benefited from integration, most citizens are undecided about this, a perplexity which is most pronounced among the lowest income categories (those who are supposedly the most Eurosceptic) (McLaren 2006). Secondly, even if one assumes that individuals may be able to evaluate how general policy orientations affect them, the impact of occupation and/or individual skill levels on attitudes towards European integration is also mediated by the country context (see p.69).

Recent research concludes that the utilitarian theory is of wide relevance in explaining individual orientations towards the EU (McLaren 2007; Abts *et al.* 2009). However, the theory should not be understood in the sense that there are objective losers of Europeanization. This is about subjectively perceived situations. As was shown in the case of anti-regulation Eurosceptics, or in the case of French No voters in 2005, Euroscepticism is limited neither to unskilled workers, nor to less-educated citizens. Moreover, utilitarian theories have been too exclusively focused on economic interests. European integration also has non-economic redistributive consequences, for instance in terms of influence between and within specific institutions or organizations (be they political parties or NGOs) (see pp.114 and 221).

The rediscovery of identities and values

Since the end of the 1990s, non-utilitarian theories emphasizing the role of identities and values in the formation of attitudes towards the EU have been rediscovered. In parallel to this, constructivist approaches have highlighted the role of non-material factors in shaping collective perceptions of European integration.

At individual level

At the individual level, attitudes towards politics (political alienation, distrust towards national and EU institutions), understandings of national identity (exclusive national identity and lack of attachment to 'Europe') and values (ethnocentricity or xenophobia) have been identified as highly relevant variables shaping Eurosceptic orientations. Compared with the post-materialist theory, which relied on the rather general notions of materialist versus post-materialist world views, recent research emphasizes the correlation between individuals' and parties' positions on specific issues (such as immigration, minority rights and abortion) and their attitudes towards European integration. These issues can be grouped into three categories: civil liberties and the rule of law, tolerance towards normative pluralism (e.g. sexual minorities) and attitudes towards ethnic minorities (and hence towards cultural and religious pluralism).

Leonard Ray (2001), for instance, contends that an individual's position on the authoritarian/libertarian axis strongly influences his/her degree of support for the EU, as libertarians seem to be more prone to support integration. A similar correlation was highlighted in the case of support for specific institutions, such as the ECJ (Gibson and Caldeira 1995). In the French case, individuals upholding conservative positions on a range of issues (such as the death penalty, the rights of sexual minorities and of immigrants) seem more likely to oppose European integration than others (Grunberg and Schweisguth 2002). However, this should not at all be understood as a systematic correlation between normative conservatism and Euroscepticism, notably because of the role of the country context in mediating the influence of normative variables. In the ECE countries, for instance, earlier studies highlighted the existence of a negative correlation between post-materialism and support for integration (Gabel 1995).

At country level
At the country level, theories of 'bounded integration' (Cederman 2001) have drawn lessons from the limitations of earlier theories that predicted a massive erosion of nationalism. While acknowledging that national identities are politically and culturally constructed, they point to the fact that collective identities are perpetuated in administrative practices, policies and cultural practices. Consequently, they argue that the development of a post-national European identity is not likely to occur and that the EU should not venture into constitutional politics. On the issue of identity, we have seen in earlier chapters that the study of Euroscepticism has benefited considerably from the interest taken in it by different disciplines. Historians and specialists of nationalism especially illustrate how current national perceptions of the EU are influenced by collective perceptions of 'Europe' that have been forged during century-old processes of nation- and state-building. Specialists in cultural and media studies explain how these perceptions have been perpetuated by educational systems or by domestic media. Similarly, constructivist approaches to European integration show how different understandings of 'Europe' are conveyed by language or how specific concepts (such as *Kerneuropa*) can have a positive meaning in one country, while conveying a negative meaning once translated into another cultural context (Schäfner 2001). They illustrate how attempts to 'Europeanize' national identities might be constrained

by collective meanings embedded in discursive practices (Marcussen 1999).

Implications for the study of international governance

There is a gap in the literature on Euroscepticism relating to parallels with patterns of public support for international cooperation or institutions of global governance.

Existing literature establishing a comparison between support for the EU and support for other forms of international cooperation is scarce. The literature on 'new value cleavages' (Inglehart 1977; Dalton 1996) touches upon this issue, by interpreting increased support for EC integration and for international cooperation as the result of a broader value change. For instance, Dalton points out that value change increased support for European integration, for international peacekeeping missions (under the aegis of the UN) and for the setting up of an international agency for environmental protection. However, the question of whether strong support for the UN is conducive to support for the EU or whether it negatively affects support for the EU (the latter being disparaged as a more inward-looking organization) remains unanswered. In addition to this body of literature, Niedermayer and Sinnott's book *Public Opinion and Internationalized Governance* (1995), although extremely valuable for the study of European integration, addresses the comparison with other forms of international governance to a limited extent.

Euroscepticism and hostility towards global governance

First of all, as we have noted already, Euroscepticism is often embedded in a more general hostility towards institutions of international governance.

For instance, defiance of EU norms often expresses a principled opposition to the Europeanization (via the Council of Europe) or internationalization of domestic law. Euroscepticism among conservatives in the UK and the US is a case in point. In the field of criminal justice especially, the Europeanization of domestic law triggers resistance because it is perceived in the broader context of the internationalization of criminal justice. Reluctance towards the implementation of the EAW in the UK illustrates this, some MPs having raised concerns over the principle of universal extra-territorial jurisdiction in criminal matters which is exercised by courts in Belgium and Spain. This principle illustrates a wider, global trend – the internationalization of criminal justice, as embodied, for instance, by the setting up of the International Criminal Court (an institution which the UK and France initially welcomed with mixed feelings). Consequently, in the act implementing the EAW framework decision, the British Parliament decided not to apply the principle of mutual recognition to cases implying the principle of universal extra-territorial jurisdiction (Sievers 2008).

Moreover, as the EU develops as an international actor, so does its transforming impact on the international system. This is one of the key reasons underlying US neo-conservative Euroscepticism. First, as a member of (some) international organizations (like the WTO), the EC might affect US influence in these organizations, but also induce a change in the membership of international organizations, at the expense of states. This is why, to the neo-cons, the US should 'oppose plans to change the membership of multilateral institutions to reflect a single "European" identity. There should be no talk of a UN Security Council seat for Europe' (Bolton 2008:2). Moreover, the EU promotes multilateralism at the expense of traditional interstate alliances: 'The European Constitution goes far beyond creating a modest European identity; it supersedes traditional tools of foreign policy-making, such as alliance building' (McNamara 2006:2). This refines the idea, expressed by scholars of the EU's external relations (see Leonard 2005), that as a non-state actor and 'civilian power', the EU is less likely to trigger hostile reactions among third countries than traditional state actors like the United States. It is precisely the civilian component of the EU's international identity that can foster hostility among those actors who cling to traditional understandings of international relations and foreign policy.

Trade policy preferences and European integration: the specific relevance of identities

Drawing on the vast literature on the formation of individual preferences regarding global trade liberalization, one can identify interesting parallels with patterns of support for the EU. First of all, research on Euroscepticism and on attitudes towards trade liberalization concludes that a structured public opinion on these issues exists. Contrary to widespread assumptions, recent research has shown that hostility towards trade liberalization does not necessarily reflect an individual's ignorance of trade issues. A study of American public opinion showed, indeed, that large segments of the American public were well aware of the gains derived from free trade according to economic theory, but that, at the same time, they were worried that free trade would drive down wages and destroy employment (Scheve and Slaughter 2004). Similarly, in the EU's case, Euroscepticism cannot be reduced to the public's mere ignorance of EU issues. In fact, higher levels of information are not necessarily conducive to stronger support for the EU; they may actually be less so (Abts *et al.* 2009).

Second, research on the variables influencing attitudes toward trade liberalization in twenty-three countries (including non-EU countries such as the USA, Japan and other Asian countries) offers interesting parallels with research on Euroscepticism. Concerning the respective relevance of interests and values, nationalist orientation has been identified as being correlated with protectionist preferences in almost all countries. Chauvinism (defined as an exclusive understanding of national identity) has been identified as the most relevant variable underlying hostility to free trade, ahead of occupation, skills or education (O'Rourke and Sinnott 2001). This is consistent with recent developments in research on Euroscepticism.

One can thus conclude that hostility towards trade liberalization and European integration are neither driven by mere ignorance, nor by some form of social determinism. In this respect, utilitarian and normative theories accounting for Eurosceptic attitudes can easily lead to stereotypical views about Eurosceptics as 'losers of globalization' and parochial nationalists. As we have seen, Euroscepticism is a much more complex and multifaceted phenomenon, in which country context and elite/public relationships also play a decisive role in the activation of exclusive identities. There is still a need for a better understanding of how exclusive identities take root and how they can be activated in specific contexts (for example, in times of recession).

Conclusion

To conclude, two avenues for further research on Euroscepticism are suggested, pointing towards a less 'Eurocentric' direction. First, the study of Euroscepticism could benefit from more systematic comparisons of public opinion on trade liberalization and other forms of regional cooperation, such as NAFTA (the North American Free Trade Area). A second promising avenue for further research is to enhance our understanding of Euroscepticism in non-EU countries (for example, China and Russia) and assess to what extent the development of the EU as an international actor might produce Euroscepticism in other parts of the world.

Chapter 10

Conclusion: The Future of Euroscepticism and the Future of the EU

In late 2005, as EU leaders decided on a 'pause' in the ratification process of the EU Constitutional Treaty in reaction to the Dutch and French referenda, the European Commission put forward an initiative called Plan D (Democracy, Dialogue, Debate) aimed at fostering a wide-ranging debate on EU policies between EU institutions and citizens (European Commission 2005b). This initiative, interpreted as the 'starting point of a long term democratic process' (European Commission 2006b), aimed at empowering citizens on EU issues. In parallel to this, the Commission announced it would engage in a new type of communication, relying on more interactive, bottom-up interactions with citizens (European Commission 2006a). However, the ability of the Commission to address Euroscepticism by trying to foster deliberative democracy at EU level is limited. As was argued elsewhere (Moracksik 2007) in the case of the convention which drafted the EU Constitutional Treaty, the conventional method neither boosted public support for the treaty, nor brought EU institutions closer to citizens. To begin with, EU institutions neither have the resources, nor the competences to articulate wide-ranging communication campaigns targeting large number of EU citizens; national governments remain the gate-keepers of communication on EU issues. This actually suits the preferences of a majority of EU citizens, who think national governments should be the main providers of information on the EU (FEB 189a:33). In the 1960s and 1970s, successive attempts by EC institutions to boost their communication activities were already triggering a backlash among some member states' goverments, as did interventions by the Commission's President during the French referendum campaign thirty years later. Secondly, as explained in Chapter 9 (see p.251), utilitarian support does not easily translate into diffuse support for the EU.

260

Consequently, communicating more on the gains derived from integration at regional or country level will not necessarily boost support for major institutional or political reforms, as the first Irish referendum on the Lisbon Treaty illustrated. Thirdly, the sheer diversity of national concerns underlying hostility towards the EU or specific policies make it impossible to define EU-wide communication strategies beyond a set of very general principles.

Would it not be wiser, then, for the EU not to communicate? As we have seen in the case of the media, increased visibility does not necessarily improve the EU's image in the eyes of citizens. In fact, ad hoc communication strategies with a necessarily very limited outreach cannot replace more long-term reflection on how forms of opposition to the EU may evolve in the future and how the EU will accommodate this opposition. To sum up, the EU cannot avoid wider reflection on the role of opposition within its political system – a question which the founding fathers of the EC had deliberately brushed aside in the early days of integration (Zellentin 1967). This concluding chapter outlines different scenarios as to the future of Euroscepticism. It also envisages three options for the evolution of the EU and how it can respond to the phenomenon of Euroscepticism.

The future of Euroscepticism: three scenarios

There are three possible scenarios for the future of Euroscepticism: marginalization, mainstreaming and reformist reorientation.

First scenario: marginalization

In the first scenario, the confinement of Eurosceptics within domestic political arenas condemns them to enduring marginalization. Scattered across these arenas and unable to transnationalize their action, Eurosceptics cannot seize the new opportunity structure linked to the emergence of a new level of political and interest representation within the EU. The poor performance of the single-issue, transnational Eurosceptic party Libertas, which got only one EP seat following the 2009 European elections, illustrates this. Even when they obtain access to the highest national offices, strongly Eurosceptic leaders have limited room for manoeuvre, as they face both peer pressure at EU level and the political and legal constraints deriving from the Europeanization of domestic law and institutions at the national level. This was illustrated, for instance, by the Czech President's failure to halt the ratification process of the Lisbon Treaty in 2009. Not only did the Czech Constitutional Court declare the Lisbon Treaty compatible with the Czech constitution, thus perpetuating case law favourable to the primacy of EU law over constitutional law, but Vaclav Klaus and other Eurosceptic leaders, including Polish President Lech Kaczyński and British Tory leader David Cameron, were unable to coordinate action to prevent the treaty from entering into force on 1 December 2009.

What is more, the Lisbon Treaty entails reforms that might limit Eurosceptics' influence or answer some of their criticism of the democratic deficit of the EU. First of all, the extension of the scope of majority voting will reduce the ability of one single member state to paralyze the EU or block major initiatives. Second, the enhancement of the role of national parliaments (which become guardians of the subsidiarity principle) and the legal provision allowing states to withdraw from the Union might mitigate the criticism of those Eurosceptics defending parliamentary and national sovereignty. Similarly, the extension of EP powers and the possibility of citizens forwarding initiatives to the Commission meet some of the claims of left-wing Eurosceptics, who denounce the under-developed state of the EU as a union of citizens.

However, this scenario ignores the fact that softer forms of Euroscepticism have reached the core of domestic party systems, affecting the cohesion of mainstream political parties.

Second scenario: mainstreaming

In the second scenario, Euroscepticism is likely to remain an enduring phenomenon in national and EU politics, channelling its influence via mainstream national political parties, as the latter accommodate soft Eurosceptic ideas. As long as EP groups remain largely dependent on their national member parties (for instance, for the selection of candidates for EP elections), the mainstreaming of soft Eurosceptics might also extend to the EP.

In this way, the second scenario hypothesizes that soft Eurosceptic parties will eventually be able to transnationalize their action, while making the integration/independence cleavage one of the most salient dimensions of party competition at national and EU levels. At the domestic level, it would thus become increasingly difficult for mainstream political parties to maintain intra-party cohesion on EU issues (Bartolini 2001). At EU level, the EP could also be affected by this evolution. Until now, the salience of the integration/independence cleavage has been limited in the EP, as it is dominated by the two largest pro-European groups. This could be challenged if large Eurosceptic groups were formed in order to put forward alternatives to further integration and attract Eurosceptic delegations or factions from the three main groups. In this respect, the consequences of the creation of the European Conservatives and Reformists (ECR) group remain to be seen. If it were to attract conservative member parties of the EPP group, such as Forza Italia (renamed the People of Freedom in 2009), the Spanish People's Party or segments of the French UMP, its influence could become significant. Strongly Eurosceptic and extremist parties are likely to remain marginal actors in the EP. This applies, for instance, to the new Europe of Freedom and Democracy (EFD) group, which is deeply divided over EU issues (its overall internal cohesion rate being only 47 per cent over the six month period following the EP elections in June 2009) (Votewatch.eu 2009). However, mainstream Eurosceptic parties are much more united in their preferences on EU issues, including institutional reform. For instance, over the same period, the internal cohesion of the ECR group was 87 per cent (Votewatch.eu 2009).

What is more, some of the Lisbon Treaty's provisions that democratize the Union might equally well strengthen Eurosceptics' actual influence in EU decision-making. Provisions on the role of national paraliaments especially can be double-edged. On the one hand, they counter claims that European integration weakens national parliaments. On the other hand, parliaments dominated by Eurosceptic forces could use some of these provisions to delay decision-making or block major initiatives. Reluctant national parliaments could also provide a useful pretext for governments unwilling to support specific initiatives at EU level.

Third scenario: reformist reorientation

The third scenario starts with a simple statement: Eurosceptics are unable to come up with common concrete alternatives to the EU. This was exemplified by recent EU referenda, when no coherent set of demands emerged from No campaigners. Similarly, grassroots organizations, like those of the alter-globalization movement, do not come up with any specific institutional model for the 'other

Europe' they call for. In this context, as no alternative to the EU emerges, actors displaying more or less hard forms of Euroscepticism will mitigate their Euroscepticism and shift to a reformist strategy, trying to reform the EU from inside. In parallel, social mobilizations will be absorbed into the EU political system, as they develop Europeanized collective identities. In this scenario, institutional reforms aiming at improving citizens' and civil society's participation in EU decision-making processes may help convert hard forms of Euroscepticism into milder forms of intra-systemic opposition. Euroscepticism would thus become progressively irrelevant, as was predicted a decade ago by scholars of social mobilizations (Tarrow and Imig 1999). There are, however, important limitations to this scenario. First, as we have already seen (p.237), social mobilizations display Europeanized identities to a limited extent. Second, participation in EU decision-making processes is not necessarily conducive to a more pro-European outlook as in the case of MEPs (see p.133). Third, absorption into the EU political system and reliance on lobbying strategies can cut off organization leaderships from their members which remain confined to the national arena, as in the case of ETUC (see p.234).

How can the EU respond to Euroscepticism?: three options

How can national and EU decision-makers respond to Euroscepticism and should they do so at all? Opinions differ widely as to how the EU should develop after the failure of its constitutionalization process. Depending on the type of scenario that materializes in the near future, different options exist. While the first scenario could support the arguments of those in favour of a status quo option, the second scenario could justify the choice of a bolder approach, that of a radical reform of the EU and the third scenario could fit within a middle-ground, intermediate option of incremental reform.

The reforms entailed in the Lisbon Treaty do not address the core issue of the permanent ambiguity relating to the goals and the nature of the Union. This ambiguity is twofold: is the EU an economic or political project? Is it a union of states or a union of states *and* citizens? Regarding the first question, the illusion has been maintained that deep market integration can proceed without affecting social, fiscal, environmental, cultural or normative issues.

Recent controversies surrounding ECJ rulings in 2007–08 (see p.230) show that this illusion can no longer be cultivated. Regarding the second question, the EC/EU has developed, officially, as a union of both states and citizens. Official discourses about a 'citizens' Europe' have abounded since the 1980s, in an attempt to legitimize the EU in the eyes of citizens. In fact, the union of citizens dimension has long lagged behind the union of states dimension, as the late conferment of legislative powers on the EP attests. Even today, EP powers remain limited in a number of respects. For instance, the EP does not have a right to legislative initiative and its role in the nomination of the Commission's president is in fact limited to approving or disapproving a pre-selected candidate (Majone 2006:619). This discrepancy between discourse (the 'citizens' Europe' motto) and reality (the continuance of interstate opaque bargaining, for instance for nominations to the EU's top posts) feeds Euroscepticism. This was clearly illustrated by the Lisbon ruling of the German Constitutional Court, in its sobering comments on the EP which, in the Court's view, could not act as a forum 'for the supranational balancing of state interests' if the Union was to develop into a federal state (BVerfGE 2009:s.279).

Opinions on how to address this twofold ambiguity vary. While some argue that it is time to put an end to the indeterminate nature of the EU, others warn that a too clear-cut choice could be fatal to the Union.

Three different options have been outlined since the failure of the EU's constitutionalization process; they start from different interpretations of the evolution of public support for the EU in the post-Maastricht period.

Proponents of the first option argue that the permissive consensus (in the sense of passive public indifference towards the EU) endures in the post-Maastricht period, although there might be a selective decline in support for integration in specific policy areas. They put forward four arguments in support of this thesis: in 2009, those who saw EU membership as a good thing outnumbered those who evaluated it negatively in all countries, except the UK (EB71:91); trust in EU institutions is higher than trust in national elected institutions (in most countries); EU issues are not salient for most citizens, because the EU has no or little influence on the issues that matter most to them (see p.161); and voters' level of information on the EU is very low (Moravcsik 2007:38–44).

By contrast, advocates of the two other options see a qualitative change in the attitude of public opinion towards EU membership in the post-Maastricht period. As elites' strategy relying on the de-politicization of European integration reaches its limits, there is a demand for more open and contentious political debates on EU issues. In this context, public Euroscepticism may easily translate into a form of principled opposition to EU membership due to citizens' inability to alter the direction and the policies of the EU (Mair 2007).

As far as policy-oriented proposals are concerned, these options differ on three core issues: the politicization of the EU political system, the type of policies that the EU should develop and the 'constitutive issues' of the EU (i.e. the nature of the Union, its ultimate goals and its external borders, as described by Stefano Bartolini (2006:34)) (see Table 10.1).

The first option, the status quo, relies on enduring de-politicization and the low saliency of EU issues as pre-conditions for maintaining the permissive consensus. The EU should leave aside highly divisive constitutive issues and focus instead on improving its output-based legitimacy, without however venturing into highly salient policies (those linked to social redistribution and identity). Since Euroscepticism is a non-issue, resulting mainly from dissatisfaction with domestic politics, it should be addressed by member states tackling their own democratic deficit.

The second option, radical reform, on the contrary, relies on the assumption that the EU could and should live up to the challenge of politicization, by transforming into a full-blown parliamentary system and developing a post-national form of democracy. Since Euroscepticism originates in a lack of collective identity and solidarity at EU level, the EU should develop those policies that have hitherto been reserved for the member states, thus increasing the saliency of EU issues in the eyes of citizens. As far as constitutive issues are concerned, proponents of this option argue that uncertainty as to the EU's nature and borders feeds Eurosceptic attitudes (Habermas 2007:27–8). Consequently, the EU has to opt for clear choices, which implies drawing its final borders and, eventually, choosing between intergovernmental cooperation and federation.

The third option, incremental reform, argues instead in favour of a gradual (as opposed to full) politicization of the EU. From an institutional point of view, a partial parliamentarization of the EU political system would enhance feedback mechanisms between citizens and EU institutions within the EU political system. Indeed, to

TABLE 10.1 *Three different options for the future of the EU*

Options	Main cause of Euroscepticism	General direction of the integration process	Reform of EU institutions	Evolution of EU policies
Status quo	Dissatisfaction with national governments or with EU's capacity to deliver on policies → Euroscepticism as 'proxy'	– Leave debate on constitutive issues open-ended – European identity artificial – Do not increase the salience of EU issues → avoid politicization	– Streamlined Union (no democratic deficit) – Democratization of EU counter-productive; tackle democratic deficit at national level	– Refocus on negative integration – Focus on specific areas (e.g. climate change, energy)
Radical reform	Community/identity/ solidarity deficit → Euroscepticism is identity-based	– Settle the constitutive issues of the EU – Promote a European identity – Increase the salience of EU issues → increase politicization	– Federal Union – Direct democracy on EU issues	– Enhance positive integration – Develop redistributive policies
Incremental reform	De-politicization of EU issues and waning of opposition at EU level → Euroscepticism as dissatisfaction with the EU political system	– Subsume constitutive issues into left/right cleavage on policies → control/ channel politicization	– Gradual politicization (more majoritarian, more contentious, more transparent)	Policy choices better linked to citizens' preferences

proponents of this approach, Euroscepticism is particularly due to insufficient connections between citizens' preferences and EU-level decision-making (Hix 2006:23), as well as to the lack of visibility of EU politics in the eyes of citizens. From this standpoint, the gradual politicization of the EU's political system will progressively subsume divisions on constitutive issues into traditional left/right cleavages relating to policy content.

Option 1: status quo

The first option – keeping the institutional status quo while refocusing the EU on core tasks – derives from a precise analysis of the failure of the constitutionalization process of the EU. It is argued that this failure is due to a false interpretation, by elites, of the evolution of public opinion in the post-Masstricht era (wrongly seen as the end of the permissive consensus) and to the incorrect assumption that the EU suffers from a democratic deficit (Moravcsik 2002). These two mistaken assumptions have led governments to try to legitimize the EU by democratizing it. However, attempts to democratize the EU (for instance, by extending the powers of the EP and of national parliaments), neither boosted public support for the Constitutional Treaty, nor for the Lisbon Treaty. Furthermore, reforms aimed at enhancing the legitimacy of the EU as a union of citizens risk undermining its legitimacy as a union of states. This was illustrated by attempts to reduce the size of the College of the Commission, which has exacerbated national concerns over a diluted representation of member states in the EU political system. In this context, attempts to democratize the EU risk undermining the permissive consensus, rather than perpetuating it (Hurrelman 2007:351).

Consequently, advocates of this option suggest abstaining from ambitious institutional reforms. The idea of transforming the EU into a fully-fledged parliamentary system (with a Commission president directly elected by citizens) and thus politicizing it further is deemed particularly risky. First, it would result in a wide-ranging politicization of the EU's constitutive issues (enlargement and institutional reforms), leading to unmanageable divisions between countries and inside European party families (Bartolini 2006:35). Second, for the time being the EU has neither a European public sphere allowing for the emergence of a clear majority, nor 'solid political structures' (in terms of a party system and interest representation) which could channel this politicization (Bartolini 2006:37). Third, further politicizing the College of the Commission risks undermining its legitimacy in the eyes of national governments (Dehousse 2005:179).

Moreover, these authors suggest that attempts to create a European identity are counter-productive. For instance, the institutionalization of EU symbols in the Constitutional Treaty triggered a backlash against the EU allegedly developing into a 'super state'. Controversies surrounding the lack of reference to Christianity in the preamble of the EU Constitutional Treaty also illustrated this. Consequently, it is precisely by trying to create an artificial European identity, thus perpetuating the fallacious parallel between the EU and the state, that one fosters Euroscepticism (see Leonard 1999:24).

As far as EU policies are concerned, it is argued that the EU should do less, but better. Giandomenico Majone, for instance, argues that 'the Union is doing too much', thus generating dissatisfaction among voters about its general performance (2007:621). In this context, the solution is not to enlarge EU power to highly salient issues, as suggested in the second option. Indeed, except for the fight against inflation, the issues that rank among citizens' top concerns in 2009 (the economy, the fight against unemployment, health, pensions and taxation) (EB 69:22) are those which, for a majority of citizens, are better managed at the national level (EB 69:7). Instead, the EU should re-focus on core tasks, such as the regulation of the internal market, the common trade policy and the fight against crime and climate change (see Leonard 1999:22), and give up attempts at promoting positive integration when it has insufficient means to do so (Majone 2007:624).

More generally, the status quo option relies on a powerful argument: it is precisely the indeterminate nature of the EU's institutional model and its membership that secures its acceptance within and outside the Union. Nonetheless, the status quo option has two limitations. First, it does not address the fact that Euroscepticism is not only output-based, but also input-based. Dissatisfaction with the way democracy is perceived to work at the EU level is a significant dimension of Euroscepticism. Second, it fails to address demands for more politicization and participation in EU issues, as has been expressed, for instance, in the high electoral turnout during the French and Dutch referenda on the EU Constitutional Treaty. If these demands are persistently left unaddressed, there is a risk that mass politicization may occur anyway, but in the form of principled opposition to the EU.

Option 2: radical reform

Proponents of radical reform argue that the EU must choose between a free-trade area and a regulated market (implying some degree of social and fiscal harmonization), as well as between inter-governmental cooperation and a deeply integrated community, eventually developing into a federation. While the positions of advocates of a free trade area have been outlined in previous chapters, the positions of proponents of a tightly integrated polity are outlined below.

The underlying assumption of proponents of an acceleration of integration is that Euroscepticism is not due to too much Europe but rather to too little integration. From an institutional point of view, the current EU system favours the representation of states at the expense of individuals. In that respect, advocates of this option tend to favour the development of the EU as a federation, as was outlined, for instance, in Joseph Fischer's Humboldt speech in 2000 (see Fischer 2000).

Regarding policies, the problem lies in selective Europeanization, as the potentially disruptive consequences of market integration must be balanced with 'positive integration'. Consequently, some authors have argued in favour of the development of more clearly redistributive policies at EU level, for instance by replacing the CAP and the structural funds with an EU-wide minimum wage for the poorest citizens (Schmitter 2002). Others have emphasized the need for some tax harmonization. This approach analyzes Euroscepticism as the expression of an identity or 'community deficit' (see Etzioni 2007). This community deficit underlies reluctance towards institutional deepening. For instance, an extension of majority voting in the Council is likely to meet with resistance as long as there is no perceived sense of common identity and solidarity. As a way of addressing the community deficit, this approach emphasizes the need to foster the development of a European public sphere, by organizing EU-wide debates. Following the 2005 referenda, Jürgen Habermas argued, for instance, in favour of an EU-wide referendum, in which citizens would be able to decide on the policies and institutional model they wish for the EU (2007:27–8). Others have suggested referenda on specific EU policies (such as the common immigration

policy) or on ethical issues (Etzioni 2007). This approach has implications for future EU enlargement, since collective redistribution and
democratic decision-making imply eventually drawing the external
borders of the EU (Habermas 1993:61)

There are, however, a number of limitations to the realization of
this option. First, mixed reactions to Joseph Fischer's 2000 speech
illustrate that there is no majority support for the development of a
federal EU at the elite level. Moreover, public support for bold institutional reforms and deeper institutional integration is lacking. For
instance, nearly 80 per cent of EU citizens think the Commission
should be composed of Commissioners from each of the member
states (an option which contradicts the supranational character of
the institution) (EB 62:159). This suggests that, to large numbers of
EU citizens, the legitimacy of the EU relies on its 'union of states'
component. In a similar vein, no majority has emerged in favour of
enhanced cooperation among a group of countries. In 2009, EU citizens appeared to be split on this option, which is opposed by a small
majority (42 per cent) (EB 71:162). Secondly, the development of
new redistributive policies at EU level might elicit little public
support in a context where two-thirds of citizens think that social
welfare is better managed at national level (EB 69:7). Nor does it
seem feasible in view of governments' unwillingness to increase the
size of the EU budget. Third, defining common values beyond a set of
universal fundamental rights might prove more divisive than unify-
ing. Controversies surrounding the EU Charter of Fundamental
Rights exemplify this point.

Option 3: incremental reform

Defending an intermediate position between status quo and radical
reform, advocates of an incremental reform of the EU think that
further politicization of EU issues is inevitable. This is why it might
be preferable to anticipate this trend by promoting a gradual, as
opposed to mass, politicization of the EU.

A mass politicization of the EU would result from the transformation of the EU into a fully-fledged parliamentary system involving direct election of the President of the European Commission by
voters. It would imply a mass mobilization and strong polarization
of voters and parties on EU issues, especially if full parliamentarization was associated with the development of redistributive policies
at the EU level.

By contrast, gradual politicization would meet voters' demand for more open competition on EU issues, while requiring only incremental institutional changes (see Hix 2006:23–4). First, the idea is to inject more majoritarian logic into the EU political system – for instance, by changing the internal organization of the EP, which is still dominated by power-sharing agreements between the two largest groups. Second, political competition for the nomination of the Commission's President would be fostered, implying clear alternatives between different candidates and a clear positioning on the part of national governments and EP groups in favour of one candidate. Third, transparency rules in the Council should be improved (as foreseen in the Lisbon Treaty), in order to allow media and citizens to hold ministers accountable for their voting behaviour in the Council. These changes, it is argued, would allow citizens to associate specific candidates for the Commission's presidency with clearly identifiable programmes and, possibly, sanction those national politicians or MEPs who have supported a poorly performing candidate. This would compensate for the inability of voters to directly sanction a European executive with which they are dissatisfied and would hence reduce forms of principled opposition to the EU. Instead of generating anti-system political conflict by maintaining the institutional status quo, proponents argue that it is better to inject some controlled political contention into EU politics.

New meta-narratives or back to functional legitimacy?

Finally, beyond the respective relevance of the different options, a remaining question is the type of legitimacy on which the EU can rely: should it reinvent meta-narratives on the goals and normative ideals underlying European integration or rely on a more modest type of functional legitimacy, emphasizing the added value of EU-level action on very specific issues?

Some EU scholars have argued indeed that the Euroscepticism of the 1990s was due, in part, to the erosion of the meta-narratives that used to underpin European integration. In its early decades, European integration was indeed associated with the three ideals of peace, prosperity and supranationalism (Weiler 1999). Some of these ideals have been affected by a perceived loss of relevance. By the same token, the meta-narrative relying on Franco-German reconciliation as the normative cornerstone of the integration process now finds limited echo in an enlarged EU; in some countries, it is even equated with a form of Franco-German domination, which sometimes fosters Euroscepticism. In a similar vein, the meta-narrative linking European integration to the post-war, anti-fascist consensus has not only been analyzed as a myth by historians such as Tony Judt (1992), but more recently it has been challenged by politicians from the eastern and central European member states, who argue that Europe's collective memory underestimates the gravity of communist crimes and thus fails to integrate the specific historical experience of the new democracies (for instance, in the otherwise controversial Prague Declaration on European Consciousness and Communism; see Prague Declaration 2008).

What type of new meta-narratives can today's EU refer to in order to legitimate European integration, and should it do so at all? Two potential pitfalls should be mentioned. First, there is a risk that the EU defines itself negatively against an 'other', thus repeating the logic of exclusion underlying the construction of nation states. Second, in a very heterogeneous Union, inventing new meta-narratives in order to make sense of European integration might prove more divisive than inclusive.

These potential problems were ilustrated, for instance, by the debate that followed the publication of an article written by Jürgen Habermas and co-signed by Jacques Derrida in 2003. Reflecting on 'what binds Europeans together', the article heralded the mass demonstrations against the US-led intervention in Iraq that took place simultaneously on 15 February 2003 in several European cities as the emergence of a European public opinion. This, it was argued, should prompt the countries of 'core Europe' (those where governments opposed the military intervention) to forge a common foreign policy. Certainly many Europeans could subscribe to the goal of this core Europe to 'counterbalance the hegemonic unilateralism of the United States' under the Presidency of G. Bush Jr' (Habermas and Derrida 2003). However, such an initiative would have left out those governments who were supportive of the US-sponsored military intervention and would certainly have split the Union.

The other problem relates to the fact that on many current issues, Europeans appear divided. The case of collective perceptions of economic globalization illustrates this. In the late 1980s, the relaunch of integration via the completion of the internal market was justified by the European Commission in reference to a more global context (that of increasing trade competition from the US and Japan) which required the competitiveness of European economies to be boosted. The '1992 objective' was thus inserted in a wider discourse appealing to a sense of collective destiny and shared solidarity among EC Europeans, which had a dynamizing impact on sections of European societies. Today, it is doubtful that a similar discourse could elicit a consensus in the current EU. While EU institutions try to boost their popularity by presenting the Union as protection against unbridled trade liberalization, countries differ widely in their evaluation of globalization and of the EU's protective role. There appears to be a quite clear north/south divide in that respect, as northern countries evaluate globalization and the EU's protective role much more positively than most southern countries (EB 71:181, 200).

Consequently, it seems that attempts at forging new, encompassing meta-narratives that could make sense to a large majority of EU citizens are likely to find only a limited echo. As we have seen in the case of EU-related referenda, large numbers of today's young voters tend to assess European integration on the basis of very practical concerns; general perceptions about 'the European cause' in general play a limited role in their voting behaviour. In this context, why not consider a revival of the functionalist method, focusing on issues that crystallize clearly discernible collective preferences? The fight against climate change is a case in point, as there clearly is a European public opinion on that particular issue. (Indeed, more than two-thirds of citizens in the EU consider climate change as a very serious issue (SEB 322:44).) In a similar vein, as it was still uncertain whether the Lisbon Treaty would enter into effect, some scholars had argued in favour of sector-based treaties in policy areas where support for EU-level action is strong (for instance energy, scientific research, police and justice cooperation, etc.) (Costa and Magnette 2007).

As for now, the most plausible development as to the future of the EU points to the continuance of the status quo. This option is the most likely in view of the evolution of political elites' attitudes towards integration. Indeed, elites have tended (with a few exceptions) to accommodate soft Eurosceptic claims – especially in order to dampen intra-party divisions on issues of integration. In this respect, public Euroscepticism is matched by a parallel lack of strong, collective leadership at government level, as has been illustrated by successive European Councils in the last couple of years. At the same time, much also depends on external developments. While the impact of Turkey's EU accession on public support for the EU is unpredictable, so are the consequences of global challenges, such as financial and economic instability, geopolitical insecurity and environmental degradation. Whether they can act as a stimulus for enhanced integration or whether they will foster centrifugal tendencies (as countries are unequally affected by challenges such as illegal immigration or climate change) remains to be seen.

Further Reading

Chapter 1

There is very little literature on the impact of Euroscepticism on the integration process. Hayward (1995) and Banchoff (1999) provide initial starting points, by giving two of the first accounts of the evolution of Euroscepticism in the early 1990s, showing how it evolved in parallel with different stages of the integration process. Providing a useful and comparative overview, Harmsen and Spiering (2004) analyze how the emergence of Euroscepticism has influenced the terms of public debate on European integration in several countries. Recent publications – notably by Dehousse (2005), Magnette (2006), Majone (2006), Mair (2007) and Moravcsik (2007) – provide more conceptual but very stimulating analyses of the failure of the EU's constitutionalization process.

Chapter 2

There is no general work comparing different varieties of Euroscepticism. Readers can find more about specific forms of Euroscepticsm in the following references. Gabel (1998) provides an in-depth analysis of the utilitarian theory and how it can help understand patterns of public support for the EU. Analyzing the discourse of French essayists on European integration, Lacroix (2005) articulates a stimulating and original reflection on the underlying logic of political Euroscepticism. Introducing the concept of value-based Euroscepticism, Madeley and Sitter (2005) provide an interesting account of the normative underpinning of Euroscepticism in the Nordic countries, while Chamorel (2006) makes a useful contribution to the debate by distinguishing between Euroscepticism and anti-Europeanism in his excellent case study on Euroscepticism in the United States. Based on a variety of contributions by self-declared Eurosceptics, the two volumes of the *Eurosceptical reader* (Holmes 1996, 2001) offer eclectic but valuable material, as they gather speeches, essays, articles (including the famous Bruges speech) highlighting different varieties of Euroscepticism as they are articulated in the UK.

Chapter 3

Emphasizing the role of history, Diez Medrano (2003) and Ichijo and Spohn (2005) provide fascinating analyses of how collective representations of Europe have informed specific understandings of national identity influencing current perceptions of the EU in different countries. Works on specific countries, like those of Gifford (2008) or Hansen and Waever (2002) also provide very interesting accounts of how specific understandings of national identity (defined in opposition to the EU) become embedded in discursive practices. Lubbers and Scheppers (2006) offer an original perspective on the geography of Euroscepticism by mapping out different varieties of Euroscepticism across regions and countries in the EU.

Chapter 4

The two volumes compiled by Taggart and Szczerbiak (2005, 2008) offer the most comprehensive, well-informed review of party-based Euroscepticism across the EU, addressing theoretical issues as well as case studies in older member states (2005, volume 1), new member states and in the EP (2008, volume 2). Concerning the evolution of party-based Euroscepticism over time, Hix and Lord (1997) provide a very clear and useful starting point, emphasizing attitudes towards European integration inside different European party families. More recent works, like Hooghe and Marks (2002) and Marks and Steenbergen (2004) provide stimulating analyses of how different ideological cleavages influence party positions on EU issues.

Chapter 5

In the absence of general references addressing Euroscepticism among state institutions, readers can rely on two separate bodies of literature: that on compliance and Europeanization. In a comprehensive and detailed study covering several countries, Falkner *et al.* (2005) test alternative theories explaining why member states fail to comply with EU law in the field of social legislation. Assessing compliance in different policy areas, Conant (2002) develops a stimulating thesis, explaining how state institutions 'contain' the impact of EU law on domestic policy-making and administrative practices. Among the vast literature on Europeanization, the book by Green Cowles *et al.* (2001), based on the 'goodness of fit' theory, provides a good overview of how national institutions try to adapt to the challenges of European integration.

Chapter 6

Several works introduce the different theories accounting for public Euroscepticism and test their respective relevance. Gabel (1995) provides a very clear overview of the different theories, while McLaren (2006), on the basis of a very extensive dataset, tests the respective relevance of utilitarian versus identity- and value-based theories. Abts *et al.* (2009) also provide an interesting, up-to-date account of different theories, relying on latest research results. As far as specific theories are concerned, in addition to Gabel's work on utilitarian Euroscepticism mentioned under Chapter 2, Inglehart's seminal book chapter (1977) is a 'must': based on the 'post-materialist' theory, it emphasizes for the first time the role of skills and values in shaping attitudes towards European integration. Regarding the evolution of public Euroscepticism across time, the article by Eichenberg and Dalton (2007) provides a very nuanced and stimulating analysis of the evolution of patterns of public support for the EU since Maastricht.

Chapter 7

Kevin (2003) provides a very good starting point, by offering a broad and extensive overview of the issue of national media and their relationship to European integration. Based on rich empirical data, the book assesses the degree of Europeanization of domestic media according to a range of indicators, from a comparative perspective. It also addresses wider theoretical issues, such as media contributions to the development of a European identity. Several studies by de Vreese *et al.* (2006) and de Vreese and Boomgarden (2006) concretely illustrate how media reporting affects citizens' positions on specific EU issues. Latest research by de Vreese (2007) and Vliegenhart *et al.* (2009) put forward stimulating hypotheses, by showing how specific types of news framing negatively affect public views on integration.

Chapter 8

Tarrow and Imig (1999) and Balme *et al.* (2002) are two reference works on the issue of social mobilizations in the EU. Covering different types of social mobilizations against EU policies, they include useful empirical data on their degree of Europeanization, as well as interesting insights on why mobilizations remain predominantly national. In a similar vein, Marks and Steenbergen's book (2004), which covers a wide range of actors (notably citizens and social movements) exhaustively investigates emerging patterns of conflict in the EU. More recently, research by Della Porta (2006) and Bursens and Sinardet (2005) fill in a gap in the literature by focusing on perceptions of the EU among new social movements, especially the alter-globalization movement.

Bibliography

Eurobarometer reports are referenced in the text, with the issue number and page reference, according to the following abbreviations:

EB: Standard Eurobarometer
FEB: Flash Eurobarometer
SEB: Special Eurobarometer
CCEB: Candidate Countries Eurobarometer.

Access to full reports can be found at http://ec.europa.eu/public_opinion.

————————

Aarts, K. and van der Kolk, H. (2006) 'Understanding the Dutch "No": the Euro, the East and the Elite', *PS: Political Science and Politics,* 39 (2): 243–6.

Abts, K, D. Heerwegh and M. Swyngedouw (2009) 'Sources of Euroscepticism: Utilitarian, Interest, Social Distrust, National Identity and Institutional Distrust', *World Political Science Review,* 5 (1).

Agence Europe (1986) 'EU/Italy/Austria. Proposals on Fundamental Rights and on Citizenship', press release, 2 October 1986.

ALDE (2008) ALDE Group in the European Parliament, press release: 'Liberal leader expresses dismay at social populism over Lisbon Treaty', 3 July.

Alexandre-Collier, A. (2000) *La Grande-Bretagne eurosceptique? L'Europe dans le débat politique britannique* (Paris: Editions du Temps).

Anderson (1998) 'When in doubt, use proxies. Attitudes towards domestic politics and support for European integration', *Comparative Political Studies* 31 (5): 569–601.

ATTAC (2007) *Traité modificatif européen: une copie du TCE;* http://www.france.attac.org/spip.php?article7576, accessed 1 July 2009.

ATTAC (2009) *ATTAC's Ten Principles for a Democratic Treaty;* http://www.attac.org/en/campaign/another-europe-possible/attac%E2%80%99s-ten-principles-democratic-treaty, accessed 1 July 2009.

Aylott, N. (2008) 'Softer but Strong: Euroscepticism and Party Politics in Sweden', in A. Szczerbiak and P. Taggart (eds), *Opposing Europe? The Comparative Politics of Party Euroscepticism* (Oxford: Oxford University Press).

Baisnée, O. (2007) 'The European public sphere does not exist (At least it's worth wondering ...)', *European Journal of Communication* 22 (4): 493–503.

Baisnée, O., C. Belot and B. Cautrès (2006) *La vie démocratique de l'Union européenne* (Paris: La documentation française).

Baker, G. (2003) 'Against United Europe', *The Weekly Standard*, 22 September.

Banchoff, T.) and Smith, M. (1999) *Legitimacy in the EU. The contested polity* (London: Routledge).

Bartolini. S. (1999) *The consequence of European integration for national political representation*, Florence: European University Institute, seminar paper.

Bartolini, S. (2001) 'La structure des clivages nationaux et la question de l'intégration européenne', *Politique Européenne*, 4: 15–45.

Bartolini, S. (2003) *A comparative political approach to European integration*, unpublished paper.

Bartolini, S. (2006) 'Should the Union be 'politicized'? Prospects and risks', *Politics: the right or the wrong medicine for the EU? Two papers by Simon Hix and Stefano Bartolini* Paris: Notre Europe, Policy Paper no.19.

Belien, P. (2005) *A Throne in Brussels: Britain, the Saxe-Coburgs and the Belgianisation of Europe* (Exeter: Imprint Academic).

Bellier, I. (2000) 'A Europeanized Elite? An Anthropology of European Commission Officials', *Yearbook of European Studies*, 14: 135–56.

Belot, C. and Cautrès, B. (2004) 'L'Europe invisible mais omniprésente', in B. Cautrès and N. Mayer (eds), *Le nouveau désordre électoral. Les leçons du 12 avril 2002* (Paris: Presses de Sciences Po).

Benedict XVI (2007), *Address of His Holiness Benedict XVI to the participants in the convention organizaed by the* COMECE, 24 March 2007, //www.vatican.va/holy_father/benedict_xvi/speeches/2007/march/documents/hf_ben-xvi_spe_20070324_comece_en.html, accessed 1 December 2009.

Bering, H. (2000–01), 'Denmark, the Euro and Fear of the Foreign', *Policy Review*, December 2000–January 2001: 63–72.

Beyers, J. and Dierickx, G. (1998) 'The working groups of the Council of the European Union: supranational or intergovernmental negotiations?' *Journal of Common Market Studies* 36(3): 289–317.

Bocklet, R. (2000) 'EuGH-Urteil zum Dienst von Frauen in der Bundeswehr ist eklatantes Beispiel für Kompetenzüberschreitung der EU', 11 January 2000; http://www.bayern.de/Presse, accessed 1 July 2003.

Bolton, J. (2008) 'Europe and the United States after Lisbon', American Enterprise Institute, 10 July.

Booker, C. (1996) 'Europe and Regulation – The New Totalitarianism', in M. Holmes (ed.), *The Eurosceptical Reader* (Basingtoke: Macmillan).

Börzel, T. (2001) 'Non-Compliance in the European Union: Pathology or Statistical Artifact?' *Journal of European Public Policy* 8 (5): 803–24.

Boy, D. and J. Chiche 'Les structures sociales et politiques du vote 'Non'', in A. Laurent and N. Sauger (eds), *Le référendum de ratification du Traité constitutionnel européen: comprendre le 'Non' français* (Paris: Cahiers du CEVIPOF no.42): 92–2109.

Brinegar, A. and Jolly, S. (2005) 'Location, location, location. National contextual factors and support for European unification', *European Union Politics*, 6 (2): 155–180.

Brinegar, A., Jolly, S. and H. Kitschelt (2004) 'Varieties of capitalism and political divides over European integration', in G. Marks and M. Steenbergen (eds), *European Integration and Political Conflict* (Cambridge: Cambridge University Press).

Brouard, S. and Sauger, N. (2005) 'Comprendre la victoire du 'Non': proximité partisane, conjoncture et attitude à l'égard de l'Europe', in A. Laurent and N. Sauger (eds), *Le référendum de ratification du Traité constitutionnel européen: comprendre le «Non» français* (Paris: Cahiers du CEVIPOF, no. 42): 121–141.

Brouard, S. and Tiberj, V. (2005) 'Les nouveaux Français et l'Europe'. Enquête TNS SOFRES/CEVIPOF.

Brown, G. (2005) *Global Britain, Global Europe: a presidency founded on Pro-European Realism*, speech delivered at Mansion House, London, 22 June 2005; http//www.hm-treasure.gov.uk/newsromm_and_speeches/press/2005_57805.cfm, accessed 30 June 2009.

Brüggemann, M., Sifft, S., Kleinen-von-Königslöw, K, Peters, B. and Wimmel, A. (2006), 'Segmentierte Europäisierung. Trends und Muster der Transnationalisierung von Öffentlichkeit in Europa', in Langebucher, W. and Latzer, M. (eds), *Europäische Oeffentlichkeit und medialer Wandel: eine transdisziplinaere Perspektive* (Wiesbaden: Verlag für Sozialwissenschaften).

Bruneteau, B. (2000) 'The Construction of Europe and the Concept of the Nation State', *Contemporary European History* 9 (2): 245–260.

Bursens, P. and Sinardet, P. (2005) *The anti-globalization movement, perspectives on European Politics and Society* 6(1): 55–78.

BVerfGE (Bundesverfassungsgericht) (2009), *Entscheidung vom 30.6.2009. Preliminary version*, http://www.bundesverfassungsgericht.de/entscheidungen/es20090630_2bve000208en.html, accessed 1 September 2009.

Cabinet Office (2007) *Global Europe. Meeting the Economic and Security Challenges* (London: Foreign and Commonwealth Office), http://webarchive.nationalarchives.gov.uk/20071204125941/http://www.fco.gov.uk/Files/kfile/FCO_BEU_DOC_GlobalEurope71022.pdf, accessed 29 June 2009.

Caldeira, G. and Gibson, J. (1995a) 'The legitimacy of the Court of Justice of the European Union: models of institutional support', *American Political Science Review* 89 (2): 356–76.

Caldeira, G. and Gibson, J. (1995b) 'The legitimacy of transnational legal institutions: compliance, support and the European Court of Justice', *American Journal of Political Science* 39 (2), 459–89.

Cameron, D. (2009) 'Fixing broken politics', speech on 26 May 2009: http://www.Conservatives.com/News/Speeches/2009/05/David_Cameron_Fixing_Broken_Politics.aspx., accessed 28 June 2009.

Carbonell, C.-O. (1999) *Une histoire européenne de l'Europe* (Paris: Privat).

Cassen, B. (2005) *The Democratisation of European Institutions*; http://www.anothereuropeispossible.net/wiki/index.php/Democratisation_of_European_Institutions_%28FR%29, accessed 5 July 2009.

Catholic Bishops of Ireland (2008) *Pastoral Reflection from the Catholic Bishops of Ireland on the occasion of the referendum on the Treaty of Lisbon*; http://www.catholiccommunications.ie/lisbon08/lisbon08-pastoralreflection.pdf, accessed 2 June 2009.

Cautrès, B. (2000) 'Les attitudes vis-à-vis de l'Europe en France', in B. Cautrès and D. Reynié (eds), *L'opinion publique européenne 2000.* (Paris: Presses de Sciences Po).

Cautrès, B. (2005) 'Les clivages socio-politiques sur l'intégration européenne et le vote du 29 mai 2005', in A. Laurent and N. Sauger (eds), *Le référendum de ratification du Traité constitutionnel européen: comprendre le «Non» français* (Paris: Cahiers du CEVIPOF, no.42): 142–55.

Cautrès, B. and Denni, B. (2000) 'Les attitudes des Français à l'égard de l'Union européenne: les logiques du refus', in Bréchon, P., Laurent, A. and Perrineau, P. (eds) *Les cultures politiques des Français* (Paris: Presses de Science Po).

Cautrès, B. and Monceau, N. (2008) 'Une résistance à l'Europe inattendue? L'euroscepticisme en Turquie', *Revue internationale de politique comparée* 15 (4): 573–87.

Cayla, P. (2009) 'Les médias nationaux contre l'Europe', *Le Monde*, 2 January.

CDU (1968) *Das Berliner Programm,* available at http://www.grundsatzprogramm.cdu.de/doc/1968_Berliner-Programm.pdf, accessed 20 May 2009.

CDU (1978) *Grundsatzprogramm. 'Freiheit, Solidarität, Gerechtigkeit',* available at http://www.grundsatzprogramm.cdu.de/doc/1978_Ludwigshafen_Grundsatzprogramm-Freiheit-Solidaritaet-Ger.pdf, accessed 20 May 2009.

CDU (2009) *Starkes Europa – Sichere Zukunft. Programm der Christlich-Demokratischen Union zur Europawahl. Berlin, 16 March 2009,* available

at http://www.cdu.de/doc/pdfc/090316-europa-wahlprogramm-2009.
pdf, accessed 20 May 2009.

CDU-CSU (2002) CDU-CSU- Arbeitsgruppe: 'Europäischer
Verfassungsvertrag': *Vorschläge von CDU und CSU für einen europäischen Verfassungsvertrag*, available at http://users.ox.ac.uk/~busch/
data/europapolitik.pdf, accessed 25 April 2009.

CEC (2001) *Les Eglises et le processus d'intégration européenne*, Brussels,
May 2001; http://www.cec-kek.org/Francais/IntegrationprocF-print.
htm, accessed 30 June 2009.

CEO (Corporate Europe Observatory) (2002), *Asia-Europe Business
Forum – ASEM's Corporate Bias* Issue briefing: September 2002;
http://www.nadir.org/nadir/initiativ/agp/free/asem/corporatebias.htm,
accessed 28 July 2009.

Cederman, E. (2001) 'Nationalism and bounded integration. What it would
take to construct a European demos', *European Journal of International
Relations* 7(2): 139–74

Chabanet, D. (2002) 'Les marches européennes contre le chômage, la
précarité et l'exclusion', in Balme, R., Chabanet, D. and V. Wright (eds),
L'action collective en Europe. Collective action in Europe (Paris: Presses
de Sciences-Po).

Chalmers, D. (2001) *The Much Ado about Judicial Politics in the United
Kingdom: A Statistical Analysis of Reported Decisions of United
Kingdom Courts Invoking EU Law 1973–1998*; Academy of European
Law online, http://www.jeanmonnetprogram.org/papers/00/000101.
html, accessed 4 May 2009.

Chamorel, P. (2006) 'Anti-Europeanism and Euroskepticism in the United
States', in T. Ilgen (ed.), *Hard Power, Soft Power and the Future of
Transatlantic Relations* (London: Ashgate).

Chaouad, R. (2008) 'L'Europe selon Gordon Brown ou la globalization
pour horizon', *Actualités européennes* (Paris: Institut de Relations
Internationales et Stratégiques), no. 20, 7 May 2008.

Charentay (de), P. (2003) 'Les relations entre l'Union européenne et les religions'. *Revue du Marché commun et de l'Union européenne*, no. 465:
90–100.

Chirac, J. (1978), *Appel de Cochin. 6 Décembre 1978*,
http://fr.wikisource.org/wiki/Appel_de_Cochin_6_d%C3%A9cembre-
1978, accessed 20 March 2009.

Christiansen, T. (1997) 'Tensions in European governance: politicized
bureaucracy and multiple accountability in the European Commission',
Journal of European Public Policy 4(1): 73–90.

Cini, M. (1996) *The European Commission. Leadership, organisation and
culture in the EU administration* (Manchester: Manchester University
Press).

COMECE (2007) *Message de Rome. Valeurs et perspectives pour l'Europe de demain. Les 50 ans des traités de Rome*, Rome, 24 March 2007, www.comece.org, accessed 1 October 2009.

COMECE (2003) *Déclaration du Comité Exécutif de la COMECE sur le projet de Traité instituant une Constitution pour l'Union européenne* Brussels, 19 June 2003. http://www.comece.org/content/site/fr/presse/communiquesdepresse/newsletter.content/739.html, accessed 25 June 2009.

COMECE (2006) Press release: COMECE *dismayed that the European Parliament promotes the instrumentalization and destruction of human embryos*', Brussels, 15 June 2006, http://www.comece.org/content/site/fr/presse/communiquesdepresse/newsletter.content/679.html, accessed 1 October 2009.

Conant, L. (2002) *Justice Contained? Law and Politics in the European Union* (Ithaca and London: Cornel University Press).

Costa, O. and Magnette, P. (2007) *How could the EU overcome the constitutional crisis?* Garnet Policy Brief no.4, May 2007, available at: ceri-sciencespo.com/cerifr/publica/garnet/garnet/php, accessed 30 August 2009.

Council of the European Communities (1973) *Copenhagen Declaration on European* Identity. Copenhagen, 14 December 1973, available at http://www.ena.lu/declaration-european-identity-copenhagen-14-december-1973-020002278.html, accessed 15 July 2009.

Council of the European Union (1992) *European Council, 11–12 December 1992. Conclusions of the Presidency, Part B. Annex 3. Unilateral Declarations of Denmark to be associated to the Danish Act of Ratification of the Treaty on European Union. Declaration on Citizenship of the Union.* Edinburgh, 11–12 December 1992.

Council of the European Union (2007) *Brussels European Council, 21–22 June 2009. Presidency Conclusions*, Brussels, 22 June 2007.

Council of the European Union (2009), *Brussels European Council 18–19 June 2009. Presidency Conclusions*, Brussels, 19 June 2009.

Cram, L. (2001) 'Imagining the Union: a case of banal Europeanism?', in Wallace, H.(ed) *Interlocking dimensions of European integration* (London: Palgrave).

Crum, B., Hollander, S. and Van Kessel, S. (2007) *Why there is (also) No Domestic Public Opinion on Europe: Three Case Studies from The Netherlands* Paper presented at the Dutch-Flemish Political Science Annual Conference, Antwerp, 31 May–1 June 2007.

CSU (1968), *Leitsätze einer Politik für heute und morgen. CSU-Grundsatzprogramm*, http://www.hss.de/fileadmin/migration/downloads/1968-Grundsatzprogramm.pdf, accessed 25 June 2009.

CSU (1976) *Grundsatzprogramm der CSU*, http://www.hss.de/fileadmin/migration/downloads/1976-Grundsatzprogramm_2.pdf, accesed 25 June 2009.

CSU (1993) *Grundsatzprogramm der CSU in Bayern,* http://www.hss.de/fileadmin/migration/downloads/1993-Grundsatzprogramm.pdf, date accessed 25 June 2009.

CSU (2009), *Europawahlprogramm 2009. Beschluss des CSU Parteienausschusses vom 9. Mai 2009,* http://www.csu.de/dateien/partei/beschluesse/090509_europawahlprogramm.pdf, accessed 25 June 2009.

Daddow, O. (2006) 'Euroscepticism and the culture of the discipline of history', *Review of international studies,*32: 309–28

Dalton, R. (1996) *Citizen politics. Public opinion and political parties in advanced Western democracies* (Chatham: Chatham House Publishers).

Daniels, P. (1998), 'From Hostility to Constructive Engagement: The Europeanisation of the Labour Party', in Berrington, H. (ed.) *Britain in the 1990s. The Politics of Paradox* (London: Routledge).

Dargent, C. (2001) 'Identités régionales et aspirations politiques: l'exemple de la France d'aujourd'hui', *Revue française de science politique* 51 (5):787–806.

Dassetto, F. and Dumoulin, M. (1993) *Naissance et développement de l'information européenne,* (Bruxelles: Peter Lang).

De Volkskrant (2005) Results of the referendum on the EU Constitutional treaty; http://www.volkranst.nl:80/images/voortegen550,0.gif., accessed 25 March 2009.

De Vreese, C. (2007) 'A spiral of Euroscepticism: the media's fault?', *Acta Politica,* 42: 271–86.

De Vreese, C. and Boomgaarden, H. (2005), 'Projecting EU referendums. Fear of immigration and support for European integration'. *European Union Politics,* 6(1): 59–82.

De Vreese, C. and Boomgaarden, H. (2006) 'Media effects on public opinion about the enlargement of the EU', *Journal of Common Market Studies* 44 (2): 419–436.

De Vreese, C. and A. Schmuck (2006) 'Le 'non' néerlandais: motivations de vote parallèles et apogée du nouvel euroscepticisme aux Pays-Bas', in J. Maarek (ed.) *Chronique d'un 'non' annoncé: la communication politique et l'Europe (juin 2004–mai 2005)* (Paris: L'Harmattan).

De Vreese, C., Banducci, S., Semetko, H. and Boomgaarden, H. (2006), 'The news coverage of the 2004 EP elections campaign in 25 countries' *European Union politics* 7 (4): 477–504.

Dehousse, R. (2002) 'Un nouveau constitutionnalisme?, in Dehousse, R. (ed.) *Une Constitution pour l'Europe?* (Paris: Presses de Sciences-Po).

Dehousse, R. (2004) *L'Europe sans Bruxelles? Une analyse de la méthode ouverte de coordination* (Paris: L'Harmattan).

Dehousse, R. (2005) *La fin de l'Europe?* (Paris: Flammarion).

Delbos, G. (1994) 'De l'isolement comme déterminant du 'non' à Maaastricht', *Revue française de science politique* 44 (1): 3–22.

Della Porta, D. (2006) *The Anti-globalization movement and the EU: critics of Europe* Paris: Notre Europe, policy paper no. 22.

Delorme, H. (2002), 'Les agriculteurs et les institutions communautaires: du corporatisme agricole au lobbying agro-alimentaire', in Balme, R., Chabanet, D. and Wright, V. (eds) *L'action collective en Europe* (Paris: Presses de Sciences Po).

Déloye, Y. (2005) *Dictionnaire des élections européennes* (Paris: Economica)

Der Spiegel (2009) 'Brussels put firmly in the back seat', 7 June.

Der Tagesspiegel (2007) 'Berlin fordert weniger Bürokratie', 14 November.

Deutsche Welle (2006) 'Stichwort: EU-Tabakrichtlinie', 12 Dezember 2006

DGB (Deutscher Gewerkschaftsbund) (2008), *Les revendications du DGB en réponse aux arrêts de la CJCE (Viking, Laval, Rüffert, Commission/Luxembourg)*, Décision du directoire fédéral du DGB du 7 octobre 2008.

Die Zeit (2009a) 'Wir Kinder Europas', 4 June.

Die Zeit (2009b) 'Keine Einmischung!', 10 June.

Diez Medrano, J. (2003) *Framing Europe* (Princeton: Princeton University Press).

Dougal, J. (2003) 'Living with press Eurotrash', *British Journalism Review*, 14 (2).

Downey, J. and Koenig, T. (2006) 'Is There a European Public Sphere?' The Berlusconi-Schulz Case', *European Journal of Communication* 21 (2): 165–87.

Drewry, G. (2007) 'The jurisprudence of British Euroscepticism: A strange banquet of fish and vegetables', *Utrecht Law review* 3 (2): 101–15.

Drulak, P. (2009) *The Czech EU Presidency: Background and priorities.* Paris: Notre Europe, Studies and Research no. 67.

Duchesne, S. and A.-P. Frognier (2002) 'Sur les dynamiques sociales et politiques d'identification à l'Europe', *Revue française de science politique* 52 (4): 355–73.

Easton, D. (1975) 'A Re-Assessment of the Concept of Political Support', *British Journal of Political Science* 5; 435–57.

Eder, K. and Trenz, H.-J. (2003) 'The making of a European public sphere: the case of Justice and Home Affairs', in B. Kohler-Koch (ed.) *Linking EU and national governance* (Oxford: Oxford University Press).

Eichenberg, R. and Dalton, R. (2007) 'Post-Maastricht Blues: The Transformation of Citizen Support for European Integration, 1973–2004', *Acta politica*, 42:128–52.

Eilders, C. and Volmer, K. (2003) 'Zwischen Deutschland und Europa. Eine empirische Untersuchung zum Grad von Europaisierung und Europa-Unterstützung der meinungsführenden deutschen Tageszeitungen', *Medien und kommunikationswissenschaft*, 51 (2): 250–70.

Electionsireland (2009) http//www.electionsireland.org/results/referendums/index/cfm, 25 June 2009.

Elsevier (2009) 'A match in Euroscepticism', 16 March.

ESF (European Social Forum) (2008) *Charter of Principles for another Europe;* http://www.fse-esf.org/spip.php?article583, accessed 2 June 2009.

Esping-Andersen, G. (1990) *The Three Worlds of Welfare Capitalism* (Cambridge: Polity Press).

ETUC (2009), *European elections manifesto* Brussels, 30 April 2009; http://www.etuc.org/a/6111#Manifesto, accessed 3 August 2009.

Etzioni, A. (2007) 'The Community Deficit', *Journal of Common Market Studies* 43(1): 23–42.

Euractiv (2007) 'Stoiber to chair new high-level group on administrative burdens', 17 September 2007.

European Commission (2001) *European Governance. A White paper.* Brussels, 25 July 2001.

European Commission (2005a) *Communication from the Commission to the Council and the European Parliament. Outcome of the screening of legislative proposals pending before the legislator,* http://eur-lex.europa.eu/LexUriServ/LexUriServ.do?uri=COM:2005:0462:FIN:en:PDF, accessed 15 August 2009.

European Commission (2005b) *Communication from the Commission to the council, European Parliament, European Economic and Social Committee and the Committee of the Regions. The Commission's contribution to the period of reflection and beyond: Plan D for Democracy, Dialogue and Debate* Brussels, 13 October 2005.

European Commission (2006a) *Livre blanc sur une politique de communication européenne.* Brussels,: 1 February 2006.

European Commission (2006b) *Communication to the European Council. The period of reflection and plan D* Brussels, 15 May 2006.

European Commission (2007a) *Communication from the Commission to the Council, the European Parliament, the European Economic and Social Committee and the Committee of the Regions. Communicating Europe in Partnership.* Brussels, 3 October 2007.

European Commission (2007b) *Communicating about Europe via the Internet. Engaging the citizens.* Brussels, 21 December 2007.

European Commission (2007c) *Communication from the Commission to the Council, the European Parliament, the European Economic and Social Committee and the Committee of the Regions. Implementing the Community Programme for improved growth and employment and the enhanced competitiveness of EU business: further progress during 2006 and next steps towards a proposal on the Common Consolidated Corporate Tax Base (CCTB).* Brussels, 2 May 2007.

European Commission (2009) *Progress in notification of national measures implementing directives already in force*, General Secretariat of the European Commission, 26 June 2009, http://ec.europa.eu/community_law/directives_transposition_en.htm, accessed 15 May 2009.

European Council (2001) *Laeken declaration of 15 December 2001 on the future of the European Union.*

European Federation of Journalists (2002) *European Media Ownership: threats on the landscape. A survey of who owns what in Europe*, available at http://www.ifj.org/assets/docs/252/115/714aafc-9039473.pdf, accessed 5 May 2009.

European Parliament (2002a) *Resolution on Sexual and Reproductive Health and Rights in Europe*. Brussels, 3 July 2002.

European Parliament (2002b) *Resolution on an updated green paper on media pluralism* Brussels, 20 November 2002.

European Parliament (2004) *Report on the Risks of Violation, in the EU and especially in Italy, of Freedom of Expression and Information.* Brussels, 5 April 2004.

European Parliament (2007) Committee on Constitutional Affairs, *Draft report on the Treaty of Lisbon*. Brussels, 3 December 2007.

European Parliament (2008) Press release: 'Lisbon Treaty: MEPS debate Irish rejection and way forward', 6 October 2008; www.europarl.europa.eu/news/expert/infopress, accessed 20 June 2009.

Evans, G. and Butt, S. (2007) 'Explaining Change in British Public Opinion on the European Union: Top Down or Bottom Up?', *Acta Politica* 42: 173–90.

Fabry, E. (2005) *Qui a peur de la citoyenneté européenne? La démocratie à l'heure de la constitution* (Paris: Presses Universitaires de France).

Falkner, G., Treib, O., Hartlap, M. and Leiber, S. (2005) *Complying with Europe. EU Harmonisation and Soft Law in the Member States* (Cambridge: Cambridge University Press).

Farrell, D., Hix, S., Johnson, M. and Scully, R. (2006) 'EPRG 2000 and 2006 MEP Surveys Dataset'; available at http://www.lse.ac.uk/collections/EPRG/, accessed 20 September 2009.

Favoreu, L. (2006) *L'euroscepticisme du droit constitutionnel* (Paris: Dalloz).Federal Constitutional Court (2009), *Judgment of June 30 2009*, Press release no. 72/2009 of 30 June 2009; http://.bundesverfassungsgericht.de/en/press/bvg09-072en.html, accessed 1 September 2009.

Fetzer, T. (2007) 'Turning Eurosceptic: British trade unions and European integration (1961–1975)', *Journal of European Integration History* 13(2):85–101.

Fischer, J. (2000) *Vom Staatenverbund zur Föderation – Gedanken über die Finalität der europäischen Integration*. Speech at Humboldt-Universität Berlin, 12 May 2000, www.auswaertiges-amt.de/www/de/infoservice/download/pdf/reden/2000/r000512a.pdf, accessed 15 July 2009.

Fischer, J. (2009) 'Ein nationaler Riegel', *Die Zeit*, 9 July.

Flood, C. (2000) 'Euroscepticism in the Ideology of the British Right' in Parker, N. and Armstrong, B. (eds) *Margins in European Integration* (Basingtoke: Macmillan).

Flood, C. and Usherwood, S. (2007) *Ideological factors in party alignments on the EU: a comparison of three cases*. Paper presented at EUSA tenth biennial international conference, Montreal, 17–19 May 2007.

Fourquet, J., Ravenel, L, Bussi, M. and Colange, C (2005) 'Au-delà d'un 'vote de classe': la permanence de spécificités régionales', in A. Laurent and N. Sauger (eds), *Le référendum de ratification du Traité constitutionnel européen: comprendre le «Non» français* (Paris: Cahiers du CEVIPOF, no.42): 110–20.

Franklin, M., Van der Eijk, C. and Marsh, M. (1995) 'Referendum Outcomes and Trust in Government: Public Support for Europe in the Wake of Maastricht', in J. Hayward (ed.), *The Crisis of Representation in Europe* (London: Frank Cass).

Fulton, L. (2007) *Worker representation in Europe. European Trade Union Institute;* http://www.worker-participation.eu/National-Industrial-Relations/Across-Europe/Trade-Unions2, accessed 5 August 2009.

Gabel, M. (1995), 'Public support for European integration: an empirical test of five theories', *The Journal of Politics* 60 (2): 333–54.

Gabel, M. (1998) *Interests and Integration: Market Liberalization, Public Opinion and European Union* (Ann Arbor, Mich.: University of Michigan Press).

Gabel, M. and Hix, S. (2002) 'Defining the EU political space. An empirical study of the European elections' manifestos, 1979–1999', *Comparative Political Studies* 35 (8): 934–64.

Gabel, M. and Hix, S. (2005) 'Understanding public support for British membership of the single currency', *Political Studies* 5: 65–81.

Gamble, A. (1995) 'Economic recession and disenchantment with Europe', in J. Hayward (ed.) *The crisis of representation in Europe* (London: Frank Cass).

Ganley, D. (2003) 'Europe's Constitutional Treaty: A Threat to Democracy and How to Avoid It', Foreign Policy Research Institute, Center for the Study of America and the West, Newsletter 4 (5); http.www/fpri.org/ww/0405.200312.ganley.euconstitution.html, accessed 15 May 2009.

Genieys, W. and A Smith (2000) 'Idées et intégration européenne: la 'grande transformation' du Midi viticole', *Politique européenne*, 2000, 1 (1): 43–62.

Gerhards, J. (1993) 'Westeuropäische Integration und die Schwierigkeiten der Entstehung einer europäischen Öffentlichkeit', *Zeitschrift für Soziologie* 22(2): 96–110.

Gerstlé, J. (2004), 'L'information entre fragmentation des espaces publics en Europe', in A. Bockel and I. Karaka (eds) *Diversité culturelle en Turquie et en Europe*: 129–43.

Gerstlé, J. (2006) *The Impact of Television on the French Referendum Campaign in 2005*, Paris: Notre Europe, Studies and Research no.53.

Gifford, C. (2008) *The making of Eurosceptic Britain: Identity and Economics in a Post-Imperial State* (London: Ashgate).

Grant, C. (2008) 'Why is Britain Eurosceptic?' (London: Center for European Reform); http/:www/cer.org-uk/essays_eurosceptic_ 19dec08.pdf, accessed 16 August 2009.

Green Cowles, M., J. Caporaso and T. Risse (2001) *Transforming Europe. Europeanization and Domestic Change* (Cornell: Cornell University Press).

Grunberg, G. and Schweisguth, E. (2002) 'La tripartition de l'espace politique', in Perrineau, P. and Ysmal, C. (eds) *Le vote de tous les refus. Les élections présidentielles et législatives de 2002* (Paris: Presses de Sciences-Po).

Haas, E. (1958) *The Uniting of Europe: political, social and economic forces 1950–1957* (Stanford: Stanford University Press).

Haas, E. (1968) *Authors' Preface to The Uniting of Europe: political, social and economic forces 1950–1957* (Stanford: Stanford University Press).

Habermas, J. (1992) 'Citoyenneté et identité nationale. Réflexion sur l'avenir de l'Europe', in Lenoble, J. and Dewandre N. (eds) *L'Europe au soir du siècle. Identité et démocratie* (Paris: Esprit).

Habermas, J. (1993) *Die postnationale Kosntellation. Politische Essays* (Suhrkamp: Frankfurt a. M).

Habermas, J. (2008) *Sur l'Europe* (Paris: Bayard).

Habermas, J. and Derrida, J. (2003) 'February 15th or What Binds Europeans Together', *Frankfurter Allgemeine Zeitung*, 31 May.

Hall, P. and Taylor, C. (1997) 'La science politique et les trois néo-institutionalismes', *Revue Française de Science Politique*, 47 (3–4): 469–96.

Hanley, D. (2008) 'Sovereignists, Sceptics and Populists: As Transnational as the Rest?', in Hanley, D. (ed.) *Beyond the Nation State. Parties in the Era of European Integration* (Basingstoke: Palgrave Macmillan) 179–200.

Hansen, L. and O. Waever (2002) *European integration and national identity. The challenge of the Nordic states* (London: Routledge).

Harmsen, R. (2004) 'Euroscepticism in the Netherlands: stirrings of dissent', *European Studies*, 20: 99–126.

Harmsen, R. and Spiering (2004) 'Euroscepticism and the evolution of European political debate', *European Studies*, 20: 13–35.

Hastings, M. (2007) 'Nordicité et euroscepticisme', in Lacroix, J. and Coman, R. (eds) *Les résistances à l'Europe. Cultures régionales, idéologies et stratégies d'acteurs* (Bruxelles: Editions de l'Université de Bruxelles).

Haverland, M. (2000) 'National Adaptation to European Integration: The Importance of Institutional Veto Points', *Journal of Public Policy* 20 (1): 83–103.

Hayes-Renshaw, F., Van Aken, K. and Wallace, H. (2006) 'When and why the EU Council of Ministers votes explicitly', *Journal of Common Market Studies* 44(1): 161–94.

Hayward, J. (1995) *The Crisis of Representation in Europe* (London: Frank Cass).

Hersant, J. (2008) 'Contourner les normes européennes grâce ... aux instruments européens. L'impératif de sécurité nationale ou les résistances à l'intégration européenne de la Grèce', *Revue Internationale de Politique Comparée*, 15 (4): 639–52.

Hix, S. (1999) 'Dimensions and alignments in European Union politics: cognitive constraints and partisan responses', *European Journal of Political Research,*35: 69–106.

Hix, S. (2005) *The political system of the European Union* (Basingstoke: Palgrave Macmillan).

Hix, S. (2006) 'Why the EU Needs (Left–Right) Politics', in *Politics: the right or the wrong medicine for the EU? Two papers by Simon Hix and Stefano Bartolini*. Paris: Notre Europe, Policy Paper no.19.

Hix, S. and Lord, C. (1997), *Political parties in the European Union* (London: Macmillan Press).

Hix, S. and M. Marsh (2005) 'Understanding European Parliament Elections: Punishment or Protest?', Conference paper, Ninth Conference of the European Union Studies Association, Austin, Texas, 31 March–2 April 2005.

Hooghe, L. and Marks, G. (2005) 'Calculation, community and cues. Public opinion and European integration', *European Union Politics* 6 (4): 419–433.

Hooghe, L. and Marks, G. (2006), 'Europe's blues: theoretical soul-searching after the rejection of the European Constitution', *PS: Political Science and Politics,* 39 (2): 247–50.

Hooghe, L., Marks, G. and Wilson, C. (2002) 'Does left/right structure party positions on European integration?' *Comparative Political Studies* 35 (8): 965–89.

Holmes, M. (1996) *The Eurosceptical reader. Volume 1* (Basingtoke: Macmillan).

Holmes, M. (2001) *The Eurosceptical reader, Volume 2* (Basingtoke: Macmillan).

House of Commons (2001) *The Treaty of Nice and the future of Europe debate*, Research paper 01/49; available at http://www.parliament.uk/commons/lib/research/rp2001/rp01-049.pdf, accessed 20 May 2009.

House of Commons (2008) *The Treaty of Lisbon: an Uncertain Future*, Research paper 08/66; available at http://www.parliament.uk/commons/lib/research/rp2008/rp08-066.pdf, accessed 10 May 2009.

Hughes, J., G. Sasse and C. Gordon (2002) 'Saying "Maybe" to the "Return to Europe". Elites and the political space for Euroscepticism in Central and Eastern Europe', *European Union Politics* 3 (3): 327–55.

Huisman, J. (2005) 'The Rejection of the European Constitution and What It Means for Transatlantic Relations', Heritage Foundation, 20 June 2005.

Hurrelmann, A. (2007) 'European democracy, the permissive consensus and the collapse of the EU Constitution', *European Law Journal* 13 (3): 343–59.

Huysmans, J. (2000) 'Contested community. Immigration and the question of the political in the EU', in Kelstrup, M. and Williams, M. (eds) *International Relations Theory and the Politics of European Integration* (London: Routledge).

Hyman, R. (2001) *Trade unions and the ambiguities of social Europe*; http://www.ilo.org/public/english/iira/pdf/congresses/world_13/track_5_hyman.pdf, accessed 27 June 2009.

Ichijo, A. and W. Spohn (2005) *Entangled Identities. Nations and Europe* (London: Ashgate).

Imig, D. (2002) 'Contestation in the streets. European protest and the emerging Euro-polity', *Comparative political studies* 35 (8): 914–33.

Impalà, F. (2005) 'The European Arrest Warrant in the Italian legal system. Between mutual recognition and mutual fear within the European area of Freedom, Security and Justice', *Utrecht Law Review* 1 (2): 56–78.

Inglehart, R. (1977) *The Silent Revolution. Changing values and political styles among Western publics* (Princeton: Princeton University Press).

Inglehart, R. (1997) *Modernization and post-modernization. Cultural, economic and political change in 43 societies* (Princeton: Princeton University Press).

Inglehart, R. and K.-H. Reif (1991) 'Analyzing trends in West European Public Opinion: the Role of the Eurobarometer Surveys', in K.-H. Reif and R. Inglehart (eds) *Eurobarometer: the Dynamics of European Public Opinion* (London: Macmillan).

Jacqué, J.-P. (2008) 'Le traité de Lisbonne: une vue cavalière', *Revue trimestrielle de droit européen* 44 (3): 439–83.

Janssen, J.H. (1991) 'Postmaterialism, Cognitive Mobilization and public Spport for European Integration', *British Journal of Political Science* 21: 443–68.

Jáuregui, P. and A. Ruiz-Jiménez (2005) 'A European Spain: The Recovery of Spanish Self-Esteem and International Prestige', in A. Ichijo and W. Spohn (eds) *Entangled Identities. Nations and Europe* (London: Ashgate).

Joerges, C. and Neyer, J. (1997) 'From Intergovernmental Bargaining to Deliberative Political Processes: the Constitutionalisation of Comitology', *European Law Journal*, 3 (3): 273–99.

Judge, D. (1995) 'The failure of national parliaments?', in Hayward, J. (ed.) *The Crisis of Representation in Europe* (London: Frank Cass).

Judt, T. (1992) 'The Past is Another Country: Myth and Memory in Postwar Europe', *Daedalus* 121 (1): 83–118.

Judt, T. (1996) *A Grand Illusion? An Essay on Europe* (New York: Hill & Wang).

Jupille and Leblang (2007), 'Voting for Change: Calculation, Community and Euro Referendums', *International Organization* 61: 763–82.

Kaeding, M. (2008) 'Lost in translation or full steam ahead? The transposition of EU transport directives across member states', *European Union Politics* 9 (1):115–43.

Kaiser, W. (1995) 'The EU referenda in Austria, Finland, Sweden and Norway', European Union Studies Association Conference, Charleston, 11–14 May.

Katz, R. and Mair, P. (1995), 'Changing models of party organization and party democracy. The emergence of the cartel party', *Party Politics* 1 (1): 5–28.

Katz, R. (2002) *Euroscepticism in Parliament. A Comparative Analysis of the European and National Parliaments*. Workshop paper, ECPR Joint Session of Workshops, Torino, 22–27 March 2002.

Keating, M. (2003) *European Integration and the Nationalities Question*. Paper presented at International Political Science Association Conference, Durban, 29 June–4 July.

Kennedy, F. and Sinnott, R. (2007) 'Irish Public Opinion toward European Integration', *Irish Political Studies* 22 (1): 61–80.

Kevin, D. (2003) *Europe in the media. A comparison of reporting, representation and rhetoric in national media systems in Europe* (Erlbaum, London).

Kissinger, H. (1973) 'Year of Europe' Speech. New York: April 23, 1973, *Department of State Bulletin*, 14 May 1973: 593–8.

Kissinger, H. (1996) *Diplomatie* (Paris: Fayard).

Klimkiewicz, B. (2005) 'Media pluralism: European regulatory policies and the case of central Europe', Florence: EUI Working paper no.19.

Knill, C. and Lenschow, A. (2005) 'Compliance, competition and communication', *Journal of Common Market Studies* 43 (5): 583–606.

Koopmans, R. (2007) 'Who Inhabits the European public sphere? Winners and losers, supporters and opponents in Europeanized public debates', *European Journal of Political Research* 46(2): 183–210.

Kopecky, P. and Mudde, C. (2002), 'The two sides of Euroscepticism. Party positions on European integration in East Central Europe', *European Union Politics* 3 (3): 297–326.

Koslowski, R. (1999) 'EU citizenship: implications for identity and legitimacy', in Banchoff T. and Smith, M. (eds) *Legitimacy in the EU. The contested polity* (London: Routledge).

Král, D., Bartovic, D. and Řiháčková, V. (2009) *The 2009 Czech EU Presidency. Contested Leadership in a Time of Crisis.* Stockholm: Swedish Institute for European Policy Studies, May 2009; available at www.sieps.se, accessed 23 August 2009.

Krastev, I. (2004) 'Balkans: enthousiasme pour une Europe imaginée et salvatice', in J. Rupnik (ed.) *Les Européens face à l'élargissement* (Paris: Presses de Sciences-Po).

Krejci, H. (2004) *Grundlagen des Skeptizismus gegenüber der Europäischen Union und dem Euro* (Wien: Österreichische Nationalbank).

Küsters, H.-J. (1989) 'The Federal Republic of Germany and the EEC-Treaty', in E. Serra (ed.) *La relance européenne et les traités de Rome.* (Bruxelles: Bruylant).

Labour Party (1983) *1983 Programme: The New Hope for Britain;* available at http://www.labour-party.org.uk/manifestos/1983/1983-labour-manifesto.shtml, accessed 27 April 2009.

Labour Party (2009) 'Leading at the Heart of Europe'; available at http://www.labour.org.uk/europe, accessed 27 April 2009.

Lacroix, J. (2005) 'Euroscepticism among the intellectuals (… and how it can help to understand the true nature of the European construct'. Conference paper. National identity and Euroscepticism: a comparison between France and the UK. Oxford University, 13 May 2005.

Ladrech, R. (1994) 'Europeanization of Domestic Politics and Institutions: the case of France', *Journal of Common Market Studies* 31(1): 69–88

Laurent, A. and Sauger, N. (2005) *Le Référendum de ratification du traité constitutionnel européen: comprendre le "non" français*, Paris, Cahiers du CEVIPOF, no.42.

Leconte, C. (2003) *Entre systèmes politiques nationaux et espace public européen: les dimensions politiques de l'intégration européenne à travers l'analyse de la crise autrichienne*, PhD thesis (Paris: Institut d'Etudes Politiques).

Leconte, C. (2005) *L'Europe face au défi populiste* (Paris: Presses Universitaires de France).

Leconte, C. (2008) 'Opposing integration on matters of social and normative preferences: a new dimension of political contestation in the EU', *Journal of Common Market Studies* 46 (23): 1071–91.

Le Monde (1992) 'Interview with German Chancellor Helmut Kohl', 24 September 1992.

Leonard, M. (1999) *Network Europe: the New Case for Europe* (London: Foreign Policy Center), available at: http://fpc.org.uk/publications/network-europe, accessed 1 May 2009.

Leonard, M. (2005) *Pourquoi l'Europe dominera le 21ᵉ siècle* (Paris: Plon).

Lewis, J. (1998) 'Is the 'hard bargaining' image of the Council misleading? The Committee of Permanent Representatives and the local elections directive', *Journal of Common Market Studies* 36 (4): 479–504.

Lindberg, L. and Scheingold, S. (1970) *Europe's Would-Be Polity: Patterns of Change in the European Community* (Cambridge, Mass.: Harvard University Press).

Loth, W. (1989) 'Deutsche Europa-Konzeptionen in der Gründungsphase der EWG', in E. Serra (ed.) *La relance européenne et les traités de Rome* (Bruxelles: Bruylant).

Lord, C. and Magnette, P. (2004) 'E pluribus Unum? Creative Disagreement about Legitimacy in the EU', *Journal of Common Market Studies* 42(1):183–202.

Lubbers, M. (2008) 'Regarding the Dutch "Nee" to the European Constitution. A test of the identity, utilitarian and political approaches to voting "No"', *European Union Politics* 9 (1): 59–86.

Lubbers, M. and P. Scheepers (2006) 'Political versus Instrumental Euroscepticism. Mapping Euroscepticism in European countries and Regions', *European Union Politics* 6 (2): 223–42.

Ludlow (1998) 'Frustrated ambitions. The European Commission and the formation of a European identity', in M.-T. Bitsch (ed.) *Institutions européennes et identités européennes* (Brussels: Bruylant).

Luedtke, A.(2005) 'European integration, public opinion and immigration policy', *European Union Politics* 6 (1): 83–112.

Maarek, J. and Bras, A. (2006), 'Les spots de la campagne officielles des élections au parlement européen de 2004: une occasion manquée', in P. Maarek (ed.) *Chronique d'un 'non' annoncé: la communication politique et l'Europe (juin 2004–mai 2005)* (Paris: L'Harmattan).

Madeley, J. and Sitter, N. (2005) 'Differential Euroscepticism among the Nordic Christian Parties: Protestantism or Protest?', Conference paper, annual meeting of the Norwegian Political Science Association, 11–13 August.

Magnette, P. (2006) *Au nom des peuples. Le malentendu constitutionnel européen* (Paris: Cerf).

Mair, P. (2000) 'The limited impact of Europe on national party systems', *West European Politics* 23 (4): 27–51.

Mair, P. (2007), 'Political Opposition and the European Union', *Government and Opposition* 42 (1): 1–17.

Majone, G. (2006) 'The common sense of European integration', *Journal of European Public Policy* 13 (5): 607–26.

Marcussen, M., Risse, T., Engelmann-Martin, D., Knopf, H.-J. and Roscher, K. (1999) 'Constructing Europe? The evolution of French, British and German nation state identities', *Journal of European Public Policy* 6(4).

Marks, G. and McAdam, D. (1996) 'Social movements and the changing structure of political opportunity in the European Union', *West European Politics* 19(2): 249–78.

Marks, G. and Steenbergen, M. (2004) *European Integration and Political Conflict* (Cambridge: Cambridge University Press).

Marquand, D. (1979) *Parliament for Europe*. (London: Jonathan Cape).

Maurer, A., Mittag, J. and Wessels, W. (2003) 'National Systems' Adaptation to the EU System: Trends, Offers and Constraints', in

Kohler-Koch, B., *Linking EU and National Governance* (Oxford: Oxford University Press).

Mayer, F. (2005) 'Supremacy Lost? Comments on Roman Kwiecie?', *German Law Journal* 6 (11): 1497–505.

Mead, W.(2002) 'The Case Against Europe', *The Atlantic Monthly*, April 2002.

Mény, Y. (2004) 'The EU and the challenge of a post-national constitution', in Fabbrini, S. (ed.) *Democracy and Federalism in the European Union and the United States* (London: Routledge).

Mény, Y., Muller, P. and Quermonne, Y. (1996), *The Impact of the European Union on National Institutions and Policies* (London: Routledge).

Meyer, C. (1999) 'Political Legitimacy and the Invisibility of Politics: Exploring the European Union's Communication Deficit', *Journal of Common Market Studies* 37 (4): 617– 39.

Milner, S. (2004) 'For an alternative Europe: Euroscepticism and the French Left since the Maastricht treaty', *European Studies* 20: 59–85.

McLaren, L. (2002) 'Public support for the European Union: cost/benefit analysis or perceived cultural threat?', *The Journal of Politics* 64 (2): 551–66.

McLaren, L. (2006) *Identity, Interests and Attitudes to European Integration* (Basingstoke: Palgrave Macmillan).

McLaren, L. (2007) 'Explaining Mass-Level Eurocepticism: Identity, Interests and Institutional Distrust', *Acta Politica* 42: 233–51.

McNamara, S. (2006) 'The EU Constitution: Will the EU Force a Way Forward?', Heritage Foundation, 14 December 2006.

McNamara, S. (2008) 'The EU Reform Treaty: A Threat to the Transatlantic Alliance', Heritage Foundation, 20 February 2008.

Mignot, A. (2008) 'L'UPM au rabais, un marqueur de la puissance craintive de l'Allemagne': www.voxlatina.com; 21 March 2008, accessed 6 April 2009.

Milliyet (2006) 'Surveys alarm signals for the EU', 26 October.

Milward, A. (1992) *The European Rescue of the Nation-state* (London: Routledge).

Milward Brown IMS (2008) *Post-Lisbon Treaty Referendum*. Research findings. September 2008.

Moravcsik, A. (1993) 'Preferences and Power in the European Community: A Liberal Intergovernmental Approach', *Journal of Common Market Studies* 31(4): 473–520.

Moravcsik, A. (2002) 'Reassessing legitimacy in the EU', *Journal of Common Market Studies* 40 (4): 603–24.

Moravcsik, A. (2007) 'The European Constitutional Settlement', in S. Meunier and K. McNamara (eds) *The State of the European Union Volume 8: Making history* (Oxford: Oxford University Press): 23–50.

Nederlands election (2009a), Results for the referendum on the EU Constitution, 1 June 2005, per province, http://www. nlverkiezingen.com/Ref2005.html, accessed 1 September 2009.

Nederlands elections (2009b), Results of the 2009 EP elections, per province, http://www.nlverkiezingen.com/EP2009P.html, accessed 1 September 2009.

Nelsen, B. and Guth, J. (2000) 'Exploring the Gender Gap. Women, Men and Public Attitudes toward European Integration', *European Union Politics* 1(3): 267–91.

Nelsen, B. and Guth, J. (2003) 'Religion and youth support for the European Union', *Journal of Common Market Studies* 41 (1): 89–112.

Neunreither, K. (1998) 'Governance without Opposition: the Case of the European Union', *Government and Opposiiton* 33 (4): 419–41.

Neyer, J. and Wolf, D. (2000) 'Compliance in the Multi-level System of the EU: Measures to Combat BSE and State Aid Control'. Conference paper. International Conference 'Linking EU and National Governance', Mannheim Centre for European Social Research, 1–3 June 2000.

Niedermayer, O. and Sinnott, R. (1995) *Public Opinion and Internationalized Governance* (Oxford: Oxford University Press).

Nugent, N. (2001) *The European Commission* (Basingtoke: Palgrave Macmillan).

Österreichische Gesellschaft für Aussenpolitik (2008) *Österreichische Gemeinden im Fokus. EU-Volksabstimmung und Beteligung an Europawahlen im Vergleich*, Wien.

Olivi, B. (2001) *L'Europe difficile* (Paris: Gallimard).

O'Rourke and Sinnott (2001) *The Determinants of Individual Trade Policy Preferences: International Survey Evidence*, in Collins, S. and Rodrik, D. (eds) *Brookings Trade Forum: 2001* (Washington, DC: Brookings).

Panke, D. (2007) 'The European Court of Justice as an agent of Europeanization? Restoring Compliance with EU law', *Journal of European Public Policy* 14(6): 847–66.

Pantel, M. (1999) 'Unity in diversity: cultural policy and EU legitimacy', in Banchoff, T. and Smith, M. (eds) *Legitimacy in the EU. The contested polity* (London: Routledge).

Papier, H.-J. (2006) *Das Subsidiaritätsprinzip als Bremse des schleichenden Zentralismus in Europa?* Ringvorlesung im Rahem des studium generale an der Universität Tübingen. Tübingen, 28 November 2006.

Parsons, C. (2006) 'The Triumph of Community Europe', in Dinand, D. (ed.) *Origins and Evolution of the European Union* (Oxford: Oxford University Press).

Parti Socialiste (2007) *Programme du Parti Socialiste pour les elections legislatives des 10 et 17 juin 2007*, available at http://hebdo.parti-socialiste.fr/2007/05/14/762/, accessed 20 April 2009.

Paterson, W. (1996) 'The German Christian-democrats', in Gaffney, J. (ed.) *Political Parties and the European Union* (London: Routledge).

Pernice, I. (2005) *Europäische Justizpolitik in der Perspektive der Verfassung für Europa* Berlin, Humboldt Universität: Walter Hallstein Institut, WHI Paper 03/05.

Perrineau, P. (2005) 'Le référendum français du 29 mai 2005. L'irrésistible nationalisation d'un vote européen', in P. Perrineau (ed.) *Le vote européen 2004–2005. De l'élargissement au référendum français* (Paris: Presses de Sciences Po).

Peterson, J. and Bromberg, E. (1999) *Decision-making in the European Union* (London: Macmillan).

Pfetsch, B. (2004) 'The Voice of the Media in European Public Sphere: Comparative Analysis of Newspaper Editorials', Europub Project Report, at: europub.wz-berlin.de/Data/reports/WP3/D3-4%20WP3% 20Integrated%20Report.pdf, accessed 19 May 2009.

Piar, C. and Gerstlé, J. (2005) 'Le cadrage du referendum sur la Constitution européenne: La dynamique d'une campagne à rebondissements', in A. Laurent and N. Sauger (eds) *Le référendum de ratification du Traité constitutionnel européen: comprendre le «Non» français* (Paris: Cahiers du CEVIPOF, n°42): 42–73.

Pollicino, O. (2008) 'The European Arrest Warrant and the Constitutional Principles of the Member States: a Case Law-Based Outline in the Attempt to Strike a Balance between Interacting Legal Systems', *German Law Journal* 9 (10): 1313–54.

Prague Declaration (2008) *Prague Declaration on European Consciousness and Communism* Prague: 3 June 2008, Senate of the Czech Parliament.

Priollaud, F.-X. and Siritzky, D. (2005) *La constitution européennes. Textes et commentaires* (Paris: La Documentation française).

Quaglia, L. (2003) *Euroscepticism in Italy and Centre-Right Wing Political Parties*, Sussex European Institute (Brighton: Sussex European Institute), working paper no.60.

Quaglia, L. and Moxon-Brown, E. (2004) *What makes a good presidency? Italy and Ireland compared*. Paper presented at the UACES Conference, March 2004.

Rabier, J.-R. (1977) *La confiance mutuelle entre les peuples: un indicateur de l'intégration européenne?* Bruxelles: Commission des Communautés Européennes, document de travail.

Rabier, J.-R. (1989) 'L'opinion publique et l'intégration de l'Europe dan les années 50', in E. Serra (ed.) *Il rilancio dell'Europa e i trattati di Roma* (Bruylant: Bruxelles).

Raunio, T. (2000), 'Losing Independence or Finally Gaining Recognition? Contacts betwenn MEPS and National Parties', *Party Politics* 6(2): 142–68.

Raunio, T. (2002) 'Why European Integration Increases Leadership Autonomy within Political Parties', *Party Politics* 8(4): 205–422.

Raunio, T. (2007), 'Softening but Persistent: Euroscepticism in the Nordic countries', *Acta politica* 42 (2/3): 191–210.

Ray, L. (2001) 'The ideological structure of mass opinion about European level policy-making', Conference paper, annual meeting of the American Political Science Association, San Francisco, 29 August–1 September.

Ray, L. (2004) 'Expectations, fears and oposition to EU-level policymaking', in G. Marks and M. Steenbergen (eds) *European integration and political conflict* (Cambridge: Cambridge University Press).

Ray, L. (2007) 'Mainstreaming Euroskepticism: Trend or Oxymoron?', *Acta politica*, 42: 153–72.

Reichel, S. (2006), 'Luxembourg: eine kleine Geschichte der Ernüchterung', (Berlin: Stiftung Wissenschaft und Politik), available at http://www.swp-berlin.org/transfer/Lissabon/pdf/Luxembourg.pdf, accessed 2 May 2009.

Reif, K. and Schmitt, H. (1980) 'Nine second-order national elections – a conceptual framework for the analysis of European elections results', *European Journal of Political Research* no.8: 3–44

Robinson, B. (2001) 'Greek Orthodox Church and identity cards', http://www.religioustolerance.org/chr_orthi.htm, accessed 30 August 2009.

Roger, P. (2002) *L'ennemi américain. Généalogie de l'anti-américanisme français* (Paris: Seuil).

Rohrschneider, R. (2002) 'The democratic deficit and mass support for an EU-wide government', *American Journal of Political Science* 46 (2): 463–75.

Ruiz Jimenez, A. And Egea de Haro, A. (2004) 'Spain: Euroscepticism in a pro-European country?' unpublished paper, http://www.uned.es/dcpa/invest/eu_consent/AMRJ_2006_SESP_draft_euroescepticism.pdf, accessed 4 April 2009.

Rupnik, J. (2004) *Les Européens face à l'élargissement. Perceptions, enjeux, acteurs* (Paris: Presses de Sciences-Po).

Sàdaba, T. (2005) 'Le cas particulier des élections législatives en Espagne: un 'second tour des légsialtives', in Maarek, P. (ed.) *Chronique d'un 'non' annoncé: La communication politique et l'Europe (juin 2004–mai 2005)* (Paris: L'Harmattan).

Sanchez-Cuenca, I. (2000) 'The Political Basis of Support for European Integration', *European Union Politics* 1 (2): 147–71.

Sauger, N., Brouard, S. and Grossmann, E. (2006) *Les Français contre l'Europe?* (Paris: Presses de Sciences Po).

Saurwein, F. (2006) *Europäisierung der österreichischen Öffentlichkeit: Mediale Aufmerksamkeit für EU-Politik und der veröffentlichte Diskurs über die EU-Erweiterung*, Universität Wien: Institut für Publizistik- und Kommunikationswissenschaft; http://www.univie.ac.at/Publizistik/Europaprojekt/datei/pub/europaeisierung-final-rep.pdf, accessed 14 April 2009.

Schäfner, C. (2001) 'Attitudes to Europe – Mediated by Translation', in A. Musolff, C. Good, P. Points and R. Wittlinger (eds) *Attitudes towards Europe. Language in the Unification Process* (Aldershot: Ashgate).

Scharpf, F. (1997) 'Economic integration, democracy and the welfare state', *Journal of European Public Policy* 4 (1): 37–55.

Scheve, K. and Slaughter, M. (2004) *Public Opinion, International Economic Integration and the Welfare State,* http://www.yale.edu/macmillan/globalization/KSMS_Carnegie_PubOp.pdf, accessed 10 August 2009.

Schild, J. (2001), 'National v. European identities? French and Germans in the European Multi-Level System', *Journal of Common Market Studies* 39 (2): 331–351.

Schlesinger, P. (1993), 'Wishful thinking: cultural politics, media and collective identities in Europe', *Journal of Communication* 43 (2): 6–17.

Schlesinger, P. (1999) 'Changing Spaces of Political Communication: The Case of the European Union', *Political Communication* 16: 263–79.

Schlesinger, P. (2007) 'A Cosmopolitan Temptation', *European Journal of Communication* 22 (4): 413–26.

Schmitt, H. (2005) *The European elections of June 2004: still second order?* Working paper (Mannheim: Zentrum für Europäishce Studien), available at http://www.mzes.uni-mannheim.de/publications/papers/HS_EP_ParElec_2004.pdf, accessed 2 March 2008.

Schmitter, P. (2002) 'Una propuesta pera expandir la ciudadania social en la EU y al msimo tiempo ampliar hacia el Este', *Sistema* 3 (167): 3–17.

Schoen, H. (2008) 'Identity, instrumental self-interest and institutional evaluations. Explaining public opinion on common European policies in foreign affairs and defence', *EU Politics* 9 (1): 5–29

Schout, A. and Vanhoonacker, S. (2006) 'Evaluating Presidencies of the Council of the EU: Revisiting Nice', *Journal of Common Market Studies* 44(5):1051–77.

Scully, R. (2005) *Becoming Europeans? Attitudes, behaviour and socialization in the European Parliament* (Oxford: Oxford University Press).

Sédillot, R. (1967) *Survol de l'histoire de l'Europe* (Paris: Fayard).

Semetko, H., Van der Burg, W. and Valkenburg, P. (2003), 'The Influence of Political Events on Attitudes Towards the European Union', *British Journal of Political Science* 33: 621–34.

Sievers, J. (2008) 'Too Different to Trust? First Experiences with the Application of the European Arrest Warrant', in E. Guild and F. Geyer (eds) *Security versus Justice? Police and Judicial Cooperation in the EU* (London: Ashgate).

Sinnott, R. (2001) *Attitudes and behaviour of the Irish electorate in the referendum on the treaty of Nice. Results of a survey of public opinion carried out for the European Commission Representation in Ireland* (Dublin: European Commission's Representation).

Sitter, N. (2001) 'The Politics of Opposition and European Integration in Scandinavia: Is Euro-Scepticism a Government–Opposition Dynamic?', *West European Politics* 24 (4): 22–39.

Smith, A. (2005) '*Set in the silver sea*': *English national identity and European integration* Conference paper, Conference on 'National identity and Euroscepticism: a comparison between France and the UK', Oxford University, 13 May 2005.

Smith, A. (2004) *Le gouvernement de l'Union européenne. Une sociologie politique* (Paris: LGDJ).

Smith, M. (1999) 'EU legitimacy and the 'defensive' reaction to the Single European market', in T. Banchoff and M. Smith (eds) *Legitimacy and the European Union. The contested polity* (London: Routledge).

Smith, T. and Seokho, K. (2006) 'National Pride in Cross-national and Temporal Perspective', *International Journal of Public Opinion Research*, 18: 127–36.

SPD (1959), *Grundsatzprogramm der Sozial-Demoraktischen Partei Deutschlands*, beschlossen in Bad Godesberg, vom 13. bis 15. November 1959, http://library.fes.de/pdf-files/bibliothek/retro-scans/fa-57721.pdf, accessed 20 March 2009.

SPD (2001) Beschluss des SPD-Parteitages vom 20. November 2001: 'Verantwortung für Europa – Deutschland in Europa', 2001.spd-parteitag.de/servlet/PB/menu/1002021/index.html, accessed 20 March 2009.

SPD (2007) *Hamburger Programm-Grundsatz-programm der Sozial-Demoraktischen Partei Deutschlands,* http://www.spd.de/de/pdf/parteiprogramme/Hamburger-Programm_final.pdf, accessed 20 March 2009.

Spence, J. (1996) *The EU. 'A View from the Top'. Top Decision Makers and the EU*; http://ec.europa.eu/public_opinion/archives/top/top.pdf, accessed 5 March 2009.

Spinelli, A. (1967) 'European Union in the Resistance', *Government and Opposition* 2(3): 321–29.

Steinbrecher, M. and Rattinger, H. (2007) *Turnout in European and national elections*, IntUne Papers, Paper no. MA07-06, http://www.intune.it./articles/papers, accessed 25 April 2009.

Stone, A. (1992) 'Le néo-institutionalisme. Défis conceptuels et méthodologiques', *Politix*, 20: 156–68.

Strøm, K. and Mueller, W. (1999) *Policy, offices or votes? How political parties in Western Europe make hard decisions* (Cambridge: Cambridge University Press).

Taggart, P. (1998) 'A touchstone of dissent: Euroscepticism in contemporary Western European party systems', *European Journal of Political Research* 33: 363–88.

Taggart, P. and Szczerbiak, A. (2002) 'The Party Politics of Euroscepticism in EU member and Candidate States', Brighton: Sussex European Institute, working paper no.51.

Taggart, P. and Szczerbiak, A. (2003), 'Theorizing party-based Euroscepticism: problems of definition, measurement and causality', Brighton: Sussex European Institute, working paper no.69.

Taggart, P. and Szczerbiak, A. (2005) *Opposing Europe. The comparative party politics of Euroscepticism. Volume 1: Case studies and country surveys* (Oxford: Oxford University Press).

Taggart, P. and Szczerbiak, A. (2008) *Opposing Europe. The comparative party politics of Euroscepticism. Volume 2: Comparative and theoretical perspectives* (Oxford: Oxford University Press).

Tarrow, S. and Imig, D. (1999) *Contentious Europeans. Protest and Politics in an Emerging Polity* (New York and Oxford: Rowman & Littlefield).

Teubert, W. (2001) 'A Province of a Federal Superstate, Ruled by an Unelected bureaucracy-Keywords of the Eurosceptic Discourse in Britain', in A. Musolff, C. Good, P. Points and R. Wittlinger (eds) *Attitudes towards Europe. Language in the Unification Process* (Aldershot: Ashgate).

Thatcher, M. (1988) Speech at the College of Europe (Bruges: College of Europe), 8 September 1988, http://www.margaretthatcher.org/speeches/displaydocument.asp?docid=107332, accessed 2 March 2008.

The Irish Times (2008a) 'Doing nothing to upset the voters', 22 April.

The Irish Times (2008b) 'Craft union calls for rejection of EU treaty', 6 May.

The Irish Times (2009) 'Eurosceptic elements in Irish media', 19 November.

Theiler, T. (2004) 'The origins of Euroscepticism in German-speaking Switzerland', *European Journal of Political Research* 43 (4): 635–56.

Thieulin, B. and Senèze, V. (2006) 'La campagne française pour le referendum sur Internet', in P. Maarek (ed.) *Chronique d'un 'non' annoncé: la communication politique et l'Europe (juin 2004–mai 2005)* (Paris: L'Harmattan).

Toshkov, D. (2008) 'Embracing European Law. Compliance with EU Directives in Central and Eastern Europe', *European Union Politics* 9 (3): 379–402.

Trenz, H.-J. (2007) 'Quo vadis Europe?' Quality newspapers struggling for European unity', in J. Fossum and P. Schlesinger (eds) *The European Union and the Public Sphere. A communicative space in the making?* (London: Routledge).

Trouvé, M. (2005) 'Les parlementaires aquitains et l'Europe', *Parlement[s]* 3: 99–108.

TUC (2007) *The 139th annual Trade Unions Congress Congress, 10–13 September, Brighton*, http://www.tuc.org.uk/congress/tuc-15379-f0.pdf, accessed 5 August 2009.

TUC (2008) *The 140th annual Trade Unions Congress Congress, 8–11 September, Brighton. Congress report*, http://www.tuc.org.uk/congress/tuc-15645-f0.pdf, accessed 5 August 2009.

United States House of Representatives (2005), *The EU Constitution and US–EU relations: the recent referenda in France and the Netherlands and the US–EU Summit.* Hearing before the Subcommittee on Europe and Emerging Threats of the Committee on International Relations, 109th Congress, first session, 22 June Serial no. 109–68.

Usherwood, S. (2004) 'Bruges as a Lodestone of British Opposition to the European Union', *Collegium* 39: 5–16.

Vaïsse, J. (2004), 'Les néoconservateurs américains et l'Europe: sous le signe de Munich', *Relations Internationales* 120: 447–62.

Van Ham, P. (2002) *The Dutch Conservative Revolution. The Impact for Europe.* The Hague: Clingedael Institute, research paper; http://www.clingendael.nl/publications/2002/20020500_art-vanham.pdf. accessed 5 April 2008.

Vetik, R., G. Nimmerfelt and M. Taru (2006) 'Reactive identity versus EU integration', *Journal of Common Market Studies* 44 (5): 1079–102.

Vignaux, E. (2004) 'Les ressorts confessionnels de l'euroscepticisme : facteurs religieux et comportements politiques dans les pays nordiques', *Nordiques*, Summer–Autumn, 5: 83–109.

Vissol, T. (2006) 'Is there a case for an EU information television station?', report, Directorate-General Communication, European Commission.

Vliegenthart, R., Schuck, A., Boomgaarden, H. G. and de Vreese, C. (2009) 'News coverage and support for European integration 1990–2006', *International Journal of Public Opinion Research* 20 (4): 415–439.

Voessing, K. (2005) 'Nationality and the preferences of the European public toward EU-policy making', *European Union politics* 6 (4): 445–67.

Volmerange, X. (1993) *Le fédéralisme allemand et l'intégration européenne* (Paris: L'Harmattan).

Votewatch.eu (2009) http://www.votewatcheu/cx_europea_party_groups.php?vers=1, accessed 25 November 2009.

Wallace, W. and J. Smith (1995) 'Democracy or Technocracy? European integration and the problem of popular consent', in J. Hayward (ed.) *The Crisis of Representation in Europe* (London: Frank Cass).

Weiler, J. (1995) 'European democracy and its critique', in J. Hayward (ed.) *The Crisis of Representation in Europe* (London: Frank Cass).

Weiler, J. (1996) ' "Der Staat über alles". Demos, telos und die Maastricht-Entscheidung des Bundesverfassungsgerichts', *Jahrbuch des öffentlichen Rechts der Gegenwart* 44: 91–135.

Weiler, J. (1999) *The Constitution of Europe: 'Do the new clothers have an emperor?' and other essays on European integration* (Cambridge: Cambridge University Press).

Weiler, J. (2002) 'Fédéralisme et constitutionnalisme: le *Sonderweg* de l'Europe', in R. Dehousse (ed.) *Une constitution pour l'Europe?* (Paris: Presses de Sciences-Po).

Wessels, B. (2007) 'Discontent and European Identity: Three Types of Euroscepticism', *Acta Politica*, 42:287–306.

Wessels, W. and Rometsch, D. (1996) 'German administrative interactions and European Union', in Mény, Y., P. Muller and J.-L. Quermonne (eds) *Adjusting to Europe. The impact of the European Union on national administrations and policies* (London: Routledge).

Wyplosz, C. (2005) 'Les nouveaux défis de l'Union européenne', *Politique étrangère* 70(4): 715–25.

Zellentin, G. (1967) 'Form and function of the Opposition in the European Communities', *Government and Opposition* 2(3): 416–35.

Ziller, J. (2008) *Les nouveaux traités européens: Lisbonne et après* (Paris: Montchrestien).

Index